The Skousen Book of

Mormon World Records

And Other Amazing Firsts, Facts & Feats

Premier Edition

Paul B. Skousen

Skousen Book of
Mormon World Records
and Other Amazing Firsts, Facts & Feats

ISBN 1-555517-811-1

Cover design by Jeff Clawson and Nichole Shaffer
Layout by Paul B. Skousen using QuarkXPress on a computer from *Totally Awesome Computers*, the largest LDS-owned chain of computer stores, founded by Dell Schanze.

Distributed by

Cedar Fort, Inc. / August 2004
www.mormonworldrecords.com

PRINTED IN THE UNITED STATES OF AMERICA
10 9 8 7 6 5 4 3 2

Who holds the Mormon World Records?

What Latter-day Saint has the most
children, baptisms for the dead, full-time missions, dead beetles, or Olympic gold medals?

What Latter-day Saint has the biggest
family, cookie, milkshake, house cat, pie, or pen-and-pencil collection?

What Latter-day Saint has the longest
last name, pole-sitting record, continuous singing record, chess or basketball game, string of unbroken 100 percent home teaching, or set of fingernails?

What Latter-day Saint is the oldest
convert, bishop, twin, to go through the temple, world power-lifting champion, or to parachute from a plane?

What Latter-day Saint is the fastest
runner, talker, reader, walker, typist or swimmer?

What Latter-day Saint was the first
to climb Mt. Everest, launch into space, high jump seven feet, give birth to septuplets, row across the Atlantic, invent diamonds, or have a test-tube baby?

What LDS building was
the most expensive, last to have an outhouse, the oldest, the largest, or the farthest north, south, or from Salt Lake City?

Which General Authority is the first
to fly, be hijacked, have a dinosaur named after him, help build atomic bombs?

These and more than 1,600 additional Mormon world records are for the first time brought together in this premiere edition of *The Skousen Book of Mormon World Records – And Other Amazing Firsts, Facts & Feats*. Read on for the most fascinating collection of achievements ever assembled of members of the Church of Jesus Christ of Latter-day Saints. And then, turn to page 7 for details on how you can challenge an existing Mormon world record or set one of your own to be included in the next edition of *Mormon World Records*.

FOREWORD

This compilation of *The Skousen Book of Mormon World Records – And Other Amazing Firsts, Facts & Feats* (abbreviated MWR) is a book of superlatives. Some of the accomplishments stand on their own as records. Others are simply interesting tidbits gleaned from history. The collection is meant to entertain, educate and challenge, and show validation of President David O. McKay's oft-repeated statement, "What e'er thou art, act well thy part," and President Gordon B. Hinckley's declaration that the Gospel will "help make bad men good and good men better," as demonstrated in the following pages.

Sources The vast majority of records in this book have already appeared in newspapers and magazines. Unpublished entries were sent to the editors specifically for use in this book.

Accuracy If you see your name in MWR, please review the information for accuracy. These records are only as correct as the source materials, and their citations were transposed only as accurately as could be expected from a couple of thousand midnight type-a-thons by your bleary-eyed and fumblefingered compiler.

Missing Information We would like to include the ward and stake of everyone mentioned, and if yours is missing or has changed, we would appreciate you sending that to us for the next edition.

Wrong Information If you don't belong in this collection (hiding from the law, non-LDS, etc.), please let us know immediately so we can remove your entry. Please see "It's a record!" among the following pages for instructions on how to submit corrections. If you have a photo for your printed story, or can update the photo we've used, please contact us immediately.

Submitting a "Challenge" Submitting materials for the next edition of MWR does not automatically mean they will be used. The panel of reviewers weighs all submissions against existing records and other factors that fall under the categories of "firsts, facts and feats." Materials submitted to the editors become the property of *Mormon World Records*, and will not be acknowledged. If you want your materials returned, please include a self-addressed, stamped envelope. We cannot guarantee that you will receive back any submitted materials. If you send a photo but do not want it published, please let us know in writing at the same time. The instructions on the following pages provide more information.

About These Claims ... If a record is or was a world record, we indicate that by putting the year and "World Record" in the entry's title. Please note that such records may not be world records today, but were indeed world records at the time they were accomplished. Also, some records are only declared as such within the membership of the Church, for example, the longest home-teaching route or fastest mile run by a Mormon. This book and its contents are in no way endorsed by the Church of Jesus Christ of Latter-day Saints, its leadership or members.

Submissions may be e-mailed (see www.mormonworldrecords.com) or mailed to: Cedar Fort, Inc., 925 N. Main, Springville, Utah 84663.

PREFACE

Some years ago, when I was editor of the Utah edition of the Latter Day Sentinel, I began receiving some interesting correspondence about members of the Church—a man celebrating his 1-millionth proxy baptism for the dead, the longest home teaching route, the highest kite ever flown, and so much more. Such snippets didn't really qualify as hard news but they certainly were interesting, amazing and inspirational.

I began collecting such "records" in 1988, and these many years later the collection has grown to more than 2,300. I've pared it down to about 1,600, and hope you find them as enjoyable to read as I did to collect.

Many friends of old, and friends newly found, were gracious and kind about sparing time, resources and expense to aid in the gathering of this information: Sherry Tingley at the Deseret News photo library; Russ Taylor of the L. Tom Perry Special Collections at Brigham Young University; Crismon Lewis, founder and editor of the Latter Day Sentinel newspapers; the helpful hands at the LDS Family and Church History archives and Utah State Historical Society, the dedicated researchers, writers and photographers for various Church publications and other newspapers, and hundreds of others. Editing expertise was provided by good friend and Questar's own David Hampshire, and also the eagle eye of my mother, Jewel P. Skousen, whose decades of editing my father's many books was brought to bear with loving patience. Others for whom words fail to properly thank are too many for this page. Of special note is one Mormon World Record not included in the pages that follow, but hers is a perfection to which no superlative can ascend – my wife, Kathy, to whom this work and effort is dedicated, and to the ten highly creative and energetic children who gave so much support while otherwise keeping our home and lives full, busy, oftentimes confusing, but always wonderfully satisfying and complete: Jacob, Michelle, Joseph, Benjamin, Patricia, Wendy, Julie, Maryann, Joshua and Elisabeth.

I have endeavored to be as accurate as possible, but there will be mistakes. In fact, there are 17. If you see one of them, thank you for alerting me to it. I can't distribute retractions, but I can make the corrections in the next edition.

Are you a Mormon World Record? If so, let us know and we'll make room for you in the next updated edition. Records are meant to be broken. Who will set the new standard, the new record, the new level of achievement? Are you a new Mormon World Record?

Paul B. Skousen
August 2004, South Jordan, Utah

"HEY, THAT'S NOT RIGHT!"

A book of achievements is a work in progress. The volume of material from which "Mormon World Records" has been mined is massive and ever changing – mistakes happen.

If you see errors or can challenge existing records or "firsts" in this collection, you are invited to turn to "It's a record!" on the facing page for instructions on how to submit corrections or your own record or amazing tidbit. Submitting material does not guarantee inclusion in a future book.

IS IT A RECORD?

To be a "record," an event or accomplishment must be comparable and measurable so that others can challenge it. Until a challenger can prove he or she has beaten or improved upon a record in this book, the old record will stand.

Interesting accomplishments or events that seem out of the ordinary do not qualify as "records" by themselves. If the accomplishment is not comparable or measurable, for example the first couple wed in the rebuilt Nauvoo Temple or the first Mormon in space, then events such as these fall into the category of being an amazing "first," "fact," or "feat."

RULES

The performer must be, or have been, a member of the LDS Church (level of activity is not asked for). Any artifact submitted must have a clear connection to the LDS Church, and should be documented.

Marathon events are allowed one 5-minute rest period after each 60-minute interval, or 20 minutes after every four hours, and 90 minutes rest after each 24 hours of a 48-hour or longer event. A signed log book must be provided to prove constant observation during the course of the activity.

If an official organization sponsors the event, that organization should be involved in validating and ratifying the record.

Submission of a record-breaking attempt must be corroborated by independent sources (newspapers, adult witnesses, coverage by the media, official representatives of organizations, etc.).

The sole responsibility of the editors is to correct and update information in a subsequent edition.

For endeavors where variables might complicate the duplication of a record attempt, please contact us for help with laying down ground rules.

We will not publicize any activity that is or could be injurious to yourself, others, property, or living things. Activities deemed by the judges to be reckless, illegal, or contrary to LDS Church standards will not be considered for publication. Questions? Contact us at: www.mormonworldrecords.com.

CHALLENGING OR SUBMITTING A RECORD

(Photocopy this page or use separate sheets of paper and send to the address on the next page, or submit via the Web at www.mormonworldrecords.com.)

Follow the instructions on this page to:
Challenge or correct an existing entry in this book.
Submit a new record, first, fact or amazing feat, or suggest a new category.

1. Description of record or amazing first, fact or feat (Use extra sheets as necessary):

2. The Challenger: Who achieved this record (or first, fact, or amazing feat)?
Name:
Date of birth:
Church affiliation: Member/Former Member/Ethnic Mormon/Other (explain):

Home Church Unit: (Ward/Stake/Branch/Area/Mission, etc.); OR home city and state/province, country:

Is the Challenger still living? If so, please provide contact information:
Mailing address:

Phone number:
E-mail address:

3. The Source: If you are submitting this information for or about somebody else, how can we reach you?
Name:
Mailing Address:

Phone number:
E-mail address:

What is your association with the person who set the new record? (Friend, relative, quorum leader, etc.):

4. Proof. Please submit:
a. **Witnesses:** A list of responsible witnesses' names and contact information.
b. **Log books** (if applicable): A photocopy of log books used to record the event.
c. **Testimonials/Documents:** Copies of newspaper clippings and/or letters from ecclesiastical/school/seminary/mission/business or community leader, and/or other documents validating the record.
d. **Photos** (optional, but always encouraged): If no photos were taken of the event, any photo of the participant(s) is requested, but not mandatory. Any format is acceptable (electronic, print, negative, slide, video, clipping, etc.).

Note about photos: Any photo or video sent to the editors implies automatic consent to print that photo at their discretion unless a written note withholding permission is included with the photo. If a copyright of your photo is held by someone else (a newspaper, for example), please include a written release from that publication allowing the editors to reproduce the photograph. Photos clipped from a newspaper or magazine do not reproduce well, and a good quality copy of the original is preferred. Digital photos work best but any format is acceptable.

Still Looking! It was particularly frustrating and difficult to find photos of women athletes, executives and scientists. If you are listed, or should be listed, and have a photo that we may use, please contact us.

Photo Credits: We have endeavored to be as accurate as possible in giving proper credit for all photographs. Please contact us immediately if a photo was not credited accurately or if there is some other mistake or oversight.

Note about submitted materials: All submitted materials become the property of "Mormon World Records." For materials to be returned, contributors must include a self-addressed return envelope with sufficient postage. There is no guarantee the materials will be returned. Contributors are encouraged to submit copies of all materials and photographs and retain the originals. Send To: Cedar Fort, Inc., 925 N. Main, Springville, Utah 84663. Or, contact us at www.mormonworldrecords.com.

SOURCE MATERIALS

Source materials for *The Skousen Book of Mormon World Records – And Other Firsts, Facts & Feats* are cited according to a shorthand abbreviation shown below.

Author:	Unpublished submissions; or the compiler's personal interviews, correspondence, file notes, or observation.	Internet	This word is used in place of a long Web address to save space
		LDS:	*The Latter Day Sentinel*
BYU:	BYU Library, L. Tom Perry Special Collections, BYU Sports Information Services, etc.	LOC:	Library of Congress
		NASA:	Official bulletins from NASA
		This People magazine	
CN:	*Church News*	The LDS standard scriptures	
DN:	*Deseret Morning News*	SLTrib:	*The Salt Lake Tribune*
The Deseret News' *Church Almanac*		*Sunstone* magazine	
DU:	*Daily Universe*	UofU:	University of Utah Library and archives
LDS Church publications or resources		USHS:	Utah State Historical Society
	New Era	*MeridianMagazine*	
	Ensign	*The Messenger*	
	Friend	... and many others.	
	Improvement Era		

TABLE OF CONTENTS

Achievements..**10**
Largest ... Highest ... Most ... Youngest ... Oldest ... Fastest ... Longest ...
Worst ... Lowest ... Food ... Pet Superlatives

The LDS Human Being..**44**
Age ... Size ... Reproduction ... Physiology ... The Sexes ... Saints around
the world ... Asians ... Blacks ... Indians ... Military ... Scouting ... Pioneers

Fame..**98**
Movies and Stars ... TV Stars and Productions ... Animation ... Oscars and
Awards ... Beauty/Talent Pageants ... Leaders ... Thinkers ... Executives ...
Campaigns and Charities

Publishing..**142**
The Book of Mormon ... Church Periodicals ... Other Milestones ...
Postage Stamps ... Performance

Music, Art & Photography..**168**
Painting ... Sculpture Art ... Music ... Tabernacle Choir ... Radio

Courage **198**
Space Travel ... Adventure ... Lifesavers, Survivors and Heroes

The Church..**210**
Membership ... Prophets, General Authorities ... Young Women ... Seminary
Home Teaching ... Visiting Teaching ... Ordinances ... Fasting ... Welfare
System ... Genealogy ... Missionary Work ... Structures ... Business and
Real Estate

Knowledge..**294**
Education ... Inventions ... BYU Facts & Feats ... Living World ... Trees ...
Flowers ... Archeology ... Science/Engineering ... Medicine and Dentistry ...
Places ... Rocks and the Earth ... Dinosaurs ... Other Historic Items

Sports..**360**
Track ... Paralympics ... Football ... Rugby ... Basketball ... Baseball/Softball ...
Boxing ... Volleyball ... Swimming/Diving ... Gymnastics ... Wrestling ...
Martial Arts ... Cycling ... Golf ... Tennis ... Skiing ... Skating ... Mountain
Climbing ... Hiking ... Weightlifting – Men ... Weightlifting – Women ...
Rodeo/Equestrian/Jockey ... Bowling ... Automotive ... Motorcycles ...
Rowing ... Chess ... Yo-Yo

Last Minute Records **424**

About the author..**426**

Photo Credits **428**

Index..**429**

Index by Ward, Stake, Branch or Mission **453**

The Anderson family in Soldotna, Alaska, knows the perfect fishing spot. In fact, it's in a nearby river where Nate Anderson, 12, caught this world-record King salmon using 80-pound fishing line. He can hardly hold his massive catch for this historic photograph. His brother, Deryk, was fishing in the same place when he caught his King salmon, setting another world record using 6-pound line.

Achievements

Mormon Achievements – by the numbers

1 — Winners in the National Soap Box Derby
40 — Instruments mastered by one member of the Church
216 — Hours of nonstop typing by a Mormon
1,000 — Hours spent atop a pole by a member of the Church
75,000 — Most Mormons gathered in one place at one time
3,000,000,000 — Largest audience for the Mormon Tabernacle Choir

LARGEST

Largest Fish – 80-pound Line (1988 World Record). In 1988, Nate J. Anderson, a 12-year-old in the Soldotna Ward, Soldotna, Alaska, Stake, boated to his favorite fishing spot on the Kenai river. For gear he had 80-pound-test fish line spooled onto a big halibut reel, and a stiff rod loaned to him by his dad. Nate let his line dangle into a favorite underwater depression where he had found success before. Suddenly he snagged something strong that yanked hard on the line. After a 15-minute tug of war, he started reeling in a big but tired Chinook (King) salmon. Nate and his older brother, Jeremy, hauled their massive catch to a nearby unofficial scale where it weighted just under 76 pounds. Unfortunately, by the time they reached an official scale, the fish had lost a lot of blood. Still, the official weight came in at 71 pounds 4 ounces, a new world record. (Nate Anderson, e-mail)

Largest Fish – 6-pound Line (1996 World Record). In 1996, Deryk Anderson, 18, Soldotna Ward, Soldotna, Alaska, Stake, was fishing the Kenai River when a firm strike hit the bait. He set the hook and began working the fish. When he pulled in his prize, it was the largest Chinook (King) salmon ever caught with 6-lb. fishing line. The official weight was 50 pounds 4 ounces, a new world record. (Nate Anderson, e-mail)

Largest Pen and Pencil Collection. Richard and Eva Done, Tucson, Arizona, have been collecting pens and pencils – most of them personalized for advertising purposes – since 1939. By 1989, their collection of unique pencils (no duplicates) numbered more than 6,000. (LDS 11/1/86)

Largest Human Conveyor Belt (1985 World Record). On Sept. 14, 1985, a total of 823 BYU students lined up at the Helaman Halls Field to form the world's largest human conveyor belt. Ten-year-old Jim Caldwell was the first passenger, passed overhead for the 10-minute ride down. (DU 9/18/85)

John Goddard donated thousands of insects he collected from all over the world.

Largest Bug Collection. Famed explorer, John Goddard, donated his collection of beetles to BYU in 1968, raising the university's collection to 510,000 insects. Brother Goddard's specimens were gathered from around the world, and ranged in size from a speck of dirt to the palm of your hand. (LDS 1986)

Largest Lap Sit (1984 World Record). The world's largest lap sit was performed by 8,500 young women and one General Authority (Hartman Rector Jr., emeritus member of the First Quorum of Seventy) at the 1984 Area Young Women's Conference in Arizona. Six lines were formed on Skydome Drive at Northern Arizona University in Flagstaff, and with a helicopter filming the event, all 8,500 sat back on the lap of the person behind, until all 8,500 were seated. (LDS 8/84)

Longest Kick Line (2002 World Record). More than 600 students at Timpanogos High School in Utah County gathered at their football stadium one evening to simultaneously "kick to the music," in an effort to set a new world record for the longest kick line. Unofficially, they beat the old world record of 593 people. (DN 9/20/02)

Largest Legal Load Moved on a Truck. Stanley Jones, San Jose 13th Ward, San Jose, Calif., Stake, moved the largest legal load in American history in November 1979. He transported a 107-ton magnet 2,200 miles from Illinois to Palo Alto, California. The giant, horseshoe-shaped electromagnet, when activated, could yank a wrench out of a man's hand 40 feet away. Jones had a special truck built for the job – a giant green trailer almost half as

This monster load gave new meaning to "oversize" and "long." A total of 120 tires supported the 107 ton load.

long as a football field with 120 tires on 18 axles, all monitored for stress by an on-board computer. The top speed was 35 miles an hour. At a truck stop, when two truckers refused his request to move until they had finished breakfast, Jones slipped his 18.6-foot-wide load between the trucks with three inches to spare on either side. His CB call sign was "Little Wheels." (CN 11/17/79)

Largest Explosion. Melvin A. Cook, inventor of numerous explosives, developed what is believed to be the most powerful conventional (nonnuclear) weapon in history. In 1969, the U.S. military asked Brother Cook to participate in "Project Cloudmaker," an attempt to detonate a 45,000-pound bomb. Cook estimated that filling the massive casing of the huge bomb with conventional explosives would have taken weeks. But he loaded the bomb with his powerful slurry in just 75 minutes (see "Inventors: Melvin Cook"). The bomb was lofted to 52,000 feet by a B-52 bomber and released. At 45,000 feet it detonated, creating such an explosion that the crew of nearby aircraft thought that the government had violated the atmospheric nuclear test-ban treaty. Cook died in 2000, having generated more than 100 patents, six books and more than 200 articles in scientific journals. ("More Bangs for the Buck," David Hampshire, 2002)

Largest Parade. The largest LDS parade is the Days of '47 parade, now considered the third largest parade in the United States. More than 300,000 people routinely line the streets for the annual event, and more than half-a-dozen states now pick up the parade on television. More than 130 floats and numerous other entries participate each July 24 for the two-mile march through downtown Salt Lake City. (Author)

Largest Gathering of Saints. What is the record for the largest gathering of Saints in one place at one time? In 1980, it was at the beginning of a two-day conference in the Pasadena Rose Bowl when 75,000 Latter-day Saints from the Los Angeles area united for the morning session. The May 17-18 conference required translators for seven languages (Spanish, Samoan, Korean, Vietnamese, Tongan, Mandarin and Cantonese) and more than 90 interpreters. (CN 5/24/80)

Deseret Morning News archives file photo

The world's first KFC was built near downtown, Salt Lake City. It was demolished in 2004 and a new resturant and museum was built in its place.

Utah Fried Chicken? When Col. Harland Sanders went looking for a way to promote his special chicken recipe that included 11 herbs and spices, he encountered a friend who would make all the difference. Leon "Pete" Harmon had been looking for something new for the menu at his "Do Drop Inn" on State Street in Salt Lake City. When he tasted Sanders' chicken, prepared with his secret recipe in a pressure-cooker, Harmon raced out the very next day to buy several pressure cookers and hire a sign painter. He had found his new speciality. But what would he call this new chicken delight? "Utah Fried Chicken" just didn't sound right, so Harmon named it "Kentucky Fried Chicken" because Kentucky was Col. Sanders' southern home and it gave the idea of fried chicken a nice southern feel. From this small beginning, the KFC empire began to grow. Today, Harmon owns 300 franchises himself, but there are almost 12,000 others spread over 80 countries that serve 8 million people a day. The "finger-licking good" empire has $10 billion in annual sales, staying neck-and-neck with McDonald's as the fast food leader. (www.kfc.com; SLTrib 8/2/02)

Largest Balloon Release. The largest simultaneous release of helium balloons by an LDS group occurred Oct. 11, 1986, when some 300,000 young women around the world launched balloons with attached messages of love, hope and peace for the world. Two of the largest mass releases were the 6,000 launched from Lavell Edwards Stadium at BYU, and 2,000 released in Orange County, California. Responses came from Texas, Florida, Wisconsin, Oklahoma, England, Argentina, Brazil, and some locations in the Indian Ocean region. (LDS 10/23/86)

Additional balloons were released from the Washington Monument, Cape Canaveral, the United States-Canadian border, and Tonga's main-island beach. Elsewhere, messages adrift in bottles from the La Reunion Island in the Indian Ocean. In Egypt, girls went to the tip of the Sinai to release bottles into the Red Sea after snorkeling to get beyond a reef so the bottles wouldn't wash back up on shore. In one remote area in Central America, one girl went to the top of a mountain with her parents to release her balloon. (CN 10/86)

Sam Battistone

At the height of Sambo's success, more than 1,400 restaurants blanketed the U.S.

Largest Chain of Restaurants. In the 1970s, the largest chain of fast-food restaurants owned by a member of the Church was Sambo's. Sam Battistone took a beleaguered chain of fast food outlets from 60 restaurants to more than 1,400 by 1979. (Internet)

Largest Audience of Readers. The largest single audience targeted by the Church for printed material was 50 million when it published an eight-page removable insert in the April 1980 Reader's Digest. (Church Almanac 1989)

Largest Toilet Flush. The largest LDS toilet flush officially witnessed by public utility workers occurred on Jan. 22, 1984, (Sunday?!?) in Salt Lake City just when halftime started during the Super Bowl. Workers were struggling to repair a broken water main on that frigid Sunday afternoon when suddenly a tremendous rushing noise could be heard as air was sucked into the open pipe leading into the city system. The rushing noise lasted 2-3 minutes. Workers knew the vacuum represented a very high demand for water perfectly timed with breaks people were taking during half-time television advertising. The workers estimated that some 10,000 toilets had been simultaneously flushed. (LDS 2/3/84)

Largest Audience to See BYU Dancers Perform. An estimated 1 billion viewers tuned in to the opening exercises of the Seoul, Korea, Summer

Olympics Sept. 17, 1988, to enjoy BYU's folk dancers performing in western-style red-and-white checkered costumes. (CN 9/88)

Nine tons of baptismal font made some of the temple granite seem easy to these teams of oxen.

Largest Legal Load Moved by Wagon? In 1874, the Saints had the chore of moving the baptismal font built in Salt Lake City to its new home in the St. George Temple. Several teams of oxen were needed to haul the 18,000-pound load. (CN 11/13/71, 2/26/77)

Largest Users of 35mm Projectors in the World. In 1948, and for several years thereafter, the Church's media, public communications, and missionary departments held the number one spot as the largest users of 35mm slide projectors in the world. The equipment was carried by missionaries all around the world and by other members for teaching Sunday lessons, instructing investigators, and for Church history and Book of Mormon displays and expositions. (CN 11/3/48)

Larry Miller operates one of the largest car dealerships in the nation.

Largest Car Dealership. In 1993, Automotive Age listed Larry H. Miller of Salt Lake City as the 15th largest car dealer in America with 19 dealerships. He has since expanded and remains, among Mormons, the largest car dealer in the world. Miller has also gone far to enrich and improve the Salt Lake community. He owns the Utah Jazz, plus other professional sports teams, and financed the huge Delta Center. He also owns a local television station, KJZZ. (Internet)

Largest "Love Is ..." Cartoon Collection. In 1985, Debbie Keola, 20, had her purse stolen not far from her home in Hawaii and lost the 447 "Love Is ... " cartoons she had been clipping from the Los Angeles Times – one for each day her missionary had been gone. She was so heart-broken, she wrote the newspaper asking if they could help her get copies. When other media picked up the story, her simple letter blossomed into what the Los Angeles Times dubbed the "Debbie Project." The "Debbie Project" culminated in a personal visit from the "Love Is ... " artist, who flew to Hawaii with 1,800 past cartoons, a signed original, and numerous gifts. (LDS 12/21/85)

Kim Casali

Largest Cornucopia (2001 World Record). A Salt Lake City grocery store created what it said was the world's largest cornucopia. The 10-foot-tall horn of plenty had some 20,000 pounds of locally-grown food, and was part of a display to promote healthy eating of five fruits and vegetables a day. (Author)

Jeffrey D. Allred, Deseret Morning News

The largest cornucopia in the world?

Largest Audience of Viewers. An estimated 3 billion people watched the opening ceremony for the 2002 Olympic Winter Games at which thousands of LDS volunteers and performers united their talents to put on the show of all shows. Media reaction proved the opening ceremony to be one of the finest ever.

In 1987, Sister Yue-Sai Kan was seen on a Sunday evening 15-minute televi-

Deseret Morning News file photo

The Mormon Tabernacle Choir and Utah Symphony as the world saw them on television during the 2002 Olympic Winter Olympics.

sion program shown to 300 million Chinese TV viewers. The program, "One World," presented various cultures from around the world. It was aired twice, once in Mandarin and once in English. The text of the show was published in China's equivalent of TV Guide. (LDS 6/10/87)

Michael Brandy, Deseret Morning News

Crowds begin to gather for an outdoor viewing of "Independence Day" in July 2002. It is unknown how many enjoyed the film from the comfort of the world's largest sleeping bag (24 x 54 feet), but chances are it took these two brave souls most of the night to roll the thing up and pack it away

Keith Johnson, Deseret Morning News

It would take an airplane hanger to get these 252 volunteers under one roof in this 500-foot sleeping bag, and we won't even talk about getting them to sing camp songs in unison!

Biggest Sleeping Bags. Slumberjack, a large sleeping bag manufacturer, stopped by at Thanksgiving Point, south of Salt Lake City, to roll out what could be the world's largest sleeping bag. It measured 24 feet 7 7/8 inches wide and 54 feet 2 1/2 inches long.

NeboSporting Goods tried another approach to the world's biggest sleeping bag by supplying $5,000 worth of sleeping bags that were all zipped together. Some 242 people, a few families included, climbed inside the 500-foot sleeping bag to be part of another world record for the widest sleeping bag in the world.

HIGHEST

Highest Kite (1967 World Record).

A 29-cent drugstore kite and a reel of six miles of fishing line was all it took for a sociology professor and his son to set a world's record. On a chilly Nov. 21, 1967, in Laramie, Wyoming, Dr. Phillip Kunz and his son, Jay, used 32,950 feet of fishing line to fly their kite to more than 28,500 feet, more than five miles high. "We could-

Phillip Kunz and his son Jay set the world's record for the highest kite when their paper kite soared to almost 5 1/2 miles high (Dr. Kunz's hand is on the spool of fishing line used to tether the kite.)

n't see it, even with field glasses," Brother Kunz said. The fishing line reflected the sunshine, prompting dozens of curious observers to notify authorities. "People were calling the police reporting UFOs," he said. Other kites flown for weather observation include a cluster of eight that reached a record altitude of 31,955 feet by the German Weather Bureau in 1919, and a single kite that reached 12,471 feet by the U.S. Meteorological Service in 1896. But none beat the solo record by kite-flying amateurs Kunz and his son Jay. (DU 4/7/82)

Highest Flier (1990 World Record).

In 1990, explorer John Goddard, La Canada, California, took the controls of an F-106 and flew it to an altitude of 63,000 feet (almost 12 miles high), making him the only civilian to pilot an aircraft to that altitude. (DN 2/15/90)

Highest Balloon Flight (1935 World Record).

On Nov. 11, 1935, two Army Corps officers went aloft in a helium balloon to test the durability and atmospheric

In 1990, John Goddard set an altitude record for civilians in this F-106.

Construction engineers pause for a photo after completing construction of the 35-story communications tower.

survivability of humans at very high altitudes. Capt. Orvil A. Anderson and Capt. Albert W. Stevens, both former BYU men, set a new world's record in 1935 for altitude when their balloon reached 72,395 feet. (BYU archives)

Tall Tower. In 1952, Church-owned KSL Television erected a 340-foot television transmitter tower atop Coon Peak some 17 miles west of Salt Lake City. The mountain summit is 9,425 above sea level. Does this remain the tallest Church-owned tower? (CN 9/6/52)

MOST

BYU student Dianna Lyn Gibbons, of Arbon, Idaho, helped keep her ward's hamburger eaters well supplied.

Most Hamburgers Consumed. As an opening activity every fall, the BYU 4th Ward has been getting together to eat hamburgers. Since 1979, the ward has steadily increased the number of burgers consumed from 200 to 636, then 837, 1014, and by 1984, more than 1,200. Jake McCready, Saratoga, California, ate 13 in one sitting. The restaurant where the burgers are bought typically requires three hours or more to cook them all, and must order extra cases of meat and buns all the way from Salt Lake City to keep up with the annual tradition. (DU 9/27/83)

Most Miles Driven Without Accident. The most documented miles driven by a Church-employed driver is 215,000 by the four drivers of the Deseret Industries trucks assigned to the Mesa, Arizona store from 1984-1986. (LDS 6/28/86)

In 1991, Lawrence "Rusty" Acord won a trip to Hawaii for him and his wife from PST Trucking for driving 5 million miles without an accident. (DN 8/5/91)

Lawrence Acord, accident-free driver.

In 1973, Curtis C. Stapp, San Leandro, California, was named ATA driver of the year for going 4 million miles without an accident. (CN 1/13/73)

In 1979, Willard R. Holmes, a counselor in the bishopric of the Evansville 2nd Ward, Evansville, Indiana, Stake, won a national safe-driving award for driving 1,500,000 miles without an accident. The American Motor Truck Association presented the award at a dinner held in his honor. (CN 12/22/79)

Most Languages (2002 World Record). John Henry Jorgensen, a senior linguistics major at BYU in 2002, is fluent in 15 languages. His list includes fluency in: American Sign Language, Arabic, Arabic Sign Language, Eastern and Western Armenian, English, French, Georgian, German, Italian, Mandarin, Russian, Spanish, Syrian and Turkish. At the time of his graduation, he was learning five additional languages (Japanese, Ukrainian, Mongolian, Persian and Czech) and planned to learn an additional five. (BYU 8/14/02)

John Jorgensen is fluent in more languages than anyone else in the world.

Children's Drawings. The largest single collection of children's art, more than 6,500 drawings from children ages 5-12 throughout the Church, was collected and displayed by the Museum of Church History and Art in Salt Lake City in 1988. Asked to illustrate their favorite Book of Mormon theme, the children submitted works in crayon, pencil, watercolor and collage. (CN 10/22/88)

Most Money for a Toy Design. Ricky Ardmore, 11, Eatonville Ward, East, Washington, Stake, won $50,000 for winning a "Masters of the Universe" toy-design contest. His creation, suitably named "Eye Beam," was a huge eyeball with muscular legs and arms to act as a seeing-eye guardian for He-Man, leader of the good guys in the Masters of the Universe world. (CN 2/9/88)

Photos by Paul B. Skousen

K. C. Willams set another record on Sept. 19, 2004, by inflating 89 160-Q balloons, a size virtually impossible to inflate (try it at your own risk!)

Most Balloons Inflated (2003 World Record). On Sept. 21, 2003, K.C. Williams of West Valley, Utah, set a new world record for the greatest number of balloons inflated and tied in one hour: 661.

Williams says he used 260-Q balloons, a type that is hard to inflate but has been established as the standard for this world record. He held the prior world record in 2002 by inflating and tying 599 balloons in one hour. He donates hundreds of hours and thousands of balloons to fund-raising and awareness events such as walkathons and charity games. He performed 30 times at the 2002 Olympic Winter Games and Paralympics and estimates he blew up, tied, and gave away more than 100,000 balloons in 2002. (Author's interview)

Most Tourists to a Temple. The largest number of pre-dedication tourists to visit a temple is 758,328 visitors who went through the Washington, D.C. Temple Nov. 19-22, 1974. The old record was 662,401 visitors at the pre-dedication tours of the Los Angeles Temple in 1956. (Church Almanac 1989)

J. M. Heslop, Deseret Morning News

The Washington D.C. Temple opened in 1974.

Most Hair Cut for a Charitable Cause. No LDS hair-cutting record stands against the quantity of hair cut for missionaries at the Missionary Training Center in Provo, Utah, but when it comes to charity, the young women of the Redondo Ward, Torrance, California, Stake, take the prize. After watching another young lady in their class suffer through chemotherapy and lose her hair, the young women decided to help. Each donated ten inches of her hair to "Locks of Love," an organization that takes human hair to make wigs for cancer patients. One by one, the girls had their hair cut, sometimes in tears, but all to support their friend and ward member. Local media picked up on the story and soon other LDS young women in the area had joined the project. Within a few weeks, more than 150 ponytails had been clipped, with more on the way. (CN 2/5/00)

Most Instruments Played. Raul Ayllon, baptized a member of the Church in his native land of Bolivia, is a very accomplished musician. By 1980, he could play more than 40 instruments, ranging from a miniature guitar made from an armadillo to a hand-carved flute. (DU 10/2/80)

Most Birthday Cards. When Bishop Vernon S. Johnson was released in the 1950s as Bishop of the Idaho Falls 4th Ward, Idaho, an amazing legacy of birthday card greetings ended. As bishop, he had given away to members of his ward a total of 11,000 birthday cards during his six years of service. (CN11/7/70)

Most Annual Visitors to Temple Square The record for the most visitors to Temple Square in one year keeps going up. In 1990, a new high was reached with 4,838,478 visitors to the popular site. This ranked Temple Square above visitors to the Grand Canyon (3.8 million), the Washington Monument (3.5 million), Yosemite Park (3.3 million), and the Statue of Liberty (2.9 million). The Smithsonian Institute in Washington, D.C.. topped them all with more than 28 million visitors. Temple Square continues to be an important stop to millions of visitors each year, with numbers always exceeding 5 million.

Pictured above, conference goers sport their best in 1906. The size of such crowds grows larger each year – only the clothing changes. Since Temple Square opened around the turn of the century, it has remained a "must see" for travelers passing through Salt Lake City. Today, the site typically hosts more than 5 million visitors a year.

Most Visitors to Temple Square at any Given Time. The largest number of persons to crowd onto Temple Square at one time was 31,206 for the Christmas lighting ceremony on Nov. 25, 1988. Elder Russell C. Taylor of the First Quorum of Seventy flipped the switch to the 300,000-plus lights. The power surge required the installation of special transformers so circuit breakers wouldn't blow and put all of Temple Square in the dark. (Author)

Most Subscriptions with Smallest LDS Representation. A break-even point of 600 subscriptions was all that stood between the 50 families of the Reykjavik, Iceland, Branch and the revenue to print a version of the Church magazines in their native language. But 600 subscriptions didn't discourage them. The branch members got busy selling door to door, and in two months they sold more than 650 subscriptions, in addition to their own 50. As the magazines were shipped to the branch members in 1986, they became the smallest congregation in the Church to receive the largest number of Church magazines. (CN 5/25/86)

Most Hand-Delivered Christmas Cards. The most Christmas Cards given out in the shortest period of time were 280,000 during the three days prior to Christmas by 100 missionaries in Singapore, Hong Kong and Taiwan. The cards were handed to individuals, not mailed, at the rate of almost 1,000 cards a day per missionary. (CN 1/18/69)

Most Traveled Hitchhiker. By 1982, former BYU student Neil Millman had traveled some 100,000 miles by thumb. His first trip across the United States (more than 4,000 miles) took only four days. He had hitched through 49 states and 16 countries. His longest wait for a ride was five days in Alaska. (DU 2/5/82)

Most Fanatic Football Fan. We have some sports nuts, but can anyone beat this? In 1984, Gary Jensen of Sandy, Utah, put a life-size poster of Robbie Bosco on his front door, transplanted into his backyard the actual piece of turf on which Jim McMahon completed the pass that set a new NCAA total-yardage record, and renamed his son Gifford McMahon Jensen. (LDS 12/28/85)

Church Museum Visitors. The Museum of Church History and Art, across from Temple Square, welcomed its 1 millionth visitor on Feb. 13, 1989, nearly five years after opening its doors on April 4, 1984. The honored visitors were Edwin and Afton Higley of the Clearfield, Utah, North 12th Ward, who had arrived there to volunteer. "Somebody told us how nice it was and we thought we ought to come visit," said Higley, a former bishop. (LDS 3/8/89)

YOUNGEST

Hang Glider Pilot. In 1982, the youngest pilot of a motorized hang glider was John Phillips, 12, who successfully mastered his "flying kite" and whose flying skills were featured on the nationally-televised kids' show, "Kidsworld." John lived in the Alma 9th Ward, Mesa, Nevada, Stake, and soloed for the first time Dec. 26, 1980. (LDS 5/21/82)

Star Search Dance Champion. In 1988, Jim Heywood, 9, a member of the Reynoldsburg, Ohio, Ward, and his partner were named Star Search junior dance champions on the national television program called "Star Search" hosted by Ed McMahon (CN 12/17/88)

Youngest Major-League Soloist. Three-year old Rex Spjute may be the youngest singer ever to perform at a major-league baseball game. At Dodger Stadium on June 9, 1999, young Rex took center stage and belted out the national anthem a cappella and on pitch. When Rex hit "... rockets red glare," the stadium exploded in cheers, whistles and applause. It so startled him, according to his mother, that Rex almost stopped singing. (CN 6/19/99)

FLAGS

Photos: (left) Joe Rosenthal (LOC), and (below) Marine photographer, Bob Cambell (LOC).

Most Recognized Flag. The famous flag raising in 1945 on the captured Japanese island of Iwo Jima was made possible, in part, thanks to a Mormon. The original flag wasn't dramatic enough for the photographer, so Elder A. Theodore Tuttle, a marine, was sent to his ship to retrieve a larger flag. The resulting photo became world famous (above right). As for that smaller flag, it was stowed away to see glory at another island on another day (right). (www.meridianmagazine. com)

Highest Place in America. On July 9, 1984, young men of the Morgan Hill 1st Ward celebrated the country's birthday and the Statue of Liberty's rededication by climbing Mt. Whitney, the highest point in the continental United States, and planted a U.S. flag there. The climb to the 14,495-foot peak took the young men two days. (CN 9/11/86)

Moments after Elder Theodore Tuttle's flag was raised over Iwo Jima on Feb. 20, 1945 (inset), the smaller original flag (above) was retired for duty elsewhere.

Photos by W. B. Skousen

Sandy, Utah: A display of 3,031 flags, one for each person killed Sept. 11, 2001, and one for each soldier killed in the war on terror since then, was created by Colonial Flag to honor and memorialize the dead.

Largest Display of Flags. On Sept. 11, 2002, Colonial Flag of Sandy, Utah, incorporated in 1989 by brothers Paul and David Swenson, set the record for the largest number of flags in one location when they observed the first anniversary of the terrorist attacks the year earlier. Their "Healing Fields" display has been duplicated around the country and draws hundreds of thousands of people to those locations each September. (Author)

Most Recognized Proxy. Sharlene Wells Hawkes, Miss America 1984, has the distinction of being the first and possibly only person to stand proxy for the American flag during a formal public pledge of allegiance. While attending a formal function in Arizona in 1986, the governor was about to lead everyone in the pledge of allegiance when he suddenly discovered there was no flag to salute. So he quickly invited the audience: "Will you please face Miss America and salute the flag." The group then stood, faced Hawkes, and recited the pledge of allegiance to the flag. (LDS 7/26/86)

Dave Siddoway, Deseret Morning News

Sharlene Wells Hawkes was crowned Miss America in 1984.

Using a convention center in Sandy, Utah, workers finished sewing together the largest flag in the Church. It was manufactured by Colonial Flag, a company owned by LDS brothers Paul and David Swenson. Michael Brandy, Deseret Morning News

Largest U.S. Flag. This huge flag (above) measures 150 feet by 300 feet (45,000 square feet of fabric), and was manufactured in 2004 by Colonial Flag of Sandy, Utah. It took six employees more than 425 hours to complete the sewing project. The stars are 7-1/2 feet across and the stripes are 12 feet wide. If laid on a football field this giant flag would stretch from goal line to goal line, and fall five feet short of the sideline boundaries. (DN 4/9/04)

Courtesy NASA

Highest Flying Flag. The flag associated with the Church that has flown the highest was aboard the ill-fated space shuttle Challenger that blew up in January 1986. The U.S. flag, wrapped in plastic and stowed in Challenger's cabin, had been placed there by Troop 514, sponsored by Monument Ward, Colorado Springs, Colorado, North Stake. As it turned out, the flag was one of the few items recovered intact after the explosion. Prior to the launch, the troop had the flag flown over the U.S. Capitol. In 1987, the Bicentennial Committee asked the troop if the flag could be flown over Independence Hall during the bicentennial celebration of the signing of the Constitution as a symbol of the never-dying spirit of the American people. (CN 2/7/87)

(Right) Last flight of the Challenger.

27

First U.S. Flag Over Los Angeles. The first American flag raised over Los Angeles was by the Mormon Battalion in 1847. (LDS 7/21/84)

First U.S. Flag Over Arizona? Was the first American flag raised over Arizona soil hoisted above Tucson by the Mormon Battalion? They raised the flag there during their record-breaking march of 2,000 miles in 1846-67. (LDS 7/21/84)

OLDEST

Parachute Jumper–Female. Who is the oldest LDS woman to parachute out of a plane? In 1987, it was Minnie Selkirk, 70, of the Newcastle-Upon-Tyne Ward in England. She jumped at 7,000 feet for a fund-raising activity in her community. Awaiting her arrival on the ground were her bishop, several ward members, and her doctor. (CN 1/24/87)

Commercial Airlines Pilot. In 1983, Ronald G. Ottesen, Larkspur, California, was the oldest active commercial pilot in the United States at the age of 62. He had been on the job more than 40 years. Flying at age 62 is unusual because airlines have a mandatory retirement of 60. He received a two-year extension because of his excellent health. (CN 7/10/83)

Oldest Unpaid Transportation Bill. After 124 years, the oldest outstanding debt in the Church was finally taken care of. When the Thomas and Mary Ann Riley family arrived in the United States in 1856, they were among the first to have their trip financed by the Church's Perpetual Emigration Fund. In 1880, when all of these debts were forgiven, the Rileys' names remained on the ledger books for some apparent clerical error. A descendant, A. Lisle Packard, was doing research on his family when he made this discovery and, as a fitting tribute to his forbear, and a way to donate to the Church, Packard repaid the debt of $69.76. (CN 1/26/80)

Oldest Unpaid Medical Bill. When mobs broke into Carthage Jail in 1844 and murdered Joseph and Hyrum Smith, John Taylor was shot four times but survived. Dr. Thomas Barnes cared for Elder Taylor's injuries and nursed him back to health. In a letter dated Nov. 6, 1897, Dr. Barnes gave his daughter, Mirand, graphic details of the shootings, and added, "We took the best care of him (John Taylor) we could till he left us. He got well but never paid us for skill or good wishes." Many decades later, Taylor's grandson, Raymond, became aware of the unpaid debt and decided to settle things with the family. In Santa Rosa, California, he finally located Mrs. Bertha Haskett. She was a direct descendant of Dr. Barnes. Upon hearing of Brother Taylor's quest to pay his grandfather's medical bill, Mrs. Haskett declined money but suggested any funds go to Southern Illinois University to create a collection about Mormons in Illinois. She quit-claimed the bill to a history professor at the university, Dr. Stanley B. Kimball. Some time later, Taylor received this letter from Dr. Kimball: "Please consider this letter as a statement to you for the sum of $1 which will fully satisfy this more than one hundred year old medical bill." Taylor dispatched a dollar immediately. (CN 2/22/64)

Oldest Working American (2003). In October 2003, Russell Clark, 102 was officially designated the oldest working American by Experience Works, a national organization funded by the U.S. Department of Labor. The honor goes once a year to the eldest American who continues to work full time and meets other criteria. Brother Clark's home is in Orem, and he commutes on a regular basis to manage property he owns in St. George, Nevada, California, and elsewhere. He retired as a surgeon in the 1980s. He was one of 11 children and

Russell Clark, oldest worker in the U.S. in 2003.

was raised on an Idaho farm. He and his wife, Ruby, raised five children. She passed away and he remarried Donna. He's taught medicine at BYU-Hawaii, and has walked three marathons, the first one after his 99th birthday. He's also served a mission with his wife. His secret? "I don't take medications, go easy on the sweets and carbohydrates, and I eat plenty of fruits and vegetables." (CN 9/28/03)

Oldest Birthday Party. Okay, so it isn't a Mormon or Jaredite birthday, but it was billed as the world's oldest party on Oct. 15, 1971, when Iran celebrated its 2,500th anniversary. Elder Ezra Taft Benson represented the Church at the seven-day event. Elder Benson found himself among kings, queens, heads of state and more than 10,000 invited guests who participated in what Iran called "The Greatest Spectacle on Earth." (CN 10/16/71)

Working Clock. The old pioneer clock brought to Salt Lake City originated in the iron works of Robert Wood & Co. of Philadelphia in 1870. The 18-foot-tall clock was proudly placed on the corner of First South and Main Street and instantly became a focal point in downtown Salt Lake City. Its early clock works were driven by a water wheel. A tunnel was dug beneath the Zion's Bank building on the same corner and a stream of water was

Paul B. Skousen

Utah State Historical Society

This clock appears in early historical photos when downtown Salt Lake City streets were little more than muddy ruts crowded with horses and carriages.

diverted from City Creek to turn the wheel. The water wheel later was replaced with four springs that kept it going five days between windings; they, in turn, were replaced with wet-cell batteries that could keep the clock running for up to six months. By 1912, a master clock had been installed at the bank to which the pioneer clock was then attached. (CN 7/19/69)

FASTEST

Fastest Typist. Who is the fastest typist in the Church? In 1985, Von E. Christensen took first place as the fastest typist in Utah with a speed of 124 words per minute. He was a member of the Sandy 37th Ward, Sandy, Utah, East Stake. (CN 1/20/85)

Fastest Shorthand. Who takes the fastest shorthand? We don't yet have the record in "words per minute," but we do have the name of Tracy Campbell, Melba Ward, Nampa, Idaho, South Stake, who won the 1984 Shorthand I competition at the Office Educational Association's national competition. One of 12 children, she was a straight-A student in her high school. (CN 8/19/84)

Fastest Traveling Toy Balloon. A balloon with a message from the Bountiful, Utah, 39th Ward's Days of '47 Children's Parade float was released on the morning of July 19, 1986, from Salt Lake City, Utah. The following day, July 20, at about 8:30 p.m., the balloon was found in Ontario, Canada, some 1,700 miles away. Experts estimated the balloon must have sustained a speed of 50 mph to make the trip in so short a time. (CN 8/24/86)

Deseret News Morning News file photos

National Soap Box Derby. Steve Souter, 12, Midland Ward, Texas, West Stake, won the 32nd All-American Soap Box Derby in Akron, Ohio, in 1969. His racer scooted down the 974.5-foot course with a time of 27.34 seconds. (CN 8/30/69)

Fastest Civilian Flier. Flying an F111 fighter-bomber, explorer John Goddard set the civilian air-speed record in that class at 1,500 mph. He also set a civilian speed record of 1,420 mph in the F-4 "Phantom." (DN 2/15/90)

Fast Female Pilot. Actress Terry Moore, wife of billionaire Howard Hughes, and a star in more than 30 movies, was the third woman in history to win her wings as a jet pilot. (Internet)

Fastest Knot Tying. In 1974, Kenneth Purnell, 12, a member of Troop 55 in the Boy Scouts of Canada, set a new Canadian national record for tying six different knots in 10.9 seconds. The old record set in 1957 was 12.5 seconds. Kenneth was a member of the Calgary 3rd Ward, Alberta, Canada. (CN 6/22/74)

Deseret Morning News File Photo

Fastest Construction of a Fence By Hand. In 1952, 100 St. Johns, Arizona, welfare workers dug post holes by hand and strung a fence 15,840 feet in length, without any mechanical aid, in about 50 hours. (CN 12/26/51)

In 1903, some 250 men from Brigham Young Academy's student body were put to work to dig one post hole each around the new track for a fence some 2,000 feet in length. They had all 250 holes dug in under ten minutes. (CN 6/5/54)

Micah Crapo takes aim down a grocery bag. In 2001, he was the fastest groceries bagger in the world.

Deseret Morning News

Fastest Groceries Bagger. Micah Crapo, 17, Bluffdale 2nd Ward, Bluffdale, Utah, Stake, was crowned, er, bagged as Best Bagger 2001 by the National Grocers Association at its annual contest in Dallas. The youngest in the final round, Micah had been working at a grocery store for less than a year. He won $2,000 and an appearance on "The Late Show with David Letterman." (CN 3/3/01)

Fastest Selling LDS Book. On Aug. 2, 1985, the fastest selling Church book in history made its debut, selling more than 1 million copies in a short 10-month period. For its first few months in print it was rolling out the doors at about 3,000 copies a day, and was nearly always on back order. Surprisingly, this best seller wasn't any of the scriptures nor an epic tome by one of the brethren, but rather a favorite of both children and adults alike: the newly revised and improved LDS Hymnal! (CN 6/29/86)

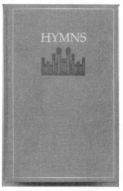

Best seller!

LONGEST

Longest Pole Sit. As of 1983, the Mormon record for pole-sitting was 1,000 hours (41 days), set by Gloria Skinner, 27, University 2nd Ward, Tempe Stake, Arizona. She sat in a 7x10-foot compartment atop four 15-foot poles from 4:30 p.m., Oct. 28, until 8:30 a.m., Dec. 8, 1983, to raise more than $100,000 for research towards a cure for multiple sclerosis. (LDS 10/28/83)

Longest Continuous Typing (1985 World Record). In 1985, Violet Gibson Burns, Ryde Ward, Sydney, Australia, Greenwich Stake, won an exhausting endurance contest, typing nonstop for 264 hours, setting a new world's record. In any human endurance contest, participants are always allowed rest periods at various stages of an activity. The typing-endurance contest, called the Australia Cup Challenge II, pitted Americans against Australians. (CN 7/21/85)

Longest Teeter-Totter Ride (1974 World Record). In 1974, Dean Walton, 12, and his buddy, Mike Furniss, 13, set a new world's record for non-stop teeter-tottering, enduring 13 straight days and nights to complete a record-shattering 300 hours. The old record was 216 hours. The boys took turns sleeping by lying lengthwise on the board while the other kept it in motion. At the end of each 60 minutes they were allowed five minutes to dash to the bathroom, stretch, and grab some food. The boys also used the marathon event to raise $700 for charity. They were members of the Redding 12th Ward, Redding, California, Stake. (CN 7/27/74)

Longest Wheelie (1977 World Record). The world record for the longest wheelie (riding on the back tire of a two-wheeled bicycle) was 5.1 miles, set in 1977 by Robert Carlisle, American Fork, Utah. He made an attempt at American Fork's Alpine Days celebration, but fell just a block short of his five-mile goal, much to his disappointment. He felt so bad he went back that afternoon and did it again, exceeding his goal by one-tenth of a mile. (Author)

Longest Chess Game. After 111 hours of play at the Salt Lake Holiday Inn, Mike Stone and Robert Tanner gave up trying to set the world's record for chess playing. But their record game, begun Sept. 10, 1979, nevertheless stands as the longest non-stop chess game played by Mormons. Though Stone passed out the last morning and couldn't be revived, the duo had raised more than $2,000 for the March of Dimes. (DU 9/18/79)

Ryan Tripp mowed down a world record in 1997 when he arrived in Washington D.C. to clean things up.

Longest Riding-Mower Trek (1997 World Record). In 1997, 12-year old Ryan Tripp, a deacon in the Beaver 6th Ward, Beaver, Utah, Stake, set a world's record when he drove a riding-lawn mower 3,116 miles between Aug, 15 and Sept. 25. Leaving Utah, he traveled cross country to Washington, D.C.. At the end of his journey he mowed part of the U.S. Capitol's west front lawn. The drive was intended to raise money for a sick friend. The old world's record was 3,034 miles. (CN 11/1/97)

Longest Unicycle Ride. On the first clear day in April 1969, Phil Hulme finished a 12-mile, 2-1/2-hour ride on his unicycle as his "reward" to his Georgetown, Washington, D.C., Elders Quorum who had met the challenge to have 100 percent home teaching during October 1968. Hulme would have made the single-wheeled trip earlier, but bad weather put the trip off for several months. (CN 5/3/69)

Longest Last Name. Who has the longest last name in the Church? In 1945, it may well have been the district Aaronic Priesthood leader and first counselor in the Wailuku Branch presidency in Hawaii. His 22-character last name could probably be put to music: Solomon Kekanakailokookoaihana. (CN 6/30/45)

Longest Bus Trip to a Temple. Who has the longest bus ride to an LDS temple? In 1979, the longest round-trip bus ride for patrons attending the Mesa Temple was for families in the Canal Zone of Panama. The 8,000-mile bus trek was over some narrow, dangerous roads through all kinds of weather and danger of attack by gangs of robbers in some areas. On Jan. 12, 1979, several families were the first to make the journey. The $160/person trip required most of them to sell many of their personal belongings to afford the once-in-a-liftime adventure. (CN 3/13/76)

Longest Lifetime Walk. Who in the Church has walked the farthest? Ranking close to the top must be Annie Starling Pilcher, Enoch, Texas. For 43 years, she walked from her home to Church and back again, a round trip of about 11 1/2 miles. This totaled more than 25,800 miles, or the equivalent of about once around the earth. (CN 3/16/49)

Longest Regular Commute to Church. For more than a year, beginning in 1959, E. Wiley Barker had to travel 2,500 miles each week to attend Church. As an assistant corporate secretary for Trans World Airlines, Barker would leave his Kansas City home for New York on Tuesday morning, be the first to MIA prayer meeting that evening (he taught the Manhattan Ward M Men-Gleaner class), and returned to his home ward in Kansas City Thursday or Friday. (CN 7/25/59)

Beginning in 1965, Josephine Maass, 63, got up at 4:15 a.m. for Church. She walked 30 minutes to the train station and took a two-hour ride to the Wels, Australia, Branch, a ride of 50 miles. She couldn't attend all of her meetings because the train schedule would have left her stranded overnight. But for eight years, she faithfully made the trek. (CN 11/17/73)

ODDS & ENDS

Best Marksman. In 1978, Addison Clark, Kalispell 1st Ward, Kalispell, Montana, Stake, out-performed the Secret Service, the Los Angeles Police Department and the Texas Rangers to win the National Shooters League handgun competition. He earned 163 out of a possible 200 points in the contest, the highest score ever, on a course covering more than 200 yards with targets 15 to 60 yards away that were only 2 to 5 inches in size. And all of this in only 3-1/2 minutes. (CN 11/25/78)

Addison Clark was the best shot in the U.S. in 1978.

Farthest Glider Soar. Gary F. Kemp of the Chico, California Stake, soared 1,000 kilometers from Parowan, Utah, in 1994, making him one of 60 people in the United States and 250 in the world to have soared so far. Kemp used a standard class Pegasus glider. At the time of the flight he also held 19 other Utah soaring records. (CN 8/20/94)

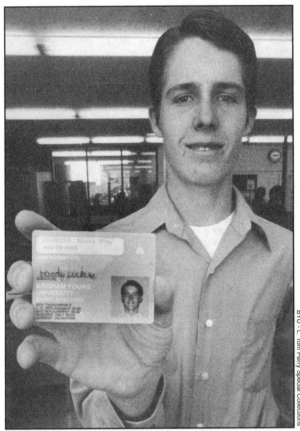

In 1976, Randy Jenkins had the lowest social security number in America: 000-0000-0001.

BYU - L. Tom Perry Special Collections

Lowest Social Security Number. The lowest Social Security Number (SSN) in the Church was 000-00-0001. It was reissued to Randy Jenkins of the Glendale, Arizona, Sixth Ward, Glendale North Stake, in 1976. The number had previously been used, of course. However, Brother Jenkins just had to have that number! With a lot of tenacity and determination, he climbed over the federal bureaucracy and, with the help of his Ari-zona congressmen and sena-tors, sparked the passage of a bill authorizing the reissue of the first 10 Social Security numbers. Congress agreed to reis-sue the numbers in 1976 "in the spirit of the Bicentennial celebration." However, a few years of having to prove the number was a real one, Jenkins became fed up with the problems of being "number one" and applied for a regular number. Every time he wrote his number down, computers or people would reject it saying the number was a phony. Even at BYU, he was constantly taking letters and forms back and forth between professors when the BYU computerized class scheduling system wouldn't accept his SSN as proper student identification. (LDS 7/16/82)

Longest Distance Traveled At Sea. During his Navy career of 28 years, Capt. Robert H. Lemmon sailed more than 500,000 miles at sea. With home base at Coronado Branch, San Diego, California, Stake, he and his wife Patricia became friends to dozens, if not hundreds, of sailors looking for a temporary "home port" among friendly LDS people. Lemmon served as branch president. Among his many distinguished Naval assignments, he commanded a destroyer escort, a destroyer, a destroyer division, a cruiser and served as an assistant to a fleet commander. (CN 2/26/70)

First Mormon to bow hunt buffalo on horse back? The only known Mormon to kill a buffalo with a bow and arrow from horseback is Lee Nelson, Mapleton 4th Ward, Mapleton Utah South Stake. In 1980, while doing research for his Storm Testament series of historical novels, Brother Nelson took down a thousand pound bull buffalo in a desert canyon near Tooele, Utah. Hunting free-range buffalo is illegal, so Nelson bought the animal to learn how hard that early Indian hunt really was. He and his companions camped for four days tanning

Lee Nelson prepares to take down a buffalo he bought for $550 as part of his research for books he was writing.

the hide and preparing the meat as early Indians did. Since the buffalo almost went extinct in the 1880s, no known person has hunted buffalo in this manner. Others have since tried to duplicate the feat but have failed. (Author's interview)

Farthest Fall. Elder Matthew Weirich, 21, originally from Texas and serving in the Australia Sydney South mission, probably holds the record for the farthest fall survived by a member of the Church. When trying to retrieve a companion's shoe while hiking near the Grand Canyon Lookout in Southwest Australia, he tumbled over the edge and fell 210 feet. "It's a miracle," said the local police spokesman. "I guess the boss was looking after him." Weirich suffered serious head and spinal injuries, but otherwise had no broken bones and not a scratch on him. The trees and underbrush are credited with breaking his fall, but the Weirich family, and millions of others believe otherwise -- it was a miracle. (DN 6/24/04)

FOOD

Largest Cookie (1985 World Record). The largest cookie in the world in 1985 was a 4,200-pound tollhouse delight that was made in the parking lot of a Salt Lake City grocery store. Eight bakers used 2 million chocolate chips, 1,200 pounds of flour, 336 eggs, and 192 pounds of butter, mixed and poured out as a 20-foot by 30-foot cookie that was rolled into a special oven to cook. Pieces were sold to raise funds for Utahns Against Hunger. (DU 10/17/85)

Longest Sandwich. Who dares claim the longest sandwich? In May 1992, President Gordon B. Hinckley was invited to cut a 20-foot sandwich at the grand opening of The Park Food Court in the ZCMI Center in Salt Lake

City. Since the food court's theme is food, the usual ribbon-cutting ceremony was replaced with the unusual sandwich slicing. (DN 5/5/92)

Tom Smart, Deseret Morning News

President Hinckley prepares to cut a 20 foot sandwich.

Deseret Morning News file photo

The world's biggest pie in 1950 was being served at a ward fundraiser.

Largest Pie (1950 World Record). The world's largest pie in 1950 could be tasted at the Park Avenue Ward building-fund carnival in Salt Lake City. Forty-two inches in diameter, the lemon-custard pie required 120 eggs, nine cases of condensed milk, 1/2 case of lemons, 60 packages of ready-to-mix pie crust, and a lot of patience. On the last evening of the fund-raising event, ward members cut it into 500 pieces and sold them at 15 cents a slab. (CN 9/13/50)

Most Holiday Cookies. Every holiday season for the past two decades, Sid L. Walker, Salt Lake City, has cooked about 10,000 cookies as gifts to family and friends. He started his tradition while his boys were on missions and continues to this day. He estimates that over the past 15 years alone he has used more than 3,400 pounds of flour, 1,600 pounds of sugar and 2,600 pounds of butter. For Christmas 2002, Brother Walker rose daily at 4 a.m. to bake. His 15,000 cookies were packaged and express-mailed to locations across the United States, Korea, New Zealand, the Netherlands, Canada, the Dominican Republic and elsewhere. The cookies typically cost him $1,500 for ingredients and $500 for shipping – all donated to the cause of holiday giving. (Author)

Pillsbury Bake-off. In 1992, a record total of four Utah contestants to that year's Pillsbury Bake-off made it into the top 100 finalists. Maureen Pinegar, Vilah Peterson, Carol Winder, all of Salt Lake City, and Penelope Weiss, Provo competed against more than 40,000 contestants. To better appreciate this accomplishment, con-

Kristan Jacobsen, Deseret Morning News

In 1992, a cook from Utah had a .7 percent chance of making the Pillsbury Bake-off. That same year, four Utahns were selected.

sider that the home-cooking state of Utah had only four finalists in the prior 10 years, and no one even entered in 1986 or 1988. The ladies figured their chances of getting at least one entry from Utah in the top 100 was .7 percent! Of the 40,000-plus recipes entered, 1,500 were chosen for testing, and from those, 100 were chosen as finalists. When the flour dust had settled, Carol Winder was the only cash winner, receiving a prize of $2,000 for her Super Lemon Pie. (DN 2/18/92)

Champion Cooks in the Pillsbury Bake-off. Judy Moon, Jacksonville Beach Ward, Jacksonville, Florida, East Stake was one of 13 national winners in the 1980 Pillsbury Bake-off with her entry of "Easy-as-Pie Almond Fingers," winning $2,000. (CN 6/28/80)

Judie Boyd Miller, Mesa, Arizona, won one of three $5,000 awards given at the 1975 Pillsbury Co./General Electric bake-off contest in San Francisco with the best wheat rolls in the country. (CN 1/3/76)

Largest Milkshake (1986 World Record). The largest milkshake in the world in 1986 was made by the BYU 7th Stake. Using 60 gallons of ice cream, 30 gallons of milk, two gallons of syrup, and 33 pounds of Oreo cookies, the 92-gallon shake shattered the previous world's record of 50 gallons set in 1986. (LDS 7/9/88)

Ice Cream Consumption. Utah is still in the top five ice cream-eating states in the country on a per capita basis. Californians eat the most ice cream in total (193 million gallons), but Utah's 14.1 million gallons eaten each year, and its smaller population, keeps it neck and neck with California as the greatest consumers. In 1991, Utah residents were eating 7.12 gallons of ice cream per person, compared to the national average of 5.5 gallons. In 2000 that number had dropped to 6.3 gallons per person. But with the Olympic games and a growing population, the numbers are way up again. (Census)

Utah State University

Nobody cooks turkey like Stephanie Hughes, and a nation-wide contest proved it.

Best Turkey Cook. In November 2002, Stephanie Hughes, Spanish Fork, Utah, won the National 4 H Turkey Barbecue contest in Louisville, Kentucky. She competed against 13 other finalists from around the country and won a $500 savings bond. Her secret list of herbs and spices? Just one: a bottle of teriyaki sauce straight from the grocery store, and a slowly marinating turkey. The judges were smitten! (DN 7/2/03)

Biggest Milk Drinkers. Utah residents drink more milk per capita than anyone else in the nation. The average Utah resident gulps down milk at the rate of 130 or more gallons per year, compared to the national average of about 100 gallons per person per year. (Utah Dairy Commission, USA Today 7/19/91)

Greatest Consumers of Cracker Jacks. So, which state loves Cracker Jacks the most? For several years the Cracker Jack consumption capital of the world continues to be Utah. And if not on top, Utah continues to remain among the top five. In the Beehive State, Cracker Jacks is particularly popular among youth ages 3 to 11. (LDS 9/6/89; author)

Hooked on Candy Bars. Salt Lake City was the candy bar and marshmallow consumption capital of the nation in 1985. On a per-capita basis, Salt Lakers swallowed more candy bars than anyone else in the United States, prompting the editorial cartoonist for the Deseret News, Calvin Grondahl, to comment, "We don't spend a lot on light beer, so we go heavy on the chocolate. That's the way it is with people, you crack down on one vice and they go to something else!" (DU 9/4/85)

Best-Selling Cookbooks. The most famous Mormon cooks are most likely Karine Eliason, Madeline Westover and Nevada Harward. These three Mormon mothers were walking partners before deciding to collaborate on what became in 1987 the ever-popular "Make A Mix" books. Today, Sister Eliason and Sister Harward report that their combined total book sales exceed 2 million copies. (LDS 6/28/87; www.make-a-mix.com/aboutus.asp)

Puzzling Cookies. Jessie Carlile's cookie recipe isn't that complicated, but the thousands of people who bought her cookies are spending hundreds of hours trying to put them together. Well, not the real cookies, but photographs of them. Sister Carlile, of the Pittsburgh Ward, Joplin, Missouri, Stake, used 10 different recipes, making a dozen of each, for puzzles by Hallmark Cards. "I had cookies running out of the house," she says. Hallmark Cards' jigsaw puzzle representatives took the cookies to the Kansas City office to arrange them and photograph them. Presumably, the cookies were eaten afterwards by the staff. (CN 11/25/78)

SEWING

Largest Sewing Project. The largest sewing project in Church history was organized by volunteers preparing for a multi-regional dance festival during the Rose Bowl activities in 1985. More than 16,000 LDS dancers had to be outfitted with costumes. Men's waist sizes ranged from 26 to 50, and women's sizes ranged from 4 to 38. Supplies included 100,800 buttons, 70,000 yards of satin, 35,000 yards of netting, 25,000 yards of crinoline, 20,000 yards of shearing and baby hemming, 15,000 yards of polyester gabardine, not to mention 16,200 T-shirts, 6,000 petticoats, and 6,000 pettipants. Oh, yes, and also 1,900 hats. Dancers paid $40 apiece for their costumes; the workers performed the labor for free. (LDS 7/20/85)

Most Prolific Seamstress. Who in the Church sews the most? Over a 50-year period, Mary Peters, 17th Ward, Salt Lake Stake, contributed to Mormon Handicraft 13,986 hand-sewn items for sale. "When I started," she said, "I hardly had money to pay for thread." Her earnings were invested and helped support her in her retirement years. (CN 3/28/87)

Most Needlework by an Individual. Audria Butler, Garland, Utah, 1st Ward, crocheted 73 items (tablecloths, altar cloths, doilies) for 10 temples on three continents over a 15-year period. "The most important thing was getting the articles perfect," she says. "If I knew there was a mistake, I'd correct it even if I had to undo three- or four-day's work." (CN 1/26/86)

Most Widely-traveled Quilt. In a Church of quilt-making experts for the last century and a half, Beverly Melrose, Medina, Ohio, Ward, has risen to the top with her award-winning quilt entitled, "Dress Up." The Great American Arts Festival selected her quilt in 1989 as the Ohio winner and one of 61 to take a three-year tour around the world. There were more than 1,200 quilts entered from all over the world. (CN 7/15/89)

ANIMAL SUPERLATIVES

Leonard and Harriet Arrington

Leonard and Harriet Arrington wondered if KFC offered a finders fee ....

Largest Chicken. Former Church historian and long-time chicken farmer Leonard Arrington and his wife, Harriet, of Parleys 1st Ward, Parleys Utah Stake, were the proud owners of the largest chicken in the Church in 1987. Okay, so this wasn't a live chicken, but where else do we put a chicken 6 feet tall and looking like it won't take no for an answer? This plastic-and-fiberglass bird showed up on the Arringtons' front porch on Christmas Eve, 1987. Stepson Rick Sorenson had the bird flown in overnight as a Christmas present. When the bird was discovered out front on Christmas morning, Brother Arrington said "We just laughed and laughed for two hours straight." (Author)

Largest Cow. The largest real cow among LDS is yet to be determined, but a bigger-than-life plastic-and-fiberglass cow that stood 10 feet high was delivered to a BYU student's new in-laws. It was payment, he explained, for their daughter's hand in marriage, a la Johnny Lingo style. (Johnny Lingo was the title of an old Church film about a plain-looking and scorned young woman whose self image is rescued when Johnny Lingo buys her with eight cows, a payment higher than that offered for any other wife in the village.) (LDS 2/11/83)

Nation's "First Puppies." When President Gerald R. Ford's dog, Liberty, gave birth on the third floor (the residence) of the White House to a litter of nine puppies, he gave the first one to Jennifer Brown, 15, of Tremonton, Utah. As suggested by President Ford, she named the golden retriever "Liberty's Pride." President Ford had a close association with Jennifer's father, James E. Brown, who was an FBI agent and Ford's skiing partner. (CN 11/29/75)

Heavyweight House Cat.

Where does a 54-pound house cat lie down to sleep? Anywhere he wants to, says Adam H. Didra, a high priest in the Winder 9th Ward, Winder, Utah, Stake. Adam's cat, Sneaky, was the heaviest cat in the Church, and possibly in all of north America. Featured on local Utah news, and worldwide on CNN, Sneaky was one VERY large cat. Most neighborhood kids couldn't even pick him up, Adam said. "Sneaky" was so named because he snuck into the Didras' car while they were on their way to Church. As a kitten, he put on weight rapidly. The seven-year old cat weighed 39 pounds 12 ounces in 1990, and would later tip the scales between 45 and 55 pounds depending on the season. (DN 2/10/92; author)

Don Grayston, Deseret Morning News

Sneaky the cat broke the world's heavy-cat record, but each time an official weight was taken, sneaky had snuck off more pounds.

Most Popular Birds. Salt Lake City's Tracy Aviary, established in 1908, has more than 300,000 visitors per year, the highest number of visitors to an aviary in the world. More than 240 species of birds are on display. (Tracy Aviary)

Largest Fish Caught in Downtown Salt Lake. Pulling a 13-1/2 inch rainbow trout from State Street in downtown Salt Lake City isn't what you'd call a classic fish story, but that's exactly what Alma Allred did on May 31, 1983. When State Street was turned into a canal with sandbags during the spring flooding of 1983, Allred spied the trout swimming in the murky water. He reached in and grabbed it, much to the dismay of passers-by, and preserved it in a basin of water until he could go home and present it to his mother for dinner. (DU 6/2/83)

Paul B. Skousen

"You gotta shave, grandpa."
The Church's emphasis on family and its eternal nature attracts converts from all walks of life. It helps members build the best and most secure nurturing environment for raising Saints young and old. And from such work comes a unique and positive force for good in the earth – *the LDS Human Being.*

The LDS Human Being

The LDS human being – by the numbers:

1— Number of septuplet (7) births by an LDS couple
26 — Inches difference between tallest Mormon and his wife
118 — Years old when oldest woman was baptized into the Church
750 — LDS soldiers killed in World War I
100,000 — Words per minute read by a Mormon speed-reader
12,000,000 — Members of the Church in 2004

With a life span 8-11 years longer than the average American, a very low incidence of life-threatening diseases, and a reputation as one of the hardest-working, happiest, and most prolific groups in the world, the LDS human being is indeed a wonder to behold. Here is a sampling of some of these extraordinary LDS in the world of today or recent past.

AS FOR THE SAINTS IN UTAH ...

From the U.S. 2000 Census, the Saints in Utah have a pretty good thing going, numbers wise.
- The largest household size: 3.06 persons per household (U.S. average is 2.59).
- The highest birth rate: 21.7 births/1,000 per year.
- The youngest population: average age 26.7 years.
- The highest literacy rate: 94 percent.
- Violent crime in Utah is 238 per 100,000 compared to 505 per 100,000 nationally.
- One of the healthiest populations: third in the United States
- The lowest number of smokers: 16.8 percent compared to an average of 22.7 percent in the U.S.
- The lowest consumption of alcohol: 21.47 gallons per capita (Nevada averages 61).
- The third-longest life expectancy: males 74.93 (U.S.: 71.83), females 80.38 (U.S.: 78.81).
- Among America's top ten in high school graduation rates at 83 percent.
- One of the lowest infant mortality rates: 5.6 per 1,000 (U.S. average is 7.2).
- One of the lowest heart-disease mortality rates: 190 per 100,000 per year (U.S. is 268 victims per 100,000).

• One of the lowest overall death rates: 787 per 100,000 per year (U.S. average is 882 per 100,000).

AGE

OLDEST

Sister Rampas became the oldest woman in the Church when she was baptized in 1983.

Bill Stuart, Deseret morning News

Oldest Woman. Who has been the oldest living woman in the Church? In 1984, the oldest woman was 118 years old at the time of her baptism. Encarnacion Banares Rampas of Cuzco, Peru, was born in March of 1865, in Anta, Peru. She was baptized October 1983. She told the missionaries during her first visit to a Church meeting, "I just like the feeling there." (CN 2/26/84)

Oldest Man. Who has been the oldest living man in the Church? In 1980, the oldest man was 116 years old at the time of his baptism. Nicholas Santucho of Canada de Gomez, Argentina, was baptized in the fall of that year; his wife was baptized a week later at the age of 86. They were the parents of 17 children. "There is no secret to long life," Santucho said. "I have lived because God has wished it so." (CN 12/13/80)

Longest-Wed Couple (1960 World Record). On Dec. 11, 1960, Peter (100) and Celestia Terry Peterson (99) set a new world record as the longest-married couple, having been wed 82 years. They married Dec. 11, 1878, in the St. George Temple and lived long enough to witness each of their ten living children all marry in the temple. (CN 12/6/58; www.proutah.com)

In 2002, Marion and Erma Winn were recognized at a ceremony during the Olympic Winter Games in Salt Lake

Nicholas Santucho was the oldest man in the Church in 1980

Deseret Morning News file photo

City as the longest-wed couple in the United States at 78 years. They were married in the Logan Temple on Dec. 24, 1924. (CN 2/02)

Oldest Twins. The oldest twins in the Church turned 93 April 17, 1991. Margaret Olson Davidson and Mabel Field Nielson made their Utah homes in Manti and Pleasant View, respectively. (LDS 5/31/91)

Oldest Male-Female twins. Orlando Erickson and his twin sister, Amanda Binks, both Utah LDS, celebrated their 92nd birthday Jan. 28, 1991. (LDS 2/22/89)

Oldest Native Armenian. Venus Aposhian Orullian, believed to be one of the oldest living Armenians, turned 101 on May 16, 1991. She emigrated to the United States in 1908 with her brothers and sisters. They were met in New York by LDS missionaries. Because of a mixup, the family was accident-

Margaret and Mabel Olson

Oldest twins in the Church in 1991.

ly sent to a polygamist colony on the Mexican border. But when the parents arrived in the United States a short time later, the mess was straightened out and the whole family settled in Utah. Venus married Joseph Orullian on July 2, 1909, and the couple had nine children. Joseph, a gardener on the Salt Lake Temple grounds, died in 1955. (DN 5/14/90)

Fewest People Over 65. According to the 2000 Census, there are not many people 65 and older in Summit County, Utah. In fact, that county ranks near the bottom (3,125 out of 3,141 counties) in the United States, with only 4.9 percent of its population older than 65. Utah County ranked 3,088 with 6.4 of its population older than 65. Compare this with the oldest county in America: Charlotte County, Florida, where 34.7 percent of its population was over 65.

Among the 245 cities of 100,000 or more, West Valley City, Utah, had 5.4 percent of its population over 65, placing it at the 241st spot out of 245. Provo ranked 236th with 5.7 percent. Salt Lake City was close to average with 11 percent of its population 65 or older (ranked 119).

Fewest People Over 85. Despite the youthful population of Utah, there are still a few people 85 and older in the state. According to the 2000 Census,

Alaska had the fewest people 85 and older (.4 percent), and Utah came in next with 1.0 percent, or 21,751.

Among the 245 largest cities, West Valley City, Utah, was third from the bottom with 399 citizens (0.4 percent of the population) 85 years or older. Salt Lake City had most of Utah's 85+ year-old senior citizens with 3,155, ranking it 62 out of 245 cities. (Census 2000)

Fewest People Over 100. Are you a centenarian? If so, you're a rare breed! The most people 100 years old or older were found in California (5,341) and the fewest in Alaska (34). Utah had 155 in the year 2000, putting it 46th in the nation. There were 50,454 nationwide. (Census 2000)

SIZE

Tallest Man. Shawn Bradley, who stands 7 feet 6 inches, is the tallest living Latter-day Saint, and possibly the tallest LDS ever. He was a very highly recruited basketball star from Emery High School in Castle Dale, Utah, and signed on with BYU where his reputation as a rebounder and shot-blocker followed him through a successful first season. After serving a mission, he signed on with the Philadelphia 76ers. (CN 9/23/89; author)

Tallest Woman. Who is the tallest LDS woman? Teresa Spaulding, originally of Idaho, was a star player on BYU's women's basketball team in 1983. She stood 6 foot 7 inches tall. (DU 11/11/83)

Shawn Bradley turned a lot of heads up during his mission to Australia.

Shortest. Billy Barty, well known on TV and in movies, was 3 feet 9 inches tall. He served as an assistant ward clerk in his Studio City Ward, Hollywood, and was very active in the movement to stop discrimination against short people. He joined the Church in 1963, two years after marrying his LDS wife from Idaho. He appeared in more than 150 motion pictures and several hundred TV shows beginning in the 1930s. Some of

Billy Barty poses at the unveiling of his star on Hollywood's Walk of Fame.

his last starring roles included the movies "Willow" and "Rumpelstiltskin." (LDS 2/11/83; DN 3/90)

Wayne T. Shaw, University Ward, Portland, Oregon, Stake, stood 3 feet 9 inches tall. Born in Ontario, Ore., the youngest of seven children, he was afflicted as an infant with a bone disorder called osteogenesis imperfecta. He couldn't walk until he was 26 and, as an adult, got around on crutches, drove a car, and designed his own dune buggy. A talented draftsman for the Bonneville Power Administration in Portland, he was selected as one of 10 outstanding handicapped federal employees for 1976. (CN 11/20/76)

Chuck Wing, Deseret Morning News

Shortest Brothers. Brothers Kim and Kent Page, Tucson, Arizona, each stood 3 feet 9 inches. (CN 7/31/76)

Greatest Size Difference. Professional basketball player Shawn Bradley, and his wife Annette, may have a larger difference in height than any other married couple in the Church. Shawn towers to 7-foot-6 while Annette stands at 5-foot-4, a size difference of 26 inches. (Internet)

Heaviest Baby. Who is the heaviest baby born into the Church? In Utah, the heaviest tipped the scales at 16 pounds 13 ounces. Mrs. Renee Kelsch of Salt Lake City gave birth to Jodie K., her twelfth child, at Cottonwood Hospital on Jan. 25, 1979. (DN 1/27/79)

Shawn Bradley and his wife Annette

Paul Barker, Deseret Morning News

Healthy baby at 16 pounds!

REPRODUCTION

Most Families. In 1991, South Jordan, Utah, took the title as "Family City of America" with 93.4 percent of households filled with families, the highest percentage in America (both single parent and married couples were included in the number). Families headed by married couples again put South Jordan at the top in America, with 87.1 percent. Years after the fact, not a lot has changed. The southern end of the Salt Lake Valley continues to stand out as one of the youngest regions in the nation. (CN 6/4/91)

Most Married-Couple Households. From Census 2000, Utah led the nation in households headed by a married couple at 63.2 percent compared to the United States average of 51.7 percent.

Fewest Unmarried-Partner Households. Utah tied with Alabama for having the lowest percentage of unmarried couples heading up a household at 3.4 percent compared with Vermont and Alaska (7.5 percent) at the other end of the scale. In California, more than 684,000 unmarried couples were heads of household, as of 2000. (Census 2000)

Church Goers Have Better Marriages. LDS couples who attend Church services together have a divorce rate of about 20 percent compared to the national average of 50 percent. If only one spouse attends Church, the divorce rate soars above the national average. (Research by Tim Heaton, BYU, 1995)

Education and Family Size. The more education an LDS woman has, the larger her family. This is just the opposite of the national norm that shows that more educated women choose fewer children. (Tim Heaton, BYU, 1995)

Largest Household. In 2000, Utah had the largest average household among all United States cities with 3.13 people per household while the national average was 2.59. (Census 2000)

Youngest City. According to the 2000 Census, Provo, Utah, had the youngest population with an average age of 22.9 years. West Valley City, Utah, ranked eighth youngest at 26.8 years. The retirement cities in the Sun Belt states had the oldest residents on average.

Youngest County. In 2000, Utah County was the youngest in the nation at an average of 23.3 years old compared to the national average of 35.3 years old. (Internet)

Youngest State. The median age of 27.1 in Utah is about eight years younger than the national median of 35.3, according to the 2000 Census.

Family Friendly. The percentage of people in Utah who live in a household is the highest in the nation at 76.3 percent (68.1 percent for the United States). Utah ranks close to the bottom (47th out of 50) in households led by a single parent with children. (2000 Census)

Most Babies in One Delivery. The first septuplet (7) birth in the U.S. was by Samuel and Patti Oragenson Frustaci, Riverside, California, on May 21, 1985. Sister Frustaci, a 30-year-old English teacher at the time, had been taking a fertility drug. One baby was stillborn and only three survived. The birth-weights were between 1 pound 1 ounce and 1 pound 3 ounces. The three surviving children won lifelong monthly payments following a $6.2 million malpractice settlement against the fertility clinic that treated Mrs. Frustaci. Shortly after the law suit was resolved, the Frustacis' attorney announced that she was pregnant again and in late 1990, she gave birth to healthy twins. Her babies were named Patricia Ann, James Martin, Stephen Earl, Bonnie Marie, Richard Charles, David Anthony, and Christina Elizabeth. (LDS 5/85, 6/85, CN 7/11/90, Internet)

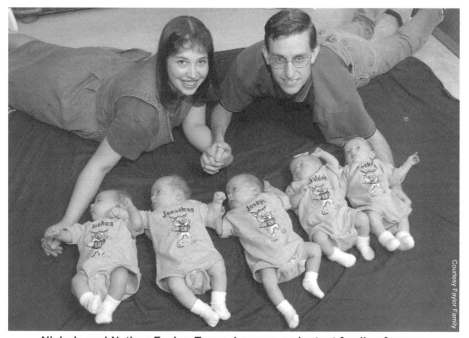

Courtesy Faylor Family

Nichole and Nathan Faylor, Texas, became an instant family of seven.

Quintuplets. On Sept. 1, 2002, Nichole and Nathan Faylor of the Plum Creek Ward, Austin, Texas, Oak Hills Stake, gave birth to quintuplets (5). The five babies weighed from 2 pounds 12 ounces to 4 pounds 5 ounces, and were named Joshua, Jonathan, Joseph, Nataleigh and Cathryn. It was quite the chore to care for the children. Besides the five cribs, highchairs, and car seats, plus a new minivan to transport the family, the babies required 40-50 diapers a day and at least 30 bottles of formula. Sister Faylor said the child-rearing had become a stake-wide project. "They are so kind," she said. "A stake diaper drive keeps us supplied with diapers each week. Donations are funneled through the Relief Society presidents. And then a dozen or so sisters come each week at appointed times to help change and feed the children." She said that when the family moves on foot they have a triplets' stroller and a twins' stroller. "For us, it's normal life. We don't know what it's like to have just one child, so this is normal ... I have no idea why the Lord wanted us to have five at one time, but we're so very grateful." (Author's interview)

Quadruplets. On Jan. 15, 2003, Melynie and Tom Meeks, Provo, Utah, welcomed quadruplets. Their babies were all about 16 inches long with weights from 3 pounds 3 ounces, to 3 pounds 9 ounces. They were named Spencer, McKay, Hunter and Tanner. (DN 1/17/03)

Kirsten and Rob Hinton, McKay Creek Ward, Hillsboro, Oregon, Stake, gave birth to quadruplets on Aug. 28, 2002. The babies weighed in at 5 to 8 1/2 pounds and were named Isabel, Aerin, Olea and Ethan. (CN 11/16/02)

In 2002, the Searle family literally grew from 4 to 8 members overnight.

Jennifer and Scott Searle, Butler 20th Ward, Salt Lake City Butler West Stake, gave birth to quadruplets on July 25, 2002. The babies were named Alec, Alyse, Brooke, and Bryson. (CN 11/16/02)

Laurie and John Hansen, Provo, Utah, gave birth to four babies Aug. 1, 1990: John Christopher, Jason Kent, David Alden, and Nathan Seth. Little David died after a valiant nine-week struggle. (CN 12/10/90)

Denise and John Cross, Fairfield, California, Stake, had quadruplets on Christmas Eve 1988: Daniele Gem, Robert George, David Randall and Merinda Noel were born at Travis Air Force Base. John Cross says the Church was a big help – he had been assigned to the ward nursery for all of the previous year. (LDS 2/14/88)

On Jan. 5, 1982, quadruplets were born to Jolene and Jeff Welch of the Sandy, Utah, Crescent Sixth Ward: Andy, Natalie, Ashley and Tiffany. They joined two siblings aged 5 and 3. (CN 4/17/82; DU 1/6/82)

Longest Surviving Triplets. Vinal Grant Mauss, Velma Mauss Torp and Vilda Mauss Hughes became the longest-lived triplets in United States and Church history when they celebrated their 85th birthdays in 1985. Born Oct. 16, 1900, the triplets averaged 3 pounds. Their mother helped them survive their first winter by putting all three in a basket in the warming oven of the family's old coal stove. (CN 8/23/75; CN 11/24/85)

First Triplets – Tahiti. The three little girls born to Garff and Ura Tehoiri Mariteragi, Papeete First Branch, French Polynesian Mission, on March 18, 1960, are also believed to be the first triplets ever born in Tahiti. (CN 10/1/60)

Tahiti's first-ever triplets weighed 2, 3, and 4 pounds, respectively.

TWINS, BABIES, FAMILY

Deacons Quorum. The Moses Lake 4th Ward, Grand Coulee Stake in Washington, had six sets of twins in its deacon's quorum in 1968. Lawrence Smith, their advisor, said each twin boy was nearly identical to his brother, making it nearly impossible to tell them apart. (CN 10/19/68)

Seminary. Seminary Principal Leroy Whitehead, Juab, Utah, Stake Seminary, Nephi, reported in 1948 that among his student body of 280 students, he had 12 sets of twins. (CN 10/20/48)

Four sets of twins in the Dodge family.

Most Twins – Family. The Delos Dodge family of Mesa, Arizona, had four sets of twins. In total, Sister Dodge gave birth to 18 children. (Richard Dodge; LDS 7/1/83)

Other "Twins" Records. In 1966, the Santa Barbara Stake had three sets of twins among the presidency: President and Sister Halderman had 10-year-old twin sons; First Counselor Joseph F. Chapman and wife had 18-year-old twin daughters; and Second Counselor Leon V. Evans and wife had eight-year-old twin daughters. (CN 4/2/66)

The Sandy, Utah, First Ward Sunday School had eight sets of twins in 1948. (CN 9/15/48)

The Temple View Ward, Hamilton Stake, New Zealand, had six sets of twins among members in 1967, with two sets from the same family. (CN 2/11/67)

The Thatcher 1st Ward, Thatcher, Arizona, Stake had six sets of twins in 1983. (LDS 5/20/83)

In 1957, people were seeing double at the East Mill Creek, Utah, Ward

Deseret Morning News file photo

Most Twins – Ward. In 1957, the East Mill Creek, Utah, 3rd Ward, East Mill Creek Stake, boasted nine sets of twins ranging in age from 14 months to 13 years old. (CN 3/9/57)

Multiple Births – Arithmetic Progression? Michael and Laura Daut, Littleton 6th Ward, Columbine, Colorado, Stake, were not too sure if they wanted a fourth pregnancy. The first pregnancy produced one baby, the second produced two babies, and the third produced, yes—you guessed it—three babies. The family of six children, all under age four, attracted much attention. "We love them and they love us," the parents said. "All of us have to work hard and nurture one another." (CN 9/14/86)

Most Twins Born in the Shortest Time. The small San Juan, Utah, Stake, set some kind of record for the birth of twins within its stake boundaries in 1972. It began Oct. 15, 1971, with the birth of Donnie and Darren Keith into the Blanding Indian Branch. On Dec. 4, 1971, Tarra and Tomara Jack were born into the Blanding 3rd Ward. On Feb. 14, 1972, Nathan and Richard Henderson were born into the Blanding 1st Ward. On March 17, 1972, Bryan and Ryan Halliday were also born into the Blanding 1st Ward. A day later, Kevin and Damon Orr were born into the Blanding 3rd Ward. And lastly, on Sept. 9, 1972, Janae and Bruce Shumway were born into the Blanding 1st Ward. A grand total of six sets of twins were born in 15 months. Statistically speaking, Blanding shouldn't have had any twins! (CN 1/27/73)

Largest Living LDS Family. Lenora Huntsman Lamoreaux, at age 100 in 1986, counted 337 in her posterity, including six children, 46 grandchildren, 166 great-grandchildren, and 119 great-great-grandchildren. (CN 7/27/86)

Most Multi-Generational Births in Shortest Time.

On Oct. 23, 1972, Maureen Johnson, Riverton, Utah, and her two daughters all gave birth to children on the same night, at the same hospital, and the babies were delivered by the same doctor. Maureen's baby, a girl named Shannon, came first. She was the new-born aunt. Two hours later, Kim Kelsch gave birth to a son named Kerry, and eight hours after that, Cherrie Morrison gave birth to a daughter named Krista. The "triplets" make a point of meeting up to celebrate their birthdays. (DN 11/2/89)

17 years later: A mother and two daughters mark the birthday of their "triplets."

First LDS Test-Tube Baby.

The first test-tube baby born to LDS parents, and the 14th test-tube baby born in the U.S., was a healthy 7 pound 9 ounce, 20-1/2-inch boy. He was delivered Jan. 11, 1983, at 8:08 a.m., to Claudia and Steven Allen. The Centerville, Utah, parents had conceived the baby outside of the womb at an in-vitro fertilization clinic in Virginia. (LDS 2/11/83; DU 1/12/83)

First LDS Test-Tube Twin Babies.

Michael and Shauna Poulsen, Cody, Wyoming, are the proud parents of twins conceived outside of the womb and born April 8, 1984. Michael Chandler weighed in at 6 pounds 2 ounces, and his sister Apryl Shanel, arrived at 5 pounds 3 ounces. (LDS 7/14/84)

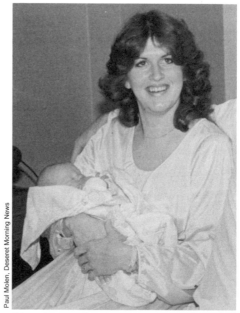

Claudia and Steve (not pictured) Allen, were the proud parents of the first LDS "test tube baby."

Delos Allred Dodge and Allice Ann Allred married Sept. 15, 1909, and gave birth to 18 children and raised an adopted son. As of January 2003, the family had grown to 632. Pictured here (front, l-r): Nellie, Alice Lou, Zola, Lola, Velda, Bell, Naomi, and Alice (mother); second row: Herbert, Thurbert, Veldon, Hugh, Oren, Loren, Alvin, Russ, Leo, Albert and Delos (father). Insert: Denny Varis (adopted) (left), George Edsil (right).

Photo courtesy of Richard Dodge

Most Children In One Family. Hats off to all the mothers and fathers who invite children into their homes and survive to tell about it! Here are a few of the largest families we've been able to identify.

18: The Delos Dodge family, Mesa, Arizona, set the Church record for the most children born to one mother – 18. There were 10 single births intermingled with four sets of twins. Great-grandson Richard Dodge said only a few of the original 18 lived to see the year 2000, but the family was always very close and frequently met for reunions. (Author)

17: Maikeli and Vake Wolfgramm, originally of Tonga, are the parents of 17 children who make up the famous THE JETS singing group. The older children formed the first group that made its reputation in the 1980s; now the younger children are touring and recording under the name, "JETTS17." (www.jettsmusic.com)

16: In 1974, the Richard Coburn family watched proudly as their daughter was selected Miss Hawaii to compete in the Miss America pageant. She was one of their 16 children. (CN 8/13/74)

15: At a family reunion in 1974, John M. and Elsie Paulson of Orem, Utah, enjoyed the company of their 15 children (8 boys, 7 girls), plus 59 grandchildren, 65 great-grandchildren, and one great-great-grandchild. (CN 8/17/74)

Largest Combined Family. It was a story of learning to love and learning to trust all over again. On June 20, 2003, widower Bob Memmot and divorcee Corinne Hanks were married in the Provo, Utah, Temple. The union brought together Brother Memmot's 13 children and Sister Hanks' 13 children for what appears to be the largest LDS combined household with 26 children ranging in age from 13 to 34. But that isn't all. Some of the older children were married with children, so the family also includes another 13 children-in-law and 34 grandchildren. The couple was introduced on a blind date set up by the sisters of Memmot's deceased wife. After several months of dating, he proposed on bended knee in the lobby of the Joseph Smith Memorial Building, and she was thrilled to say yes. (DN 6/20/03)

5-Billionth Human. Eric Scott McHenry, born 8:17 a.m., July 7, 1986, to LDS parents, was declared the 5-billionth human born onto the planet. The "guesstimate" of when this event would take place was made by the Population Institute of Washington, D.C.. Eric weighed in at 7 pounds 4 ounces. Said his mother, "It'll be fun to put in his baby book!" (LDS 7/13/86)

PHYSIOLOGY

Best Lungs in the World. Following a test on a treadmill, Kip Mibey, a native of Kenya and a member of BYU's 1982 track team, was declared to have the best lungs on the planet. The test showed he had the highest oxygen count of anyone yet tested in the world. His Swedish doctor told him that in the realm of sports, "The sky's your limit – you can break world records!"

BYU track coach Clarence Robison said that such tremendous lung power gave the young runner endurance capabilities unequaled by anyone. (DU 2/16/82)

Neatest Handwriting. Who are the neatest handwriters? In a nationwide contest that drew entries from thousands of elementary-school-aged children, Natalie Horne, Bountiful 46th Ward, Bountiful Utah Mueller Park Stake, won first place in a handwriting contest among all third graders. Josh Lamoreaux, Goshen, Utah, was the winner of the national fifth-grade competition. The children had to write, "This is my best cursive handwriting. Can you read it easily?" on a blank piece of paper. First prize was a framed certificate, a $500 savings bond, and a winner's T-shirt. (DN 6/11/92, CN 9/12/92)

Neatness was worth $500 to Natalie Horne.

For years, Elder Milton H. Ross, Forest Dale Ward, Granite, Utah, Stake, under assignment from President David O. McKay, wrote the inscriptions on more than 30,000 individual awards and 825 quorum award certificates (by 1956). The 32,000+ missionaries who served from 1936 to 1956 and beyond also enjoyed the beautiful penmanship of Brother Ross – each name on every missionary certificate was written by him. He taught penmanship for 52 years. Side note: Among his students were Presiding Bishop Joseph L. Wirthlin and Elder LeGrand Richards. (CN 8/25/56)

Superlative Memory Skills, Junior Division. Being able to quote 265 verses of scripture, plus an explanation of each, won Charles Lon Talksdorf, age 9 (in 1950), first place in a scripture memory contest sponsored by the Bible Memory Association of Shreveport, La. He competed against 100 other contestants. (CN 8/23/50)

Longest Hair. Who has the longest hair in the Church? In 1980, Helen Arave's hair measured 35 inches, and was woven into a hat for a BYU fashion show. It took two hours 45 minutes to arrange the hair and another 45 minutes for the setting gel to dry. (DU 10/7/80)

He could quote 265 scriptures from memory.

Loudest Mormons. Except for any given ward nursery, how can anyone establish who the loudest Mormons are? One attempt was made by Robert Burgener, a BYU professor who made measurements during a 1983 BYU-University of Utah basketball game at BYU. Prof. Burgener took a portable noise meter and periodically checked the noise level at critical times during the game. The loudest noise a person can withstand for eight hours without eardrum damage is 90 decibels. The average cheer in the Marriott Center was 94 decibels. Devin Durrant's behind-the-back bank shot that put BYU ahead brought the loudest response at 112 decibels. (DU 3/9/83)

Quickest Talker. Joseph Anderson, general authority emeritus, says of the many speakers for whom he has taken shorthand, President Heber J. Grant was by far the fastest talker. Elder Anderson, an extremely fast and accurate shorthand taker, could barely keep up with President Grant's admonitions to the Saints. (Author's interview with Elder Anderson, October 1988)

Most students of BYU professor Hugh Nibley would agree that he could deliver more facts per second than any other speaker or teacher in the Church.

Hugh Nibley can race through the amazing and the historical faster than a drive home after fast meeting.

Loudest Talker. (We mean this in a nice way.) It appears that many are in agreement that in April 1984 when the power went out during General Conference and the microphones went dead, Elder L. Tom Perry was still heard both inside and outside of the Salt Lake Tabernacle. Said one listener on Temple Square, "I could hear him better without the microphone than with," and others lounging on the grass outside the Tabernacle said his booming voice penetrated the open windows and doors just fine. (LDS 4/13/84)

L. Tom Perry, a soft-spoken man unless he wants to be heard.

Most Prolific Reader. More than 300 books a year made Marba C. Josephson, the associate editor of the Improvement Era in 1948, the most prolific reader in the Church. And she read – not skimmed – all of her books and did most of her reading after midnight! (CN 8/29/48)

Courtesy Lee Redmond

Lee Redmond has the longest set of fingernails in the world. A "set" means all ten. She hasn't cut them since 1979.

Longest Fingernails (2003 World Record). In 1979, Lee Redmond, Winder 7th Ward, Winder, Utah, Stake, decided not to file her 1-1/4 inch fingernails. "I wanted to see how long they would grow before they would twist out of shape," she said. And grow they did! In 1999, she was declared the record holder for the longest set of fingernails in the world with an average length of 27 3/4 inches. Today, she owns that world record with nails that now exceed 31.5 inches. "I grew them as an experiment," she said, "and I had no intentions of becoming some record holder. Somebody else had to tell me about that." She is gratefully amazed at the opportunities her long nails have created. "They give me a chance to speak at schools to help hundreds of teens every year deal with their self-esteem struggles. When I tell them that it's okay to be different so long as you're not hurting anyone, they listen and nod. I ask them, 'Who is to judge that long nails are bad when chewing short ones is not? Who can judge?'" Sister Redmond's nails have not slowed her one bit. Happily married, she is the mother of three grown children and grandmother to six. "I recently taught the Sunbeams in Primary, and the children fought to see who could sit next to me," she said. Her celebrity status has carried her around the world for television shows, and promotional and charity events, and she has been written about in numerous national publications. "Oh, I'll cut them off some day," she said. "But not yet!" It's a story that just keeps growing. (Author's interview, 6/12/03)

Highest IQ - Youth. How about 200+ for an 11-year-old? Arnold Sasaki could read and write by age 2, took up chess at age 6, and was ranked among the world's top 50 chess players in the 13-and-under age group. He became the youngest ever to enroll at BYU-Hawaii in 1985, at the age of 11. He planned post graduate studies after college. (DU 2/6/85)

Fastest Reader. In 1966, 11-year-old Tanya McBride was clocked at reading 100,000 words a minute with comprehension above 90 percent. Her father, the branch president of the Dunn Branch, Raleigh Stake, North Carolina, was a teacher of speed reading along with English courses in Methodist College in Fayetteville. He developed his speed-reading system by trial and error. Calling it Panoramic Reading, he taught students to see entire paragraphs at once, as one sees a picture. Sister McBride said a book with pages that were difficult to turn really slowed her down – to about 50,000 words a minute. (CN 7/16/66)

Deseret Morning News file photo

50,000 words a minute on a slow day!

Best Health in the U.S.A. The Northwestern National Life Insurance Company determined in late 1989, after an extensive study of all 50 states, that Utah has the healthiest population in the nation. Utah ranked first in good health habits, lowest for premature death, and best in avoidance of disease. It ranked third in life expectancy and 10th in productivity least affected by illness. (DN 11/2/89)

Most Livable State. For the past 10 years of the Morgan Quinto "Most Livable State award" rankings, Utah has maintained the highest average score and always ranked among the top five except in 1994 when it was ranked seventh. It was ranked the most livable state in 1992 and 1996 and second most livable in 1993. Morgan Quinto uses a formula that weighs 43 factors, from crime and marriage rates to road and bridge maintenance problems. Scott Morgan, president of the firm running the survey, said, "Utah simply has what people and companies are looking for ... the state has healthy, highly educated citizens; relatively low taxes and very little poverty." (DN 3/9/92; www.morganquitno.com/srml91-00.htm)

THE SEXES

The male-female ratio

There's a record in the making as fewer and fewer men are around compared to the growing number of women in the Church. BYU sociology professor Tim Heaton showed that, the older you are, the fewer LDS men you'll find. Some of his findings show that:

At age 20-29, there are 89 men for every 100 women
At age 40-49, there are 53 men for every 100 women

At age 50-59, there are 35 men for every 100 women
At age 60+, there are 24 men for every 100 women.

Professor Heaton attributes the low number of men in the Church to:
• Men dying at a faster rate then women;
• Most men marrying women younger then they are — an average of two years younger;
• More women converting to the Church and women remaining more active. (LDS 7/23/89)

The Best Husbands? Where is the best place to find a husband in America? After nationally-syndicated newspaper columnist Ann Landers asked readers to disclose where the good men might be found, one reader wrote: "The Decency Capital of the USA is Salt Lake City. The Mormon Church produces faithful, compassionate husbands and wonderful fathers. Signed, Found Mine in Utah." (CN 9/5/81)

SAINTS AROUND THE WORLD

*References to Asians, Blacks, Indians, etc., include African Americans, Asian Americans, American Indians, etc.

Howard C. Moore, Deseret Morning News archives

Elder and Sister Komatsu, first Asian general authority.

First Asian General Authority. Adney Y. Komatsu was the first man of Japanese descent to be called as a general authority. He was sustained an assistant to the Twelve April 4, 1975, and to the First Quorum of Seventy Oct. 1, 1976. (Church Almanac)

Japan Media. Kent Gilbert, a former missionary to Japan, returned to Japan in 1985-86 to become a media star. He had his own TV game show, fan clubs, a weekly TV drama series and hosted radio shows. His rise to fame in Japan was featured in People magazine. (LDS 10/4/86)

First Black General Authority. The first black called as a general authority was Helvica Martins, Rio de Janeiro, Brazil. He was sustained as a member of the Second Quorum of Seventy by the general membership during April Conference, 1990. (Church Almanac)

First Black Missionaries. Marcus H. Martins, Rio de Janeiro, Brazil, who served in the Brazil Porto Alegre Mission 1978-80, was the Church's first black missionary. Brother Martins went on to serve as the Chair of the

Helvica Martins, first black general authority.

Religious Education Department at BYU-Hawaii. Shortly after his mission call, two sister missionaries were called – Mary Sturiaugson, Rapid City, South Dakota, and Jacques M.G. Jonassaint of Haiti on Sept. 22, 1978, to serve in the Texas San Antonio Mission, and the Florida Spanish Mission, respectively. Sister Sturiaugson authored the book "A Soul So Rebellious" following her conversion. (DU 1/8/81; LDS 6/4/88)

First Black Elder. The first black to be ordained an elder was Elijah Abel on March 3, 1836.

First Blacks to Settle in San Bernardino. The first African-American settlers in San Bernardino, California, arrived with the first Mormon wagon train. Some of them were already baptized members of the LDS Church and included Grief Embers, Charles Rowan, Elizabeth Flake, and Biddy and Hannah Smith. It is not known if Biddy was LDS, but she took the surname of Mormon Apostle Amasa Mason Lyman. She became one of the richest women in Los Angeles and donated the land for the first African Methodist Episcopal Church in Los Angeles. (Church Almanac)

First Black BYU Law Student. Keith Hamilton, North Carolina, was the first black law student at BYU's J. Reuben Clark law school. He was accepted in 1983 but postponed schooling for two years to serve his mission to Puerto Rico. (LDS 9/16/83)

First South African Missionary. Hilda Benans of East Paarl, South Africa, was the first South African non-white sister missionary in the

Church. She accepted her call to Birmingham, Alabama in 1986, some 3-1/2 years after her baptism. (CN 4/20/86)

First Missionaries from Western Africa. The first black full-time missionaries from western Africa were Elders Benjamin Crosby Sampson-Davis, 23, and Samuel Eko Bainson, 24, sent to the Manchester, England, Mission in 1980. Both had an interesting introduction into the Church. Several pamphlets and articles about the Church made their way to some towns in western Africa and were warmly accepted by several individuals. For lack of any formal Church organization or representation, some dozens of people came together and began calling themselves Latter-day Saints. Missionaries were sent in 1978 to formally baptize the new converts and organize them into Branches. (CN 2/28/81)

First Black Mission President. The first black mission president was Helvicia Martins, 56, from Rio de Janeiro, Brazil. The former bishop and stake president's counselor was called in 1986. (LDS 1/21/87)

First Mission Among Blacks. The first mission created in a predominantly black area was the Africa West Mission. It was created April 1, 1980, and later renamed the Nigeria Lagos Mission. (LDS 6/4/88)

First Stake Among Blacks. The first stake in the Church in which all priesthood leaders were black was the Aba, Nigeria, Stake organized in western Africa on May 15, 1988. (Church Almanac 1989-90)

First black given the Priesthood after the revelation: Joseph Freeman Jr., pictured here saying goodbye to son Alexander and his wife, Toe, before leaving for work.

Priesthood Extended to the Blacks. On June 9, 1978, the Church announced a new revelation authorizing that all worthy male members, including blacks, could receive the Priesthood. The announcement sparked a great deal of interest in the Church. All major TV networks featured the announcement that evening, and NBC made it the lead story on its network news. Time and Newsweek magazines held up deadlines to get a report for their upcoming issues, and the New York Times, Washington Post and Los Angeles Times carried the story on the front page. U.S. President Jimmy

Carter sent a telegram to President Spencer W. Kimball commending him for his "courage in receiving a new doctrine." And the 17 Church telephone operators found themselves suddenly swamped with thousands of phone calls. (CN 6/78)

In the July 23, 1978, edition of the Salt Lake Tribune, a group called "Concerned Latter-Day Saints" headed by Joseph Jensen published a full-page ad entitled, "LDS Soon To Repudiate A Portion Of Their Pearl Of Great Price?" in which the group challenged the revelation. (SLTrib 7/23/78)

Black Panther. Eldredge Cleaver, a prominent black activist and member of the Marxist group "The Black Panthers," was baptized into the Church on Dec. 11, 1983, at the Oakland, California, Stake Center. "I feel real good," Cleaver said. "I'm sure and clear about it ... It was worth waiting seven years for." Cleaver was a fugitive in communist countries for eight years, but returned to the United States to pay his debt to society. "I'd rather be in jail in America than free under communism," he said. He later ran unsuccessfully for several political offices in California. (LDS 12/20/83)

Eldredge Cleaver, converted Black Panther

First Convert from Western Africa. The first black convert in western Africa was Anthony Obinna, a schoolmaster who had been investigating the Church on his own for eight years. He was baptized in 1978 and was subsequently called as branch president. (LDS 6/4/88)

First Branch Among Blacks. The first all-black branch in the United States was the Southwest Branch, Downey Stake, in Southern California. After several years of industrious service, it was dissolved in 1988. (LDS 6/4/88)

Highest Public Office by an LDS American Indian. Ed Brown, Pagedale Branch, St. Louis, Missouri Stake, was nominated by President George Bush and confirmed by Congress in 1990 to serve as Assistant Secretary of Indian Affairs in the Department of the Interior, in Washington, D.C. He served for all of Pres. Bush's term and six month's into Pres. Clinton's term. (Author's interview)

Dr. Eddie F. Brown helped lead Indian Affairs until 1993.

George P. Lee, first Indian general authority.

First Indian General Authority. George P. Lee, a Navajo, was the first American Indian called to serve as a general authority. He was sustained to the First Quorum of the Seventy Oct. 3, 1975.

First American Indian Bishop. In January 1939, Moroni Timbimboo became the first American Indian bishop in the Church. Brother Timbimboo, of the Shoshoni in northern Utah, was bishop of the all-Indian Washakle Ward, Malad, Idaho, Stake. (CN 3/28/70)

Oldest Baptized Indians

Kate Crozler, oldest baptized American Indian.

Kate Crozler was approximately 110 when he was baptized by elders of the Southwest Indian Mission in 1955. An interesting sidelight to Brother Crozier's life was his job as scout for General George Crook and his replacement, General Nelsen Miles. Both were sent to Arizona to put down several uprisings by the American Indians led by Chiricahua Geronimo. Crozier helped with the eventual capture and exile of the rebel chief, Geronimo. (CN 3/19/55)

Hosteen Ele Yen (Cle Yani), a Navajo Indian, was baptized at Sawmill, Arizona in June 1954 at the age of 101, becoming the oldest Navajo man to join the Church. (CN 6/26/54)

Mrs. Charlie Largo, Southwest Indian Mission, was baptized in September 1952 in New Mexico at the age of 86, becoming the oldest Navajo woman to join the Church. (CN 9/13/52)

First Micmac Baptized. Freeman Knockwood, Oxford, Nova Scotia, is the first of his tribe to join the Church on March 5, 1972. "I hope there is some way my baptism can help bring the restored gospel and the true history of the Indians to my people, the Micmacs," Knockwood said. (CN 5/20/72)

First Chapel. The first chapel built in the Indian mission in Utah was named "Tseh Kin," meaning "Rock House." (CN 8/28/49)

Athlete of the Year. Eddie Hakala, a three-time state wrestling champion from Anchorage, Alaska, was named National Indian Athlete of the Year in 1987. The 5-foot 9-inch 142-pound young man attended Anchorage's East High School. (CN 3/28/87)

First Cherokee Baptized. After the labors of four missionaries among the Cherokees on the Qualla Reservation in western North Carolina in 1948, the first baptism finally resulted when Nellie Lucille Burgess Tahquette, Dorothy Elaine Moles, Lillian Lyedella Stanley Neely and Shirley Ann Neely joined the Church. The tribe was a band of only 3,200 on 63,000-acre reservation, down from a mighty people of tens of thousands 150 years before. (CN 5/8/48)

First Harvard Law School Graduate. Woodrow Blaine Sneed, a Cherokee, earned his way into Harvard after scoring 97 percent on the law-school entrance exam. He turned down offers from Stanford, George Washington, Chicago and Duke universities. After graduation, he became the assistant legal counsel for the Navajo Tribe at Window Rock, Arizona. (CN 10/31/64)

First BYU Law School Graduate. The first LDS Indian to graduate from the J. Reuben Clark Law School was Carolyn Seneca Steele, a Seneca Indian from Idaho, in June 1982. (LDS 7/16/82)

First Engineering Student. In 1983, Marlene Begay, a Navajo from Salt Lake City, became the first LDS Indian woman to graduate in engineering from BYU. (LDS 8/12/83)

First in Placement Program. The Church's Indian placement program grew out of an effort in the 1940s to give American Indian children a chance to experience new educational experiences. The first American Indian to become involved in the placement program could also be credited with starting the program. When Helen John Hall, who was then a 17-year-old Navajo, decided her future held more than just working in the fields, she sought out a family in Richfield, Utah, to stay with while she attended school. This first visit in 1947 was formalized into a Church program by 1954 as the Indian Placement Program. By the time the program was ended in 1996, more than 70,000 Indians had followed in her footsteps. (CN 4/17/83; LDS 9/2/82; various Internet sources)

Education Firsts. Janice White Clemmer holds a number of extraordinary records in the Church. By 1980, she was:
• The first Indian woman in the United States to earn two doctorates;
• The first Indian woman in Utah to earn a doctorate in history and cultur-

al foundations of education;
- The first to achieve this academic stature among both males and females of her tribes (her mother was of the Wasco tribe of central Oregon, and her father was of the Shawnee and Delaware tribes).
- The third Indian woman in the nation to receive a doctorate. (CN 5/24/80)

Most LDS Tribe Outside of Utah. The Catawba Indian tribe in South Carolina is 95-percent LDS. (CN 1/10/76)

First Doctorate Degree. In 1975, George P. Lee became the first LDS American Indian to earn a doctoral degree. At the time, Brother Lee was president of the Holbrook, Arizona, Mission. His degree was in educational administration. (CN 9/6/75)

First in Scouting. Who is the first Indian to earn his Eagle Scout award? In 1971, Orville Eriacho, Zuni, New Mexico, became the first Zuni Indian Boy Scout to earn his Eagle. (CN 5/10/71)

MILITARY

Dec. 8, 1941, the Deseret News announces the declaration of war by the U.S. against Japan after its suprise attack on Pearl Harbor. Not many years later, when the war had ended, the Church's missionary program would flourish in that country bringing many new friends and faithful members into the Church.

Saints of all nationalities, races, and ages have served and died for their countries. The two great world wars were costly to all nations involved, and took the lives of thousands of Latter-day Saints on both sides.

WWI (all numbers are approximations)

Members of the Church worldwide at the outbreak of war: 370,000

U.S. LDS members in the war: 22,500

LDS killed: 750 (116,708 total U.S. soldiers killed)

Most LDS unit: First Utah Field Artillery Regiment with 1,016 LDS among 1,313 total men.

LDS chaplains commissioned: 3

The Relief Society donated 250,000 bushels of wheat to the cause, for which they received a personal letter of thanks from U.S. President Herbert Hoover.

WWII (all numbers are approximations)

Members of the Church worldwide at the outbreak of war: 803,000

U.S. LDS members in the war: 100,000

LDS killed (worldwide): 5,000 (408,306 total U.S. soldiers killed)

LDS Chaplains commissioned: 46

Two ships named after LDS prophets: the S.S. Brigham Young and S.S. Joseph Smith

Of the 12,000 German LDS, 600 died including three mission presidents, and 2,500 listed as missing. At least 80 percent were left homeless.

Highest Ranking. Admiral Paul A. Yost (who served as the commandant of the U.S. Coast Guard), Air Force General John K. Cannon, Lt. General Robert C. Oaks (assigned as commander-in-chief of the U.S. Air Forces Europe in 1990), and Admiral C. Monroe Hart (Navy), are the only known LDS to attain the four-star ranking in the military. Admiral Hart also received the Legion of Merit, the nation's highest peacetime award, for his supervision of the design and development of the Polaris submarine. (LDS 5/3/86, CN 5/24/90, CN 6/6/70)

U. S. Navy

Paul Yost, one of the highest ranked officers in the military.

Firsts – World War II. Lt. Col. Reuben E. Curtis, LDS chaplain, was in on several significant firsts as World War II came to a close. He was in the unit that retook the first captured American territory (Attu), he was with the unit to capture the first Japanese soil (Kwajalein), and was with the first unit to land in the Philippines. (CN 12/23/44)

Lucy Gates Bowen christens the SS Brigham Young and sends it sliding down the planks to sea.

SS Brigham Young slips into the sea to join hundreds of other Liberty class ships.

Photos: U S Navy

Naval Ships. The first Liberty ship named and christened after a member of the Church was the SS Brigham Young, launched Aug. 17, 1942. It was followed nine months later by the SS Joseph Smith, launched on May 22, 1943.

The SS Brigham Young was built in a record 38 days; a 10,500-ton ship, it was the 58th to slide down the ways at Calship near Los Angeles. Twenty minutes after "Brigham" hit the water, workers were laying the keel of another ship. Lucy Gates Bowen, granddaughter of Brigham Young, was called upon to christen the ship. "May it sail the seas till it has reached the ripe maturity which he attained!" she said. "And may those who man it ever be filled with the same fidelity to purpose, the same unflinching courage to battle for the right, the same consecration to the cause of freedom, and the same devotion to God and country, as actuated him throughout his long eventful life." After WWII, the Navy changed the ship's name to SS Muzim and gave it a new number, AK95. In 1973, the Navy sold it for $68,113 to the Nicolai Joffee Corporation, San Jose, California, for scrap. (CN 11/6/83)

The SS Joseph Smith was launched May 22, 1943 from Permanente Metals Corporation of Richmond, California It saw active duty for almost two years. It was lost in heavy seas while in a North Atlantic convoy en route to New York City from Liverpool, England, on Jan.11, 1944. After removal of all 41 crew members and 26 Naval Guard personnel, the vessel was purposely sunk. It now lies 15,000 feet deep on the ocean floor. "The Smith was abandoned when she appeared to be breaking up after severe fractures in the hull," according to the book, "A Careless Word ... A Needless Sinking." Survivors were picked up and the ship was blasted into its watery grave by gunfire from an escort vessel. (CN 9/25/83)

SS Joseph Smith was launched in 1943, but was scuttled after two years' service.

The USS Utah was the first ship to be sunk during the Pearl Harbor attack in 1941. Here it lies partly submerged.

Naval Submarine. The $340 million nuclear attack submarine, "Salt Lake City" was launched Oct. 16, 1982, from the Newport News Shipbuilding yard in Virginia. Utah Senator Jake Garn's wife, Kathleen Garn, christened the 360-foot submarine that carried 12 officers and 115 enlisted men. (www.chinfo.navy.mil/navpalib/factfile/ships/ship-ssn.html)

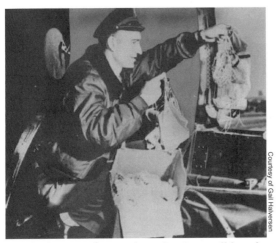

Gail Halversen dropped candy via small hand-made parachutes to thousands of children in war-torn Germany.

Most Welcome Bomber. In 1948, Gail Halversen found himself part of the great Berlin Airlift that brought food and supplies to the starving people of war-torn Germany. Seeing so many homeless children and orphans, Brother Halversen started a special food drop of his own. He made little parachutes out of handkerchiefs and attached all kinds of candy bars and treats. He would signal children on the ground that he was ready to make a drop by waggling the wings of his C-47 "Gooney Bird," earning him the nickname, "Uncle Wiggle Wings." To their parents, he became known as the "Candy Bomber." As Halvorsen's candy-drop project caught the attention of the world, people from just about everywhere began sending him candy and parachutes. It became known as Operation "Little Vittles." The Candy Bomber was one of the most famous names associated with the Berlin Airlift. (Author's interview; CN 3/14/70)

Close Call for Chaplain Durham. Chaplain L. Marsdan Durham became the first LDS chaplain wounded in World War II after a mortar shell exploded next to him during the conquest of Okinawa. "Others standing near me, at my very elbow, were killed instantly while my life was spared," Brother Durham said. "I feel that my guardian angel was working overtime once again." With four Mormon chaplains and numerous LDS soldiers in the

Okinawa area, Durham predicted, "Once it (Okinawa) is taken from the Japanese, it may have to be retaken from the Mormons!" (CN 6/9/45)

Most LDS Graves. In one day, Chaplain Eldon Ricks dedicated ten LDS graves at the height of World War II fighting. (Internet)

Bataan Death March. The only LDS we've located who were on the Bataan death march are Harold Poole, Robert Strasters, V.O. "Johnny" Johnson, and Franklin T. East. On April 7, 1942, the men found themselves with more than 20,000 soldiers and marines fighting a losing battle on the island of Bataan. With only 24 hours of food, medicine and ammunition remaining, Maj. Gen. Edward P. King Jr. surrendered to the Japanese. Thousands of U.S. troops were herded into hot open fields at Mariveles Air Field at the very tip of Bataan. They were searched by Japanese servicemen, relieved of all personal belongings, humiliated and given little food, water or medical care and no sanitary facilities. Already suffering from three months of half rations, they were lined up and forced to march. Said Brother East, "If you fell out, they'd kill you. There were dead soldiers all along the route." They marched for 50 miles and reached a railhead where the survivors were jammed into windowless stall boxcars, and lived the horrors of the "iron warehouse." Less than 10 percent of those who surrendered on Bataan and Corregidor were still alive when the war ended. Ironically, Brother Poole's son later traveled to Japan as a missionary. (CN 1/23/83; LATimes 12/14/99)

Harold Poole

Robert Strasters

First Branch at West Point. Organized in the summer of 1946, the West Point Branch, under direction of the Eastern States Mission, had a rough beginning. Reported one young cadet in 1947, "While there are seventeen cadets, one officer and two enlisted men who are members of the Church on the post, their various military duties reduce the general attendance from eight to 12 men depending on the weekend. Though these meetings are small, they are a great inspiration and a great source of comfort to these men." (CN 5/31/47)

Library of Congress

Stimpson was the first American to know Japan's surrender terms that ended World War II.

First Person to Know How WWII Would Finally End. After the atomic bombs were dropped on Hiroshima and Nagasaki, bringing the Japanese to the negotiating table, super-secret documents were quickly prepared to announce Japan's surrender. The documents had to be carefully crafted to stop hostilities and, at the same time, seek some degree of respect for the Japanese people. And when all was ready, only one man in the world besides the Japanese leadership knew what that document contained. It was Joseph H. Stimpson, Washington, D.C. Stake, the U.S. government's official Japanese translator. He translated the documents into English so the world could learn Japan's terms of surrender. Brother Stimpson gained his expertise in Japanese while serving in Japan as a missionary for 5-1/2 years, and later as mission president for six years. Even the Japanese accepted his accuracy and devotion to detail above that of other translators. During the war trials that followed, the Japanese chose Stimpson's translations above all others to be submitted as official court documents. (CN 5/2/64)

U.S. Air Force

Flying Ace Chesley Peterson didn't like how the Air Force was fighting in Vietnam and quit at age 49 rather than take a desk job.

Most Highly Decorated LDS Flying Ace. Chesley Peterson, a former BYU student from Salmon, Idaho, became the most highly decorated LDS flying ace after bluffing his way into the Air Force at age 19. After his forged birth certificate was discovered two months into pilot training school, Peterson went to England in 1940 and joined the Royal Air Force's Eagle Squadron, flying Hawker Hurricanes and Supermarine Spitfires into battle against the German Luftwaffe. He advanced to squadron commander at age 21 and colonel at 23. When he moved to the U.S. Army Air Corps to fly P-47 Thunderbolts in 1943, he retained his title of colonel and was the Air Force's youngest-ever colonel. In more than 200 combat missions, Peterson claimed nine kills and nine more probably kills, and twice parachuted from damaged Spitfires. He is the only American to win both the U.S. Distinguished Service Cross and Britain's Distinguished Service Order, each country's second-highest military decoration. (DN 1/30/90)

First VFW National Chaplain. The first LDS to serve as the Veterans of Foreign Wars (VFW) national chaplain was Boyd W. Winterton, East Millcreek 4th Ward, Salt Lake East Millcreek Stake. He held the position twice, 1987-88 and 1991-92. (CN 11/2/91)

Dog Tags. New "dog tags," for Mormons only, were issued in 1951 to all LDS serving in any branch of the armed forces. Authorized for wear by the Church Servicemen's Committee, the tag has written on one side, "I am a member of the Church of Jesus Christ of Latter-day Saints," followed by the word "MORMON" in quotation marks. The opposite side has a depiction of the Salt Lake Temple and the words, "In case of need notify L.D.S. Chaplain or member." (CN 5/9/51)

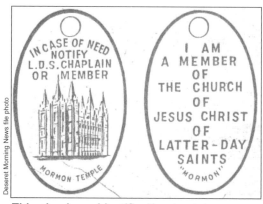

This aluminum identification tag (shown front and back), a third set of dogtags soldiers could wear, was issued by the Church, along with a serviceman's copy of the Book of Mormon, beginning in 1951.

Pilot for the VP. Stephen J. Snow, Springfield Ward, Annandale, Virginia, Stake, was one of 12 elite pilots who flew the Vice President's Air Force 2 in 1986. (CN 9/7/86)

Military – Dental. The highest-ranking dentist in the military was also the chief of the U.S. Naval Dental Corps in 1989. Adm. Milton C. Clegg, originally of Salt Lake City, was promoted to rear admiral on March 1, 1989, and became responsible for the dental health of 750,000 sailors and marines and their 5,200 dental officers and dental technicians around the world. (CN 7/15/89)

Best Tow in the Air Force. U.S. Air Force Captain Robert Goodman used towing skills he learned as a civilian to save the lives of two men and a $4 million aircraft. In 1981, Brother Goodman, Caribou Branch, Massachusetts Boston Mission, was flying a refueling tanker over the chilly North Atlantic when an accompanying F-4 fighter plane lost power. Goodman dropped to the fighter, hooked his refueling pipe to it, then towed the fighter as if it were a glider. After the engines fired up, he dropped the fighter, but engines failed again. After yet a second try, which failed again, he pushed his plane to its maximum speed of 500 mph, caught the F-4 once again just before the two pilots would have had to eject into the frigid waters, and towed the craft to the nearest airport 160 miles away, where the planes landed safely. The fighter pilots were so grateful, "they kissed the ground and Goodman," a spokesman said. (CN 1/82)

First Married Couple to Enlist. In 1973, Gregory L. Lee and Susan Lee, Brigham City 7th Ward, Utah, were sworn into the U.S. Army. They were the first LDS couple to simultaneously enlist voluntarily in the Army, and only the second couple to do so in U.S. history. (CN 1/13/73)

Most Languages. The 142nd Military Intelligence Company of the Utah National Guard has the unique distinction of being comprised of nearly 100 percent of LDS returned missionaries whose language expertise makes the group conversant in at least 26 languages. It was expanded to full battalion size on April 1, 1980, and played key roles in translations services for U.S. involvement in the Iraq and Afghanistan wars. (CN 4/26/80; various Internet sources)

First LDS Among the Queen's Guards. In 1973, Gary Wells, London, England, became a member of the Queen's Guards, more formally known as "The Blues and Royals, Household Calvary, in Knightsbridge, London." The horse-mounted guards perform actual as well as ceremonial security for the Queen of England and her household. Brother Wells joined the British Army in 1971 and worked his way into the 14-month Guard's Training Course at Pirbright, Surrey. Only one out of five who take the course are selected. Wells did not meet the minimum calvary experience of five years, but this was overlooked because of his superb horsemanship. (CN 1/27/73)

Only LDS to Lobby World's Drug King. In 1987, Lt. Col. Bo Gritz, Sandy Valley Branch, Las Vegas South Stake, gained the distinction of being the first American to sit in the jungle headquarters of international drug overlord General Kuhn Sa in Burma for an interview. Gritz was there to locate U.S. POWs. His chance meeting with Kuhn Sa allowed Gritz to question the man about the problems drugs were creating around the world, especially in the U.S., Kuhn Sa's role in the drug problem, and a discussion about exchanging U.S. financial support for an end to Burma's drug trade. (LDS 11/12/88)

First Navy Chaplain. Was Lt. Edward R. Gwynn, a native of Washington, D.C., the first LDS chaplain? He began sailing the seas with the Navy in 1954. (CN 3/6/54)

Best Fighter Pilots in the U.S. Are Capt. Larry L. Kemp and Maj. Tom Tutt the first LDS "Top Guns"? The team was awarded the "Top Gun" trophy in the F-4 fighter category of the William Tell 1986 Top Gun competition at the LA Center in Washington state in 1987. (CN 3/28/87)

Helicopters. In 1987, Kenneth Ivan Kiger, Fort Eustis, Virginia, became the first among more than 5,000 to complete the advanced individual training in helicopter mechanics at Fort Eustis with an average score of 100 percent. He was presented with the Army Achievement Medal and a certificate of achievement. (CN 8/29/87)

High Achiever. Lt. Graydon K. Calder, one of about 500 officer candidates graduating from the U.S. Air Force Officers Candidate School at Lackland Air Force Base, set a record never before achieved in Air Force history. He was awarded simultaneously the "Academic Award" and the "Distinguished Graduate Award," the first time in the school's history that one man has won both awards. (CN 2/13/54)

Utah State Historical Society

Fifty years later: A group of surviving Mormon Battalion marchers unite for this reunion photo in 1896.

Longest Military March (1847 World Record). On July 1, 1846, Brigham Young prophesied at Council Bluffs, Iowa, that if 500 men would form the Mormon Battalion, their only fighting would be with wild animals. At the beginning of their march, 497 of the 541 in the battalion were LDS. They left Council Bluffs on July 20, 1846. In early December, Young's prophecy came true as the Mormon Battalion was attacked by a large herd of wild bulls on the San Pedro River near Tucson, Arizona. Eighty bulls were killed, some wagons were overturned and a few mules were gored. The Mormon Battalion completed its march, arriving in San Diego Jan. 29, 1847, after traveling 2,000 miles. It was disbanded in Los Angeles on July 16, 1847. Returning soldiers to Salt Lake Valley testified to the fulfillment of Brigham's prophecy that their only foe had indeed been animals. Today, the Fort Moore Memorial in the Civic Center of Los Angeles honors the Mormon Battalion for raising the flag of the United States there on July 4, 1847.

Utah State Historical Society

The Mormon Battalion Bugle Corps led the Mormon volunteers.

Utah Parks and Recreation

Today, Camp Floyd is a Utah State Park.

Largest Pre-Civil War Military Base. Built almost next door to the newly founded settlement for the Saints along the Wasatch Front, Camp Floyd, near Fairfield, Utah, was the largest pre-civil war military base in the country in 1858. It was established by Col. Albert Sydney Johnston's 3,000-man army sent to bring LDS settlers under government control. In 1985, a BYU archaeological excavation team uncovered the foundations of three buildings at the camp, yielding numerous artifacts including a large key, cannonballs, pipe fragments, military buttons, percussion caps, shoulder boards, hairbrushes, a toothbrush, knife handles, bottles, pitchers, cups, plates, and a Masonic emblem. The Masonic emblem was the most significant find because Camp Floyd was the site of the first Masonic lodge west of the Mississippi River. (DU 7/2/85)

Nuclear Attack: The Mormon Relocation Plan. The only relocation plan in the United States based on local church boundaries is in Utah. The relocation plan, prepared by the Federal Emergency Management Agency, is continually updated but could save 80 percent of Utah's population. In the event of pending nuclear attack, people within any given stake boundary would be directed to their stake center where predetermined evacuation routes would be assigned. People would depart en masse to the mountains or away from high-risk target areas. The plan doesn't apply to BYU stakes because students would be sent to their homes far in advance of hostilities. Three days is required under this current plan for such an evacuation. (DU 2/14/83)

The official government photogarpher forgot to open the shutter on his high-speed movie camera. An illegal camera smuggled on board by a crew member was used for this photo.

Photographer of the First A-Bomb. George W. Marquardt, Murray, Utah, 1st Ward, piloted the plane that photographed the atomic bomb blast over Hiroshima on the morning of Aug. 6, 1945. Brother Marquardt, an Army major, was at the helm of the B-29 Superfortress that was designated No. 91, but was named Necessary Evil by the crew. It was one of the seven-aircraft group that escorted Col. Paul Tibbets Jr.'s Enola Gay that dropped the bomb. "It seemed as if the sun had come out of the Earth and exploded," he frequently commented. "It felt as if a monster hand had slapped the side of the plane." On the 50th anniversary of the event, he told The Salt Lake Tribune in 1995, "I have never for one moment regretted my participation in the dropping of the A-bomb. It ended a terrible war." (DN 8/24/03; Internet)

George Marquardt

The light from the 9,700-pound uranium bomb blast was so intense, Marquardt could not see his co-pilot.

LDS sailors participating in nuclear weapons tests at Bikini Atoll witnessed this 21-kiloton explosion known as Operation CROSSROADS.

Atomic Bomb Testing. While some Mormons were busy in Oak Ridge, Tennessee, designing and building America's first atomic bombs, other Mormons took part in the first atomic tests at Bikini Island. LDS sailors aboard ships anchored near the island to participate in the bomb tests found time to hold church services on Sundays. Acting Group Leader, Sgt. James Shelby Arrigona of Salt Lake City wrote home to say that of the 40,000 personnel aboard some 150 vessels involved in the tests, they had managed to locate six members for their first Church meeting on June 9, 1946. The group soon grew to 30. "Nearly every man comes from a different ship," Arrigona said, "and each man has his own transportation problems ... so you can be assured that the attendance of these men in church evidences real sincerity and genuine faith." (CN 8/3/46)

Photos: Deseret Morning News

"By the Rockets' Red Glare..."

During the years of above-ground nuclear testing in Nevada, Salt Lake City enjoyed an occasional light show. Shown here, the sleepy skyline in 1955 just one second prior to a massive nuclear explosion at the Nevada test site more than 370 miles away. Instantly, a brilliant orange-red flash silhouetted the distant mountains and the Salt Lake Temple.

SCOUTING

The LDS Church was the first organization in the United States to sponsor a Scouting unit. After thoroughly investigating the Scouting program, which was relatively new at the time, the Church adopted it in 1913. Sponsorship has continued uninterrupted since then, and today the Church sponsors more units than any organization in the world. (CN 3/78)

The Church has more than 25,000 packs, troops, teams and posts chartered with the Boy Scouts of America (BSA).

Almost 400,000 LDS youths are registered Scouts. This is about 10 percent of total BSA membership in the United States

The first troops were chartered through the Church in June 1913. (BSA-Mormon Relations)

First LDS Scout. Arthur Sadler registered with the Scouts in 1908 with the Colchester First Troop in England and remained continuously registered his entire life. Sadler had a personable association with Scouting's founder, Sir Robert Baden-Powell. Baden-Powell awarded Sadler his second- and first-class awards, plus the "All-round Cord." Sadler recalls starting a fire in the rain with only two matches under the watchful gaze of Baden-Powell. Sadler and his family were baptized in 1910 and emigrated to America in 1915. (CN 8/20/77)

Oldest Scout. Until his death on February 11, 2003, the oldest Boy Scout in America was George Elton Freestone, 104 years old. He was a member of the Tempe 1st Ward, Tempe, Arizona, West Stake. Brother Freestone was also the last surviving member of the first Boy Scout troop in America. Born July 28, 1898, in Safford, Arizona, he was 12 years old and living with his family in Los Angeles, California, when he joined the original Boy Scout troop, and he remained an active member for 92 years. He was honored on the David Letterman television show, and was the oldest person to carry the torch for the 2002 Winter Olympics Torch Relay. (Internet)

George Freestone, oldest Boy Scout in America in 2003, was a member of the first troop in the U.S.

In 1995, the oldest Boy Scout was Fred Reese, 96, St. George, Utah. Brother Reese joined the Scouts in 1910. Even though he joined a year before he was old enough, BSA recognized him in 1995 as having the longest consistent membership, 85 years. He also helped design the Church's Duty to God award that is given to Scouts who meet certain Church requirements. Reese said his wife, Elva, would often welcome the Scouts to the house to teach them how to cook. She was the best "assistant Scoutmaster" there ever was, he said. (DN 6/28/95)

Richard S. Best

First LDS Troop. In 1911, T. George Woods, Waterloo Ward, Granite Stake, Salt Lake City, an enthusiastic teacher and leader of boys, organized the first LDS troop (pictured above) two years before the Church officially adopted the program, and several years before England's Scouting system was officially launched. He also volunteered as the first Scoutmaster and served for 15 years. He died in Raymond, Alberta, Canada, on Jan. 5, 1964, at age 76. (CN 2/3/68)

Highest Scouting Award – Spain. Elder W. Wayne Prince, a 54-year veteran in the Boy Scouts of America, became the first recipient of the Don Quixote award, Spain's highest honor to the person making the greatest contribution to the Scouting program. The award is equivalent to the BSA National Silver Buffalo award.

Mario Robles del Moral, national Scouting representative for Spain and a member of the Malaga District in the Seville mission, was the first recipient of the Sancho Panza award, equivalent to the BSA Silver Beaver and Antelope award combined. (CN 10/27/90)

Highest Medal Earned. Scouting's highest medal, the Honor Medal for Lifesaving with Crossed Palms, was awarded to Steve Fisher, San Bernardino 2nd Ward, San Bernardino Stake. Steve risked his own life to jump into raging flood waters to save the life of a friend who had been swept away in the torrent. (LDS 4/13/84)

International Scouting's Highest Awards. The Silver World award was presented to President Spencer W. Kimball during April Conference, 1977. (CN 4/9/77)

Oldest to Earn Silver Beaver. The oldest LDS recipient of the Silver Beaver is Chester Sease, 93, of the Exeter, California, Ward. He was not a Scout himself, but became involved when his son joined the Scouts in 1947. From that time forward, Brother Sease actively served in dozens of various Scouting positions. (CN 3/18/89).

First National Director of the Boy Scouts. Rees A. Falkner, Sharon 2nd Ward, Orem, Utah, Sharon Stake, became the first Church member to serve as national director of the Boy Scouts of America on July 6, 1992.

Silver World recipient Spencer W. Kimball.

Falkner took over the job of overseeing more than 1 million Scouts, ages 11-17, and other programs including national jamborees, adult leadership training, and administration and program development of varsity Scouting. (CN 6/20/92)

The Bronze Wolf award was presented to President Ezra Taft Benson during October General Conference, 1988. He received every one of Scouting's honors, including international scouting awards.

First Jamboree in Japan. The first LDS Jamboree in Tokyo took place in August 1981 as 350 Cubs and Scouts assembled to help commemorate the Church's 80th anniversary in Japan. The Scouts camped at a U.S. Army depot and the Cubs at a youth center in town. To address the group, Visiting Elder

Bronze Wolf recipient Ezra Taft Benson.

Yoshihiko Kikuchi of the First Quorum of the Seventy climbed one of the signal towers the Scouts had lashed together, a scene reminiscent of King Benjamin's tower. In Japan, Scouts strive to become a "Fuji Scout," the equivalent of an "Eagle" rank. (CN 8/29/81)

First Explorer President. In 1973, Steven K. Pollei, Salt Lake City, was elected national Explorer President of the Boy Scouts of America. Some 19 years later, in 1992, another LDS took the same post – Brett Braithwaite of the Manti 3rd Ward, Manti, Utah, Stake. The president is selected from candidates in eight regions representing Explorers throughout the United States (CN 5/12/73; 3/14/92)

Graduate College and Eagle Scout Award. Jeffrey Ryan, Ft. Lauderdale, Florida, became the first LDS Scout to earn his college bachelor's degree before completing the requirements for his Eagle Scout award in 1987. He achieved this unusual honor by finishing high school early and enrolling in a community college at age 14. (CN 9/5/87)

Most Eagle Scouts in One Family. In 1974, the James R. Boone family welcomed youngest son Michael as its ninth Eagle Scout. Preceding him were James, Columbus, Frederick, Daniel, Joseph, Hyrum, David & John. (CN 4/27/74)

In 1994, the Clyde and Afton Gardner family of the Grand Junction 6th Ward, Grand Junction, Colorado, Stake, saw its eighth son, Jared, receive his Eagle Scout award. He joined ranks with brothers Marlin (1969), Teryl (1972), Wayne (1973), Shanon (1978), Rowan (1982), Lanier (1985), and Bryant (1987). (CN 12/24/94)

European Scouts. The largest gathering of LDS European Scouts was more than 2,500 from 18 European countries at Brexbachtal, near Koblenz, Germany, for Triangle '89. The group had to be divided into 12 subgroups with an average three languages per group so that activities and talks could be translated and coordinated. (CN 9/23/89)

Fuji Scout Award. The highest honor given to Scouts in Japan is the Fuji Scout award, similar to the Eagle Scout award. The Fuji Scout award carries more prestige and recognition because only one is awarded each year, and the prime minister and crown prince are always on hand to make the presentation. In 1984, Kei Osako, a student at BYU-Hawaii, became the first LDS to receive it. He was a member of the BYU-Hawaii 2nd Ward, BYU-Hawaii 1st Stake. (CN 6/18/84)

First Christian to Receive Rover Badge in Pakistan. Iqbal Bhatti of the Islamabad Branch, Asia Area, and president of the Christian Scouting program in the Punjab Province of Pakistan, received the President's Rover Badge at a ceremony Aug. 11, 1991. The president of Pakistan, Ishaq Khan, presented the award to Bhatti, making him the first Christian Scout to receive the award in the predominantly Moslem country that had 110 million people at the time. Pakistan's Rover Scouting program is part of the Boy Scout program for young men over age 18. (CN 8/17/91)

Youngest to Earn All Merit Badges. The Boy Scouts of America doesn't track ages for earning merit badges, but it appears that Christopher Haskell, Elk Ridge, Utah, First Ward, is the youngest to earn all 120 offered badges by age 13. (DN 7/29/03)

Hollywood Honors Scouting. In Disney's feature-length movie about the Boy Scouts, "Follow Me, Boys," co-star Vera Miles, Hollywood, California, Stake, played not only the wife of the Scoutmaster (played by Fred McMurray), but as "mother" to dozens and dozens of Boy Scouts. The Boy Scouts of America honored the film production company and actors for depicting in a realistic manner the positive influence Scouting can have on a community and a boy's life. (CN 4/8/87)

Howard C. Moore, Deseret Morning News

Vera Miles, star of Disney's "Follow Me, Boys," was a frequent visitor to Salt Lake City.

Most Merit Badges. Who earned the maximum number of merit badges first? Since the number of available merit badges has changed, the records have been difficult to nail down. Here are those we know of:

1958: Byron G. Mills, 22nd Ward, Salt Lake, Utah, Stake, is believed to be the first LDS Scout to earn all 101 Boy Scout merit badges. He completed his last merit badge, Agriculture, in December 1958 after a seven-month effort to grow two varieties of cotton. (CN 2/14/59)

1974: Craig Carson, 16, and his brother Chad Carson 15, Ogden 55th Ward Ogden, Utah, Weber Heights Stake, each earned all 127 merit badges. (CN 9/14/74)

1981: Kent Bates, 15, Heber City 5th Ward, earned all 119 offered merit badges.(CN 1981)

1984: John T. Alquist, 15, and his nephew, Joshua J. Peterson, 14, both of the Hunter 6th Ward, each earned all 119 offered merit badges, plus two no longer available, for a total of 121 by 1984. (CN 2/12/84)

1988: Steve Sweat of the Iona, Idaho, 1st Ward, earned all 119 offered merit badges. (CN 2/28/88)

1988: Art Finch of the Idaho Falls, Idaho, 25th Ward earned all 121 offered merit badges. (CN 12/17/88)

1990: Troy Jens Pugh, Ferndale 2nd Ward, Bellingham, Washington, Stake, earned all 126 offered merit badges. (CN 7/14/90)

1993: Michael Arsenault, 17, of Oakridge 1st Ward, Farmington, Utah, Oakridge Stake, earned all 131 offered merit badges. (CN 5/29/93)

1993: Jared Toone, Crystal 1st Ward, Minneapolis, Minnesota, Stake, earned all 127 offered merit badges. (CN 7/19/93)

1996: David Wilson, 15, South Hill 3rd Ward, Puyallup, Washington, South Stake, earned all 124 offered merit badges. (CN 9/21/96)

1996: Jacob Walters, of the Hyrum 3rd Ward, Hyrum, Utah, North Stake, earned all 124 offered merit badges. (CN 9/21/96)

Youngest Eagle Scout? Who is the youngest to receive the Eagle Scout award? In 1985, the youngest was David Heidenreich who, at age 12, had completed all the requirements for his Eagle. He was presented his Eagle by his father, Richard Heidenreich, who was the Scoutmaster. They were members of the Freeport Ward, Rockford, Illinois, Stake. (CN 2/24/85)

Highest-altitude Boy Scout Camp (1930 World Record). As of 1930, the highest official Boy Scouts of America Scout camp continues to be Camp Steiner at 10,400 feet above sea level in the Uinta Mountains of Northern Utah. The camp was acquired for the Boy Scouts in 1930. Today, more than 55,000 Scouts use the facility each summer. (DN 2/6/02)

Largest Encampment. More than 9,000 LDS Boy Scouts and leaders, the largest such gathering ever, came together at Camp Pendleton, California, for the Sept. 3-6, 1982 "Mormon Trails Encampment." Sunday sacrament service required 100 priests, 100 teachers and 300 deacons to bless and pass the sacrament. Opening day was 100 degrees in the shade, prompting the sale of 120,000 soft drinks, 80,000 chocolate malts, 50,000 chocolate milks, 81,000 big stick Popsicles, 75,000 cartons of milk, 15,000 cartons of orange juice, 30,000 bags of chips and 25 tons of ice. (CN 9/11/82)

Cub Scout Officer. The highest position held by a Mormon in the Cub Scout program was chief executive over the entire program. Rodney H. Brady, at the time the Los Angeles, California, Stake president, was appointed "Top Cub" in July 1977. His task was to oversee the 1.9 million Cubs in the United States and their 625,000 leaders, plus prepare for the 50th anniversary celebration of Cub Scouting in 1980. (CN 8/6/77)

First Cub Scout Three-Time "World Athletic Champs."
Gregory Weichers, Derek Schiffman, and Kevin Armstrong of Pack 353, Union 5th Ward, Sandy, Utah, Willow Creek Stake, won the 1978 National

Physical Fitness Championship from among 100,000 competitors. But that's only a third of the story. In 1979, the same pack won again, and then again in 1980. Gregory Weichers was a member of all three winning teams before he became too old to compete. (CN 12/16/78, CN 12/27/80)

The first Cub Scout pack in the nation to win back-to-back Cub Scout National Physical Fitness Championships occurred in 1975 and 1976 by Church-sponsored Pack 411, St. David Ward, St. David, Arizona. (CN 1/3/77)

Deseret Morning News file photo

The winners of the National Physical Fitness championships.

Most Wolf Electives. The highest number of electives earned by any Cub Scout in the Church is 110, by Vance McKim, 9, Afton, Wyoming, 3rd Ward. He earned his last elective in December 1982. (CN 1/30/83)

Christopher Severson, 9, Orinda Ward, Oakland, California, Stake had earned all 106 possible Wolf electives available in early 1982. (CN 1982)

Deseret Morning News file photo

One of Utah's earliest Girl Scout troops heads for an outing in the mountains. The uniforms may have changed over the years, but the scouting principles have remained the same.

First Girl Scouts President. In 1990, LaRae Orullian, Lakewood, Colorado, Stake, was named president of Girl Scouts of the U.S.A. At the time, there were more than 3.2 million Girl Scouts ages 5 to 17 under her stewardship. Sister Orullian had previously served as national treasurer, first vice president, and chairwoman of the Girl Scouts' executive committee. (CN 7/13/91)

Deseret Morning News file photo

LaRae Orullian took charge of millions of girl scouts in 1990.

PIONEERS

Utah State Historical Society, Geo. Ed Anderson

First Pioneer Company. Departing Winter Quarters April 7, 1847, the first company of pioneers, under the leadership of Brigham Young, set out with 143 people, including three women and two children. The group included farmers, mechanics, carpenters, blacksmiths, and wheelwrights. In the 72 wagons they carried plows and tools; they had 93 horses, 52 mules, 66 oxen, 19 cows, 17 dogs and a few chickens. Advance riders scouted for camping and grazing spots, and watched over the company for Indians or other troubles. Pictured above, pioneers from 1847 celebrate a reunion 50 years later in 1897.

William Carter's plow (right) that suceeded where the other wooden plows failed, is on display at the Church History Museum in Salt Lake City.

First Half-Acre Plowed. At noon on July 23, 1847, a 26-year-old English convert, William Carter, stood with his oxen and plow at a five-acre plot near present State Street and 200-300 South in Salt Lake City, and went to work. Two other men, Shadrach Roundy and George W. Brown, had rigged up plows to turn the sod, but as their plows cut into the hard dirt, the wooden beams on the plows broke. Before they had time to repair them and return to try again, William Carter had plowed the first half acre. He credited the steady pull of his oxen with cutting through the firm turf without snagging the plow and snapping the beam. They continued plowing and on Saturday, July 24, when Brigham Young arrived in the valley just 15 minutes before noon, George A. Smith planted the first potatoes. By July 31, more than 52 acres of land were under cultivation. And with help from several rainstorms and water diverted from City Creek, sprouts soon began showing above the ground. (CN 3/10/90)

Longest Sea Voyage by Religious Colonists. On Feb. 4, 1846, the sailing ship Brooklyn departed New York Harbor bound for California with 238 Latter-day Saints led by Sam Brannan. The trip of 24,000 miles around South America was the longest ever attempted by religious colonists. Coincidentally, the departure date was the same day the Saints abandoned Nauvoo and began their trek across the frozen Mississippi River. The sea voyage was successful and the ship arrived safely in Yerba Buena (now San Francisco) on July 31, 1846. (Church Almanac 2001-02; Internet site for California LDS "Firsts")

Mob Destruction. The most LDS homes destroyed by mob action in any single year occurred in 1833 when mobs ruined 200 homes in Jackson

County, Missouri. The early Saints endured similar hardships for more than another dozen years before plans to move out west were finally formulated. (Deseret News Church Almanac; Internet)

Jim Bridger Bets Against Mormon Corn. On June 28, 1847, the pioneers had just reached the point where the California and Oregon trails branched off. Taking the left-hand route, they suddenly came upon the great western scout, Jim Bridger. He cautioned the Saints against going to the Great Salt Lake Valley, saying a group their size shouldn't go there until it was proven grain could grow and ripen. Said Bridger to Brigham Young, "Mr. Young, I would give a thousand dollars if I knew an ear of corn could be ripened in these mountains. I have been here twenty years and have tried it over and over again." (CN 4/13/57)

Last of Utah Pioneers Before 1850. James William McDaniel, age 100 on Sept. 13, 1946, was honored as the last of the pioneers to cross the plains from Illinois to Utah before 1850. At the age of three he came to Utah with his parents and served in the Blackhawk War when he was 18. His wife died just one day before their 70th wedding anniversary. Brother McDaniel died in January, 1947. (CN 2/1/47)

Deseret Morning News file photo

Richard Ballantyne started the first Sunday School

First Sunday School. Richard Ballantyne, a Scotsman who formerly taught Sunday School to some 75 children for his Presbyterian Church in Earlston, Scotland, founded the first LDS Sunday School on Dec. 9, 1849. With no room large enough to accommodate the 30 children in his ward, Ballantyne built the Sunday School building himself. He hauled red sandstone from Red Butte Canyon for a foundation, mixed adobe for the walls, cut timber in Mill Creek Canyon, and added a thick layer of sod over the sheathing to complete the roof. The little 18-by-20-foot room was built as an addition to the kitchen he had erected on the corner of Third South and First West in Salt Lake City. After visiting the children's homes to invite them to Sunday School, he greeted the shy youngsters Sunday morning with a roaring fire in the fireplace and an opening song they all knew. Then he raised his arm and, bowing his head, dedicated the little room for the teaching of children. And then he began, "Let me tell you a story about Jesus ..." (CN 12/8/62)

First Primary. Aurelia Spencer Rogers was concerned the children were not benefitting from any program to teach and guide them during the long summer days. She expressed a desire that an organization be started to teach the children during the weekdays. When word reached the Twelve, President John Taylor wrote to Sister Rogers' bishop giving permission to organize such a program. On Aug. 11, 1878, Rogers was sustained by her ward in the new calling, and after two weeks of canvassing the ward and personally inviting the children, the first Primary meeting was held Aug. 25, 1878, with more than 200 children in attendance. "Never find yourselves in the neighbors' orchards ... and you shouldn't catch rides on wagons," she told her young flock. (CN 8/25/62)

First primary presidency in 1878.

The house in Farmington, Utah, where the first Primary was held.

Last Handcart Company. From 1856-1860, 10 handcart companies with 2,945 pioneers made the 1,300-mile trek from Missouri to Utah. The last, led by Oscar Orlondo Stoddard, had 126 emigrants, 22 handcarts and 6 wagons. Captain Stoddard celebrated the successful trek by marrying his sweetheart, Elizabeth Taylor, on Oct. 2, 1860, only eight days after their arrival in Salt Lake City.

The handcart era ended after it was discovered that oxen raised on the nutritious grasses of the Rocky Mountains could make the trip to Missouri and back to Utah with a company of pioneers. Oxen raised on the more abundant but less nutritious grasses of the prairies of Iowa and Nebraska could only make the trip one way. The completion of the railroad in 1869 ended the slow 3-4 month trips by animal- or human-pulled wagon. (CN 9/24/60; CN 6/28/58)

The handcarts typically carried 400-500 pounds of flour, bedding, cooking utensils and a tent. In addition, they frequently carried children and sick wives or husbands. A wagon or two accompanied the handcart companies to haul supplies and assist the elderly, infirm and the little children. The handcart companies could typically cover 30 miles a day, almost twice what the wagon groups could average.

Two men atop poles during telegraph construction in Weber Canyon in 1861.

Meeting of the Telegraph Wires. Mormons who contracted to provide trees for the first transcontinental telegraph helped bring the project together in Salt Lake City. As with the first transcontinental railroad, two companies worked from the east and west, fighting against time to cover as much ground as possible. On Oct. 24, 1861, the two lines joined in Salt Lake City, marked by a monument at 63 South Main Street. Mormons provided poles for 750 miles of telegraph wire. In addition to a lack of trees in many areas, the companies faced many trials including buffaloes rubbing the poles down, Indians cutting up the wire for trinkets, snowdrifts completely burying the poles at high spots, and bears attracted by the bee-like humming noise from the wires clawing poles down. Brigham Young was honored to send the first message over the completed line. "Sir: Permit me to congratulate you," were his first words.

Beginning in 1864, Brigham Young instigated a north-south telegraph to link Mormon settlements up and down the continent. By 1869, telegraph lines had linked St. George, Utah, to Franklin, Idaho. (CN 10/28/61)

First telegraph office on Main Street in Salt Lake City.

The historic "meeting of the rails" was made possible in part by LDS workers.

Largest Rail Construction Effort.

When Union Pacific Railroad representatives approached Brigham Young for Mormon help to finish a 120-mile stretch of railroad grade, the prophet gladly accepted. The $2 million payment to Mormon contractors was a badly needed shot in the financial arm of Utah. But later that year, representatives from the Central Pacific Railroad approached the prophet asking for Mormon help on a 200-mile stretch of track, most of it paralleling the Mormon-built Union Pacific job. Brigham didn't complain. The people needed the work and the money, even though it meant that some 200 miles of parallel redundant grade would be constructed.

By March 1869, both companies were fervently at work at Promontory, Utah. The lines were often just a few feet from each other, and criss-crossed here and there. Frequently, the blast from one Mormon company would shower the other with debris. By April, it was appar-

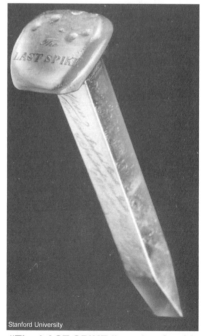

"The LAST SPIKE," made of gold with a fineness of 17.6 carats, shows hammer dents from its pounding on May 10, 1869. It is in the care of Stanford University.

ent that the Union Pacific had won the race into Ogden, and the two companies agreed on a meeting place. When it came time for a final settlement, the Union Pacific found itself short of ready cash and paid off its debts to the Mormons with $700,000 of equipment. (CN 5/1/65)

Utah State Historical Society

The first train to enter Salt Lake City in 1870 was photographed during this maintenance stop in Farmington.

Deaths Along the Mormon Trail. During the years 1846 to 1869, more than 6,000 immigrants were laid to rest along the Mormon Trail from Nauvoo to Salt Lake Valley. (CN 3/2/49)

First Sugar Beet Factories. The Saints' first attempt to produce sugar in 1852 ended in failure. But efforts continued. Shortly after the first branch in France was organized in April 1860, Elder Taylor of the Council of the Twelve arrived in that country to study the sugar-beet industry. Eventually he purchased and shipped to the United States sugar-beet-processing equipment in a vain attempt to launch a sugar producing plant among the Saints. In 1879, the first successful beet sugar factory in America was started in Alvarado, California. Encouraged by the success there, Church leaders again pushed the project. Members of the Dyer family finally collected enough funds to erect a sugar plant in Lehi, Utah. In October 1891, as the first white crystallized sugar poured down the spout into waiting bags amidst the cheers of the assembled workers, the first all-American-constructed and tooled sugar plant was finally opened. (CN 11/8/58; CN 11/9/57)

First Flour Mill in Salt Lake Valley. John Neff and his family arrived in Salt Lake Valley on Oct. 2, 1847, with intentions of building a flour mill. In the spring of 1848, Brother Neff began to locate a suitable site for his mill. He began constructing a mill on Mill Creek, about two miles from the mouth of Mill Creek Canyon, and moved his family there in the fall of 1848. It was said he was a very benevolent man, refusing to take $1 per pound of flour during the famine of 1856, but accepted 6 cents a pound from those truly in need. He died at his home on May 9, 1869, at age 74. (CN 7/2/55)

Most Important Bird. The most important bird in Church history is the California gull, credited with coming to the rescue of the Saints when a plague of crickets began devastating badly needed crops in the spring of 1848. Having barely survived the winter on meager food supplies including wolf meat, crows, sego lily bulbs, tree bark, thistle tops, and hawks, the Saints were looking forward to a bounteous harvest. The appearance of the black swarms of crickets, described by one as "wingless, dumpy, black, swollen-headed, with bulging eyes in cases like goggles, mounted upon legs of steel wire ... a cross of the spider and the buffalo ..." was horrifying, to say the least, to the starving Saints. When the seagulls miraculously arrived in great white swarms to ingest the crickets and spare the crops, the Saints knew divine intervention had once again spared their lives. The Seagull Monument was erected on Temple Square in 1913 to honor and express gratitude to God for sending the seagulls. (Internet)

Paul B. Skousen

The Seagull Monument honors the miracle that saved settlers from starvation.

PIONEER HOLIDAYS

First Thanksgiving. The first Thanksgiving among the Saints in the Salt Lake Valley involved two celebrations in 1848. The first occurred Aug. 10 when a

Ravell Call, Deseret Mornig News

The infamous "Mormon Cricket" – a crop-killing foe, or dinner for a gull?

public feast was held under a bowery in the center of the fort. The Saints ate freely of bread, meat, butter, cheese, cakes, pastry, green corn, melons and almost every variety of vegetables. There was prayer and thanksgiving for the bounteous harvest. The second Thanksgiving was held at the beginning of the October General Conference session. After preliminaries, there was a great friendly festival held as a "thanksgiving" for the safe return of the members of the Mormon Battalion. After the returned soldiers marched behind the martial band, with their wives and families at their sides, all were seated at tables under the bowery for a delicious thanksgiving meal. (CN 11/24/48)

Courtesy Church History Museum

The "Old Sow" cannon hauled from the east and used for defense ... or to wake up a travel-weary band of pioneers.

First Christmas. The first Christmas in Salt Lake Valley began early on Dec. 25, 1847, with a "BOOM!" It was the "old sow," a cannon hauled across the plains that announced Christmas morning had arrived. In the 10-acre log enclosure, people arose to go about their usual Saturday labors. The children stayed in their warm beds while adults built up the fires, prepared breakfast, milked some cows, and gathered eggs. It was chilly, but since Dec. 19, the weather had been clear and sunny. This meant the melting snow on the sod-and-rush cabin roofs would seep through and drip everywhere. One mother spent Christmas Day sewing a canvas cover for the baby's cradle so the youngster would be protected from the muddy, cold drops. The men spent the day plowing up the softened ground so as to get an early start on the spring planting. In some of the cabins, guests were invited over for a special Christmas dinner to include perhaps a rabbit. In the evening, young people gathered for singing, games and dancing. There were hardships aplenty, but on this day it was good to be alive. (CN 12/25/65)

ODDS & ENDS

Hands Across America. The "anchor" for the famous 1987 "Hands Across America" fund-raising event to help the hungry and homeless was Church member Bill Jones, 35, a father of five. He was taken from a relief shelter in Long Beach, California, to be the beginning of the chain that stretched from the Pacific to the Atlantic coast. Unfortunately, Brother Jones never received any of the money that the giant event was staged to raise. (LDS 5/87)

Prisoners. Where were the most LDS prisoners held at any given time? In 1990, about 1,600 of the 2,300 prisoners incarcerated at Utah's prison facilities said they were LDS. Of the total prison population, about 850 of them were convicted on charges of burglary, theft and robbery. About 225 others were imprisoned for murder, and another 118 were there for drug-related crimes. (DN 3/21/90)

Most Service-Minded. How can anyone gauge the most service-minded among a church geared to service? Perhaps, in the 25-and-under category, Ken Kuykendall, Seattle, would take top honors. He was named in Time magazine in 1986 as one of "America's 100 Outstanding College Juniors." As a student at BYU he centered his life around community service and his output of energy and time was enormous. Beginning at age 9 he organized the first of more than 60 large service projects that stretched over the years and over the miles to give aid, comfort and help to those in need. One project he started at age 16 called "Christmas in May" was a campaign that netted more than $8,000 in food and cash for the needy in Seattle. (LDS 4/19/86)

Photos courtesy Kathy B. Skousen

Most Widely Circulated LDS Joke. In 1989, a story was submitted to Reader's Digest's "Life in these United States," by Kathy Skousen of South Jordan, Utah, River Ridge 3rd Ward. The editors called the local school to verify its accuracy, and then published it in their July 1989 issue that went to 16 million subscribers. Over the years the joke has spread to no fewer than 85 web sites with funny variations on the sex, age and setting. Here is the original joke:

Patricia Skousen, age 5

For Drug Awareness Day, the school asked each child to bring a white T-shirt so an anti-drug slogan could be ironed onto it. After a frantic search, I found my daughter's only clean shirt, which already had something on the front. The back was blank, however, and I sent her off with it. When she came home that afternoon, she proudly displayed the shirt. The front of it proclaimed, "Families Are Forever." On the back was "Be Smart, Don't Start!" (Author)

Fame can last an eternal 15 minutes or a blazing 15 decades, and among LDS men and women, there are plenty who have achieved both. In 1960, Linda Bement (center) became the first member of the Church to be crowned Miss Universe. She is one among hundreds of Mormons who have won national and international acclaim and *fame*.

Photo courtesy of Linda Bement

Fame

Famous Mormons and Church-related accomplishments – by the numbers:

1 — Mormons winning the title of Mr. Universe
8 — Book of Mormon verses quoted in an Alfred Hitchcock movie
80 — Number of "B" movies in which the same LDS actor appeared
42,000 — Dollars won by a Mormon on a television game show
463,400 — Lodging rooms offered worldwide by the Marriotts
1,700,000,000 — Dollars grossed from movies produced by an LDS

MOVIE STARS AND MOVIE MAKERS

Utah, Mormons, and the LDS Church have been portrayed in movies for almost 100 years. Hollywood's treatment of the Saints and their culture has ranged from outrageous to hilarious.

According to Chris Hicks, former movie critic for the Deseret News, the Church has been the target of some 30-40 anti-Mormon propaganda films. The first was the 1905 "A Trip to Salt Lake City," a two-minute gag about a polygamous family aboard a train. The father solves the problem of giving his many children a drink by using a milk canister with dozens of straws.

In the years that followed, a push to produce negative films about the Church caught hold in Hollywood. During the 1920s and '30s, cheesy films appeared with such titles as "A Mormon Maid," "Trapped by the Mormons," "A Victim of the Mormons," and "Marriage or Death."

Then, in 1940, the tide began to turn with the 20th Century Fox production of "Brigham Young," starring Dean Jagger. It was a dramatic presentation that made a good attempt at retelling the LDS story without the usual focus on polygamy. According to Hicks, the real contribution of "Brigham Young" was to change public perception of Mormons. Hollywood began to emphasize the greatness found in the Mormon pioneers and their leaders – people of great faith, determination, and family values. Over time, Mormons became heroic figures in many westerns.

Television picked up the Mormon story by airing episodes of encounters with Mormons in the old West. In the '50s and '60s, the positive "pioneer" image was perpetuated in episodes of "Bonanza," "Death Valley Days," "Wagon Train," "The Big Valley," and others.

However, comical jabs at Mormons were renewed in "Paint Your Wagon," "They Call Me Trinity," "The Duchess and the Dirtwater Fox," and other movies produced during the late '60s and '70s.

By the '80s and '90s, Hicks says, Mormons became subjects of "based on a true story" movies, usually in positive portrayals that showed them to be "regular folk." A good example was the 1988 made-for-TV film "Go Toward the Light," depicting a California family whose son contracts AIDS through a blood transfusion.

And then, in 2001, independent LDS movie producers entered the feature-length movie business with the launch of Richard Dutcher's "God's Army." It was a surprising smash hit among LDS audiences, taking in almost $3 million in sales. Dutcher followed this with a murder mystery called "Brigham City," and has other Church-themed films in the works.

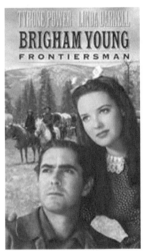

Other Mormon-produced movies include the spoofs "Singles Ward," "RM," and "The Home Teacher." More serious treatments of LDS culture and belief were captured in the true story of Elder John H. Groberg in "Other Side of Heaven," and the ongoing "The Book of Mormon" series. (Author; Chris Hicks; DN 2/26/93)

Tyrone Power and Linda Darnell, starred as two pioneer lovers in this 1940 drama.

First Feature-Length Movie. "Brigham Young—Frontiersman," starring Dean Jagger as Brigham Young, was the first and certainly the most expensive film at the time to focus on a specific aspect of Church history. Produced in 1940, the film has been late-night movie fare for decades. Brother Jagger joined the Church in 1972 and became a member of the Studio City 1st Ward, Hollywood, California, Stake. (CN 5/1/83)

Courtesy of Gerald R. Molen

Gerald R. Molen's movies have grossed close to $2 billion at the box office.

Highest Grossing LDS Producer at the Box Office. Gerald R. Molen is the most successful LDS producer in Church history with a string of big-hit movies that have grossed more than $1.7 billion at the box office in North America. He won the Best Picture Academy Award for "Schindler's List" (1993). He was also producer (or executive producer) of Mitch Davis' "The Other Side of Heaven" (2001), "Lost World: The Jurassic Park" (1997), "Jurassic Park" (1993), "Rain Man" (1988), "Twister" (1996), "Casper" (1995), "The Flintstones" (1994), "The Little Rascals" (1994), "Little Giants" (1994), "A Far Off Place" (1993), "Hook" (1991), "Days of

Thunder" (1990), "Bright Lights, Big City" (1988), "View from the Swing" (2000), and "The Trigger Effect" (1996). Brother Molen was the unit production manager for: "Hook" (1991), "*batteries not included" (1987), "The Color Purple" (1985), "A Soldier's Story" (1984), "Let's Spend the Night Together" (1982), "Tootsie" (1982), "The Postman Always Rings Twice" (1981), and more. (Author's interview, Internet)

Most Leading Roles. Laraine Day, a native of Roosevelt, Utah, performed in 45 feature-length movies, and had starring roles opposite such leading men as John Wayne, Kirk Douglas, Spencer Tracy, Robert Mitchum, Gregory Peck and Ronald Reagan. She was always active in the Church, and spent the later years of her life serving as a worker in the Los Angeles Temple. (LDS 7/13/85)

1961: Laraine Day and Tabernacle Choir director Richard P. Condie prepare for a program featuring the choir.

Biggest Money-Generating Actor. As of 2002, the movies in which LDS actor Paul Walker starred had generated U.S. box office sales of more than $322 million. He was the leading star in "Timeline" (2003), "The Fast and the Furious" (2001) and its sequel, "The Fast and the Furious II" (2003), and played leading roles in "The Skulls" (2000), "Joy Ride" (2001), "Varsity Blues" (1999), "She's All That" (1999), "Pleasantville" (1998), "Meet the Deedles" (1998), "Tammy and the T-Rex" (1994), and "Monster in the Closet" (1986). (www.ldsfilm.com/bio/bioW.html)

Most Prolific Cinematographers. Dal Clawson, one of Hollywood's early motion-picture cameramen, filmed 58 motion pictures during his career.

Robert W. Stum filmed more than 150 motion pictures, most of them for the Church, including the classics "Johnny Lingo" (1969), "Windows of Heaven" (1963), and "Man's Search for Happiness" (1964)

First "Best Picture" Featuring a Mormon. In the feature film "Rainman," Dustin Hoffman's Academy-award-winning portrayal of Kim, a Utah-native autistic savant, helped the film win the Oscar for "Best Motion Picture of the Year," in 1988.

Screen Writer. Samuel W. Taylor, San Francisco, wrote the screenplays for Disney's "The Absent Minded Professor" (1961), and "Son of Flubber" (1963), among others. The "Absent Minded Professor" was the fourth-highest-grossing film in the United States in 1961. In total, Brother Taylor's films have grossed more than $115 million. (www.ldsfilm.com/bio/ bioT.html)

John Gilbert was once one of Hollywood's "great lovers."

First "Movie Star." John Gilbert was born July 10, 1899, in Logan, Utah, into an LDS home and environment but didn't practice the religion as an adult. One of the first movie stars in Hollywood history, he became known as the "Great Lover of the Silver Screen." One movie critic called him the "Tom Cruise of the silent era." One list of the 100 most influential people in cinema history ranked him number 28. He appeared in more than 100 films and is best known for his role in "The Big Parade" (1925), one of the last great silent films. It was the top box office earner until "Gone With the Wind." He drank himself to death in 1936.

Robert Clarke, king of "B" horror movies.

Most Prominent in "B" Horror Movies. Robert Clarke, originally of Oklahoma City, Oklahoma, appeared in more than 80 movies. He is best-known as the star of B horror movies such as: "Frankenstein Island" (1981), "Terror of the Bloodhunters" (1962), "The Astounding She-Monster" (1957), and "The Man from Planet X" (1951), just to mention a few. He also made numerous TV guest appearances on "Adam-12," "Dragnet," "Knight Rider," "Marcus Welby, M.D.," "Matt Houston," "Murder, She Wrote," "Perry Mason," "Simon & Simon," "The Lone Ranger," "Wagon Train," and others. In 1996 he published his autobiography To "B" or Not to "B": A Film Actor's Odyssey. (Internet)

Most Popular Christmas Film: "It's A Wonderful Life." It should come as no surprise that LDS artists migrate to projects that reflect their personal standards and beliefs. So was it with the 1946 James Stewart/Donna

Reed holiday classic, "It's a Wonderful Life." The film score was created by LDS composer Leigh Harline, winner of 2 Academy Awards. Mormon actors Moroni Olsen and Joseph Kearns provided voices for two of the angels and another native Utahn, Charles Meakin, had an on-screen role. (Internet)

James D'Arc (left), curator of BYU's Arts and Communications Archives, was integral in securing Jimmy Stewart's papers. Stewart made several visits to Utah, pictured here in 1985, meeting with a BYU film class.

Most Watched (TV) – Holiday Story.

In 1980, "Mr. Krueger's Christmas," starring Jimmy Stewart, became a Christmas-season favorite almost overnight. Broadcast nationwide in nearly every local market, "Mr. Krueger's Christmas" still finds itself among regular viewing fare for nearly all of America. The film featured the Mormon Tabernacle Choir, which was directed by Mr. Stewart in one of the dream scenes. When he finished leading them through a hymn, the choir spontaneously broke into applause and gave him a standing ovation. This scene was not part of the original script but was included in the final version. (Author)

Longest Book of Mormon Quote.

Alfred Hitchcock's "Family Plot" features the longest quote from the Book of Mormon in a major motion picture. During a funeral scene, a priest is heard reading verbatim eight verses (20-27) from 2 Nephi 9. Some of the producers and writers who collaborated with Hitchcock were LDS, and their influence can be spotted in several of his masterpieces. (Internet)

Jimmy Stewart frequently spoke of "Mr. Krueger's Christmas" as one of his favorite projects from his later years.

Large Format/IMAX Films.

Reed Smoot is one of the world's leading cinematographers for large format/IMAX films including "Grand Canyon: The Hidden Secrets" (1984). "Grand Canyon" may end up being the top-grossing documentary in world box-office history. (Internet)

Most Prominent Voice in Commercial Movies. What greater role is there than the voice of God in "The Ten Commandments?" Delos Jewkes, formerly of the La Cienaga Ward, Santa Monica Stake, California, was the voice of God speaking out of the burning bush to Moses in the Cecil B. DeMille classic film. He sang or had small roles in 15 movies including "The Music Man," "Paint Your Wagon," and "The Wizard of Oz." He sang in the Mormon Tabernacle Choir, and was in great demand as voice-over in hundreds of movies. (CN 1/15/72)

Deseret Morning News file photo

The making of Cecil B. Demille's "The Ten Commandments" involved several members of the Church. Arnold Friberg's paintings influenced set designs, Delos Jewkes was the voice of God, and an unidentified assistant on the set helped the director portray the bestowing of the priesthood from Moses to Aaron. They had been experimenting with more dramatic actions such as Moses raising his hands over his head or using his staff to anoint Aaron. The Church member suggested Moses simply place his hands on Aaron's head, and that's exactly how the scene was shot. Pictured above, Demille (second from left) and Charlton Heston in costume as Moses, visit with President and Sister David O. McKay in 1955.

Strangest Casting for a Mormon? When an actor was needed in 1940 to portray the Prophet Joseph Smith in the feature-length movie, "Brigham Young—Frontiersman," Hollywood producers chose somebody to help draw crowds: king of horror films, Mr. Vincent Price.

Most Widely-Acclaimed Anti-LDS Film. "Trapped By the Mormons" was banned from the United States after its release in 1922 following intense lobbying efforts by LDS Church leaders and U.S. Senator Reed Smoot (R-Utah). Though the silent film is today seen as a fantastic comedy and farce, it was serious business when it first appeared in the 1920s. It depicted missionaries going around the world to entrap young ladies and return them to Salt Lake City to live as slaves in their polygamous families. The film created a hatred of Mormons by people in the United Kingdom and other places where it showed. (DU 12/6/79)

Anti-LDS Films. For a couple of years after its release in 1983, the $100,000 production called "The Godmakers" was one of the hottest anti-LDS films on the market. Based on the book, "The Godmakers," the script was subsequently exposed and discredited in the book, "The Truth About The Godmakers." Additionally, several of the inactive LDS portrayed in the film returned to full fellowship in the Church and denounced the film as a hodgepodge of lies and deception. "The Godmakers II," released in 1992-93, became the subject of threatened court action by the Church because of gross hearsay and slander the producers allowed into the film. (Author)

Movie Novelization. Director Jim Cameron ("The Terminator," "Aliens" and "Titanic") asked famed LDS fiction writer Orson Scott Card to write the novel for "Abyss." Card initially resisted because of the stigma a writer gets for "novelizing" a movie. He eventually changed his mind when Cameron said, "I don't want a novelization. I want a novel." The book was published before movie production got underway. It became so successful that the director reportedly showed some of the chapters, in draft form, to stars of "Abyss" so they could gain a better understanding of their own characters. (LDS 8/23/89)

Hollywood's Big-Screen Lover's Love! The great-granddaughter of early Church apostle Heber C. Kimball turned out to be a talented costume designer and art director for Hollywood in the 1920s and '30s. Winifred Kimball Shaughnessy was born in Salt Lake City in 1897. She later changed her name to Natacha Rambova and married Rudolph Valentino, one of the best known romantic leading men in Hollywood history. Some of Valentino's biographers blame Rambova for dressing her husband in silly outfits for his movie roles that detracted from his manly, romantic appeal, thus hurting the later years of his career. (Internet)

Critics accuse Rambova of ruining Valentino's career.

2003: The Osmond family receives their star on the Hollywood Walk of Fame.
Photo courtesy of Crystale Richardson, TCP, International

Mormon Hollywood Stars. Mormons who have been immortalized with a star on Hollywood's "Walk of Stars" sidewalk include:

Billy Barty, Hollywood's famous little man, starred in numerous films for more than 50 years. On July 1, 1981, he was honored with his own star. Brother Barty founded the Little People of America Foundation, a philanthropic organization to which no one more than 4 feet 6 inches can become a member.

The Osmond Family. On Aug. 7, 2003, the Osmond Family was honored with a star on Hollywood's Walk of Fame in tribute to their "life-long contributions of both public and peer appreciation."

Glen Larson. In 1986, star number 1,813, was placed in honor of writer, producer, and director Glen Larson who has produced such popular television series as "Quincy," "Magnum, P.I.," "The Fall Guy," "Knight Rider," "McCloud," "It Takes a Thief," "Battlestar Galactica," "The Hardy Boys/Nancy Drew Mysteries," "Sheriff Lobo," "Alias Smith and Jones," "Six Million Dollar Man," "Buck Rogers in the 25th Century," "BJ and the Bear," and others.

Rhonda Fleming starred in more than 50 films, her first big break came fast as the female lead opposite Bing Crosby in the 1949 film, "A Connecticut Yankee in King Arthur's Court." She also co-starred with Ronald Reagan, Charlton Heston, Gregory Peck, Kirk Douglas, Burt Lancaster, Dick Powell, Mark Stevens, John Payne, Ricardo Montalban, and Joseph Cotten.

Robert Walker, famed actor in several World War II-themed movies, also starred as the psychopath in Alfred Hitchcock's "Strangers on a Train" (1951).

Marie Windsor served for 25 years on the Board of Directors of the Screen Actors Guild and starred in more than 70 movies. She was credited as one of the best "bad girls" in Hollywood history, often portraying a cold-blooded temptress who would entrap the hero. She played the leading role in many "B" movies of the late 1940s.

Joi Lansing achieved stardom in "B" movies, but made her biggest hit on television. Many would recognize her as Gladys Flatt on the television sitcom, "The Beverly Hillbillies" (1962).

Fay Wray, an ethnic Mormon (raised in a non-practicing LDS family and not baptized), appeared in almost 100 movies beginning in 1923, including the thriller "King Kong."

Mack Swain, born in 1876, was a talented vaudevillian who appeared in many early silent motion pictures and also starred with Charlie Chaplin.

Terry Moore, once married to billionaire Howard Hughes, starred in more than 30 movies and was one of the most popular actresses in Hollywood in the 1940s and 1950s.

Joi Lansing, from Salt Lake City, was "Gladys Flatt."

TELEVISION STARS & PRODUCERS

Youngest Child Star in a Leading Role. At age 6, Johnny Whitaker starred in the series, "Family Affair," and played the orphan Jody for five years. His character lived with his Uncle Bill, played by Brian Keith. Brother Whitaker later served a mission to Portugal from 1979-81, married the former Symbria Wright, and graduated from BYU with a bachelor's degree in motion picture television directing. (CN 10/5/86)

1973: Johnny Whitaker, 13, starred in "Tom Sawyer" and several "Homefront" spots for the Church.

Michael Lookingland became familiar to tens of millions in his role as Bobby in the popular television series, "The Brady Bunch." He played the part for five seasons. He, his talented sisters (they starred in advertising), and his parents were members of the Harbor Ward, Torrance, California, Stake. (CN 10/19/74)

Youngest Twins in a Sitcom. The youngest LDS twin regulars ever to appear on television were Mike and Joe Mayer. They alternately played the part of "Little Ricky" on the "I Love Lucy Show." They stayed with the series for about three years, taking part in such classics as the episode in which Lucy desperately tries to get John Wayne to put his footprints in cement as a souvenir. As "Lucy" fans will recall, after Lucy's usual antics and problems to get Wayne's cooperation, one of the toddlers playing "Little Ricky" crawls through the wet cement, ruining it before it could dry, much to Lucy's horror. Joe says that particular set of footprints was made from oatmeal, and after the toddlers crawled through it, they were allowed to eat some. (LDS 8/9/89)

Merlin Olsen as "Father Murphy" in 1981.

First Mormon to Star in His Own Regular TV Series. Merlin Olsen, the former NFL star and NBC commentator, was the star in two series, "Father Murphy" and the short-lived "Aaron's Way." He also played a minor role in the long-running "Little House on the Prairie."

Dan Blocker (played Hoss on Bonanza) and other LDS greats helped pioneer the success of several television series for millions of Americans. (LDS 1988)

First Woman Regular in a TV Series. The only female to join the all-male household on "My Three Sons" was Tina Cole, a member of the Church from Los Angeles. She became Robbie's bride during the 1967-68 season and starred on the show for eight seasons. (CN 11/4/67)

Tina Cole, the only woman in an all-male TV family.

Most Widely Distributed. The Church's Homefront television and radio series has been winning awards for more than 30 years. It has been honored with more than 300 distinguished national and international awards including Emmys, Clios, and a Bronze Lion at the Cannes Film Festival. By 2002, Homefront had aired on 9,138 radio and 1,973 television and cable stations in the United States and Canada and another 8,013 radio stations and

2,071 television stations in Australia, New Zealand, Fiji, Tahiti, Samoa, Latin America, Brazil, United Kingdom, Philippines, Spain, Portugal, Italy, Russia and Czech Republic (CN 2/14/87; CN 6/8/02)

Best TV Spot. "Try Again," a public-service announcement sponsored by the Church and produced by Bonneville Productions, was judged the best public service television spot of the year 1980. The competition included 5,000 entries from 50 countries. "Try Again" had already won three CLIO awards. (CN 5/17/80)

Highest Nielsen Ratings for a Movie. "Side by Side," the story of how the Osmond family began their phenomenal musical career, captured a 32-38 percent market share in New York, Chicago and Los Angeles, surprising many critics who had panned the film. (LDS 5/21/86)

Grant and Chris Oyler's ordeal with the death of their son, "Go Towards the Light," ranked second in all programming in 1988 with a 24 percent share of the audience and a 14.9 rating equaling 13,469,000 homes. The CBS-TV movie was based on the true story of nine-year-old Ben Oyler and his losing battle with AIDS. It was later awarded the prestigious Christopher Award by the National Association of Religions Broadcasters, and Reader's Digest published the book in condensed version in its November 1988 issue.

Marie Osmond played the part of her mother in the TV movie, "Side by Side" in 1981.

Third Rock from the Sun. Nashville Bishop Tony Martin wrote a "chart-topper" song he called "Third Rock from the Sun." A television comedy series of the same name bought the rights to the name (not the song). "They pay to use that title for the TV shows," Martin said. "It's a nice part-time job, let's put it that way." (CN 6/10/00)

Most Watched (TV) – 30-Minute Story. O. Henry's classic short story, "The Last Leaf," was produced by the Church in 1983-84. It starred Oscar-winner Art Carney as Verlaine, whose lifelong desire was to paint a masterpiece. More than 100 markets throughout the United States and Canada scheduled the 30-minute presentation during the Easter time period in 1984. It has remained popular ever since. (CN 3/11/84)

Most Money Won by LDS on a TV Game Show. In June 2004, Ken Jennings, 30, of Murray, Utah, shattered records for "Jeopardy," a quiz show in which an answer is given and the contestant must provide the question. Brother Jennings, a returned missionary from Madrid, defended his championship for 70+ consecutive games and won more than $2 million. At BYU he was once ranked seventh in the nation among college quiz bowl teams. (Internet)

Ken Jennings' "day job" is a computer programmer for a health care company.

Longest-Running TV Commercial with an LDS Star. The longest-running TV commercial starring a Mormon actress was the "Pearldrops" ad which featured Suzanne Barnes, Phoenix 21st Ward, West Maricopa Stake. Barnes' sparkling white teeth were flashed across America's televisions for more than seven years, a record in the advertising industry. She has performed in more than 100 television ads. (LDS 3/12/82)

Soap Character Named for LDS. When "Days of Our Lives" aired an episode about kidney disease, a mistake in the medical facts prompted Jodi Butler, a BYU student and kidney patient from Springville, Utah, to write a letter to the program's producers explaining their mistake. Unfortunately, Jodi died from her kidney disease before she could mail her letter. Jodi's mother later found the letter and sent it with a death notice to the writer of the soap opera. In honor of Jodi, the writer named a new character after her: "Nurse Jodi Butler." (LDS 3/12/88)

First Game-Show Host. The first LDS game-show host on network television was Ray Combs, Los Angeles. On July 4, 1988, Brother Combs became the host of "Family Feud," replacing Richard Dawson. Dawson's trademark kiss (he kissed all of the women) didn't carry over with Combs. "I won't kiss all the women," he said, "I'll just be funny!" (LDS 5/17/89; LDS 9/17/89)

Deseret Morning News file photo

Ray Combs on Family Feud. 'No kissing!'

Game-Show Announcer. Nearly every American who has seen daytime television in the past 30 years would probably recognize the voice of Bob Hilton. Brother Hilton had been a game-show host or announcer at one time or another for "Let's Make a Deal," "The Guinness Game," "Truth or Consequences," "The Match Game," "The Challengers," "Win, Lose or Draw," "The $10,000 Pyramid," "Double Talk," "The New Dat-ing Game," "Body Language," "The Price is Right," "Trivia Trap,"

Bob Hilton doing his dad job during home-work time. 'Okay sweetie, then Let's Make A Deal, but it better be Truth ... or Consequences!'

"Child's Play," "Block-busters," "Password Plus," "Card Sharks," and "The New Tic Tac Dough." (Internet)

National "Mormon" Work-out. Produced for BYU's television station, KBYU, the "Hooked on Aerobics" morning exercise show became so popular in 1983 that it was released nationally. Said Ellen Mathias, program hostess, "'Hooked on Aerobics' is different than any other exercise program on the air because it demonstrates low, medium and high efforts of aerobic endurance." This was the first major program from BYU to go national. (DU 3/29/83)

Morning Show Host. Jane Clayson joined Bryant Gumbel as co-host on CBS's The Early Show in 1999; the duo remained popular until the show's format changed in 2002 and the cast was let go. The Sacramento, California, native attended BYU on a music scholarship. After graduation in 1990, she anchored and reported for Salt Lake City's highest-rated news station, KSL-TV. She has won an Emmy and an Edmund R. Murrow Award. (www.cbsnews.com)

Jane Clayson on CBS's "The Early Morning Show."

The first LDS talk show hostess of a program extending beyond just local broadcasting was June Cain Miller, La Canada 1st Ward, La Crescenta, California, Stake. Her program began airing in the mid-'80s and was carried by stations across the United States (LDS 5/7/88)

Largest TV Contract (1989 World Record). In 1989, the highest rate for any TV contract ever signed was $7 million for seven hours of transmission with NBC, by Marie Osmond, announced March 9, 1981. The price also was to cover talent and production costs. (Author)

Documentary. In 1986, the Voyager Team from the Voice of America visited Salt Lake City to do a radio program about the Mormons and their place in American history. Including interviews with Church leaders, the program was broadcast around the world over Voice of America in 42 languages, an audience that could have reached more than one billion people. The Voyager Team travels all over the country, focusing on various aspects of American life, "warts and all," a team member said. (CN 10/26/86)

Surviving the Survivor Craze. The 2000 CBS hit series "Survivor" spawned a whole generation of reality television programs that featured teams of competitors who had to survive the trials and hardships of nature while outwitting co-stars. The last survivor would ultimately win a huge cash prize, usually $1 million. Kelly Wiglesworth, a non-active member of the Church, managed to outsmart and out-luck her 15 challengers to finish second in the hugely popular final episode in 2000.

On May 19, 2002, Neleh Dennis, 22 (Layton, Utah), also finished in second place in "Survivor: Marquesas." She took home $100,000 for her efforts. Sister Dennis brought along her scriptures as her only-allowed luxury item. Even though her membership in the Church wasn't made known at the first, toward the end of the show it became public. She was criticized as being too much of a sweet, next-door girl, and for not backing down on her Christian standards. She told the Deseret News that from the start, "everybody on the show knew I was Mormon." (CN 5/25/2002)

Dave Letterman's Stupid Human Tricks. The best "stupid human trick" performed on national television by members of the Church is probably that done by Ryan and Merilee Barker of Murray, Utah. Their trick, which aired in December 1999, involved Sister Barker putting a balloon in her mouth and Brother Barker blowing through her nose to inflate the balloon. The feat won groans and applause from the audience, plus an instant replay. The nine-month-married couple developed the trick while studying anatomy and physiology at BYU-Idaho. Barker said that one day, after studying air passages, "... she had some bubble gum in her mouth and ..." The rest is history. (DN 12/31/99)

Mexican Martyrs. In the sleepy town of San Marcos, Mexico, two LDS men, Rafael Monroy and Vicente Morales, were killed by firing squad on

Sunday July 17, 1915. Their crime? Refusing to renounce their faith in the restored gospel. The two big ash trees they stood by are now gone, but older residents of the town still remember and can point out their location to visitors. The story of their valiant stand for truth is powerfully retold in the Church movie, "And Should We Die." (CN 10/21/67)

Boycott. Stirring up the ire of major network bosses, Terry Rakolta of Bloomfield Hills, Michigan, happily married and mother of four, was thrust into the national limelight when she single-handedly took on "trash television." Sparking the largest consumer backlash against trash TV in late 1988 and 1989, "that woman from Detroit," — as Norman Mailer called her — succeeded in persuading major sponsors of "Married With Children" to cancel or suspend their advertising contracts. Rakolta has been interviewed, quoted, referred to, or attacked in TV Guide, The New York Times, USA TODAY, The Washington Times, and on Nightline with Ted Koppel, the Phil Donahue show, Entertainment Tonight, Good Morning America, Financial News, The Larry King Show, and others. (LDS 4/19/89)

Disney Sunday Movie. A Thanksgiving movie based on the book, "Chester, I Love You," by Brent and Blaine Yorgason was televised in 1986 under the title, "The Thanksgiving Promise." The Yorgason brothers both served in their respective stake and mission presidencies. (Internet)

CARTOON ART & ANIMATION

Earliest Cartoon Artist. Floyd Gottfredson, originally of Kaysville, Utah, gained fame as the artist for Walt Disney's Mickey Mouse comic strip. His early renditions of Mickey, beginning May 5, 1930, was a close rendition of a mouse – with pointed nose and beady eyes. By 1933, Mickey had become puffier and more details had been added, but he was still very mousy. By 1936, Mickey began to take on his more familiar appearance. Brother Gottfredson took away the wiry, pipe-cleaner legs and added joints that moved more easily and human-like. Other changes were introduced after 1955. Gottfredson continued working on the strip until 1975. (Internet)

Floyd Gottfredson gave Mickey Mouse immortality on comics pages around the world.

Photo Courtesy of Don Bluth

Above, Don Bluth in studio. His company is now working on animations for video games and at least 7 feature-length films.

Most Prolific Animator. Don Bluth has numerous feature-length films to his credit representing the painstaking work of several million drawings. Brother Bluth produced numerous films from studios in Ireland, California, and Arizona. Among his works are the classics:

"An American Tail" (1986) won two Grammy awards—Song of the Year and Best Song for a Motion Picture: "Somewhere Out There." The movie grossed $48.7 million.

"The Land Before Time" (1988) grossed $42.2 by the end of 1988. (LDS 2/22/89)

"Secret of NIMH" (1982) won the Saturn Award and was voted Best Animated Feature of 1982.

"Banjo, The Woodpile Cat" (1979) won the Golden Scroll Award and the National Film Advisory Board Award of Excellence.

"All Dogs Go To Heaven" (1989)

"A Troll in Central Park" (1992)

"Thumbelina" (1993)

"The Pebble and the Penguin" (1994)

"Anastasia" (1997)

"Bartok the Magnificent" (1999)

"Titan AE" (2000)

First Animated Film of the Book of Mormon. "Animated Stories from the Book of Mormon" was a $2.3 million project by Living Scriptures that was released in June 1987. Combining the talents of composer Lex de Azevedo, cartoonist Richard Rich, and writer Orson Scott Card, the producers presented, in a very believable and touching manner, some of the rich history and biography contained in the Book of Mormon.

"Peanuts" Voice. The LDS voice behind the "Snoopy" character in the televised animated cartoon "Peanuts" was that of Cam Clarke of the Studio City 2nd Ward, North Hollywood, California, Stake. (LDS 11/23/85)

OSCARS & AWARDS

Kieth Merrill has filmed and directed a number of feature-length movies including his Oscar-winning documentary, "The Great American Cowboy."

First Oscar. Kieth Merrill, Los Altos, California, 2nd Ward, won an Oscar for his 1974 documentary, "The Great American Cowboy." His other feature films include, "Harry's War," "Take Down," and "Windwalker." That same year, LDS-Church member James Payne, Woodland Hills, Califor-nia, won an Oscar for best set design for "The Sting," the movie that also received Oscars for "Best Picture" and in six other categories. (CN 4/27/74)

Most Oscars. Edwin Catmull has won three Academy Awards for his pioneering work in developing the computer-graphics technology used in such blockbusters as "Toy Story," "A Bug's Life," and "Monster's, Inc." (Internet)

Kieth Merrill has also produced several Church films including "Testaments," continuously shown at the Joseph Smith Memorial Building.

Deseret Morning News file photo

Jim Koford won an Emmy for sound effects.

First Emmy. Who won the first Emmy in the Church? In 1985, Jim Koford, Cerritos 1st Ward, California, won an Emmy in 1985 for his sound effects work on the miniseries, "Wallenberg." He also won a Golden Globe award for sound effects for "Ellis Island." (LDS 7/7/85)

First Emmy for the Church. A Homefront series spot, "The Practice," won an Emmy from the National Academy of Television Arts and Sciences in 1987. This was the first time ever the coveted award was given to a public-service spot. (CN 9/12/87)

The Church's Homefront series won a second Emmy in August 1988 for "Braces and Glasses." An estimated 147 million viewers nationwide saw the spot. (Church Almanac 1989-90)

The Church's Homefront public-service announcements are broadcast worldwide in multiple languages, and have won more than 300 national and international awards. The singular message heard over and over again: "Family – Isn't It About Time?"

Most Emmy Awards. Anthony Geary, star of soap opera TV, movies and television, was nominated six times for Emmys and won three. He was nominated four times for Soap Opera Digest awards and won two. His awards were all for his performances on "General Hospital." He also played on "The Young and the Restless" (1973) and a host of other daytime and prime-time programming including "Burke's Law," "Roseanne," "Murder, She Wrote," "Hotel," "Starsky and Hutch," "Barnaby Jones," "The Streets of San Francisco," "Marcus Welby, M.D.," "Mannix," "The Partridge Family," "All in the Family," and several made-for-TV movies. (Internet)

The 2002 Olympic Winter Games in Salt Lake City captured six Emmy awards for its opening ceremonies at which more than 1,000 local skaters and performers participated. (DN 9/16/02)

Emmy for Styling. Dorothy Andre of the Santa Clarita Stake in California won an Emmy in 1997 for her work on the television musical, "Mrs. Santa Claus." She was responsible for styling and arranging hair, including that of Angela Lansbury, the principal actor in the show. This was Sister Andre's second Emmy award. (CN 11/29/97)

Best-Known Non-LDS Stars in LDS Films

Dr. Wernher von Braun, Rocket Scientist. In a Church-sponsored film, "Search for Truth," some of the Church's most distinguished scientists joined Dr. Wernher von Braun to present their views on science and religion. Dr. von Braun expressed his views on God and the universe and man's effort to understand them through science. (CN 12/23/61)

B.J. Honeycut, Surgeon Elite from M.A.S.H. Mike Farrell, star of the hit television series, M.A.S.H., made a film for the Church in 1971, starring as an elder's quorum president. Farrell says he has read the Book of Mormon and has many friends who are LDS. While Farrell has been called a Mormon by many journalists who say he portrays a typical Mormon image, Farrell told a BYU audience, "I am surprised if I have a typical Mormon image since my position on many political issues is different from the LDS Church." (DU 11/16/83)

Tony Award. Keene Curtis made his performing debut at age 2 when he sang "Red, Red Robin" for a talent show at the Bountiful, Utah, 2nd Ward in 1925. When the enthusiastic audience applauded and called for more, "I started to cry," he said. He had nothing more to perform. But that has changed. In a life of acting on stage, in movies and on television, he won a Tony in 1971 for four roles that he played in "The Rothschilds." He is best known for his recurring role on "Cheers" as John Allen Hill. He also is known for his stage productions of "Annie," "La Cage aux Folles," and "The Fantasticks." He has made many appearances in other television shows including "M.A.S.H.," "Lou Grant," "Benson," and "Hawaii Five-O." Recent movies include "Richie Rich's Christmas Wish," "I.Q.," "Gypsy," and "Lambada." (SLT 9/20/00)

Deseret Morning News file photo

Keene Curtis (pictured with Patricia Ann Patts and Sandy the dog) pose for a rehearsal photo for the stage production of Annie.

BEAUTY/TALENT PAGEANTS

The number of beauty and talent pageants won by members of the Church is so large we had to limit the list to winners of major national and international contests. Mormons have had many turns winning or placing high in just about every contest. Listed below is a partial list.

Largest U.S. "Family of the Year" The largest LDS family to be named America's Family of the Year (there have been several) is the Charles Brown family of Mesa, Arizona, with 14 children. The family also included five nieces and nephews who were adopted when they were orphaned by a plane crash (their parents were returning from a temple trip). (LDS 5/18/85)

All American Family
1957: F. W. (Bill) Bergeson family, Shelley, Idaho. (CN 1/11/58; CN 6/8/57)

All American Family Search
1957: E. Peter Grigsby family, Martin, Kentucky. (CN 7/6/57)

YMCA Family of the Year
1955: Ora O. Call family, Appleton, Wisconsin, South Wisconsin District, Northern States Mission. (CN 2/26/55)

Linda Bement, the first LDS Miss Universe, is congratulated by her parents, Charles and Elaine Bement.

Photo courtesy of Linda Bement

Miss Universe
The first member of the Church to win the Miss Universe Pageant was Linda Bement, Parleys 1st Ward, Parley's Stake, Salt Lake City, in 1960. Months after graduating from high school, Sister Bement won the Miss Utah and Miss USA contests and was crowned Miss Universe that same year. Bement tells of the counsel she received from Pres. David O. McKay shortly after returning home from the pageant in Florida: "We met in his office one day, and he was so happy about me winning," she said. "He looked me in the eye and said, 'Don't forget you represent the youth of America.' I was so impressed that he wanted me to be a good example to more than Mormon youth ... he was thinking of America's youth." (Author's interview)

Non-American Miss Universe

The first non-American LDS to win the Miss Universe title is Miss Thailand, Porntip Nakhirunkanok, 19, crowned Miss Universe in June 1988. Nakhirunkanok moved to Bangkok after living in the Glendale Stake in Southern California. She won $250,000 in cash and prizes. (LDS 7/9/89)

Mrs. America

1984: Deborah Wolfe, Huntington, West Virginia. (CN 5/13/84)

1970: Alice Beuhner, East Mill Creek 14th Ward, Utah. (CN 5/2/70)

1969: Joan Fisher, Winder 20th Ward, Salt Lake County. (CN 12/6/69; CN 5/2/70)

Deborah Wolfe

Mrs. National U.S.A.

1990: Allyson Tenney, Bennion, Utah. (DN 6/5/90)

1989: Sheri Tate, Fruit Heights, Utah, 1st Ward. (CN 10/28/89)

Mrs. U.S.A.

1993: Sandra Earnest, Laguna Niguel 1st Ward, Laguna Niguel, California, Stake. (CN 7/24/93)

Lady of the Year

1957: Mrs. Reed H. Richards, Salt Lake City. (CN 1/11/58)

Mrs. International U.S.A.

1994: Margo Watson, Salt Lake Holladay Stake, (CN 10/2/94)

American Young Mother

2003: Carole B. Gates, Henderson, Nevada (CN 5/10/03)

1991: Wendy Goodrich McKenna, Farmington 19th Ward, Farmington, Utah, South Stake. (CN 5/18/91)

1988: Janet K. Bud, Medford, Oregon. (LDS 5/21/88)

1985: Suzanne Ballard, Walla Walla, Washington. (LDS 4/27/85)

1984: Lezlie Noel Porter, Sparks, Nevada. (LDS 5/18/83)

Catherine Peterson, and family, was crowned American Young Mother in 1983.

1983: Catherine Cryer Peterson, Pennsylvania. (LDS 4/83)

1982: LaDawn Anderson Jacob, Orem, Utah. (LDS 5/82)

1979: Susan Brown, Mesa 38th Ward. (LDS 3/12/82)

National Young Mother
1991: Wendy McKenna, Salt Lake City, Utah. (CN 5/20/91)

1985: Suzanne Webb Ballard, Wall Walla, Washington, 3rd Ward. (CN 5/5/85)

1979: Susan Elizabeth Wright, Mesa, Arizona. (CN 6/2/79)

1972: Mrs. Merrill C. Oaks, BYU 49th Ward, Provo, Utah. (CN 5/13/72)

1971: Mrs. Billy Casper, Chula Vista II Ward, San Diego, California, South Stake. (CN 5/15/71)

Sharlene Wells, Miss America 1984, visits the Reagan White House.

Miss America
1984: Sharlene Wells, Utah. (LDS 7/27/85)

1952: Colleen Kay Hutchins, Salt Lake City, Utah. (CN 1/11/58; 3/12/52)

National or American Mother of the Year
2003: Mervlyn Kitashima, Pearl City, Hawaii (CN 5/24/03)

1990: Nadine Thomas Matis, Ogden, Utah. (KSL TV 4/29/90)

1979: Frances Davis Burtenshaw, Logan, Utah. (CN 5/19/79)

1974: Phyllis Brown Marriott, Washington, D.C.. (CN 5/18/74)

1965: Lorena Chipman Fletcher, Provo, Utah. (CN 5/8/65)

1955: Lavina Fugal, Pleasant Grove, Utah. (CN 5/8/65; CN 1/11/58)

Miss U.S.A.

1986: Christy Fichtner, a former Miss Texas U.S.A., was a member only 7 months when crowned. She later finished second in the Miss Universe pageant that same year. (LDS 6/14/86)

1960: Linda Bement, Utah. (LDS 10/15/89)

1957: Charlotte Sheffield, Salt Lake City. (CN 1/11/58; CN 7/27/57))

Charlotte Sheffield, Miss U.S.A. 1957

Miss Indian America

1988: Bobette Kay Wildcat, Fort Hall, Idaho. (CN 11/4/89)

1976: Kristine Rayola Harvey, Sheridan, Wyoming. (CN 9/18/76)

1971: Nora Begay, Provo, Utah. (CN 8/28/71)

Miss Indian World

2001: Ke Aloha May Cody Alo, White Mountain Apache Tribe, Arizona. (CN 6/9/01)

Miss Navajo

1969: Rose McCabe, Leupp, Arizona. (CN 11/2/68)

Miss New Zealand

1981: Vicki Hemi, New Zealand; also fifth runner up in the Miss World Pageant. (LDS 4/13/84)

Ke Aloha May Cody Alo, Miss Indian World 2001.

Miss Cambodia
1986: Oun Ros, 20, Irvine 2nd Ward, Santa Ana, California, Stake. (LDS 8/2/86)

Miss Chinatown U.S.A.
1963: Shirley Fong, 20, Honolulu, Hawaii. (CN 2/16/63)

Miss U.S. Latina. Lydia Acuna, a sophomore at BYU, was crowned Miss U.S. Latina in Cancun, Mexico in September 2003, and represented the U.S. in the international competition. (CN 10/18/03)

Miss Pioneer (Days of '47 Queen)
1931: The first "Miss Pioneer" was Margaret Young, crowned in 1931. She was the first "Covered Wagon Days" queen; the name was changed to "Days of '47" in 1943. Her great-great-grandfather was Brigham Young. (CN 1984)

First Non-GA-Descendant Days of '47 Queen
Hard to believe, but the first queen of the Days of '47 who was NOT a descendant of a general authority was Tammy Cederlog whose reign began in 1986. However, she did have Mormon pioneer blood in her. (LDS 8/9/86)

Miss Teen USA. There are at least 10 different titles for a "Miss Teen U.S.A." pageant. Here are the LDS teens who have won national "teen" pageants.

2004: Kristen Tanner, El Centro Ward, Sacramento California North Stake (National Miss Junior Teen) (CN 4/3/04)

2000: Jesika Henderson, St. George, Utah, Green Valley Stake (Miss Junior America). (CN 7/8/00)

1994: Elaine Thomas, Mountain Shadows Ward, North Las Vegas Stake. Also named Miss Photogenic. She was the only girl in a family of 12 children (Miss Junior America West Coast Teen).

1992: Tera Michele Allen, Colleyville Ward, Hurst, Texas, Stake (National Miss TEEN USA). (CN 3/14/92)

1987: Carol Lyn Dickson, Salt Lake Mount Olympus 3rd Ward (Miss Junior America). (CN 10/24/87)

1986: Katie Adams, Kalispell, Montana, 1st Ward (Miss U.S. Teen). (CN 3/2/86)

1984: Tiffani Baker, 14, Salt Lake Millcreek, Utah, 2nd Ward (Miss National Teen Continental). (CN 1984)

1984: Laura Baxter, Danville, California (Miss Teen America). (LDS 3/16/84)

1983: Becky Hollingsworth, 16, Grass Valley 2nd Ward, Auburn, California, Stake (Miss American Teenager). (CN fall 1983)

1982: Deborah Dutson, 16, Highland Ward, Ogden, Utah, East Stake (Miss Teenworld). (CN 3/82)

1977: Ann King, Las Vegas 31st Ward, Las Vegas, Nevada, Stake (Miss United Teenager of America). (CN 4/5/80)

1976: Kimberly Ann Jensen, Caldwell, Idaho (Miss National Teenager). (CN 9/11/76)

1971: Janene Forsyth, Falls Church Ward, Potomac, Virginia, Stake (Miss American Teenager). (CN 11/13/71; CN 6/24/72)

Miss Black U.S.A. Scholarship Pageant
1996: Tina Johnson, a returned missionary from Arkansas Little Rock Mission, and originally of Pennsylvania, represented Utah. She lived in the Salt Lake Central Stake and attended the University of Utah. (CN 5/25/96)

Miss La Petite
1977: Lindsay Brooke King, 6, Fresno 9th Ward, Fresno, California, Stake. (CN 11/5/77)

Future Homemakers of America
1980: Amy Montierth, Basin City Ward, Pasco, Washington, Stake. (CN 10/80)

1971: Marsha Bowen, Spanish Fork 3rd Ward, Palmyra, Utah, Stake. (CN 11/20/71)

1967: Lynn Hunsaker, St. Anthony Ward, St. Anthony, Idaho, Stake. (CN 10/28/67)

Miss Gorgeous Eyes
Christy Ann Cheney, 2, daughter of Catherine Cheney of the Yucaipa 2nd Ward, San Bernardino, California, East Stake, won the Miss Gorgeous Eyes 1983 contest. Previously she had won the Miss Dream Girl California contest. (LDS 10/21/83)

Deseret Morning News file photo

Lindsay King, Miss La Petite.

Pee Wee Miss of America
The 1988 National Pee Wee Miss of America was Brittany Lynn Harper, 13 months old, of the Las Vegas 23rd Ward. She received a fur coat, scepter, satin monogrammed sash, a U.S. savings bond, and a wardrobe. (LDS 10/22/88)

Miss Cheerleader U.S.A.
1975: Sandy Blackwell, Charleston 2nd Ward, Charleston South Carolina Stake. (CN 1975)

Miss All-American Cheerleader
1985: Phuong-Anh Doan, Westminster, Rhode Island, 1st Ward. (LDS 5/25/85)

Miss Dance/Drill International
1994: Kellie Hansen, Willow Canyon 3rd Ward, Sandy, Utah, East Stake. (CN 9/3/94)

World's Majorette Queen – 8 Year Olds
1973: Earlet Phillips, Royal Oaks Ward, Detroit, Michigan, Stake. (CN 11/17/73)

Connie Lucia, Miss Rodeo America.

Miss Rodeo America
1974: Connie Della Lucia, West Weber Ward, Ogden, Utah, Weber North Stake. (CN 12/14/74)

1971: Susan Merrill, Ogden 41st Ward, Ogden, Utah, East Stake. (CN 11/20/71)

Miss Rodeo Queen
1992: Tanya McKinnon, Randolph 2nd Ward, Kemmerer, Wyoming, Stake. (CN 11/7/92)

American Royal Livestock, Rodeo and Horse Show Queen
1980: Jan Gladene Parcell, Heber 3rd Ward, Heber City, Utah, East Stake.

Ms. United Nations
2003: Karen Schultz, Bryan 1st Ward, College Station Texas Stake (CN 10/4/03)

Miss American Honey Queen

1995: Ester Wright, Dallas 4th Ward, Richardson, Texas, Stake. (CN 5/20/95)

Prettiest Schoolgirl

1954: Lorna Young, Salt Lake City, Utah. (CN 1/11/58)

Miss National Contact Lens

1958: Bonnie Brown, Lomita Ward, Redondo, California. (CN 12/6/58)

Least Expensive Gown. The best bargain in gowns ever worn by a winning participant in a state beauty pageant is the $1.48 gown purchased from a Deseret Industries store by Andrea Lund for Idaho's 1982 Miss Teen contest. She spent hours altering it for the formal evening-gown judging. She won the Miss Teen Idaho title and went on to the nationals. The wire services picked up the story of her "rags-to-riches" gown and the resulting media attention brought an estimated $1 million of new business to Deseret Industries. (LDS 3/26/82)

America's Perfect Couple

1993: Pat and Julee Brady of the Citrus Heights Ward, Mesa, Arizona, Red Mountain Stake. (CN 11/27/93)

Mr. Olympia

1964, 1965: Larry Scott, Bountiful 54th Ward, Utah Height Stake. Brother Scott won the first two Mr. Olympia contests and was inducted into the Joe Weider Bodybuilding Hall of Fame in 1999. (www.larryscott.com)

Mr. Universe

1963: Larry Scott, Bountiful, Utah (see "Mr. Olympia" above).

Mr. America

1962: Larry Scott, Bountiful, Utah (see "Mr. Olympia" above).

Mr. Natural America

1987: Paul Devine, branch president in the Southwest, Arizona, Branch won the

Courtesy Larry Scott

Larry Scott, the first LDS Mr. Olympia, Mr. Universe and Mr. America.

1984 Natural Mr. America contest, and placed fourth in the Mr. America contest. He has power lifted more than 1,500 pounds. (LDS 11/21/87)

Mr. U.S.A. National "Natural" Body Builder.
In 1992, Jared Kuka, 19, Brainerd Ward, Chattanooga, Tennessee, Stake, won first place in the Mr. U.S.A. National "Natural" Body-Building Championships, teenage division. Not only did Kuka have to go through the strenuous efforts of the competition, but he also had to take a polygraph test to certify he was free of drugs, steroids, and diuretics for the prior five years. (CN 2/22/92)

A pageant is a pageant! Mike Bice, winner of BYU's Ugliest Man contest in 1975.

First and Only Mr. Clean.
The only LDS to win the distinction of resembling Mr. Clean is Wayne O'Dell, Mesa, Arizona. His shining bald head, prominent ear lobes and glistening smile helped him wipe away the competition in the 1985 Southwest regional of the Mr. Clean look-alike contest. (LDS 8/24/85)

President of Miss America Pageants.
Norman L. Neilsen, Orem, Utah, Lakeridge Stake, was appointed national president of all Miss America state pageants in 1992. One of the changes he brought to the competition was to require that some 70,000 young women across America do community service in order to be part of the national competition. (CN 1/18/92)

Modest Prom Dresses.
In 2000, more than a dozen teenaged girls from the Olathe, Kansas, Stake decided enough was enough. They banded together to demand a change from the sexy, revealing prom dresses filling department-store racks. Their campaign for attractive but modest attire was an instant success among like-minded people around the globe. A large groundswell of support caught the attention of the media. One of the girls, Ashley Hamrick, appeared in the Wall Street Journal in what one of her friends called a "hot but still modest" red dress. They were also featured on the television tabloid news program, Inside Edition. Today the girls' efforts continue to grow. They are well on their way to gathering 250,000 signatures on a petition asking department-store chains to offer modest clothing. See their Web site at www.goodworks.net.

Bathing Suits.
For a long time, Utah was the only state that didn't hold a swimsuit competition for its Miss Utah/America contest. The broken rule was excused by Miss America Pageant officials in Atlantic City in 1979 only

because of "strong objections" in Utah, but there is no such exemption when Miss Utah arrives for the Atlantic City pageant. (DU 9/7/79)

Most Beautiful Swimsuits. Rose Marie Reid, originally of the Westwood Ward, Los Angeles Stake, was world renowned for her Rose Marie Reid swimsuits that were modest but beautiful. Born in Canada, Sister Reid didn't like the skimpy swimsuits of her day and designed one herself. An executive of The Hudson's Bay Company saw her design and helped her launch the Rose Marie Reid Company. At its peak in the 1950s, the company was producing 5,000 swimsuits a day, 365 days a year, and shipping them around the world. (CN 12/24/55)

Photos courtesy Rose Marie Reid family

Rose Marie Reid (above) received the sports fashion world's most prestigious honor, the American Sportsware Designer Award, in 1958 (left).

Most Beautiful Girls – According to an Independent Judge. Bert Parks, the host of the Miss America Pageant for two decades, was asked by newspaper reporters where the most beautiful girls in America were. "It's Salt Lake City," he said. "We have models there who make Miss America contestants look like Phyllis Diller." (LDS 6/30/84)

Ugliest LDS Swimsuit. The BYU-issued swimsuit for women was, for two decades, a baggy, shapeless, blue ugliness worn and abhorred by nearly every coed who dared wear one to swim in the indoor pools. The suit prompted one single BYU male to boldly declare: "If I ever see a coed who looks good in one of those suits, I'm going to marry her." But by 1988 a more stylish suit was approved, much to the relief of males and coeds alike. (LDS 3/22/86)

PERFORMANCE

Hill Cumorah Pageant is the oldest and longest running Church pageant. It premiered in the summer of 1937. The pageant today attracts more than 100,000 visitors each summer for the week-long production. (Church Almanac)

Ruth and Nathan Hale

Hale Center Theaters. Ruth and Nathan Hale, pictured here (left) in 1990 at the opening of the Hale Center in Orem, pioneered live theater in Utah and California. Their Glendale, California, theater was opened in 1947 and today is the longest continuously operating theater in the round in the United States, and longest theater of any kind in California. Their popular Hale Center Theater in West Valley, Utah, is second only to the Utah Symphony for attendance for the arts in Utah. And Sunday nights, they frequently did a show – but at no charge to patrons and the performers shared their talents at no charge to the theater. It was a missionary performance, and they attracted thousands. Brother Hale passed away in 1994, and Sister Hale passed away in 2003, but their legacy for the performing arts continues strong and clean to this day. (Internet)

Dance Festival. The largest Mormon dance festival featured some 16,000 dancers on July 20, 1985. The performers, from throughout Southern California, put on a show for more than 100,000 spectators seated in the Rose Bowl. (LDS 7/85)

Dance festivals involved thousands.

Some of the BYU-Hawaii college students who perform daily at the Polynesian Center.

Photo courtesy Polynesian Center

Hawaii's Top Paid Attraction. The Polynesian Center, established in 1963, is today the largest paid attraction in all the Hawaiian islands. On April 25, 2003, it welcomed its 30 millionth visitor. About 1,000 employees work at the Center, and at least 700 of these are students at BYU-Hawaii. The students perform on stage or in other capacities to earn tuition money. The center shows off the various Polynesian cultures of the South Pacific with traditional songs, dances, fun and entertainment – not to mention very delicious food. Was it worth building this facility on an obscure north shore of Oahu more than four decades ago with the expectation that tourists would one day flock to its doors? That outlandish idea turned out to be both profitable and prophetic.

World's Best Disco Dancer. In 1985, Ezra Levi, 18, succeeded in "stay'n alive" through a tough competition against 96 other disco dancers from 12 countries to win the International Disco-Dancing Championship. He was a member of the Milton Keynes Ward, Northampton, England, Stake. (CN 1985)

Ballroom Dancers. In 2001, the BYU Ballroom Dance Company placed first in both the Standard and Latin divisions at the British Formation Championships in Blackpool, England. The performance marked the 15th and 16th first-place championship medals won by BYU. That dance competition is ranked among the most prestigious in the world, and is also one of the longest-running competitions. (CN 6/16/01)

Ballroom Dancer, Senior Division. In 1994, Doris Scott, Ft. Myers 2nd Ward, Ft. Myers, Florida Stake, won the United States Ballroom Scholarship championships, amateur division, at a national dance competition in

Arkansas. The 75-year-old grandmother danced with her teacher/partner to win a four-foot tall trophy and a scholarship for — what else? More dance lessons! (CN 2/26/94)

Clogging. Scott Asbell, 19, and his little brother Robbie, 14, of Draper, Utah, are the first brothers ever to win first-place honors in the 1986-87 Western United States Clogging Championships in their individual age categories. (CN 3/28/87)

The Steele family, Ogden, Utah, took top honors in 1985 at the National Cloggers Festival in Orem, Utah. They beat out 300 dancers in the event. The Utah team had captured various age championships and toured such places as Australia, New Zealand, Japan, Europe, Canada, Mexico, and all 50 states. (DU 7/2/85; CN 9/21/86)

Highland Dancing. Hugh Bigney, 18, a BYU student from Lynnfield Ward, Boston, Massachusetts, Stake, shocked highland dancers from Scotland, and around the world when he won the adult world championship in highland dancing in 1973. The competitions were held in Dunoon, Scotland, and attracted the best dancers in the world. Everyone was amazed that an American could perform the traditional dances with such precision. (CN 11/24/73)

NATIONAL AND WORLD LEADERS

Deseret Morning News file photo

Ezra Taft Benson visits with Ronald Reagan in 1985.

Highest Appointed. Determining the highest appointed Latter-day Saint in the government depends upon which office is considered the highest. Ezra Taft Benson served as secretary of agriculture, a cabinet position, to President Eisenhower for eight years. Others have since served in the cabinet. Brent Scowcroft served as national security advisor for President George Bush in 1989. Brother Scowcroft briefed the president daily at 9 a.m. and kept an office just down the hall from the Oval Office in the West Wing. More recently, Michael Leavitt, Utah's former governor, was appointed as director of the Environmental Protection Agency, a post being considered for promotion to cabinet level at the time. (Internet)

National Security Advisor. In November 1988, President George Bush appointed Ret. Gen. Brent Scowcroft, 63, to be national security advisor. Brother Scowcroft, a native of Ogden, Utah, told the press shortly after his appointment not to worry about his Mormon roots. "I'm not a strict Mormon. I enjoy coffee. And I frequently have a glass of wine with dinner. ... There is a notion among the Mormons that at the end of each day you ought to be able to say, 'I've made myself a better person or I have made things better by what I have done today.'" And that was what he tried to do, every day. (LDS 2/8/89; LDS 12/10/88)

Brent Scowcroft, national security advisor.

Youngest Elector. In 1984, the youngest elector (a person in the Electoral College that elects the United States president) in the history of the United States was David Fowers, Bountiful, Utah, 56th Ward, Mueller Park Stake. He won the honor of "youngest ever" when he cast his vote Dec. 17, 1984, at age 19, for President Ronald Reagan and Vice President George Bush. When Brother Fowers was elected at the GOP state convention at age 18, he also became the youngest presidential elector ever chosen. (CN 12/23/84) (Author)

First Mormon Senator. Reed Smoot was the first member of the Church elected to the Senate, in 1902. Anti-Mormon efforts delayed his being seated in the Senate, but after an investigation, he was allowed to begin his duties. (Internet)

Congress With the Most. The most LDS elected to serve in Congress at any given time (as of this writing) is 17 in 1999-2000.

The first LDS senator, Reed Smoot, congratulates Charles Lindburg after his historic one-man flight across the Atlantic in 1927.

Gregory Newell, youngest ambassador at age 39.

Youngest Assistant Secretary of State. At age 36, Gregory J. Newell became the youngest assistant secretary of state when he was appointed in 1982. (LDS 11/30/85)

Youngest Ambassador. At age 39, Gregory J. Newell became the youngest ambassador ever selected when he was appointed United States Ambassador to Sweden in 1985. (LDS 11/30/85)

Foreign Service Language Test. In 1990, Douglas McOmber, Cantonsville, Maryland, Ward, had the highest score ever recorded in Chinese reading in the State Department's Foreign Service Institute language test. McOmber was proficient in reading a wide variety of difficult materials including cursive, script, literary Chinese, modern Chinese literature and documentary Chinese. (CN 12/22/90)

First Woman State Senator. In 1896, Martha Hughes Cannon became the first woman elected as Utah state senator, and also the first woman state senator in the history of the United States. (Church Almanac 1989)

David M. Kennedy, ambassador to NATO.

First Ambassador to NATO. In 1972, David Kennedy was the first Latter-day Saint appointed as United States ambassador to the North Atlantic Treaty Organization (NATO). He had served as secretary of the treasury in 1969, leaving his previous job as president of America's seventh largest bank, Continental Illinois National Bank and Trust Co., Chicago. He was President Richard M. Nixon's ambassador at large in 1971.

First Write-in Winner. Congressman Ron Packard won his seat in the California legislature in 1982 with 66,000 write-in votes, 10,000 more than his opponent whose name was printed on the ballot. He is only the fourth person to win a write-in campaign in the history of Congress. His slogan: "Bring your pencils to the polls!" He served for 18 years, and though assured a win in the next election, he chose to step down in 2000 so he could "go back and be a father, grandfather, and husband again." (LDS 11/26/82; Internet)

United States Treasurer. The first LDS United States treasurer was Ivy Baker Priest, who served eight years during the Eisenhower Administration. (Internet)

David Kennedy was appointed secretary of the treasury in the Nixon Administration for two years, beginning in 1969. Afterwards, he was an ambassador-at-large for the United States where his negotiations on trade and monetary issues took him to capitals all over the world.

Bay Buchanan, Irvine 2nd Ward, Santa Ana, California, Stake, served for two years (1980-82) as United States Treasurer during President Reagan's first term. At age 32, she was the youngest ever in that position. Her older brother, Pat Buchanan (not LDS), was known to many at the time as a media communications director in the Reagan White House. (LDS 4/6/84)

AP/WIDE WORLD PHOTOS

Bay Buchanan, one of three LDS to hold the office of secretary of the treasury, visits with Donald Regan. He is pointing out where her signature will appear on an estimated $4 billion in U.S. currency.

Highest Among United States Postal Service Workers. Reva Beck Bosone became the first woman to hold a judicial position in the United States Post Office Department. (CN 7/25/64)

First Secretary of the Interior. Stewart Udall served as secretary of the interior for eight years under presidents John F. Kennedy and Lyndon B. Johnson. (CN 1/17/81)

BLM Director. In 2001, Kathleen Burton Clarke was the first woman ever to become the director of the Bureau of Land Management. (www.adherents.com)

First LDS Baby Born in Congress. Enid Greene Waldholtz, Parleys 3rd Ward, Parleys Utah Stake, has the distinction of being the first LDS mother to give birth to a child while serving in the United States House of Representatives. On Sept. 1, 1995, she took an early "Labor Day" outing to LDS Hospital in Salt Lake City, Utah, to deliver a baby girl. Rep. Waldholtz is only the second woman to have a child while serving as a representative in Washington, D.C.

Returning to the Mission Field. The first LDS to return to the land of his missionary work as an official United States government representative was Keith Foote Nyborg, Ashton, Idaho, who was appointed by Ronald Reagan as United States Ambassador to Finland in 1981. (LDS 5/3/86)

First Women to Vote. In February 1870, the Utah territorial legislature passed a statute permitting women to vote, making them the first female citizens in the nation to vote in a regular United States election. (DU 11/2/82)

Highest in Department of Labor. During the Lyndon B. Johnson administration, Ester Eggertsen Peterson served as assistant secretary of labor, the highest appointed position for a Mormon during Johnson's tenure. (CN 7/25/64)

Gerald W. Silver, Deseret Morning News

Nathan Eldon Tanner, "Mr. Integrity."

Canada. The first LDS cabinet minister in Canada was Nathan Eldon Tanner. He served from 1936 to 1952. He was appointed Minister of Lands and Mines, a position that was enlarged to include mines and minerals, and lands and forests. He pushed through legislation that helped protect Canada's natural resources, especially petroleum. He helped Alberta become the first province to be free from public debt. Brother Tanner had a nickname during his term as minister—"Mr. Integrity." He was known as a strictly honest man who refused to be bribed by accepting gifts from anyone while in office. (Internet; CN 1/83)

Argentina. Roberto A. Cruz, Ramos Majia 2nd Ward, Buenos Aires, Argentina, West Stake, became the first Mormon in Argentina's parliament when he was appointed to serve as a member of the Chamber of Deputies (similar to the U.S. House of Representatives). The appointment came after a vacancy was created when another man was assigned to be Argentina's ambassador to the United States. Said Cruz, "I believe that this is a great opportunity to serve my homeland and defend correct principles that will benefit my fellow citizens and the future of our nation." (CN 9/8/90)

Brazil. Moroni Bing Torgan, president of the Fortaleza, Brazil, Stake, was elected a national congressman to serve in the House of Representatives in Brazil in 1990, becoming the first LDS ever to be elected to a Brazilian post. Prior to running for office, he became the youngest man ever appointed as secretary of public security in the state of Ceara when he took the assignment at age 31. (CN 3/16/91)

Moroni Torgan, Brazilian folk hero, was honored for arresting 3,000 criminals.

From Basketball Court to World Court. In 1992, Kresimir Cosic, former BYU basketball star and member of three Olympic medal-winning teams from Yugoslavia, was named deputy ambassador to the United States for the newly independent nation of Croatia. The 6-foot 11-inch Cosic could be heard on radios across the United States promoting tourism in his part of the world with

that distinct voice and accent that many BYU fans grew to love. After earning all-American honors at BYU, he returned to his native land to promote his country and serve as a district president for the Church. Brother Cosic died in his homeland in 1995. (LDS 8/23/86, DN 1995)

Kresimir Cosic, medal-winning ball player and ambassador.

Great Britain. Terry Rooney, elders quorum president in the Bradford 2nd Ward, Huddersfield, England, Stake, became the first Mormon elected a member of parliament ("MP") in Great Britain in the Nov. 9, 1990, national elections in England. Brother Rooney's vote tally nearly doubled his next closest rival. He represented Bradford North, an area comprising about 400,000 people in northern England. The full-time "MP" office is similar to a congressman in the House of Representatives in the United States. Sister Rooney said her husband's membership in the Church is well known, and people call him the "orange juice king" because at social gatherings he is always being offered orange juice since he won't drink alcohol. At a pre-election public forum, he was widely applauded when he stated: "I cannot be bought, and I will buy nobody. I will promise nobody anything except that I will do my best for Bradford North. When I go out of this room, I will go out with my integrity." (CN 11/17/90)

South Africa. Olev Taim became the first LDS in the history of Benoni, South Africa, and possibly all of South Africa, to be elected to a civic office when he won the election to the town council in 1989. He also served as his ward's gospel doctrine teacher in the Benoni, South Africa, Ward. (CN 7/8/89)

Samoa. In 1970, Iofipo R. Kuresa became the first LDS to win a seat on Western Samoa's national legislative assembly. At the time, there were 42 members of the governing body. (CN 5/2/70)

Highest-Profile Secretaries. In 1967, two LDS sisters commanded the best view of the country when they found themselves working in the White House as personal secretaries to the United States president and vice president. Connie Gerrard was on President Lyndon B. Johnson's staff, and her sister, Judy Gerrard Haeder, was on Vice President Hubert H. Humphrey's staff. (CN 8/5/67)

Keeper of the Nation's Journal. Dr. Wayne C. Grover, Silver Springs, Maryland, Ward, Washington, Stake, celebrated his 10th year as archivist of the United States in 1958. His job was to keep the personal journal of the United States by overseeing the National Archives and Records Service in Washington, D.C.. (CN 7/12/58)

Mormon Work Ethic at the White House. An informal poll by the Washington Post suggested that the two hardest working people at the White House during the George Bush administration of 1988-92, next to President Bush himself, were both LDS and native Utahns. Roger Porter, President Bush's economic and domestic policy adviser, and National Security Advisor Brent Scowcroft were both placed in the "insomniac" and "vampire" category by White House workers. Typical days in the office for these two men ran from 15 to 20 hours. Scowcroft was known as the man who took out time to jog — at midnight! (DN 5/30/90)

First National Political Party Chairperson. In 1981, Richard Richards, Ogden, Utah, South Stake became the first LDS national chairman of the Republican Party. (CN 2/21/81)

In 1972, Jean Westwood became the first woman, and Latter-day Saint, to serve as chairperson of the National Democratic Party. (Internet)

Richard Richards

First Husband Among Senator Wives. When Paula Hawkins was elected senator in Florida in 1980, her husband, Gene, had an interesting role to play. Brother Hawkins became the first husband of a United States Senator. Two previous female senators were appointed to fill a vacancy for a few months, and all other female senators were widowed or single during their appointment. Brother Hawkins found himself suddenly bringing havoc to the most exclusive club in all of Washington, the Senate Wives Club. Suddenly the club had to admit its first male member. This quandary prompted club organizers to change the club's name to the Senate Spouses' Club. Having his wife serve in the Senate was an honor, but Hawkins made it clear to the press, "I have but one wife to give to my country." (CN 2/14/81)

In 1979, Ronald Reagan campaigned for Paula Hawkins in her bid to become Florida's first woman senator.

Top Firefighter. In 1982, Dr. B.J. Thompson was appointed to the top firefighting post when he became administrator over the Federal Emergency Management Agency's United States Fire Administration. (CN 1/82)

Smokey's LDS Mom. Smokey the Bear's adopted mom, Gladys D. Daines, Alexandria, Virginia, Ward, says it's Smokey Bear now. The Forest Service's mascot dropped his middle name ("The") some time in the early 1980s, Daines says. In her capacity as Smokey Bear's adopted mom, Daines travels all across the country, in parades and at special activities, promoting fire safety in the forests. Smokey Bear was born on Aug. 9, 1944, when the

War Advertising Council was trying to help the public save wood and prevent forest fires. After borrowing Walt Disney's Bambi for a year, the council developed its own symbol, and Smokey Bear was born. (CN 8/26/84)

"Oyez, oyez, get thee hence to Church, young'n!"

Deseret Morning News file photo

LDS Town Criers. (And we're not talking about the ward nursery, either). The trade of Town Crier dates back to the Romans, when he or she would ring a bell to draw everyone's attention and then read a proclamation or conduct other community business. Town criers in Great Britain and Canada often dress in the traditional 17th-century knickers, cape and three-cornered hat when they clang a hand bell for various civic events or stand to draw attention with, "Oyez, oyez, oyez."

Vic Garth, 90, was perhaps the oldest active town crier in the United Kingdom in 2003. He lives in Hobart, Tasmania, and besides being perhaps the most recognized and respected of its citizens, he might also be the most photographed man in Tasmania. People love to pose with him for the camera, and he makes regular appearances to hospitals, gatherings and Parliament. Among his many public duties as town crier is the task of greeting dignitaries and visitors, close to 30,000 of them in a year, who pass through the area. Brother Garth and his late wife Irene have been great missionaries, having established branches in Southampton and Reading, England, and Fort Erie, Canada. Today, there are 2,600 members in Tasmania. (CN 7/5/03)

Brenda Willison, Peterborough 2nd Ward, Northampton England, was the official town crier for the towns of Orton Waterville and Market Deeping in Great Britain. Does the shouting bother people? "My bishop sometimes gets annoyed, because if I'm shouting on Saturday night I'm a bit hoarse for singing in the choir the next morning," she says. (CN 8/14/93)

Scott Fraser, Woodstock Branch, Ontario, became the official town crier of Woodstock in March 1992. He used his part-time job to spread good news about town and encourage good conduct among the people. (CN 8/14/93)

Anti-LDS Real Estate Law. It took more than 100 years but the 1862 anti-LDS real-estate law barring any Church from holding more than

$50,000 worth of real estate in a United States territory was finally repealed by President Jimmy Carter in 1978. The change removed a cloud on Church plans to build a temple in Samoa. The law was adopted by Congress in 1862 as part of a measure outlawing plural marriages. After polygamy was abolished in 1890, only portions of the federal law were repealed. (CN 11/11/78)

Infamous Extermination Order. It took 138 years, but in June 1976, Missouri Gov. Christopher S. Bond rescinded the extermination order issued by Missouri Gov. Lilburn W. Boggs in 1838. Boggs' extermination order stated, "The Mormons must be treated as enemies, and must be exterminated or driven from the State if necessary, for the public peace — their outrages are beyond all description." Up to that time the order was legally in effect. Gov. Bond said Gov. Boggs was clearly outside his legal and constitutional bounds and expressed "deep regret for the injustice and undue suffering which was caused by this 1838 order." (CN 7/3/76)

First LDS Mayor in Modern Nauvoo. In 1977, Walter Hugh Pierce, a former branch president in Nauvoo, Illinois, became the first Mormon mayor of Nauvoo since 1845. Joseph Smith was the town's first mayor. After Smith's martyrdom on June 27, 1844, Daniel Spencer was elected to finish out the prophet's term. By January 1845, the state legislature had revoked Nauvoo's city charter and the fastest growing and most industrious city in the state began to fall into obscurity. (CN 6/77)

Prison Warden – Utah's First. The first Mormon penitentiary warden, Daniel Garn, knew quite a bit about prisons. He had been in prison himself. His crime? Being a Mormon. He was falsely arrested in Richmond, Missouri, and had a near brush with the law doing missionary work in Hamburg, Germany. Later in life he led 400 Saints from Britain to the Salt Lake Valley in the fall of 1854. The new territorial prison had just been completed and Brother Garn was appointed warden, a position he held for six years. He died in 1872 at the age of 70. (CN 8/19/67)

A Real Mickey-Mouse Ambassador. Connie Jean Swanson, a vivacious 21-year-old from Anaheim, California, became Walt Disney's first "world ambassador" in 1966. Sister Swanson's job was to travel the world as an official representative of Mr. Disney. She was selected from among all the Disneyland tour guides. (CN 7/9/66)

Largest Taxpayer Revolt. Howard Jarvis launched the largest taxpayer revolt in the country when his 1978 "Proposition 13" was passed by two-thirds of voters in California. The proposition cut property taxes by 57 percent. Prior to Proposition 13, property taxes were out of control and people were losing their homes because they couldn't pay. The tax-revolt momentum carried on into the 1980 presidential election campaign and well into Reagan's tenure. Jarvis, though not active in the Church, nevertheless was proud of his Utah roots. He died at age 82 on Aug. 12, 1986. "We taught people that if you're willing to fight, you can win," he said. (LDS 9/3/86)

Most Recognized Billboard Star. As part of 30-day effectiveness test for billboard advertising, the image of Sharlene Wells, Miss America in 1985, was placed on 36 billboards in Tucson, Arizona, and 36 billboards in Albuquerque, New Mexico. The study found that recognition of the queen rose 700 percent after the test. The real question is, who wouldn't notice the beautiful countenance of Sister Wells smiling down at them, larger than life? (DU 6/27/85)

Most Recognized Do-It-Yourselfer. Dian Thomas's creativity has taken her across the country on every media. More than 1 million copies of her books, "Roughing it Easy" and "Today's Tips for Easy Living," have been sold. She has taken her ideas onto the Tonight Show with Johnny Carson, Phil Donahue, Mike Douglas, "Good Morning America," the "Today Show," and the "Home Show." "You can always wrap an idea in a fun way," Dian said. "I offer about 150 ideas to build family unity. I do ordinary things in an unordinary way. I try to teach how to cook without power, how to make do without." (LDS 11/88)

Dian Thomas can cook just about anything anywhere using anything, and that's only part of what she can do.

NAME GAMES

Most Common LDS Names. The most common first names used in predominantly LDS Utah (as of 2000) are (most common first) BOYS: Jacob, Joshua, Ethan, Tyler and Zachary; GIRLS: Madison, Emily, Hannah, Abigail and Samantha. (DN 2003)

Brigham Young. In a 1980 national survey, more people in the United States recognized the number-two man's name, Brigham Young, than the name of the founder, Joseph Smith.

Jack Mormann. In 1971, Jackson F. Mormann, known as Jack to his friends, was baptized with his wife after six months of lessons from the missionaries. They became members of the Audubon 2nd Ward, Philadelphia Stake. (CN 8/12/72)

The First Mormon Moorman. For years, Esther Moorman was kidded about being a Mormon. Though the kidding didn't exactly encourage her to investigate the Church, it didn't stop her either. She (a widow) inquired about Mormons from a co-worker, and later, took her two sons to visit the Washington, D.C. Temple. They invited the missionaries for more discussion, and were baptized in 1984. The family resided in the Medina Ward, Akron, Ohio, Stake. (CN 2/12/84)

LAST MINUTE WORLD RECORD

Longest Continuous Singing – Individual (2003 World Record). On June 27-29, 2003, Ace Anderson, St. George, Utah, landed in the world record books when he sang continuously for 49.5 hours at the Washington County, Utah, Fair Grounds. He performed more than 500 songs karaoke style. His titles ranged from rock and roll to Olivia Newton John. He was required to take a 15 minute break every four hours, but otherwise wasn't allowed to talk more than 30 seconds. Various audiences came and went as the singing continued. Anderson said the second day was just miserable. He began falling asleep and nearly dropped his $400 microphone. At one

Ace Anderson, non-stop singer.

point, the fatigue was so severe he started to fall asleep. He began doing squats and then ran around through the seating area trying to kick in enough adrenaline to keep going. "For some reason 8 to 11 a.m. was the hardest," he said. "If I could make it through those three hours, the other 21 hours of the day went okay." He actually fell into a sleep and dreamed he was talking to someone and asked her, "Did you do it?" The words came out over his microphone and woke him right up. What about those vocal cords? "They'll take about a year to heal," he said. In the mean time, he sprays his throat with medication and enjoys listening to music instead of making it. "I'm going to break my own record when I'm better," he said. Sixty hours? "Easy!" (Author's interview; DN 10/27/03.)

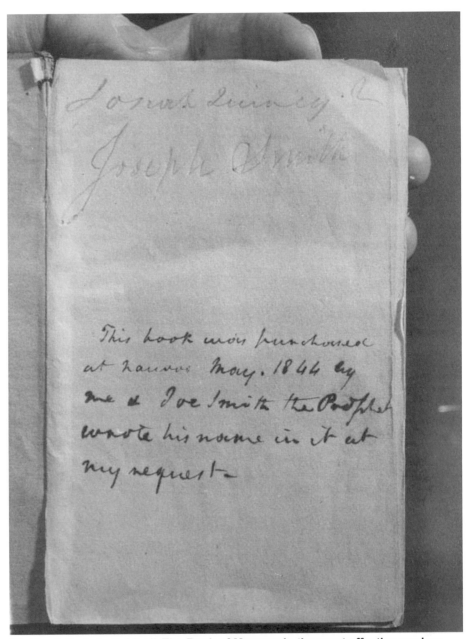

The book that started it all. **The Book of Mormon is the most effective modern-day missionary ever, appearing in places far and wide where millions of casual and serious readers have been drawn into its pages with the peaceful promise that enlightenment would surely follow. This copy of the Book of Mormon was autographed by Joseph Smith to Josiah Quincy. "This book was purchased at Nauvoo May 1844 by me & Joe Smith the Prophet wrote his name in it at my request."** Deseret Morning News, J. M. Heslop

Publishing

Printing and publishing – by the numbers:

1— Book of Mormon recovered from the collapsed World Trade Center in 2001
130 — Years of nonstop publication for one Church periodical
1,845 — Number of books autographed nonstop by a Mormon
5,700,000 — Copies of the Book of Mormon distributed in one year

BEST-SELLING BOOKS

Classical – "The First 2,000 Years," "The Third Thousand Years," and "The Fourth Thousand Years," by W. Cleon Skousen, Parley's 1st Ward, Parley's Utah Stake, introduced two generations of readers in the Church to the amazing stories of the Old Testament. The first in the series was initially published in 1953. With more than 45 printings, the books have sold in excess of 1 million copies. (Author)

W. Cleon Skousen

Novels – Anne Perry, who makes her home in Scotland, had more than 7 million books in print as of 2002. She began publishing her hugely popular Victorian mysteries in 1979, and beginning in 1990 she tried to write two books a year. Her books have been made into movie and television mysteries shown around the world. She was baptized in 1967 and most recently has been a gospel doctrine and Young Women's teacher in her small branch in the rolling highlands of Scotland. (Internet)

First Pulitzer. In 1948, Bernard DeVoto (1897-1955) won a Pulitzer Prize for his history book, "Across the Wide Missouri." It was part of a trilogy that also included "The Year of Decision: 1846," and "The Course of Empire." Born to a Mormon mother and a Catholic father in Ogden, Utah,

Brother Skousen's "Thousand Years" series became the most widely-read books on the Old Testament among Church members beginning in 1953. Photos courtesy Skousen family

DeVoto built an international reputation as a fighter for freedom of thought and speech. He was an early conservationist and presented passionate arguments and insights about the development of the West. He gained fame with his grating attacks against social and political ills of his day. (Internet)

Ina Coolbrith befriended a young and promising writer named Jack London.

First Poet Laureate – California. Ina Coolbrith (1841-1928), whose birth name was Josephine Donna Smith, was the Prophet Joseph Smith's niece. She was only an infant when he and Hyrum were martyred. After the Saints were driven out of the East, Coolbrith's family moved to California when she was 10. She had a deep love of writing poetry and all through her growing years tried to capture life and scenes around her. Her prolific and honest writing influenced generations of writers and poets and won her the honor as poet laureate of California in 1915. (Internet)

Most Book Signings (1999 World Record). When Dave Wolverton sat down in 1999 for a book signing for his new best-selling novel, "A Very Strange Trip," he didn't get up again until he had autographed 1,845 copies, a new world record for book signings. Brother Wolverton and his family live in Orem, Utah. He served his mission in South America. (www.adherents.com/adh_sf.html)

Dave Wolverton, recuperating from writer's cramp.

Best Beer Advertisement. Not only did BYU students Brent McKinley and Paul Forsey sweep first and second place in the Rocky Mountain College Press Association advertising contest in 1986 with a required marketing campaign for beer, but they did it having never tasted beer! (LDS 4/19/86)

TOP SCIENCE FICTION WRITERS

Orson Scott Card has several books among the top 100 science-fiction books of all time, including "Enders Game," "Speaker for the Dead," and "Seventh Son." He is always ranked high on lists of writers considered most popular by their peers and readers. As of 2000, Brother Card stood at the top of the list of most science fiction "novels of the year" awards (Hugo, Nebula, and Locus awards) with nine number-one books. Farther down the list are such famed authors as Isaac Asimov (six), Arthur C. Clarke (five), Robert A. Heinlein (five), and Frederik Pohl (four), just to mention a few. Card served a mission in Brazil. (Internet)

Raymond F. Jones was listed among the top 200 writers of all time in "A Reader's Guide to Science Fiction," published in 1979 by Avon Books. The biggest science-fiction movie of the 1950s, "This Island Earth," was based on Jones' book by the same title. Two of his books were nominated for Hugo awards, and for several decades his stories appeared in the classic science-fiction periodicals published monthly across the U.S. and beyond. (Internet)

Tracy Hickman has more than 12 million copies in print of his "Dragonlance" series. These best sellers topped the must-buy lists of the New York Times, Walden and B. Dalton Books, and others. Brother Hickman served a mission in Indonesia.

THE BOOK OF MORMON

Printings. As of 2004, more than 120 million copies of the Book of Mormon had been printed and translated in whole or part into 100 languages. In July 2004, the Church announced that Doubleday Books would become the first ever commercial publisher of the Book of Mormon, with redesigned copies appearing in late 2004. (DN 7/8/04)

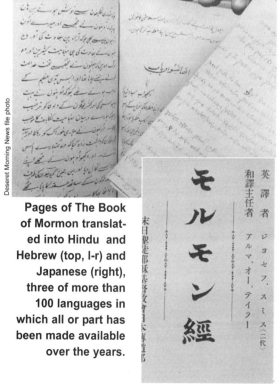

Deseret Morning News file photo

Pages of The Book of Mormon translated into Hindu and Hebrew (top, l-r) and Japanese (right), three of more than 100 languages in which all or part has been made available over the years.

Book of the Month Club. More than 2,000 Book-of-the-Month Club voters ranked the Book of Mormon number eight in a 1991 national survey among a list of books that had enhanced their intellectual or spiritual understanding of life. (DN 11/21/91)

Top 20 Most Influential Books in American History. The July/August 2003 issue of Book magazine (circulation of more than 150,000) ran an article listing the top 20 books that changed America. Several noted authors were asked to choose "crucial books that have shaped America along the way." Among the selections that included Thomas Paine's "Common Sense," "The Communist Manifesto" and "Silent Spring," was "The Book of Mormon." In their summary of the book the authors wrote that The Book of Mormon "launched the country's biggest homegrown religion. ... Today, Mormonism has 11 million followers around the world; in the United States alone, its adherents outnumber Episcopalians or Presbyterians. The book provides the theological underpinnings for one of the world's most vibrant religions." (DN 7/10/03)

J. Willard Marriott with Harold B. Lee at the dedication of the BYU Marriott Center in 1973.

Largest Family-to-Family Placement Program. By 1989, the largest private Book of Mormon placement program had grown to more than 100,000 copies given away, with some 10,000 being added each year. The source of this remarkable distribution was the J. Willard Marriott family, whose chain of Marriott hotels provides the outlet. Don Ladd, Marriott executive and bishop of the Washing-ton, D.C. 2nd Ward, said that at the time, Marriott had about 108,000 rooms in their North American hotels, each with a copy of the Book of Mormon. He said they had to replace about 10,000 copies annually. The Church donates the books, the Marriotts ship them, and the hotels place them, free of charge. (LDS 2/22/89)

Greatest Number Distributed – One year. In 2000, the Church gave out 5,700,000 copies of the Book of Mormon. Its family-to-family Book of Mormon program distributed 1.8 million in 1986. (CN 7/13/86; Internet)

Volunteers for the Church's "Family to Family" Book of Mormon distribution program paste written testimonies into the books for distribution to investigators.

In Space. The first copy of the Book of Mormon to go into outer space was carried aboard the space shuttle Discovery on April 12, 1985, when Senator Jake Garn (R-Utah) launched into orbit.

When Astronaut Don Lind took his trip in the space shuttle on April 29, 1985, he carried with him his scriptures. That particular copy of the Book of Mormon has the distinction of traveling 2,511,592 miles through space during 110 orbits around the earth. Brother Lind donated the scriptures to the Church where they were put on display at the Church museum. (CN 6/16/85)

Photo by NASA

Jake Garn carried a Book of Mormon into space in 1985.

RMS Titanic in 1912.

Aboard the Titanic. The only known Book of Mormon aboard the ill-fated Titanic was that carried by Irene Colvin Corbett of Salt Lake City. Sister Corbett had left her husband, Walter, and three children to study nursing in London. Although warned by both her husband and Church President Joseph F. Smith not to leave her family, 28-year-old Corbett did so anyway. Her grandson, Don Corbett, said his headstrong grandmother also wanted to do missionary work and asked for a blessing from President Smith. In her hometown of Provo, Utah, friends criticized her for going against the prophet. Corbett, her Book of Mormon, and all of her belongings sank in the Titanic after it struck an

Tom Smart, Deseret Morning News

Don Corbett shows photo of his grandmother and a postcard she sent from England prior to boarding the Titanic in 1912.

iceberg in the morning hours of April 15, 1912, some 300 miles off the coast of Newfoundland. She was among the 1,513 people who died in the tragedy. (DN 7/29/91)

Surviving the Sept. 11 Attack on the World Trade Center. An Episcopal priest helping with the cleanup at ground zero of the destroyed World Trade Center buildings also collected dozens of Bibles and other sacred books from amidst the smoldering rubble. Among the items found was a copy of the Book of Mormon, smelling of burnt plastic but still in pretty good shape. The book most likely belonged to one of the hundreds of LDS who escaped the buildings before their collapse.

What we watched on TV: One copy of the Book of Mormon is known to have survived the Sept. 11, 2001, terrorist attack in New York City.

Three Mormons died in the attack – two in one of the planes that hit the buildings, and another who was on the 108th floor of Tower 1. (Internet)

Japanese Book of Mormon in Braille. One of the more remarkable translations of the Book of Mormon was that done by Haruko Sakamoto, Juso Branch, Osaka, Japan. She painstakingly translated the entire Book of Mormon from Japanese into Japanese braille, finishing in 1953. It took more than 16 months to complete the project, and the final product was 11 volumes long. "It was the love of Jesus Christ that gave me encouragement whenever I found myself facing hardships which almost overwhelmed me," she said. "I shall be very glad if my humble work will give hope to the handicapped and help them to understand the love of God." (CN 2/7/53)

Sister Sakamoto (right) stands by as her 11-volume braille version of the Book of Mormon is read.

Broadcast. In 1988, K-STAR (KSRR) radio in Orem, Utah, was the first to broadcast a reading of the Book of Mormon. Station Manager Bob Morey said, "There is such a great potential for missionary work with K-STAR. We have the opportunity to reach 7 million people." K-STAR's potential audience included all of those who might have tuned their satellite dishes onto the satellite "Spacenet 1." (LDS 11/88)

Quote on a Stamp. A Samoan postage stamp, printed in the summer of 1988, was the first known stamp with an LDS scripture quotation. The $3 stamp depicted the Apia Samoa Temple to commemorate the arrival of the first missionaries in Samoa June 17, 1888. The quote was from 2 Nephi 10:21: "Great are the promises of the Lord unto them who are upon the isles of the sea."

Quickest Read. In 1989, more than 700 Laurels and priests from nine stakes met for a regional conference in Lethbridge, Alberta, Canada. Each person was given a number and a page out of the Book of Mormon, had to find another youth with the same number, and then read to one another the page each had been given. As a group, the entire Book of Mormon was read in 11 minutes and 30 seconds. (New Era 2/90)

Marathon Reading. The largest group to engage in a Book of Mormon reading marathon were the students at the Granger High Seminary, Utah. A total of 224 students each took a turn reading aloud a chapter, while others followed along, during the nonstop all-night challenge in 1989. They began after dinner at 6 p.m. Friday, Jan. 17, and finished the following afternoon at about 3 p.m. Said one participant, "By 11 p.m., we'd had popcorn fights and somebody brought a squirt gun. At midnight, pizza arrived. By 2 or 3 a.m. a few people were dozing off, but the rest of us made it till the end." (LDS 2/8/89)

First Typesetter. In 1829, E. B. Grandin agreed to print 5,000 copies of the first edition of the Book of Mormon for $3,000. John H. Gilbert, 27, of Palmyra, set the type and did most of the actual printing. (Church Almanac)

First Newspaper Advertisement. On Friday, March 19, 1830, the most important advertisement in the Church was

Utah State Historical Society

John H. Gilbert

The press used to print the first copies of the Book of Mormon.

published in the Wayne Sentinel in New York. It heralded the coming forth of the Book of Mormon, the long-awaited second witness to Jesus Christ, and the next important phase in the restoration of the Gospel. The newspaper announcement began, "We are requested to announce that the 'Book of Mormon' will be ready for sale in the course of next week."

Modern Mormon Alphabet. In 1852, Brigham Young instructed the Board of Regents of the University of Deseret (now University of Utah) to improve on the Arabic letters and their use in English spelling. With emigrants coming into Salt Lake Valley without training in the English language, the prophet wanted

The Book of Mormon in the Deseret Alphabet.

some uniform means for them to communicate. "Anything," President Young said, "would be an improvement." By 1868, a phonetic alphabet of 38 characters was created called the Deseret Alphabet. The Utah Legislature appropriated funds for the casting of Deseret typefaces, and textbooks were printed in 1868. Deseret was taught at the university and in public and Sunday schools. For those who mastered it, it worked well. Orson Pratt could write 130 words a minute in Deseret. But most others couldn't get the hang of it, and it died out in the 1880s. Shown above, a copy of the Book of Mormon written in the Deseret Alphabet. (CN 1/18/69)

Blank Paper. Who could have guessed that a lack of writing paper was all that stood between Joseph Smith and the translation of the Book of Mormon? With the plates in hand, Joseph had nothing to write upon to make the translation. Even Oliver Cowdery, who came to help, had neither money nor paper to offer. It was at this time that R. Joseph Knight Sr., of Colesville, Broome County, New York, came to the rescue. With his own money he bought provisions so the translation process could move forward. At the top of Brother Knight's shopping list was a healthy supply of lined writing paper — paper later made famous because of the foolscap water mark on each sheet. These so-called "foolscap pages" were eventually lost because of mishandling by Martin Harris and his wife. (Imp. Era 2/69)

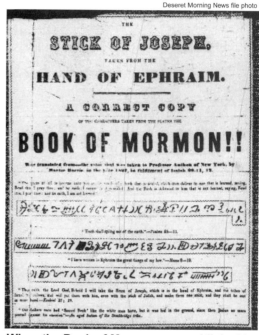

When the Book of Mormon was published in 1830, various advertising ideas were tried. This undated ad (above) tells of how a noted ancient languages expert, Prof. Anthon, was shown a few translated lines from the Book of Mormon, along with the original reformed Egyptian characters, and of how he validated the correctness of the translation. He recanted when he learned an angel was involved, fulfilling a prophecy in Isaiah 29:11-12. Shown above are some lines of text purported to be taken directly from the plates from which the Book of Mormon was translated.

COPIES GIVEN TO FAMOUS PEOPLE

The First United States President? Our closest guess as to which United States President was the first to receive the Book of Mormon is President Martin Van Buren, who was visited by the Prophet Joseph Smith on Nov. 29, 1839. The prophet had sought redress for the persecution the Saints had received in Missouri. Van Buren told Joseph that nothing could be done. Though there is no record that the Prophet gave Van Buren a copy of the Book of Mormon, it seems a very likely thing for the Prophet to have done upon first meeting the United States President. (Church Almanac 1989-90)

Photocopies courtesy Library of Congress, President's Collection

ABOVE: Book ledger from the Library of Congress showing Abraham Lincoln checked out the Book of Mormon in 1861.

Abraham Lincoln (1809-1865). On Nov. 18, 1861, Abraham Lincoln borrowed from the Library of Congress a copy of the Book of Mormon. Over a period of several weeks, he checked out four other books on Mormonism. Lincoln was already acquainted with the Church, having voted as a state legislator to give Nauvoo its city charter. He had met Joseph Smith personally. Perhaps Lincoln's interest in Mormons was sparked when Brigham Young inaugurated the newly completed transcontinental telegraph (the lines met in Salt Lake City) on Oct. 24, 1861, and sent Lincoln a message of support for the Union on behalf of the Mormons. The Civil War was then six months old. (Library of Congress, Presidents Collection)

Deseret Morning News file photo

Eldon Linschoten, Deseret Morning News

Ronald Reagan. LDS members of the California Legislature (above left), flanked by the full-time elders serving in the Sacramento area, presented Reagan with his first Book of Mormon in July 1967. Said Gov. Reagan: "I have always admired the tremendous personal integrity and self-initiative of the Latter-day Saint people, and on a number of occasions I refer to programs of your Church as outstanding examples of what I feel to be the true American way." Over the years he received additional copies, including a copy given by Pres. Hinckley during his visit to Salt Lake City in 1981 (right). (CN 7/22/67)

Courtesy Orrin Hatch and Ted Kennedy

Senator Ted Kennedy. At a fireside in Boston, Mass., in January 1989, senators Orrin Hatch and Ted Kennedy were the featured speakers. During a question-and-answer period afterwards, Kennedy was asked if he had a copy of the Book of Mormon. He replied, "No," then turning to Hatch, continued, "but I bet there's a copy on my desk Monday morning." (LDS 2/8/89)

Although at opposite ends of the political spectrum, Hatch and Kennedy have become good personal friends.

Queen Victoria (1819-1901). Lorenzo Snow, a newly baptized convert fulfilling a mission to England, had an opportunity to meet Queen Victoria by appointment in 1841. There he presented her with a copy of the Book of Mormon. He was serving as president of the London Conference at the time. (CN 2/18/61)

U.S. President Gerald Ford receives the Book of Mormon from Pres. Kimball in 1977.

Eldon Linschoten, Deseret Morning News

Pope John Paul II (1920 -) received his copy of the Book of Mormon in 1981 from famed LDS Polish pianist Vladimir Jan Kochanski. Upon receiving the book, the Pope responded: "This is a Mormon publication ... Ah, yes. Beautiful young prophet." (LDS 11/30/85)

Pope Pius XII (1876-1958) received a GI version of the Book of Mormon from Anthony I. Johnson of the Blythe, California, Stake, in the summer of 1945. The meeting was arranged through a friend of Johnson's in the American embassy. Johnson says the Pope spoke good English and was very cordial. (LDS 3/26/82)

Deseret Morning News file photo

Latter-day Saint Yuri Zvyagolasky discusses the Book of Mormon with the world's oldest man (oldest as of 2003).

Oldest Living Person (1887-2004). In celebration of Afanasy Ivanovich Tarasov's 116th birthday in 2003, local LDS members presented him with a blanket and a Russian translation of the Book of Mormon. According to Russian census records, Tarsov was the oldest living person in the world at the time. He was not LDS but local Mormons were invited to the event because of the Church's involvement in community activities in Tarasov's neighborhood. Tarasov attributed his longevity to clean living, no alcohol or tobacco, and politeness at home. "I know a lot about Jesus Christ," he was quoted as saying in the Church News. "He was the greatest revolutionary." (CN 3/1/03)

Boxing Great Muhammad Ali. During the summer of 1986, "The Champ" was intercepted at the airport in Dallas, Texas, by Bob Wilke of Chandler, Arizona. After striking up a brief conversation, Wilke presented Ali with a personalized copy of the Book of Mormon. Ali in turn autographed a "What is Islam?" pamphlet and returned the favor saying, "I'll read your book if you'll read mine." (LDS 9/20/86)

John F. Kennedy (1917-1963). When Mrs. Kennedy announced plans for a White House library of first editions, Congressman Ralph R. Harding (Idaho) and his wife decided their cherished 1830 first-edition copy of the Book of Mormon they bought in 1949 would make an excellent addition to this library. Rep. Harding made arrangements to meet with Kennedy in August 1962, and in the sunshine of the Rose Garden he presented the gift, giving also a brief history of the book and the Church. (CN 9/8/62)

Rep. Harding presents Pres. John F. Kennedy with a first editon of the Book of Mormon (1962)

Mark Twain (1835-1910). In his book, "Roughing It," (1872) Mark Twain, a.k.a. Samuel Clemens, tells of his travels through the west and his experiences with Mormons in 1861-66. In chapters 12-16, he describes his encounters with Brigham Young and other Saints, and gives his reaction to the Book of Mormon (chapter 16). In his typical Mark Twain style of biting sarcasm and genteel blasphemy, he declares the Book of Mormon to be "chloroform in print." And then he comments on the frequent use of "And it came to pass."

"All men have heard of the Mormon Bible, but few except the 'elect' have seen it, or, at least, taken the trouble to read it. I brought away a copy from Salt Lake. The book is a curiosity to me, it is such a pretentious affair, and yet so 'slow,' so sleepy; such an insipid mess of inspiration. It is chloroform in print. If Joseph Smith composed this book, the act was a miracle – keeping awake

Mark Twain tells of meeting Brigham Young.

while he did it was, at any rate. If he, according to tradition, merely translated it from certain ancient and mysteriously-engraved plates of copper, which he declares he found under a stone, in an out-of-the-way locality, the work of translating was equally a miracle, for the same reason. .... Whenever he found his speech growing too modern–which was about every sentence or two–he ladled in a few such Scriptural phrases as 'exceeding sore,' 'and it came to pass,' etc., and made things satisfactory again. 'And it came to pass' was his pet. If he had left that out, his Bible would have been only a pamphlet." [Now, now, Brother Clemens ...] (*Roughing It* by Mark Twain)

Photo courtesy of the Benson family

September 16, 1959: After Reed Benson spent 45 minutes telling Nikita Khrushchev's family about the Church, Mrs. Khrushchev said, "I give you a five (Russian for an "A") for doing a great job teaching us ... you must do more in our country." Pictured above (l-r), Reed shakes hands with Mr. Khrushchev. Between them is Reed's sister Beverly, and Reed's wife, May. Ezra Taft Benson (next to Khrushchev) had just finished giving Khrushchev a tour of the Beltsville Agriculture Experiment Station near Washington, D.C.

Nikita Khrushchev (1894-1971) and Family. During his visit to the United States in September 1959, Soviet Premier and Cold War adversary Nikita Khrushchev and his family were given a tour of Washington, D.C. Ezra Taft Benson was serving as the Secretary of Agriculture at the time, and he hosted Khrushchev for part of the visit. While Elder Benson and Khrushchev were visiting a Department of Agriculture research facility outside of Washington, Khrushchev's wife and family were hosted by Benson's son, Reed. When the conversation turned to Utah and the Mormon Tabernacle Choir, Reed took the opportunity to offer to the family copies of the Book of Mormon in Russian. Khrushchev's son-in-law, Adzhubei, then the editor of Izvestia, gave Reed the family's address where six copies of the book were later delivered, each to a member of the family. As they departed, Adzhubei took Reed aside and suggested, "Come to Russia and do some missionary work for your Church!" (CN 9/19/59; author's interview)

Sir Winston Churchill (1874-1965). Elders G. Edwards Baddley and Rodney H. Brady, serving in the British mission in August 1954, had the opportunity to visit Sir Winston Churchill at his 400-year-old country estate. They were asked to escort a visiting dignitary to Churchill's home so a gift could be presented to the British prime minister. When they arrived, Churchill greeted the threesome, offered them drinks, and exchanged pleasantries. At the appropriate time, the elders finally stepped forward to express their appreciation to Churchill for his great works and kindnesses shown toward the Church. They then presented him with a handsome leather-bound triple combination. Churchill hurriedly thumbed through the volume and thanked the givers by raising his glass and making a toast to their good health. (CN 8/21/54)

Winston Churchill raised a toast to the two elders.

Queen Elizabeth and Prime Minister Margaret Thatcher. On July 24, 1987, a commemoration of the 150th anniversary of the first Church missionary work in Great Britain was held in England. President Wendell J. Ashton of the England London Mission, with other Church representatives, presented to aides of Queen Elizabeth and Prime Minister Thatcher a modern quadruple combination of the LDS scriptures and a replica of the Book of Mormon that was given to Queen Victoria in 1841. (CN 8/1/87; Church Almanac 1989-90)

Thailand Queen Sirikit was a guest of the Church in 1981. She was given a brief tour of Temple Square and taken to meet Church leaders. During her visit, she was given a beautifully-bound set of the four standard works. (CN 10/31/84)

Thailand's Queen Sirikit.

Photo courtesy Leilani Parker

Elvis Presley received one of his several copies of the Book of Mormon from close friend and confidant, Ed Parker.

Elvis Presley (1935-1977).

Ed Parker, a member of the Church in Pasadena, California, and formerly a close friend and "protective companion" of Elvis, had many occasions to escort Elvis to concerts. When discussions drifted to religion, Parker had an opportunity to share his own beliefs with Elvis and eventually gave Elvis a copy of W. Cleon Skousen's "The First 2000 Years" and other Church books. Parker also gave him a copy of the Book of Mormon and told Elvis it contained the history of Elvis' ancestors (Elvis was part American Indian). Elvis read the Skousen book and this started a thoughtful dialogue between him and Brother Parker during trips together. One morning, Elvis consented to visit Parker's daughter in her early morning seminary class where Elvis stood to bear his own testimony of Jesus Christ. On another occasion, a young woman handed Elvis a copy of the Book of Mormon as he stood at his Graceland mansion home. After Elvis's death, the Graceland copy of the book was returned to the woman who gave it to him. She in turn gave it to Alan Osmond who donated it to the Church. In that copy, Elvis had made some notes in the margin, noting in particular a reference to Christ being king. "There is only one King," Elvis wrote. An LDS Elvis impersonator, Dr. Robert Von Moody, Orem, Utah, explained that, contrary to popular belief, Elvis was a deeply spiritual man and didn't like being called "The King." To Elvis, there was only one king (the Lord), Dr. Von Moody said, and the proof is in the margin of that dog-eared copy of the Book of Mormon in Church archives in Salt Lake City. (Author)

Russian novelist Leo Tolstoy (1828-1910)

wrote about the Church and may have read the Book of Mormon. His copy of the Book of Mormon resides in the Tolstoy museum in Chechnya. Of the Church he wrote: "If Mormonism is able to endure, unmodified, until it reaches the third and fourth generation, it is destined to become the greatest power the world has ever known." (CN 11/16/91)

Tolstoy Museum

Leo Tolstoy owned a copy of the Book of Mormon.

Sgt. Alvin C. York, World War I Hero (1887-1964). During the summer of 1949, Elder Burke V. Bastian and L. Kent Bard drove up to Sgt. York's Jamestown, Tennessee, home to pay him a visit. York was out tending his Hereford cattle, and seemed pleased to meet the elders. A friend of York's arrived during the visit and commented on what a terrible condition the world was in. Replied York, "Well this is the country where the Lord is doing His work, and don't think that God didn't have a hand in this last war. Russia closes all her doors to religion, and I don't think God will allow her to overcome this country, and I know he won't as long as people here don't forget Him. The people here can't leave God out." York told the elders he participated on a program in New York called "We The People." He remembered

Of the book he said, "I've been wanting to get one of these ...."

meeting one of the guests, the youngest daughter of Brigham Young. At the time he had heard for the first time mention of the Book of Mormon. The elders took that opportunity to present a copy to York, and related to him the history behind the book. York accepted the gift, saying, "I have been wanting to get one of these books. I'll take it home and study it some." (CN 10/30/49)

Coretta Scott King, wife of assassinated civil-rights leader Rev. Martin Luther King, received her copy from Bishop Joseph Hardy, Boulder City, Colorado, 2nd Ward at a welcoming reception for Mrs. King who had come to speak about her husband. In giving her the book, Bishop Hardy told her, "We talk of Christ, we rejoice in Christ, we preach of Christ." (LDS 5/13/87)

King of Sweden, Gustaf VI Adolf. In 1959, Gideon N. Hulterstrom, second counselor in the Swedish mission presidency, was on his way home to America. But he felt inspired to visit King Gustaf VI Adolf before he left for the States. It was one day before his scheduled departure that Hulterstrom stopped at the Stockholm palace to request an audience with the king. After struggling through several layers of interference, he finally succeeded in reaching the number three man in the government who said the request would be passed along. Hulterstrom's request was miraculously granted ("This never happens," the number-three man had told him). The following day, Hulterstrom arrived for his 11:30 appointment at the palace. During a delay while the king was detained in the Swedish parliament, Hulterstrom taught the gospel to high ranking government members and the king's son. Finally the king arrived, accepted the gift with gratefulness, and took time to read some of it. (CN 6/27/59)

Dr. Albert Schweitzer

Dr. Albert Schweitzer. A noted humanitarian, physician, and philosopher, Schweitzer was awarded the Nobel Peace Prize in 1952. Mrs. Richard O. Winkler, Garden Park Ward, Bonneville, Utah, Stake, had for so long admired Dr. Schweitzer and read so much about him that she felt he should be introduced to the Gospel. She tracked down Dr. Schweitzer's location and sent a copy of the Book of Mormon to the mission president in France, asking him to send the book to Dr. Schweitzer. Dr. Schweitzer's nurse wrote back conveying his "heartfelt thanks and kindest thoughts" for Winkler's gift. (CN 5/20/61)

Deseret Morning News file photo

Mangosuthu G. Buthelezi, Leader of six Million Zulus. In January 1988, a Church delegation headed by Elder Spencer H. Osborn presented a copy of the Book of Mormon, which had just been translated into the Zulu language, to the chief minister of KwaZulu and the leader of the Zulu people in Africa. (Church Almanac 1989-90)

Champion Ice Skater Peggy Fleming. During her preparatory work for the world figure-skating championships in Geneva, Switzerland, in 1988, Miss Fleming was met by two elders who presented her with a copy of the Book of Mormon. After a brief discussion, the elders wished her luck in the skating competition and departed. Miss Fleming won the crown, and promised the elders she would read the book on the plane trip home. (CN 4/6/68)

Jesse Jackson. Arizona Governor Evan Mecham presented a copy of the Book of Mormon to Jesse Jackson while Jackson was in Arizona to persuade Mecham not to drop the Martin Luther King holiday. "I committed him to read it," Mecham says. (LDS 2/14/87)

Queen Sophia, Spain. BYU students on the semester-abroad program to Madrid, Spain, were invited to attend a university class where Queen Sophia was visiting. After class, they stayed behind to talk with her and ask questions, at which time they presented her with a copy of the Book of Mormon and Jesus the Christ, both in Spanish. She received them with warm gratitude. (CN 5/22/76)

His Royal Highness, the Duke of Edinburgh received his specially bound four-in-one combination of the standard works in December 1961 at Buckingham Palace from Manchester Stake President William Bates. Said President Bates, "The Duke was friendly toward our Church. He knew who we were. He had seen something for which we stood and he appreciated what we were doing." (CN 1/6/62)

Juan D. Peron, President of Argentina. During President David O. McKay's tour through South America, he had the opportunity to meet with President Peron and present to him a beautiful leather-bound gold-lettered copy of each of the standard works, all in Spanish. Inside the Book of Mormon, President McKay had written, "To His Excellency, President Juan D. Peron, with appreciation from David O. McKay, President of the Church of Jesus Christ of Latter Day Saints. Feb. 3, 1954." (CN 2/13/54)

Queen Juliana of The Netherlands. Following President David O. McKay's visit to Queen Juliana in July 1952, when he presented her with a copy of the Book of Mormon, the Queen's private secretary was asked to write a note of gratitude for the gift. "Her Majesty the Queen of The Netherlands wants me to convey to you her sincerest thanks for the beautifully bound inscribed copy of the Book of Mormon, which you were so kind to present to her. It is her Majesty's wish to express once more how much the discussions during your visit have interested her. Signed, Baron van Haackeren van Moelcaten, July 28, 1952." (CN 8/6/52)

Andres Martinex Trueba, President of Uruguay. In 1951, a delegation of local Church members and nine missionaries visited President Trueba to present him with a beautifully bound copy of the Book of Mormon which had been especially inscribed for him. As they presented the gift, the missionaries said, "Your country is indeed, in every respect, a gem among the Americas." And they thanked him for the freedom they enjoyed to share the gospel in his country. (CN 12/5/51)

Vice President Alben W. Barkley. In 1950, while attending a Democratic rally and banquet at Greenville, North Carolina, Vice President Alben W. Barkley was interviewed by Elder Ray Sherwood (Phoenix, Arizona) and Donald E. Belnap (Ogden, Utah). When they presented the vice president with a copy of the Book of Mormon, Barkley said he had been asked to speak at the unveiling of the Brigham Young statue in Washington, D.C., and this book would help him prepare for the occasion. (CN 6/4/50)

Salote, Queen of Tonga. Written in her native tongue and with the personal autograph of President George Albert Smith, Queen Salote of Tonga received with warm gratitude the Book of Mormon offered her by Tongan mission president Evan W. Huntsman in 1947. This was the first copy of the Book of Mormon in the Tongan language to be distributed. Some weeks later, a case of 50 arrived for the missionaries and Saints to use. (CN 11/8/47)

Frederik IX, King of Denmark. During a special interview with King Frederik IX on April 19, 1948, Danish mission president Alma L. Petersen presented to the king a copy of the Book of Mormon and other Church literature. "I will gladly read them and also study them," the king said. He then shared with them his experience visiting Salt Lake City with his wife. "Of the trips that the Queen and I have taken, there have been none that we have enjoyed more than the time we spent in the state of Utah. It will be outstanding in our memory." (CN 5/1/48)

CHURCH PERIODICALS & PRINTING

Milestones
With the May 1987 issues of the Church magazines, the combined circulation topped 1 million worldwide — the first time ever in the Church's 155 years of publishing. (CN 5/30/87)

Volume 1 Issue 1 of the Relief Society Bulletin.

The Relief Society Bulletin started in 1872 as the Women's Exponent. In 1914 it was replaced with the bulletin and continued in print for decades. (CN 6/6/70)

The Children's Friend. In 1902, a magazine for children was started that contained lesson materials for Sunday and other teaching opportunities. When the Primary Board approved the name of The Primary Friend, an assistant secretary inadvertently wrote "Children's" instead of "Primary." The board liked the name better than their original, and the name stuck.. (CN 6/6/70)

First issue of the new Children's Friend

The Improvement Era. This magazine started out as The Contributor in 1879. By 1896, a new name was suggested and approved – Improvement Era. (CN 6/6/70)

Largest LDS Printing Press. The 100-ton Baker Perkins press attached to the Church's Salt Lake Distribution Center complex can whirl a web of paper at 1,600 feet a minute (over 18 miles an hour). In its first year it consumed 50 tons of ink and 7,000 tons of paper (enough to cover every square foot of Salt Lake County). The press prints materials for more than 120 countries, territories and possessions where Church units are located. (CN 7/27/86)

This Sept. 15, 1891, early issue of Juvenile Instructor was found among other things in a metal box in the southwest pillar of the Eagle Gate in 1961.

Oldest Press. The Cambridge University Press, the world's oldest continuous printing house and printer of more than 500 different Bibles, including the LDS edition of the King James Bible, observed its 450th anniversary on July 20, 1984. The Church's association with the press began in the 1920s when arrangements were made to produce a missionary edition of the Bible. Cambridge did all the typesetting for the 1979 LDS edition of the King James Bible and the 1981 edition of the Book of Mormon, Doctrine and Covenants, and Pearl of Great Price. The most expensive and finest quality copies of these standard works, printed on high-grade paper and bound in leather, are handled by the Cambridge press while less expensive copies are printed and bound elsewhere. In 1980, Cambridge University Press earned the graphics award for typesetting excellence in England for its work on the LDS edition of the King James Bible. (CN 7/22/84)

Longest Published. The longest lived publication in the Church was The Latter-day Saints' Millennial Star, published out of Manchester, England, beginning April 16, 1840. It finally closed in 1970 after 130 years. The paper was started two days after Willard Richards was ordained an apostle at his Preston, England, home. Parley P. Pratt was authorized to edit and publish the monthly Millennial Star, and his first issue of 24-pages cost the reader sixpence. (CN 8/9/58)

OTHER MILESTONES IN PUBLISHING

Newest Scripture. During General Conference on April 3, 1976, the newest canonized scripture which was added to the four standard works was presented to the Church for a sustaining vote. The two revelations, arranged in verses and added to the Doctrine and Covenants, include the account of the Prophet Joseph Smith's vision of the Celestial Kingdom received Jan. 21, 1836, and the vision of the redemption of the dead that was received by President Joseph F. Smith on Oct. 3, 1918. (CN 4/3/76)

Jack Anderson started investigative reporting for Drew Pearson's "Washington Merry-Go-Round" in 1947.

Columnists. The most widely read LDS newspaper columnists, Jack Anderson and Dale Van Atta, appeared in more than 1,200 newspapers across the country and around the world during the 1980s. For several years they co-authored the popular Jack Anderson investigative column, "Washington Merry Go-Round." (LDS 4/20/85)

Earliest Hymn Book. The first hymn book in the Church measured 3 inches by 4-1/2 inches and had 100 pages. There was no music in the book, only the words to hymns set up like poetry, with no titles. A "first-line" index was included in the back of the book. Nonmembers of the Church wrote the music for the most popular of the LDS hymns including "The Seer," "Come, Come Ye Saints," "O My Father," "We Thank Thee O God for a Prophet," "Praise to the Man," "The Spirit of God Like a Fire." (CN 12/29/48)

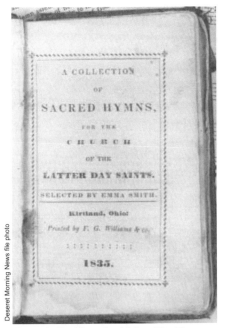

Joseph Smith asked his wife, Emma, to assemble a book of hymns that the saints could use for services. Her 1835 book was published just in time for the Kirtland Temple Dedication. The book had no music, just the lyrics.

First Non-Scripture Endorsement at General Conference Pulpit. President David O. McKay stood up during October 1959 General Conference and warned the Saints of the dark powers rising among the nations of the world, and that most people had no idea such works were underway. He recommended all LDS read "The Naked Communist," by W. Cleon Skousen. He repeated this plea at a subsequent General Conference. (Author)

POSTAGE STAMPS

Down through the years, people, events and the history of the Church have been given immortality on postage stamps. Here are some of the firsts:

Jack Dempsey. Jack Dempsey, the LDS world heavyweight boxing champion from 1919 to 1926, was pictured on a 32-cent United States commemorative postage stamp in 1998. The stamp was one of 15 that were issued on Feb. 3, 1998, as part of the "Celebrate the Century" series. (Internet)

LDS Inventor – Television.
Philo T. Farnsworth, inventor of the television, was honored with a 20-cent first-class postage stamp issued Sept. 22, 1983. He had more than 300 inventions in television and related fields, but is best known for the first all-electronic television transmission in San Francisco in

1927. He was inducted into the National Inventors Hall of Fame in 1984. He died in Salt Lake City at age 64 on March 11, 1971. (CN 9/25/83)

Seagull Monument. Featured as part of a Walt Disney series saluting well-known landmarks in the United States, a new one-cent stamp issued by St. Vincent (Caribbean), depicting Mickey and Minnie Mouse feeding the gulls near the Seagull Monument in Salt Lake City, went on sale in January 1990. (CN 1/27/90)

Tabernacle Choir. The Mormon Tabernacle Choir was one of 11 great choirs throughout the world featured by Nicaragua on its postage stamps commemorating Christmas in 1975. (CN 12/27/75)

Salt Lake Temple USA 10c
HISTORIC PRESERVATION

Sesquicentennial. A 10-cent postcard recognizing the sesquicentennial year of the Church was issued April 5, 1980. The design of the stamp was based on an original painting by an LDS artist showing the Salt Lake Temple and part of the Tabernacle with the Great Salt Lake in the background. (CN 3/29/80)

Symbols of the Early Pioneers. On April 14, 1982, a commemorative stamp was issued showing a painting of the California gull as part of a series about early pioneers. The seagull is the state bird of Utah. The stamp also depicted a sego lily. (CN 4/82)

Cancellation. The first LDS-associated cancellation of postage stamps was created in Switzerland in 1957. Two years after the dedication of the Swiss Temple on Sept. 11, 1955, a letter arrived in Salt Lake City with the Swiss cancellation that showed a line drawing of the Swiss Temple and the words beneath it: "Kirche Jesu Christi, Schweizerland Temple" (Church of Jesus Christ Switzerland Temple). (CN 12/7/57)

When Brazil helped the Church celebrate 50 years in that country, a special postage-stamp cancellation was designed. It depicted the Angel Moroni with the name and date prominently displayed. (CN 7/21/85)

Olympics. A commemorative series showing Olympic Winter Games events, and a cancellation stamp, were created for the games held in Salt Lake City in 2002. (Internet)

Only LDS Artist for a Stamp. Brian Hailes, 14, of the Millville 3rd Ward, Providence, Utah, South Stake, was one of four winners in an environment stamp-design contest sponsored by the United States Postal Service. More than 150,000 entries were submitted. His winning artwork, showing a boy planting a tree, was featured on 200 million first-class postage stamps distributed in 1995 – the largest distribution of any artwork by a Mormon. (CN 3/4/95)

The Only Mormon Word? Unless your dictionary is a fairly complete one, the word telestial isn't listed. It was unknown until 1832 when Doctrine and Covenants 76:81, 98 and 109 were published. Used to describe the kingdom of glory likened unto the stars, the word was probably edited out of Apostle Paul's Epistle to the Corinthians (I Cor. 15:40-42), since he uses celestial and terrestrial, but not a third word for the stars. Elder James E.

Talmage proposed the use of this new word to dictionary publishers in the early 1900s. (CN 4/4/51)

First English-Language Newspaper in San Francisco. In 1846, colony leader Sam Brannan led 248 Mormon settlers to California on the good ship Brooklyn. After a few weeks for the Saints to settle in, Brother Brannan started the California Star, the second English newspaper on the Pacific Coast. He printed the newspaper on a portable Franklin press that was also shipped aboard the Brooklyn. The newspaper premiered on Oct. 24, 1846, and was an instant success among saint and sinner alike. After a good 18 months of publication, the newspaper shut down for a few days in June, 1848, when the staff rushed off to the Sierra gold fields to try their hand at fame and fortune. The next year, the Star gained worldwide prominence when it announced the discovery of gold.

Sam Brannan played a key role in the early settlement and Gold Rush days of California.

The third English newspaper in California was published by George Q. Cannon, a future apostle in the Church, and was called The Western Standard. (Internet)

Florence Hansen is one of many gifted artists in the Church whose works have found world-wide enjoyment and fame. Shown here, Sister Hansen completes the clay work for a statue commemorating the beginning of the Relief Society. The finished statue has been reproduced in various forms throughout the Church. She is one of hundreds of LDS who excelled in *Music, Art & Photography.*

Music, Art & Photography

Music, Art & Photography – by the numbers:

1 — Number of dogs to conduct the Tabernacle Choir
8 — Years old of youngest LDS professional opera singer
51 — Cartoonists who drew Superman before a Mormon landed that job
1,500 — Feet underwater to which an LDS painting is regularly submerged
40,000 — Copies of "Mormon Rap" that sold in two months
80,000,000 — Osmond albums, records and tapes sold to date

MUSIC

The Recording Industry Association of America generally defines levels of sales on vinyl albums, tapes, cassettes, CDs and multi-disc sets as:

Gold: 500,000 albums or singles sold
Platinum album: 1 million sold
Platinum single: 2 million sold
Multi-Platinum: 2 million albums or singles sold
Diamond: 10 million albums or singles sold
(For more details about category anomalies and revisions of standards, see www.riaa.org)

First Platinum. Several LDS performers have produced albums that reached platinum level. One of the more recent was in June 2000, when the all-LDS group SheDaisy produced a hugely popular album that reached that level. Several of the group's hit songs were written by Jason Deere, an LDS songwriter in Nashville. The three sisters, Kristyn, Kelsi, and Kassidy Osborn, are originally from Magna, Utah. (CN 6/10/00)

The Osborn sisters (SheDaisey) have been a huge Nashville hit with albums selling in the millions.

Chuck Wing, Deseret Morning News

First Gold in Classical Music. In 1985, the Mormon Tabernacle Choir earned two more gold albums, bringing their total to five among the 17 ever awarded in the classical category. Their two albums, "The Mormon Tabernacle Sings Christmas Carols" and "Joy to the World" both sold more than 500,000 copies. Their earlier gold albums were "The Lord's Prayer," "The Messiah," and "The Joy of Christmas." (CN 1/27/85)

First Musical Group. The Nauvoo Brass Band, under the leadership of Capt. E. P. Duzette, was organized at the same time as the Nauvoo Legion. The group was at first little more than a fife and drum corps. But when William Pitt took the baton, the band really flourished. Numerous Nauvoo events, including the laying of the temple cornerstone and capstone, were accompanied by enlivening music from the white-trousered bandsmen. Halfway to Winter Quarters, the musicians disbanded, some going on, some staying behind.

The King family sings "Love At Home" to President and Sister McKay in 1966.

King Family Singers and King Sisters. In 1921, William King Driggs started a vaudeville act with his wife and five children. As the family grew, so did the act. Eventually, King family members were touring, putting on shows in towns large and small. Finally, the group began an entertainment program on television that ended each week with all the cast singing "Love at Home." The King Family spawned the famous King Sisters and numerous talents that continue bringing creative music, plays and performances to audiences today. (Internet)

Jessie Evans Smith, Utah's clarion contralto is one of the Church's great first ladies of song. Having recorded more than 20 hymns and songs, Sister Smith became a national favorite whenever she performed with the Mormon Tabernacle Choir on "Music and the Spoken Word." She sang her first solo with the Mormon Tabernacle Choir in 1918 and continued for years thereafter. She performed in the old Salt Lake Theater, in the Hollywood Bowl at the California International Exposition in San Diego, and around the world including Europe, Hawaii, Canada, Mexico, Central America, Alaska, Japan, Korea, China, Okinawa, Guam and the Philippines. And to the delight of audiences, she frequently sang a song in their own language. (CN 10/6/56)

First Orchestra. In 1850, William Pitt assembled a group of musicians from among the early settlers in the Salt Lake Valley. A Professor Ballo arrived in the valley that same year and the musicians gathered around him like children to candy. As the group began to perform, the Salt Lake Theater was being completed. Charles Thomas, George Careless and others arrived in the valley to enlarge and improve on the orchestra's repertoire. (CN 3/12/66)

Gladys Knight. Best known for her smash hit, "Midnight Train to Georgia," Gladys Knight joined the Church in 1997. Sister Knight first began singing publicly at age 4. By age 8, she, her brother Merald, sister Brenda, plus two other relatives, William and Eleanor Guest, formed the Pips in 1952. Brenda and Eleanor left soon afterwards, and by 1961, when they scored their first big hit, "Every Beat Of My Heart," the group had settled on the four members that stayed together for the next 25 years. They struggled during the early '60s (changing their name to "Gladys Knight & The Pips" in the process) before coming to Motown, where they immediately scored several hits. For the past twenty

Gladys Knight performs at the 1999 Women's Conference at Brigham Young University.

years they've been up and down, with some members going off for the occasional solo outing. Sister Knight is often a featured performer at broadcast LDS gatherings or galas, something she doesn't mind one bit. In 2001, she won a Grammy for Best Traditional R&B Vocal Album, "At Last." (Internet)

O. Walace Kasteler, Deseret Morning News

The Osmond Family performs with the Salt Lake Tabernacle Choir for the Donny and Marie Christmas Special filmed in 1977.

Osmonds. One of the most successful families in the history of show business was the Osmond family singers. They were known across the United States and around the world for their energy and stylized harmonies that covered pop, rock and roll, country and gospel music. They won millions of fans of all ages, just about everywhere. Over the years they appeared in five combinations: The Osmonds (Alan, Wayne, Merrill, Jay and Donny), Donny, Marie, Donny & Marie, and Little Jimmy. The first Osmonds to make it big were Alan, Wayne, Merrill, and Jay, who began performing at Disneyland in 1962. They were discovered that year by the Andy Williams television show and appeared regularly on his program for 4-1/2 years.

George and Olive Osmond worked hard to nurture their talented children. They traveled with them on tour and taught them that staying in line with gospel teachings and personal goals would spare them the troubles and temptations to which most entertainers succumbed. The nine children included: Virl, Tom, Alan, Wayne, Merrill, Jay, Donny, Marie and Jimmy. The two oldest suffered hearing problems and they didn't perform, but they did help run the sometimes chaotic concert schedule and burgeoning family business.

When Donny joined his older brothers, the music changed to a more contemporary style, and the Osmond brothers' popularity grew enormously during the 1960s. They were also regulars on Jerry Lewis' TV show from 1967 to '69. In 1971, their "One Bad Apple" single by the five brothers occupied the No. 1 spot in the United States for five solid weeks. This was followed by several more Top 20 hits in the next couple of years. It was about this time that Donny launched a career as a soloist. He became the new international teenybopper heartthrob with a string of hits including "Sweet and Innocent," "Go Away Little Girl," "Puppy Love," "The Twelfth of Never," and "Young Love." When he and Marie teamed up, they broke into the top five with hits such as "I'm Leaving It Up To You." Marie's success in country music produced such hits as "Paper Roses."

President and Nancy Reagan sing with Donny and Marie Osmond in 1984.

In 1975, Donny and Marie co-hosted the "Mike Douglas Show" and, by chance, the president of ABC-TV, Fred Silverman, saw them. From that encounter came the "Donny and Marie Show" in 1976-1979. In 1976, they were the youngest-ever TV hosts of a variety show (Donny was 18, Marie was 16).

By 1978, the Osmonds' popularity had begun to decline, but not their hard work and enthusiasm. Marie moved into country music and made a great name for herself. A revival of the Donny and Marie Show ran successfully on network television from 1998 to 2000. Over the course of their careers, the singers sold more than 80 million records and have at least 47 gold or platinum records. Meanwhile, the rest of the family singers (Alan, Merrill, Wayne and Jimmy) continue to perform, and the family's children are becoming world-class performers as The 2nd Generation

In 1991, Marie Osmond launched a line of fine porcelain collector dolls that she personally designed. The initial line had 40 different models.

Osmonds. The family continues to run its popular Osmond Family Theater in Branson, Missouri, and on Aug. 7, 2003, the Osmond family was honored with a star on Hollywood's Walk of Fame. (LDS 4/19/86; various Internet sites)

Top Ranked in Japan. The first LDS Japanese pop singer to make it to the top of the charts in Japan was Yuki Saitoh. Yuki's recording of "Yume No Nakae" ("Into a Dream") was ranked number four on a list of most popular songs in Japan in 1989. (LDS 8/23/89)

Randy Bachman

Founding member of Guess Who, Randy Bachman, formed Bachman Turner Overdrive, or BTO, in 1972, a couple of years after joining the Church.

Randy Bachman, Rock Star. Randy Bachman, Salt Spring Island Branch, British Columbia, Canada, Stake, is the most widely known rock singer in the Church. In 1965 he formed The Guess Who, famous for such hits as "Shakin' All Over," "American Woman," "These Eyes," "Laughing," "Undun," and "No Time." By 1970, the group had sold more records than the rest of the Canadian recording industry to that point, and even outsold the Beatles that year (in Canada). Randy dropped out of the group for health reasons but later formed another group called Brave Belt that was renamed to Bachman Turner Overdrive (BTO) in 1972. Their hits included "Let it Ride," "Roll on Down Highway," "Takin' Care of Business," "Hey You," "My Wheels Won't Turn," and "You Ain't Seen Nothin' Yet," which reached number one in at least 20 countries. Bachman has earned more than 120 gold and platinum album/singles, and has appeared in small parts in movies and television. He was a guest on "The Simpsons" as himself. He and his wife are the parents of eight children. (Internet)

BYU's Janie Thompson coached the two founding members of the Lettermen while they were students at the Y.

Lettermen. The hottest LDS singing group of the Sixties could be none other than the Lettermen. Though not touted as an LDS group, the famous singing trio that brought us "When I Fall in Love," and "Goin' Out of My Head" consisted of two LDS – Jim Pike and Bob Engemann – with nonmember Tony Butala completing the trio.

Top Ranked in Thailand. Brian Blake, Springville, Utah, returned to the land of his mission, Thailand, in 1986 to become a star entertainer—as a country-music singer. His country albums became an instant hit, he performed for millions on TV, and his outdoor concert sold out with 150,000 tickets scooped up in the first five hours. He went on to star in a Thai version of "Raiders of the Lost Ark," and hosted his own TV show. (LDS 5/3/86, 8/23/86)

The Jets, a singing group made up of brothers and sisters from the Wolfgramms, this Tongan family of 17 children started an amazing climb to popularity from their roots in Salt Lake City. The Jets of the 1980s were the eight oldest children, but since the group's move to California, the younger siblings have formed a second group known as Jetts17. (Author)

Courtesy of the Jets, photo by Randee St. Nicholas

The Original Jets were the eight oldest children (shown here in 1991). Today, the younger siblings are now performing under the name Jetts17.

Fastest-Selling LDS Single. The hottest-selling single in the Mormon market was "Mormon Rap," the silly but enjoyable spoof on Mormon life by the Walter & Hayes Band. Released in 1988, it sold 40,000 copies in just a couple of months. (Author)

First Behind Iron Curtain. The first LDS musical group to perform in the DDR (East Germany) was the Mormon Tabernacle Choir in the summer of 1988. At the conclusion of the month-long tour, a German official told the group: "You conquered the hearts of the people of Berlin. With your warm culture and smiles, you brought friendship and now we shall depart friends." (LDS 9/3/88)

Violist Cynthia Phelps, another of the most outstanding violists in the Church, if not the world, won the international competition at the Lionel Tertis International Viola Competition in 1984. Held every three years on Isle of Man, United Kingdom, it attracts musicians from around the world. To add to the pressure of performing, a "D" string broke as Cynthia performed before a packed audience of listeners and judges, in the middle of the crucial final rounds of competition. She pulled through, however, finishing in first place. (LDS 10/13/84)

Brass Ensemble. Perhaps the best known quartet of "blowhards" in 1985 was the Brunson Burners — Arlon, Deron, Geynor and Raland Brunson – who took their trumpets from performing at Church events in Kaysville, Utah, to become one of the most-requested musical instrument acts in the United States in 1985, performing on many TV shows and traveling for a while as pianist Liberace's opening act. (LDS 3/9/85)

French Horn. James W. Thatcher, 1975 BYU graduate, is so respected for his mastery of the French horn that he is often requested by name by famous movie composers John Williams, Jerry Goldsmith and James Horner. He has performed the principal French horn parts in more than 900 motion pictures including Jurassic Park, Forrest Gump and Beauty and the Beast. (BYU Magazine Fall 2002)

Major League Baseball Organist. James Connors, the official organist for the Houston Astros baseball team, was the first LDS to play for a major league all-star game. In July 1986, the Major League All-Star game was played in the Astrodome. This gave Connors an opportunity to play appropriate pieces, to the delight of LDS viewers and baseball players: when Dale Murphy batted for the National League, Connors played a jazzed-up version of "Love at Home;" when Wally Joyner batted for the American League, Connors played "Popcorn Popping;" and during the post-game show, Connors played "I Am a Child of God." (LDS 8/9/86)

Youngest Soloist in Pro-Football. Kathy Ross, 12, Broadway 1st Ward, Houston, Texas, East Stake, sang the national anthem for the Houston Oilers–Dallas Cowboys preseason football game in 1991. She won the talent competition for her age division on "Star Search" and has performed many times at professional athletic events since she was 6. (CN 11/30/91)

Deseret Morning News file photo

Youngest in Opera. The youngest Mormon to sing professionally with an opera company is Rachel Youngberg, 8, of the San Jose 24th, California, Ward. In 1990, she was selected for the cast of the San Jose Civic Light Opera. She credits her vocal range of nearly four octaves and perfect pitch voice to her Heavenly Father, "because He likes to hear children sing." (CN 12/22/90)

Rachel Youngberg, 8, has a vocal range of four octaves.

First in Vienna Boys Choir. Ralph Sieger may well have been the first Mormon in Austria's world-renowned Vienna Boys Choir. He joined the choir in 1982 at 6 years of age, the same year his mother joined the Church, and continued for four more years until his father joined. The family eventually moved to the United States (CN 6/1/86)

Youngest Chorister. In 1993, Clark Golden Dalton, 10, was called to be the sacrament meeting chorister in the Apache Junction 6th Ward, Apache Junction, Arizona, Stake. (CN 9/18/93)

In 1944, Grant Horne was called to be Primary chorister in the Fairmont Ward, Granite, Utah, Stake at the age of 13. (CN 5/6/44)

Longest-serving Chorister. In 1964, Edith B. Harding, 81, was released as ward chorister after serving for 59 years. The mother of eight children had been choir director for the Willard Ward, Willard, Utah, Stake, since 1905. She served with 10 bishops. (CN 6/6/64)

Most Enduring Organist. Is 58 years, by Flora M. Church, East Erie, Pennsylvania, Branch, the record for someone to play the piano and organ for the same branch? Except for an 18-month mission with her husband, she had played for the Sunday School, Relief Society and sacrament meetings, uninterrupted for nearly six decades. (CN 3/11/84)

Lyda G. Christensen was an organist for 62 consecutive years in Utah wards in Fountain Green, Moroni and Salt Lake City. (CN 12/7/63)

Bithen C. Beagley served as organist for 57 years in Nephi, Utah. She started playing at age 13 and over the course of time served with six bishops. Once she broke her arm but kept playing; however, at age 70 she broke her leg in an auto accident and decided it was time to retire. (CN 12/7/63)

In 1963, Mrs. Marion W. West marked her 55th anniversary as organist for the Bluffdale Ward, West Jordan, Utah, Stake. (CN 11/2/63)

Oldest Ward Choir. The Fountain Green Ward Choir, near Moroni, Utah, at 142 years old in 2004 is the oldest in the Church. It was organized in 1862 by Samuel Jewkes, an Englishman, when the town was about three years old. Despite the hardships of having no building, no organ, and the outbreak of the Indian War in 1866, the choir persisted, singing in the bowery of the nearby fort until things quieted down. Many of the present choir members are direct descendants of the original choir members. (CN 7/28/62)

Deseret Morning News file photo

Fountain Green Ward Choir more than 40 years ago. The faces may change, but the choir just keeps going and going and going ....

Youngest Average Age of Ward Organists. In 1970, the Val Verda 3rd Ward in Bountiful, Utah, had the youngest contingent of pianists and organists in the Church with an average age of 15.5 years old. Roland Putts, 13, was ward organist; Wendy Sproul, 15, played for the Junior Sunday School; Asael Sorensen Jr., 16, was replaced by Greg Batenson, 14, to play for Priesthood; and Brenda Bowman, 16, was replaced by James Call, 15, for MIA. (CN 11/7/70)

Youngest Church Pianist? At nine years old, was Ley Correa the youngest ever to be sustained as a pianist in a ward or branch? She played for all meetings at the El Cajon 7th Spanish Ward in California. (CN 1/20/85)

Let the Polkas Begin! Paul Pasquali, Salt Lake City, is the only American to have designed his own accordion. Called the Concerto, it combines digital technology with traditional acoustics, and lets users record or layer up to six sounds, as well as record 350 songs. Pasquali wants only the best to make his accordions, so he has them manufactured in Italy. The Concerto sells worldwide. Pasquali has been playing the accordion since age 8. (DN 8l/23/02)

First Guitar in Carnegie. A little-known Utahn, Cornelius Daniel Schettler, made guitar history when he became the first soloist to play a recital at Carnegie Hall sometime prior to 1904. David Norton of Salt Lake City is hunting for any information on this famous but forgotten guitarist. Schettler was born in Utah in 1874, studied in Munich, Vienna and Berlin, before returning to Salt Lake where he died in 1931. He may have played an important part in the development of the classical guitar in the late 1800s. (DN 2/21/92)

Was the first-ever guitarist in Carnegie Hall LDS?

TABERNACLE CHOIR

Largest Audience. The opening ceremony of the 2002 Olympic Winter Games gave the Mormon Tabernacle Choir an opportunity to perform before a televised audience estimated at more than three billion people. (CN 1/26/02)

"Gold" Albums. The choir's "The Messiah" was not only its first gold album, but also the first classical album in history to go gold.

First Grammy. For its stirring rendition of the great traditional ballad, "Battle Hymn of the Republic," the Mormon Tabernacle Choir was awarded its first Grammy in 1959. (CN 7/25/64)

A reunion of conductors for the Choir's 50th-broadcast anniversay in 1979, were Jerold Ottley, left, Richard P. Condie, Roy M. Darley, Jay E. Welch, and J. Spencer Cornwall.
Photo: Deseret Morning News file photo

Most Enduring Tribute to a Conductor. In 1974, when famed conductor Richard P. Condie, Parley's 1st Ward, Parley's Utah Stake, directed the members of the choir for the last time, he led them in the traditional closing piece, "God Be With You." Feeling very emotional, seeing his 1957-1974 term with the choir coming to an end, he set down his baton and walked off the stage in the middle of the piece. The choir, in sadness and surprise, finished the song without a conductor and without hymn books. To this day, the choir sings "God Be With You" without a conductor, looking only into the audience, in honor of Condie, who died Dec. 22, 1985. (Author)

Oldest Conductor. The oldest known person to conduct the choir was 84-year-old Fred Waring, known best for his half century leading the world famous Pennsylvanians. In 1984, while in Salt Lake City with his choral group, Waring was invited to direct the Mormon Tabernacle Choir in a couple of numbers made famous by the Pennsylvanians. He died shortly after his visit to Salt Lake. (DN 1/9/91)

Tabernacle Organ Players. First organist: Joseph J. Daynes, a native of England who emigrated to Utah in 1862, became the first organist for the Salt Lake Tabernacle. He was 16 when the new tabernacle first opened its doors for conference in 1867, and by assignment from Brigham Young, Daynes was the first to sit at the keyboard performing the music. He served in that capacity continuously for 33 years. Daynes gave his first organ recital before Queen Victoria at the age of 6. Among the several hymns he wrote for the Church, the most popular is performed at the close of the weekly Tabernacle Choir broadcasts, "As the Dew From Heaven Distilling." (CN 3/5/55)

Frank W. Asper's retirement as Salt Lake tabernacle organist in 1965 came after more than 41 years of consecutive and uninterrupted playing: 2,495 programs for his famed "Sunday Evening on Temple Square" radio program, 10,000 noon-time recitals, and 996 nationwide broadcasts over CBS. (CN 4/10/65)

Richard L. Evans wrote and produced Music and Spoken Word from 1930 until his death in 1971.

"Mormon" Voice. For 40 years, Richard L. Evans was the voice of the "Mormons" as he introduced the choir and gave the spoken word every Sunday morning over the CBS radio network. His successor, J. Spencer Kinard, says that on many of Elder Evans' tours around the country, most people recognized Elder Evans only after he spoke, as they had grown so very familiar with his voice. Kinard was the spokesman from 1972 to 1990. In an interview, Kinard said there was no pay for the job and it was not a Church calling requiring "setting apart" by the laying on of hands. Lloyd D. Newell is today's "Mormon" voice. (CN 7/8/89; Internet)

Oldest Member. Who is the oldest living member of the Mormon Tabernacle Choir? Evangeline Thomas Beesley held the record as the oldest choir member for many years. She passed away in the spring of 1990 at the age of 95. (Author)

Largest Live Audience. During the United States Bicentennial celebration in Washington, D.C., the Mormon Tabernacle Choir performed before a crowd of an estimated 1 million people crowded onto the mall near the Washington Monument on July 4, 1976.

Marianne Fisher, the first and only blind singer in the choir, talks with Choir conductor Jerold D. Ottley in 1979. It is said the Choir's original founder was also blind.

Dog Conductor. The first and only dog to conduct the choir was Snoopy, who was in town in March 1989 to help the Boy Scouts launch their 1989 Scout-O-Rama. Dressed as a Beagle Scout, Snoopy paid a surprise visit to the choir's rehearsal to earn his music merit badge. What he got were some first-class conducting lessons from director Jerold Ottley. Handing the baton to Snoopy, Ottley said, "You have to be very careful because there's no 'paws' in this piece." (DN 3/10/89)

What a howl! In 1989, the Choir went to the dogs ... all to support that year's Scout-O-Rama.

Youngest Conductor. Ryan Machir, Fremont, California, was only 2 1/2 when he was invited to conduct the Mormon Tabernacle Choir. During a rehearsal, choir members spotted Ryan standing between his parents, mimicking the motions of the conductor. He was attracting so much attention that conductor Donald Ripplinger stopped rehearsal and invited the boy to sit on his lap and lead the choir in "I Am a Child of God." (CN 1/9/91)

At age 2 1/2, his leading was just as good as his singing.

Longest Broadcast (2004 World Record). Since July 15, 1929, the choir has performed every Sunday for its "Music and the Spoken Word" broadcast. After beginning on the NBC radio network, the choir switched to CBS and the Church-owned KSL radio three years later. KSL had only one microphone at the time, and had to temporarily drop off the air each Sunday while the microphone was rushed to the Salt Lake Tabernacle. More than 125 radio stations pick up the live feed each Sunday morning, and another 442 radio stations and 47 television stations pick up taped broadcasts. On April 20, 2004, it was inducted into the National Association of Broadcasters' Hall of Fame. And on July 18, 2004, the choir marked 75 years on radio, the longest continuous, weekly network radio broadcast in radio history. (Internet)

The great organ in the west end of the Salt Lake Tabernacle started with just this center section of pipes. The outer sections were added to give a better look, but those pipes had no voice. The beautiful music comes from less glamorous pipes, behind (see below).

John G. McQuarrie, a veteran guide on Temple Square in 1945, compares the largest and smallest pipes. The largest pipes stand 32 feet high.

All photos: Utah State Historical Society, L. V. McNeely

In 1945, photographer L.V. McNeely took this picture of Brother McQuarrie in the organ pipe room pointing out some of the smallest pipes.

International Entanglement. KSL, the Church-owned AM radio station, got caught in a pushing match with Cuba in 1986. The 50,000-watt Church-owned station, which can be heard in many parts of the United

States, found itself in the early 1980s competing with Radio Marti in Cuba. The Cuban station, set up to blast the United States with Castro doctrine, broadcast at 300,000 watts on the 1180 AM frequency. KSL is broadcast on 1160 AM. Even with its power, however, Radio Marti only penetrated as far west as Iowa and KSL executives breathed a sigh of relief as they found no evidence of KSL being jammed. (LDS 3/8/86)

The Choir and Soviet Visitors. When Soviet inspectors arrived in Utah in 1988 to witness the destruction of American nuclear missiles under the INF Treaty, they were quickly invited to visit historic Temple Square. A special Christmas program was prepared for them as part of the usual Thursday night choir rehearsal. The choir sang two traditional Russian choral pieces, surprising and pleasing the Soviet visitors. After conductor Jerold Ottley greeted them and then paused to allow the translator to interpret, there was a moment of embarrassed silence until the interpreter finally confessed that all of the visiting Soviets could speak English just fine. (LDS 12/10/88)

PHOTOGRAPHY

Photographer of the Rich and Famous. Merrett Smith, Westwood 2nd Ward, Los Angeles, California, Stake, has taken more photos of the rich and powerful than any other LDS photographer. In his resume of "official portraits," find the names of:

• Presidents (and First Ladies) Reagan and Bush
• President Benson and the First Presidency
• President David O. McKay
• The Osmonds and their families
• The official Reagan cabinet
• Actors, performers, and luminaries such as Jack Lemmon, Charlton Heston, Bob Hope, Bob Newhart, Dick Van Dyke, Peggy Fleming, Andy Griffith, Crystal Gayle, Jack Benny, Olivia Newton-John, Tom Jones, Cheryl Ladd, Dean Martin, Frank Sinatra, Wayne Newton, Jaclyn Smith,

Deseret Morning News archives

Merrett Smith poses for a spread about the many "rich and famous" he has captured on film.

Ann-Margret, Don Rickles, and more!

Reg Wilkins, a former bishop of London, England, is one of England's top photographers, having taken official photographs of the Queen of England and the Beatles, among others. Some of his works have been shown in some of the UK's most prestigious exhibits, and his work from around the world has appeared in Harpers, Queens, Vogue, Elle, the London Sunday Times and London Sunday Observer. (CN 3/84)

Thirty years after the fact: LuJean Marsh poses in 1975 with a photo taken when she was a ltitle girl. The photo continues to show up in one form or another, all over the world.

Widely Published. In 1944, the late photographer Walter Z. Lillian took a photo of a little girl with her hands clasped in reverent prayer, her beautiful eyes turned upwards, and blond curls bunched on her shoulders. LuJean Taggart Marsh was that young girl in the photograph. The prayer pose has since been copied millions of times all over the world on calendars, Christmas cards, advertisements, magazine covers, photo-frame inserts, books, brochures, subway signs, handouts, matchbook covers, you name it! Sister Marsh says the heart-shaped cut in her bangs was actually a mistake. Prior to the photo session, young LuJean took scissors to her bangs and hacked away. Her mother tried to rescue the bangs by cutting a heart shape. This mistake became a fad after the photo was published, as mothers all over the country began cutting their girls' hair that way. (Author's interview; CN 9/13/75)

Only existing photo of Joseph Smith?

Joseph Smith. A debate concerning the origins of what may be the only photograph of Joseph Smith is far from settled. In 1970, Nelson Wadsworth, a journalism instructor at the University of Utah, was going through the negative collection of an old-time Salt Lake City photographer, Charles W. Carter. Wadsworth found a negative Carter took in 1885 of what is believed to be a much earlier and now lost daguerreotype (early form of photography) of Joseph Smith. Was the daguerreotype original? Wadsworth cites a Deseret News article (August 18, 1885) reporting Carter had in his possession the daguerreotype of the prophet taken by Lucian Foster. Joseph wrote in his journal of visiting with Foster, a daguerreotypist in Nauvoo, on April 29, 1844. Joseph was nominated for the presidency of the United States just three weeks later. And the prophet's son, Joseph Smith III, wrote in 1910 that his family had an oil painting of the prophet that matched very closely a daguerreotype in their possession. While some Church historians insist the daguerreotype is a photograph of an oil painting of the Prophet, others insist the oil painting was made from the daguerreotype. (CN 12/18/71)

Deseret Morning News file photo

Library of Congress

Fifteen minutes of fame: Vincent Villamor poses with famous WWII photo in 1972.

"I have returned, Elder!" Shown in this historic 1944 photograph, Gen. Douglas MacArthur (left) and Lt. Gen. Richard Sutherland (center), wade through knee-deep water to reach Philippines soil. Escorting them out front is Vincent Villamor.

World War II. Vincent Villamor, General Santos City, Philippines, was one of the chief participants in Gen. Douglas MacArthur's promised return to the Philippine Islands in 1944. Villamor waded ashore with the general when the allied forces began the invasion of the Philippines at Palo, Leyte, on Oct. 20, 1944. The famous "I Have Returned" picture taken of the event, showing MacArthur wearing his trademark dark glasses, was front-page fare in newspapers around the world and still accompanies many encyclopedia articles about the Pacific campaign. MacArthur and his chief of staff are shown sloshing ashore with Brother Villamor leading the way. (CN 9/30/72)

PAINTING

Ed "Big Daddy" Roth wearing his classic top hat, stands next to his wife Ilene. He sports a tee shirt with his world famous anti-Mickey Mouse creation, *Rat Fink*. He told friends that the best place for serious help and inspiration was the Manti Temple.

Photo Courtesy of Moldy Marvin

Rat Fink Lives On! How do we categorize the contributions of Ed "Big Daddy" Roth, the "mad" genius whose artwork shaped an entire generation and culture of pedal-to-the-metal '50s and '60s hot-rod enthusiasts? Roth had achieved international recognition long before he joined the Church in 1974. His outrageous car designs, and his famous airbrushed creations that featured that insanely whacked-out and slobbering anti-Mickey Mouse character called "Rat Fink," spawned a radical change for plastic car models as well as their full-sized counterparts built by Roth himself or other hot-rod lovers. A child of the beatnik generation, he became the icon and mentor of Southern California hot-rod rebels. His cars were shown everywhere, copied by thousands, and reproduced by the millions as plastic models. By 1974, Roth had become discouraged with the direction his life had been going when a friend dropped off a copy of the Book of Mormon. This turned his life around and he joined the Church. He told the Salt Lake Tribune in 1997 that his best source of inspiration came from attending the Manti Temple with his wife, Ilene. (SLTrib 11/17/97)

Deepest Traveled Painting. In 1984, Leah Christiansen Hansen completed a painting entitled "Salt Lake City: Past, Present, Future," commissioned by the U.S. Navy for the new $340 million nuclear submarine U.S.S. Salt Lake City. It had to be the proper dimensions to go "down the hatch," she said. The painting is a composite depicting the pioneers and their struggles alongside a more modern view of the city. It has the distinction of being the "deepest traveled" painting in the Church (the actual depth is classified, so we guess it's been down at least 1,500 feet). When the sub launched in 1984, two of the 35-man crew were LDS. (CN 3/11/84)

A sample of the style perfected by James C. Christensen, one of hundreds he has created that are collected and loved by fantasy fans everywhere.

Magleby's poster was voted best of the year, 1986.

Most Published Fantasy Painter. The most accomplished and best-known fantasy artist in the Church is James C. Christensen, Orem, Utah, 63rd Ward, whose beautifully detailed and message-packed works of art can be found in magazines, books, and art shows around the world. (CN 6/13/87)

James C. Christensen

Most Widely Printed Poster. What must be the most famous poster created by an LDS artist was done in 1984 by McRay Magleby, Sunset 6th Ward, Provo, Utah, West Stake, entitled, "Wave of Peace." It won the Most Memorable Poster award by an international jury of artists from 40 countries who assembled in Paris in 1986 to look at thousands of entries. "Wave of Peace" was originally created for the 40th anniversary of the bombing of Hiroshima, and after a world tour went on permanent display there. Said Magleby, "Most of the peace posters I've seen have been negative. They show how bad war is and make you feel depressed. I wanted to make people feel good, to feel that peace is something worthwhile, something to strive for." Brother Magleby was the art director of the BYU Graphic Communications Department before becoming a professor of graphic design at the University of Utah. (CN 2/14/87)

Heaviest. "The Restoration," a mural by Lewis A. Ramsey, ranks heaviest in the Church at nearly three tons. Painted directly onto the plastered brick wall of the 11th

Ward chapel, Salt Lake City, the mural was for years a focal point for visitors and members entering the building. When the building was razed in 1961, efforts were made to preserve the 13x10-foot oil painting. Workers channeled through the brick and, down each side of the painting, cut off all but four inches of brick on the back, and to ensure structural integrity, the sides and back were encased in cement. A crane was needed to lift the massive, 3-ton (estimated) piece onto a truck. The mural was lost for many years but discovered in 1979 in an old shed in Salt Lake City. A $7,000 restoration project was begun to clean it up for permanent display in a Church museum. (CN 4/29/61; DU 11/28/79)

COMIC BOOKS AND ARTISTS

Above, Ric Estrada in his New York studio. Below, a souvenir of Ric's Superman evolving to prince and prophet, akin to Arnold Friberg's famous rendition of Moses.

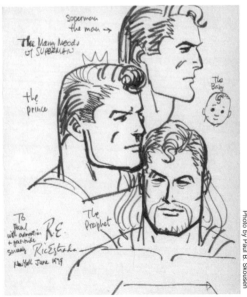

Photo by Paul B. Skousen

Superman, and others, by Ric Estrada. Perhaps the best-known comic hero of all time had been drawn by at least 52 separate artists by 1979. Ric Estrada, Scarsdale Ward, New York, was one of those artists. Estrada, a native Cuban who came to the United States in 1947 under partial sponsorship of Ernest Hemingway, has worked on such famous comic-book characters as Superman, Batman, Wonder Woman, and Flash Gordon. He also has done animation work for Hanna Barbera, Dreamworks, Warner Brothers, and Sony Tristar. His work can also be seen in "Wacky Races," "Captain Planet," "Go-Bots," "Men in Black," and "The Jetsons Movie." Estrada is especially proud of his work on "New Testament Stories for Children," a project he did for the Church. In 1999, Estrada moved to St. George, Utah, to become director of "The Princess and the Pea Animated Series." (Author's interview)

Photo by Paul B. Skousen

Washington Post Writers Group

Courtesy Brian Crane

Brian Crane

"Pickles," by Brian Crane, is a popular daily comic strip that appears in more than 340 newspapers in the United States. Brother Crane is a member of the Sparks 2nd Ward in the Sparks, Nevada, Stake. He has been drawing Pickles for more than 13 years, and bases his characters on family members. Those on the lookout will spot an occasional LDS reference in the strip such as a Church magazine being read by a character or a picture of an LDS temple hanging on the wall. (Author's interview)

"Drabble," by Kevin Fagan, is another popular comic strip now in more than 200 newspapers. Drabble depicts the ups and downs of a family beset with the challenges of raising kids and trying to make it in life, love and school. Brother Fagan has been drawing this strip since 1979. (Internet)

"Captain Canuck," by Richard Comely and Ron Leishman, both from Winnipeg, Canada, was outselling all other comic books in Canada in 1975. Shortly after his baptism in 1971, Brother Comely met Brother Leishman and the two collaborated on the comic book until Leishman left on his mission. Nearly 170,000 copies of the first Captain Canuck went to stores and newsstands in Canada and the United States. The hero's creators always had Captain Canuck bow his head in prayer before departing on a dangerous mission, and always gives credit by saying, "God is helping us." (Author's interview)

Photo courtesy Richard Comely

Richard Comely and Captain Canuck – keeping the world safe in Canada.

Gerald Silver, Deseret Morning News

Sal Velluto, an artist from Italy who joined the Church and settled in Utah, was a major artist for Marvel and D.C. comics. He created "Moon Knight," and was hired to illustrate issues of "The Justice League Task Force," a fresh series of comics that were scheduled to feature all of the great D.C. super heroes. Velluto has included in his drawings Marvel boss Stan Lee, LDS missionaries, himself, his car, and even his house which he blew to smithereens ("Luckily we were renting and not buying!" he said). (DN 6/17/92)

Sal Velluto brings "The Justice League" to life.

Breakfast Cereal Box. As most LDS parents would agree if they saw it, the best cereal box in the Church was that designed by Brent R. Evans, San Jose 9th Ward, Saratoga, California, Stake. Evans recognized that parental and home influences had a powerful impact on a child's achievement level in school. To boost parental involvement in children's lives, Brother Evans developed a sort of lesson plan for the back of cereal boxes. In 1975, Quaker Oats' "Life" and "King Vitamin" cereals were the first with the program. After initial distribution, the company was getting more than 1,000 supportive letters a month from parents. (CN 3/1/75)

SCULPTURE ART

Paul B. Skousen

PHoto courtesyChurch History Museum

Original sunstone at the Museum of Church History.

Sunstones. The sunstones from the Nauvoo Temple are among of the most recognized LDS stone sculptures in the United States. One of the stones is seen daily by thousands of visitors to the Smithsonian American history museum in Washington, D.C.. The Smithsonian bought the stone for $100,000 and put it on permanent display.

National Monument. Mount Rushmore, that mighty national monument in South Dakota, was carved by John Gutzon Borglum, the son of Mormon Danish immigrants. The world-renowned sculptor and artist was commissioned in 1927 to turn the massive granite peaks near the Bad Lands into one of the most recognized symbols in America. Gutzon's father, James, was a convert to the Church who immigrated to Salt Lake City in 1864 with his first wife, Ida. Her sister, Christina, joined the family a year later and became the second wife. The Church sent the Borglums to help settle the Idaho Territory and, in 1867, Gutzon was born to Christina. Problems with polygamy broke the family apart and Christina left for another life. James took the family to California where Gutzon studied art and eventually met Lisa Putnam, a painter and divorcee 18 years his senior. They married in 1889. After traveling the world to study, Gutzon earned a reputation as an excellent artist and caught the attention of the South Dakota state historian. The rest is rock-solid history. (Internet)

Courtesy Paul Gregory

Borglum directed the carvings until his death in 1941. Borglum's son completed the monument that same year.

Copy of photo courtesy Clawson family

Gutzon Borglum was the son of LDS immigrants from Denmark.

Presidential Medallion. Edward J. Fraughton, Jordan River 5th Ward, South Jordan River Ridge Stake, Utah, is one of the most prominent sculptors in the Church. His works can be found around the world. In 1980, he was commissioned to prepare President-elect Ronald Reagan's official inaugural medal. In preparation he made a life mask of Reagan's facial features. (DN archives)

Deseret Morning News file photo

Howard Moore, Deseret Morning News

Gary McKellar, Deseret Morning News

Avard Fairbanks, forever the teacher, shown here amazing some school children in 1985 by modeling a clay figure. His works capture LDS history in moving, touching scenes such as the tragic image of grieving pioneer parents looking down at the open grave of their child, a sculpture standing at the site of Winter Quarters near Omaha, Nebraska. His "Angel Moroni" statues adorn temples throughout the Church, and his works are recognized world wide.

Ed Fraughton works on a clay model of a Mormon Battalion figure, his first commissioned monument. The Sons of Utah Pioneers and decendants of the original Mormon Battalion members contracted with him to create this larger than life statue. It was finished in 1968 and donated to the city of San Diego in celebration of the city's 200th Anniversary.

Howard Winn

Airport Beacon. The 15-foot 5-1/2-inch Angel Moroni statue adorning the Los Angeles Temple has faithfully served as a beacon for pilots approaching Los Angeles International Airport since the temple's completion in 1956. Cast aluminum, 2,100 pounds, with an eight-foot trumpet, and covered with gold leaf, the statue can be seen from miles away by approaching pilots when it is illuminated at night with floodlights. At one time, lights were dimmed to conserve energy but numerous pilots complained. The lights were turned back on. (CN 3/27/83)

Statues. The most prominent LDS statues are probably those standing in the United States Capitol. A statue of Brigham Young was placed there in 1950, and Philo T. Farnsworth, the father of television, was placed in 1990. Each state is allowed two statues of deceased citizens for permanent display. (DN 3/7/90)

Utah State Historical Society

Artist Mahonri Young and George Albert Smith greet visitors at the unveiling of the Brigham Young statue in 1950. Brigham Young would sit here alone in Washington, D.C., for 40 years.

Utah State Historical Society

Eagle Gate in 1859

Deseret Morning News file photo

By 1960, the old wooden Eagle had developed a little dry rot under its corroded copper covering.

Wood. One of the most prominent wooden carvings in LDS history is the eagle atop Eagle Gate leading to Brigham Young's property in Salt Lake City. Truman O. Angell designed the gate and Ralph Ramsey carved the wooden eagle in 1859. The bird was carved from five blocks of wood, one for the body, one for the head and neck, two for the wings, and the fifth for the beehive on which the bird was placed. In 1890 the sculpture was sent east and electroplated. Carved on the box on which the eagle stands is an upside-down star. The star, often used in Mormon symbolism to depict man, is upside down to indicate death. The Eagle Gate led to Brigham Young's family cemetery. The gate was hit in 1960 and gave opportunity to check out the Eagle and make some adjustments to the gate's span over State Street. (Author)

A time capsule found in one of the Eagle Gate pillars contained historical documents dating back to 1891. Pres. David O. McKay, seated left; Pres. J. Reuben Clark Jr. and Pres. Henry D. Moyle take a closer look. *Deseret Morning News file photo*

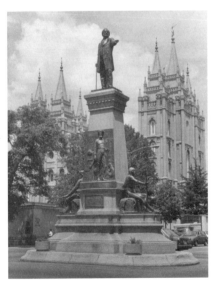

This classic view of the Brigham Young Statue (left), also world recognized, in downtown Salt Lake City was forever changed when the new Church Plaza was built, and the statue was moved back several feet to facilitate traffic flow.

Angel Moroni. It was bound to happen sooner or later. The Angel Moroni adorning the spires of so many temples has turned high tech. Newer temples no longer receive the heavier and more expensive aluminum versions, but now use fiberglass statues. Karl Quilter and LaVar E. Wallgren, who pioneered the process of casting fiberglass statues from molds, are both from Salt Lake and have produced angels for the Atlanta and many of the Pacific temples. They say fiberglass also wears better than aluminum. Several of the older statues are being replaced due in part to discoloration from lightning strikes. (CN 9/4/83)

Stained Glass. The famous stained-glass window in the old Adams Ward building, Los Angeles, California, depicting the First Vision lives now only in photographic reproductions. The work of art was removed before the Adams Ward was demolished and moved to the Los Angeles Temple and then on to Salt Lake City, where it was lost. Leland Payne, Brea 2nd Ward, Fullerton, California, Stake, is credited with preserving the image of the window. Asked by Disney to perfect a system to reduce the cartoon image of Snow White, he made sketches and images of the window as part of an experiment to reduce images. His pictures are all that remain of the stained glass window. (LDS 11/10/84)

RADIO

First LDS Radio Station. On May 6, 1922, the West's first radio station was launched when President Heber J. Grant spoke into a telephone-like microphone and delivered the first words over station KZN of Salt Lake City. In those days, the 500-watt station could only afford to stay on the air 30 minutes each day. By 1932, it had moved from a shack on top of the Deseret News building into its own facilities with a 50,000 watt transmitter and an affiliation with the National Broadcasting Company. KZN then became KSL, and switched affiliates to join the Columbia Broadcasting System (CBS), where it has remained for many decades. (CN 5/5/62)

Best Radio Spot. A public-service announcement sponsored by the Church and produced by Bonneville Productions, won best overall radio spot of the year for 1980. The competition was sponsored by the Hollywood

Radio and Television Society, and attracted 5,000 entries from 50 countries. The 30-second radio spot called "Love Plus" won both best public-service announcement and the sweepstakes award as best overall radio spot of the year. (CN 5/17/80)

Radio Talk Show Host.

The largest audience for a syndicated LDS radio talk show host numbers in the millions for Glenn Beck who talks politics for three hours on weekdays over 115 stations across the nation. Brother Beck covers just about every subject and enjoys presenting an honest if not sometimes opinionated view of life and all that it offers.

Back in the day, this radio was the latest "state of the art." Its user could tune into a half hour of great gospel from one of the Brethren ... every day.

Glenn Beck, radio talk show host.

He joined the Church in 2000, and isn't bashful about his Church membership. He makes it clear to listeners and media interviewers alike, "at last, a Church where you can ask real questions and get real answers." When he and his second wife married, one of the deals was that they'd find a Church, so they went shopping. "We must have tried on every Church there was," he told Michael Savage on national radio. "The Mormons had the answers." He and his family live in Philadelphia. (Internet)

Commander of World's Largest Network.

In 1998, Glen L. Bradey, a colonel in the United States Air Force and a member of the Moreno Valley, California, Stake, became the commanding officer of the Armed Forces Radio and Television Service.

This network serves more than 600 Department of Defense outlets in 156 countries. The network's coverage ranges from widespread bases in Europe and Asia to remote embassies, airfields and ships at sea. (CN 2/7/98)

Positive Impact. The Church's Home Front spot that says, "Sometimes the best times don't start out that way. Let love turn it around" saved a young man from committing suicide, according to the Las Vegas Sun newspaper in 1988. A Las Vegas mother found her young son sitting next to a loaded shotgun, crying. He was about to commit suicide when the Home Front commercial came on the radio, causing him to reflect and abandon his plan. Said a Home Front writer after hearing the story, "It felt better than any of those prestigious industry awards we all love to receive." (LDS 1988)

Photo by Ted Rezvoy, courtesy Richard Jones

Personal courage is the internal power to take with dignity whatever hits you, whether it comes by choice or in consequence of another's choice. In 2000, Richard Jones rowed away from the Canary Islands off the coast of western Africa to test the limits of duration and strength of his own personal courage. He wanted to row across the ocean. And he did. It was all about personal *courage*.

Courage

Courage, bravery and stamina – by the numbers:

3 — Mormons launched into orbit around the earth

49 — Days endured in Alaska's snowy wilderness without food and shelter

260 — Tribes with whom a Mormon lived during his many global adventures

4,579 — Miles rowed solo by a Mormon to cross the Atlantic

SPACE TRAVEL

First Mormon Astronaut. Major Russell L. Rogers, branch clerk at Edwards Air Force Base in 1962, became the first LDS astronaut when he was named with five others to the Dyna-Soar (X-20) man-in-space project. The Dyna-Soar was the predecessor to the Space Shuttle. Brother Rogers had been an experimental test pilot at the Air Force Flight Test Center, Edwards Air Force Base. (CN 9/62)

The First Mormon In Space. U.S. Senator Jake Garn became the first LDS launched into space when he traveled aboard the space shuttle Discovery on April 12, 1985. He completed 109 orbits and achieved his fastest speed at 17,500 miles per hour as he orbited the earth. This flight is also remembered because the LEASAT-3 satellite he helped deploy failed to fire into a geosynchronous orbit as programmed. The problem, it turned out, was a toggle switch on the side of the booster which had been left in the "off" position. The crew constructed two "flyswatter" devices meant to catch the toggle switch on the side of the satellite as it spun in space and switch on the booster rocket. However, the devices failed and a subsequent

Photo by NASA

Sen. Garn poses with shuttle pilot Karol J. Bobko while in orbit in 1985.

shuttle had to return and finish the job. Discovery completed its six-day, 23:55:23 hour trip by blowing a tire just as it touched down at Edwards Air Force Base. Sen. Garn was also the first public official to fly aboard the shuttle, and conducted medical and psychological tests while in orbit. (www.jsc.nasa.gov/Bios/)

Don Lind served as a mission specialist on one of Challenger's last flights.

Closest Call for an LDS Astronaut. LDS astronaut Don Lind's space launch aboard the Challenger on April 29, 1985, almost became a disaster, he later learned. The same problem that nine months later destroyed the Challenger and the seven astronauts aboard nearly killed Brother Lind. After an examination of the seals around the spent fuel tanks follow-

Lind takes off aboard the Challenger, nine months before a leaky seal destroyed it and all of its passengers.

ing the flight, Lind reported, "[After main tank separation] the putty was gone, the primary layer was gone and the secondary layer was 80 percent gone. We had roughly 15 more seconds and we would have had an explosion." (NASA, LDS 11/15/86)

Searfoss (foreground) chats with fellow astronauts during his 1998 flight as com- mander of Columbia.

First Mormon Commander of a Space Shuttle. Richard A. Searfoss became the first LDS to command a space shuttle when he launched into space aboard space shuttle Columbia on April 17, 1998. The seven-person crew made 256 orbits and landed at Kennedy Space Center, Florida, on May 3, 1998. This was his third shuttle trip into space.

Cool Under Fire. The terrible Columbia space shuttle disaster on Feb. 1, 2003, turned the world's attention to one man for the answers: Ron Dittemore, a high councilman and member of the Friendswood 2nd Ward, Friendswood, Texas, Stake. Since 1999, Brother Dittemore had been director of NASA's shuttle program, a position that didn't warrant much public notice – until the Columbia accident. As the spacecraft returned from a routine 16-day mission, carrying the first Israeli ever on a space flight, it broke apart at thou-

Ron Dittemore, shown here pointing out the area of damage that brought down the Columbia, was promoted in 1999 to director of the space shuttle program.

sands of miles per hour as it reentered the atmosphere some 200,000 feet above Texas. A shocked nation turned to NASA for answers and solace, and found a cool-headed, honest man whose faith and religious activity, it was said, carried him through that most pressure-filled, painful and difficult experience. As NASA's spokesman, Dittemore offered comfort: "Human spaceflight is a passion," he told the world just hours after Columbia disintegrated. "It's an emotional event. And when we work together, we work together as family members. ... It's a professional dependency, and it's an emotional dependency. And so, when we have an event like today where we lose seven family members, it is devastating to us." (Houston Chronicle 2/87/03; CN 2/8/03)

ADVENTURE

Most Adventuresome. John Goddard has created a life's book of records that is amazing to review. The La Canada 1st Ward, La Crescenta, California, Stake member is the Church's most famous explorer and adventurer. At age 15, he wrote down 127 goals he wanted to achieve in his lifetime. By age 60, he had met 107 of those goals. His life's pursuit has brought him recognition and appearances as a motivational and educational speaker to countless thousands of school children and college students across the country. He has been written up in National Geographic magazine, Life, Time, and recently in an edi-

John Goddard – Explorer!

Goddard displays a few of the ceremonial masks he has collected from around the world.

Goddard led the first expedition down the entire 4,200 miles of the Nile, the world's longest river -- a trip taking 10 months.

tion of "Chicken Soup for the Soul" that sold more than 12 million copies. Many of his experiences brought him adventures most of us will only read about in our lifetime. Among them:

• He climbed the Matterhorn during a blizzard so bad that not even the professional climbers would go along.

• He was bitten by a diamondback rattlesnake and lived.

• He retraced the route of Marco Polo.

• He fended off Hippos, crocodiles, a furious wart hog, and bloodsucking leeches in the Congo.

Goddard shows his movie camera to saucer-lipped warriors of Brazil's fierce Suya tribe.

• He has survived plane crashes, earthquakes, three rounds with quicksand, an appendicitis attack 200 miles from the nearest health-care facilities, and two near-drowning emergencies. He has faced death 38 times.

• He was the first to explore all 4,200 miles of the Nile River by kayak, and explored the length of the Congo by kayak.

• He was the youngest ever admitted to the Adventurer's Club of Los Angeles.

• He lived with 260 different tribal groups "from head-hunters of New Guinea, Borneo, ... to pygmies of Central Africa, to the hippies of Tempe," he says.

• He has climbed Mt. Ararat, Mt. Kilimanjaro, Mt. Fuji, Mt. Rainier, and the Grand Tetons.

Goddard visits natives during his trek to become the first man to explore the entire length of Africa's 2,700-mile-long Congo River.

• He has traveled to 120 countries, learned to fly a plane, and explored the underwater reefs of Florida, the Great Barrier Reef in Australia, the Red Sea, and more.

When asked which adventure has brought him the greatest joy, he says it has to be going through life with his wife and five children. (Author's interview)

Oldest Man to Row the Atlantic (2001 World Record). On Oct. 10, 2000, Richard Jones, a 57-year-old high priest from Sandy, Utah, embarked on the almost impossible goal of rowing solo across the Atlantic Ocean. His amazing trip of 4,579 miles took him 133 days, an average of almost 35 miles a day, and landed him in the world record books.

Beginning at Los Gigantes, Tenerife (among the Canary Islands, off the west coast of northern Africa), he tried to follow the same route Columbus took in 1492.

Brother Jones' home-made, high-tech rowboat was a sleek yellow torpedo aptly named "Brother of Jared." Jones had three sets of oars, the best food-storage supply

Richard Jones wasn't bashful about his Church membership, letting his hat and boat's name trigger probing questions from international press.

money could buy, and a desalinator to provide fresh water. Communication included a laptop computer with a satellite link for guidance and e-mail correspondence, and an emergency Coast Guard satellite beacon that could bring help from anyone in the vicinity.

Departure in the early dawn hours of Oct. 10, 2000.

The first few weeks quickly grew routine -- row hardest in the morning hours before sunup when the ocean was calm, take frequent breaks, take pictures and chart the day's progress, and stay in touch with home base.

At night he bundled inside his watertight compartment with a 500-pound seawater ballast that he hand-pumped in each night, and pumped out again in the morning to prevent his boat from rolling as he slept.

One night, when he was about 2,000 miles into the journey, his collision-proximity alarm jarred him from sleep. He inched his way to the door of his sleeping compartment and popped the hatch. He silenced the alarm and scanned the horizon. It was then he noticed that out towards the west the stars were blinking out. A giant black hole seemed to be swallowing them up from the horizon. Suddenly, he realized in a sickening panic that the growing black shadow was a ship plying directly towards him in stealthy silence. He quickly buckled the oars into the locks and rowed in a panic this way and then that, unable to tell exactly what direction the ship was moving. With the 500-pound ballast anchoring his progress, his pull on the oars was that

Courtesy Richard Jones

The Brother of Jared: 27 feet long, 1,100 pounds empty. Solar panels kept the batteries charged. The sleeping compartment with windows is on the right. His storage compartment that contained the wiring, battery and electrical system, cooking fuel and supplies is on the left. Jones had satellite communication gear, collision-avoidance radar, extra oars, a desalinator, a laptop computer, camera, food for six months, books, tapes and scriptures. E-mail him to learn more at www.mindspring.com/~kimball3/

Courtesy Richard Jones

Alone at sea for four and a half months.

much harder. He moved his craft far enough that when the massive ocean freighter finally churned by 60 feet away, he could almost feel the froth kicked in the air. "Had it hit, they would have never known. I would have been just a mysterious yellow streak on the bow," Jones said.

Another close encounter took place as Jones neared the western part of the Atlantic. Suddenly merging into view on his left was a huge U.S. Navy ship. He immediately grabbed for his radio and made contact. "Do you require assistance?" they radioed back. "No! Just don't hit me!" Jones called. In astonished respect he watched the seven-ship convoy of the USS John F. Kennedy aircraft-carrier battle group change course in a mighty arc to avoid The Brother of Jared. His presence in the middle of nowhere drew the respect of sailors who lined the rails of the various ships passing by, watching with binoculars in utter amazement.

Jones' trip ended a few hundred miles early when equipment failure and a storm forced him to call for help near Ragged Island,

Courtesy Lee Benson

Prayers answered: A grateful family embraces for the first time after 133 unrelenting days of work and worry.

Jones: Sea weary, weather worn, thinner, but alive.

one of about 700 islands in the Bahamas, about 60 miles off the southern tip of Florida. A local fisherman miraculously heard his emergency call for help and came to tow him in. A mishap during the tow nearly drowned Jones as his boat flipped over and flooded, ruining supplies, film, computers, and much more. Nevertheless, his trip put him in the record books as the oldest man (57) ever to row an ocean, the first American to row the entire Atlantic, and the first American to row an ocean towards his native land. (Author's Interview)

LIFESAVERS, SURVIVORS AND HEROES

Sam Cowley took five slugs from Baby Face Nelson's machine gun, but emptied his own into the murderer before collapsing.

"Bravest Man" in the FBI. "The bravest man I ever knew," FBI Director J. Edgar Hoover said, "was Samuel P. Cowley." Writing for Saga magazine in June 1952, Hoover continued, "When I say he was the bravest man I have ever known it is not because he shot it out with the cornered rat, (Baby Face) Nelson, nor yet because he directed the manhunt which trapped and finished that other public braggart, John Dillinger. ... Sam Cowley's courage was beyond heroics. He was brave enough to be scrupulously honest in little things as well as big things. He didn't accept the easy way out by a half-truth, a white lie or a turned head. ... That's the kind of courage that can carry a man proudly from the cradle to the grave." In 1934, Sam Cowley was mortally wounded in a blaze of gunfire between him, his partner, and Baby Face Nelson and his bodyguard. Cowley emptied his gun at Nelson, putting 17 slugs into him, and Cowley was left mortally wounded with a shot to the abdomin. He died shortly thereafter in a hospital, the bravest man J. Edgar Hoover ever knew. Learn more in *Sam Cowley*, by Richard L. Emery, CFI Books (www.cedarfort.com). (CN 5/28/52)

Not your typical fireside at the Little Rock 2nd Ward youth activity.

Deseret Morning News archives, Alex Brandon

Lifesaving Youths. LDS youths in the Little Rock, Arkansas, 2nd Ward were at the Stake Center, cleaning up after an activity, when someone noticed an adjoining nursing home was on fire. The youths and leaders immediately dashed to the nursing home and began evacuating the elderly patients, relocating them to the cultural hall in the Stake Center, until help arrived. By the time the fire fighters and police arrived, most of the patients were out and being attended to by several LDS young women. As television and radio began reporting the fire, LDS from all over the city descended on the Stake Center to help with food, blankets and other supplies. Said one elderly woman, "There's not anything better than going to a church to be saved." Firemen observed that many lives were preserved that night, thanks to the Little Rock LDS youth. "Little Rock is going to really sit up and take notice," one fire official joked, "the next time you Mormons have one of these firesides!" (CN 2/5/84)

Longest Wilderness Survival. Ralph Flores, San Bruno Ward, San Mateo, California, Stake, became an international hero after surviving 49 days in the icy Yukon when his plane crashed into a mountainside in a blinding snowstorm in 1963. His passenger, Helen Klaben, 21, also survived. The impact of the collision threw Brother Flores against the dashboard, dislocating his jaw and breaking his nose, cheekbone, two ribs and his sternum. His upper lip was ripped open. All he could do was to roll out of the wreckage and lie in the snow. When he discovered his jaw was dislocated, he put a stick in his mouth to reset it. Miss Klaben suffered a broken arm but otherwise was all right. In the first four days, they consumed their supply of food that consisted of two cans of sardines, two cans of fruit cocktail, and one package of crackers. For the remaining 45 days they lived on nothing but melted snow. They tried but failed to catch wildlife with slings, arrows and traps. One day, after much prayer, Brother Flores promised his Jewish companion that, if she would read the Bible cover to cover, God would send them help. Flores determined from his maps that a highway lay about 65 miles away, a hike that would take him through waist-deep snow over rugged terrain. As a last desperate act to escape their frozen encampment, he headed off to find help. On March 24, 1963, as Helen finished the very last page in the Bible, a search plane appeared overhead and spotted the 70-foot tall "SOS" that Flores had tramped sometime earlier in a frozen swamp. Flores returned to camp and a dog-sled rescue team arrived the next day and the pair became overnight celebrities. A movie was made of the incident some years later. After their rescue, Flores was able to complete his trip to California where he, his wife and six children went to the temple to be sealed as a family. (CN 4/13/63)

Michelle fully recovered.

Longest Drowned. In June 1986, 2-1/2 year-old Michelle Funk fell into a stream near her Sandy, Utah, home and lay submerged until she was found by rescuers some 66 minutes later. Emergency life-saving procedures resuscitated her and kept her alive while she was transported to a hospital. After a long stay at Primary Children's Hospital, Michelle made a complete recovery with no permanent brain damage. Doctors attributed her survival to the 40-degree water temperature, and the lowering of her body temperature to 68 degrees. Her parents give credit to someone else who knew it wasn't little Michelle's time. Michelle and her family were members of the Granite 4th Ward, Sandy, Utah. (CN 8/29/87)

Enduring a Fatal Disability. In 1974, Dean L. Miller, Hyrum, Utah, established an amazing world record in addition to an amazing record for the disabled. When Brother Miller turned 26, he became the world's longest living survivor of infantile muscular atrophy. But that's not what impressed fellow college and Church members. Also in 1974, Miller graduated magna cum laude from Utah State University with a master's degree in speech and audiology. And he accomplished this difficult feat with so little strength that he spent all his time in a wheelchair, too weak to feed himself, open a book or even turn a page. (CN 6/1/74)

An Act of Forgiveness. On April 18, 1962, 22-year-old April Aaron (Dodd) got off a San Francisco bus on her way to a youth dance at her LDS chapel. When only one block away from the church, a knife-wielding purse-snatcher attacked her, slashing her arms, legs, throat and face, and put out her right eye. For weeks Bay-area newspapers kept readers up to date on April's condition, calling for police to capture the "madman" who "viciously slashed" the "sweet and pretty Mormon girl." But when she told reporters from her hospital bed that she had forgiven the man for his crime against her, the story went nationwide. UPI reporter Neal Corbett wrote that her "compassion could not be damaged by the sharp edge of an assailant's weapon." Her story was included in Spencer W. Kimball's classic, "Miracle of Forgiveness." Said April of the incident some eight years later, "It isn't any easier for me to forgive than it is for anyone else ... But with the Lord's help, along with a little nudge from President Kimball, I'm going to keep trying to measure up." The assailant was never caught. (CN 11/8/80)

April Aaron (Dodd) looks over clippings from around the world praising her ability to forgive after a horrible personal attack.

With fewer than half a million members when Reed Smoot (left) took office as senator, LDS were viewed with a degree of suspicion by the uninformed. Today, the Church has proven its winning formula with strong families, trustworthy leaders and brilliant contributors and creatives now striving to build a peaceful world. Some of the unheralded pioneers of the Church included people like Reed Smoot and another pioneer, Ab Jenkins (right), soon to be the world renowned record holder of dozens of automotive races – two more examples of 'every member a missionary' helping to build *The Church*.

Photo: Deseret News file photo

The Church

The LDS Church, by the numbers.

1— Hijacked general authority

2— Average number of minutes between new-member baptisms

20 — Number of nationalities attending the Geneva Ward in Switzerland

85 — Years, longest streak of unbroken 100 percent home teaching by one man

180 — Record tonnage of grapes produced by a Church-owned vineyard

13,000 — Miles between Salt Lake City and the farthest-removed ward

FREQUENCY

About every two minutes, someone joins the LDS Church. At the rate the Church has been growing over the past 150 years, roughly 30 percent per decade, there could be 60 million Mormons by the year 2080. But since WWII, the rate of growth has been 50 percent per decade. At that rate, there would be 265 million LDS by 2080. (LDS 12/20/88)

MEMBERSHIP

After it was organized in 1830, growth in the Church was steady but slow. Its membership roll reached the first half million in 1919. After that, things began to accelerate.

1 million in 1947
2 million in 1963
3 million in 1971
4 million in 1978
5 million in 1982
6 million in 1986
7 million in 1989
8 million in 1991
9 million in 1994
10 million in 1997
11 million in 2000
12 million in 2004

Early International Roots. At the close of 1847, there were more members of the Church living in the British Isles than in the settlements of Salt Lake City, Winter Quarters, Mt. Pisgah, Garden Grove, Lee County, and the states of Illinois, Missouri and California combined. (CN 8/22/48)

Busiest Church. The LDS Church takes the cake as the busiest Church in the world with approximately 5,500,000 non-paying Church jobs filled by its 12 million members. This estimate is based on a more thorough study completed in 1960 when it was found approximately every-other member holds one Church job. This ratio doesn't reflect the fact that many members hold more than one job. (CN 12/31/60; Author)

Mormonism: Newest Major Religion. Dr. Rodney Stark, professor of sociology of religion at the University of Washington, said the Mormon Church is on the threshold of being recognized as the first new major world religion since Mohammed started the Moslem religion. "If Mormons hold a 30 percent growth rate per decade, they will have more than 63 million members by the year 2080," Stark predicted in 1982. "Mormon growth has gone unnoticed by people outside the Church," he said. As of 2004, the Church continues to hold its place as fifth largest in the U.S. with about 5,210,000 members. The four larger denominations in the U.S. are the Roman Catholics (63,683,000), Southern Baptists (15,960,000), United Methodists (8,341,000), and the Church of God in Christ (5,500,000). (www.adherents.com)

Mormons in the United States. There are approximately 5,210,000 members of the Church in the United States. Mormons in Utah constitute the largest religious majority in any state at 74.7 percent. The next closest is North Dakota at 73.2 percent (Lutheran). LDS are also the most "active" among Christian church-goers in the United States In a poll taken by Barna Research Group (Ventura, California) in 2000-2001, LDS respondents said they went to church once a week 71 percent of the time. The next highest were members of the Assemblies of God at 69 percent. Least active were Episcopal/Anglican and Congregationalists, all at 30 percent. (CN 5/5/91; www.adherents.com)

Mormons Worldwide. Some time during the month of February 1996, a major milestone was reached when Church membership outside of the United States exceeded that within. In the spring of 1996, there were 4.719 million members in the United States, and 4.72 million outside the United States (Almanac; SLTrib 2/10/96)

Fastest Growing Area. Where is the Church's hot spot for growth? In 1985, it was Santo Domingo, Dominican Republic. Beginning with no members in 1979, the area experienced 8,000 baptisms, averaging more than 200 per month from 1979-1985. On a per capita basis, this record-breaking pace was the highest of anywhere in the Church. The ratio of U.S. to Dominican missionaries was also quite large, with 51 Dominicans and 89 Americans serving full time in the country in 1985. (CN 8/25/85)

PROPHETS, GENERAL AUTHORITIES

The first prophet and president of the LDS Church was Joseph Smith Jr. He was sustained at age 24 as First Elder of the Church on April 6, 1830. On Jan. 25, 1832, he was sustained as president of the High Priesthood at age 26. As of 2004, a total of 15 men had served as president of the Church, and almost 100 men had served on the Quorum of the Twelve.

Longest Serving Latter-day Prophet.
The longest reign as prophet was Brigham Young, who died at age 76, having served as president, prophet, seer and revelator of the Church for 29 years and 8 months.

Shortest Serving Latter-day Prophet.
Shortest term as president of the Church was that of Howard W. Hunter, who died at age 87, having served nine months.

Longest Serving Apostle/Prophet.
President David O. McKay holds the record with service as a general authority and president that extended 63 years nine months.

Brigham Young, longest serving prophet.

Oldest General Authority.
The oldest general authority was Joseph Anderson who lived 102 years 113 days. Called to be secretary to the First Presidency in 1922, Elder Anderson was given emeritus status in 1979. "I've been nearly 67 years with the Brethren," Elder Anderson said at the time, "and there are not better men anywhere. I've loved them all, and they've loved me, I hope. There isn't a one of them I haven't admired greatly." Beginning in 1922, Elder Anderson served for seven of the Church's 13 presidents who led the Church during his lifetime. Elder Anderson passed away March 13, 1992. (Author's interview; LDS 12/24/88; CN 3/21/92)

Joseph Anderson took emeritus status at age 88 and lived 14 more years.

Hugh Cannon (left camel) and David O. McKay had a tie for every occasion.

Photo: Deseret Morning News file photo

First to Tour All the Missions. In 1920, President Heber J. Grant called Hugh J. Cannon, editor of the Improvement Era, and Elder David O. McKay to tour the missions of the Church. President Grant wanted them to assess the conditions of the missionary work around the globe. On Dec. 6, 1920, the two men left Ogden and traveled to Vancouver. From there, they sailed to Japan, China, Hawaii, and then back to San Francisco. After a couple of weeks' delay, the two sailed again, this time for Tahiti, New Zealand, Fiji, Tonga, Samoa, Australia, Java, Singapore, Burma, Calcutta, Bombay, and then to the Arabian Peninsula. While in the Middle East they toured Egypt, the Red Sea, the Suez Canal, Cairo and the Holy Land. Europe was next with stops in Germany, Switzerland, Belgium, The Netherlands, Scotland and England. By the time they returned to the United States, they had sailed every ocean but the Arctic Ocean, and crossed the equator three times. They arrived at their homes physically exhausted but exhilarated on Christmas Day 1921. They had traveled 62,000 miles in a year and 19 days. (DN 1/19/70)

Boring Train Ride. In 1938, when President George Albert Smith visited members in the Nullarbor District, Australia, as part of his 10,000-mile tour of Australia, he traveled 334 miles on a straight stretch of track that had not even a bit of curve in it. (CN 8/8/48)

President Kimball's Space-Age Mike. The tiny, sophisticated piece of equipment almost always attached to President Spencer W. Kimball's glasses was a spinoff of equipment used to put men on the moon. The tiny microphone was a pre-amplifier used to pick up the prophet's voice and amplify it before it went into the public address systems of the Salt Lake Tabernacle or other facilities where he spoke. Tests showed this was less stressful and offered better results for President Kimball, after his throat surgery, than a podium microphone. (CN 8/23/75)

Deseret Morning News file photo

Upon returning from surgery to treat cancer of the larynx, Pres. Kimball joked during General Conference: "I traveled back east and fell among cutthroats."

Longest Serving Personal Secretary to Prophets. Perhaps the closest friend to more prophets than any other person, D. Arthur Haycock served as personal secretary to seven presidents of the Church – Heber J. Grant, George Albert Smith, David O. McKay, Joseph Fielding Smith, Harold B. Lee, Spencer W. Kimball and Ezra Taft Benson. He wrote of these experiences in "In the Company of Prophets," published by Deseret Book. (LDS 3/23/85; CN 1/8/84; CN 1/19/86)

Most Deaths Witnessed. The person to accompany the most Prophets at the time of their deaths is D. Arthur Haycock who was at the side of George Albert Smith, Joseph Fielding Smith and Harold B. Lee when they died. Observing his association with the brethren at the time of their passing, he later quipped, "I'm not sure anybody wants to be alone with me anymore." (LDS 3/23/85)

Don Grayston, Deseret Morning News

Brother Haycock was loved and trusted for his devotion and integrity by the latter-day prophets and apostles for whom he served.

Longest-Serving Apostle Without Becoming President. Franklin D. Richards served 50 years and 10 months, the longest without becoming president of the Church. He was called as an apostle on Feb. 12, 1849, and served until his death Dec. 9, 1899. (CN 3/7/87)

Brother Morris was ordained at age 80.

Oldest Man Ordained an Apostle. George Q Morris was ordained an apostle on April 8, 1954, at age 80 years and 2 months. (Church Almanac)

Youngest Man Ordained an Apostle. John Willard Young became the youngest apostle when he was ordained at age 19 years and 4 months. on Feb. 4, 1864. (Church Almanac)

Most Children by General Authorities. The modern-day general authorities with the most children are Elders John H. Groberg and the late H. Verlan Andersen, with 11 children each. Four other active and released general authorities had 10 children each.

No Spanish translator needed for Elder Scott's 1989 Conference talk.

First Foreign Language General Conference Talk. The first general authority to give a non-English General Conference speech from Salt Lake City was Elder Richard G. Scott, who spoke in Spanish for his April 1989 General Conference sermon. The Spanish version was pre-taped and aired to Spanish speaking Saints in Arizona. Says Elder Scott, "The most difficult part was keeping it timed so when I finished in English, there wouldn't be any time lag until the taped Spanish version ended." (Author)

First Conference in Russian. The first Church conference conducted in the Russian language (as far as is known) was held in Nice, France, Jan. 16, 1954. Elder Andre K. Anastasion, a missionary in southern France, spoke on "What is Mormonism?" to 36 people. The film strip, "In the Tops of the Mountains," was presented and explained in

Russian. The conference concluded with repeated applause and a request for another conference. (CN 2/20/54)

Meeting of the Twelve on Foreign Soil. The unusual meeting of a majority of the Twelve Apostles outside of the United States took place on April 14, 1840, in Preston, England. The occasion was the ordination of Willard Richards as an apostle. In attendance were seven of the brethren: Brigham Young, Heber C. Kimball, Parley P. Pratt, Orson Pratt, Wilford Woodruff, John Taylor and George A. Smith. This was the meeting where Elder Brigham Young was unanimously sustained as president of the Council of the Twelve Apostles. (CN 8/22/48)

Largest Christmas Card. In 1986, President Ezra Taft Benson was surprised with an enormous 507-square-foot Christmas Card covered with greetings from thousands of BYU students. The scroll had been placed in the Wilkinsen Center for students to sign. It was also decorated with drawings from the scriptures depicting the birth and life of Jesus Christ. The scroll was three feet wide and 160 feet long. (DN 12/28/86)

Largest Happy Birthday Greeting. When President Gordon B. Hinckley turned 90, he gave a gift to the members of the Church – a televised evening filled with music and performances at the Church's Salt Lake Conference Center. The 22,000 on hand couldn't help but break out into "Happy Birthday" as he entered the hall. The celebration was broadcast to thousands, perhaps the largest birthday celebration in the Church.

Tom Smart, Deseret Morning News

BYU President Jeffrey R. Holland and other university representatives present this massive Christmas card scroll covered with thousands of greetings.

First General Authority Plane Trip. The same year George Albert Smith became an apostle, the Wright brothers made their first flight (1903). Some 17 years later, President Smith finally had the chance to fly. He took a plane over the English Channel in 1920, becoming the first General Authority ever to use an airplane for transportation. (CN 1/12/80)

'Missing in Action' When Called. The first appointee to the Quorum of the Twelve in modern Church history to be absent when his calling was announced and sustained was Elder Dallin H. Oaks in 1984. He had been excused to fulfill an obligation out of state. (LDS 4/13/84)

Last of the First. Orson Pratt was the last survivor of the original Council of the Twelve Apostles chosen in 1835. He died at age 70 in 1881, four years after Brigham Young's death. (CN 8/8/48)

O. Wallace Kasteler, Deseret Morning News

Elder Bennett's biggest worry during the hijacking: "Get me to the church on time."

First Hijacked. Elder William H. Bennett, an assistant to the Twelve in 1972, was on his way to the Newport Beach Stake in Los Angeles when the Western Airlines 737 he was in was hijacked. The plane's crew was forced to make refueling stops in Los Angeles, Dallas, and Miami before finally landing in Havana, Cuba. Elder Bennett says Cuban military officers boarded the plane to check that everyone was OK, and then gave permission for the plane to return to the US. Elder Bennett arrived in California in time to speak to the stake. (CN 5/12/72)

First Utah-Born Apostle. Heber J. Grant, born Nov. 22, 1856, was ordained a member of the Council of Twelve on October 16, 1882, becoming the first Utah-born apostle. As a six-year-old, he unknowingly hitched a ride on the back of Brigham Young's wagon one wintery day. And then 56 years later, Elder Grant found himself following once again in Brigham's path as he became president of the Church on Nov. 23, 1918. He died May 14, 1945. (CN 5/6/61)

Only Apostle Ordained in England. April 14, 1840, in Preston, England, seven of the Twelve Apostles together placed their hands on the head of Willard Richards and ordained him an apostle and a member of the Council of the Twelve. Present on that day were Brigham Young, Heber C.

Kimball, Parley P. Pratt, Orson Pratt, Wilford Woodruff, George A. Smith, and John Taylor. (CN 8/9/58)

Last Person Who Met Joseph Smith. Before her death in 1943 in Ogden, Utah, Mary Field Garner was thought to be the last living soul who personally knew the Prophet Joseph Smith. She had seen and heard him as a young girl. Shortly after Smith's 1844 martyrdom, Sister Garner recalled attending a meeting in the bowery to listen to Brigham Young address the Saints. She recorded in her diary that she was on her mother's knee and accidently dropped a tin cup. As her mother stooped to pick it up and was momentarily distracted, they both suddenly heard the voice of Joseph. They looked up and saw the form of Joseph standing before the crowd. From that time on she had no doubt, she wrote, that Brigham Young was to be their new leader. (CN 8/3/57)

Last Surviving Child of Brigham Young. Mrs. Mabel Y. Sanborn, 87, the last surviving child of President Brigham Young, died Sept. 20, 1950. One of her last public appearances was in Washington, D.C., on June 1, 1950, where she unveiled the statue of her father which now stands in Statuary Hall in the Capitol. She was one of the last links with Utah's pioneer era. (CN 9/27/50)

First Martyr To The Cause. On Nov. 4, 1833, a group of drunken mobsters in Independence, Missouri, attacked the homes of some of the Saints, throwing rocks through windows and climbing on the roofs and tearing off shingles. When the men of the homes emerged, mobsters in hiding seized them and whipped them while wives and children were left alone in the

Mabel Y. Sanborn (left) and Fannie Y. Clayton, the last two surviving children of Brigham Young, shown here at the 1949 Railroad Fair in Chicago.

darkness to fear for their safety. After one group chased several LDS men through the streets, a plea for help was issued and a rescue group of 30 Saints quickly assembled at Colesville Branch, about three miles away. When the mob, now 45-50 men strong, saw the Mormon company coming, they discharged their weapons into the Mormon group. The Mormons returned the fire. Two men from the mob were killed and two Mormon men seriously wounded. Philo Dibble survived his wound but Andrew Barber died the next day, Nov. 5, 1833. The so-called Battle of Big Blue River further inflamed the local residents' hatred of the Saints, and participants in the battle had to flee for refuge in Clay County with the rest of the Missouri Saints. (CN 6/13/59)

Most Prophets Personally Greeted. At age 100 in 1970, Matilda Andrus, St. George, Utah, could lay claim to having personally shaken hands with more Church presidents than any other person: John Taylor, Wilford Woodruff, Lorenzo Snow, Joseph F. Smith, Heber J. Grant, George Albert Smith, David O. McKay, and Joseph Fielding Smith. Her biggest regret? Not having met Joseph Smith or Brigham Young. (CN 10/10/70)

STAKES

The Church of Jesus Christ of Latter-day Saints offers leadership and direction from the top down. All leadership is sustained from the bottom up. Leaders are voted upon by the affected membership. Local units of the Church are called groups, branches or wards, depending on their size. When any group reaches ward status, it typically has 300 to 500 members, although some wards are much smaller. When a geographically close area has 2-3 wards or more, a stake is formed. A stake is led by a president, a first and second counselor, secretaries, and a high council.

The first stake was organized in Kirtland, Ohio, on Feb. 17, 1834, with Joseph Smith Jr. serving as its first stake president. The first high council was organized the same day.

From these organizations come an assortment of amazing firsts, facts and feats.

THE MOST ORGANIZED/DIVIDED

Most In One Year: is it 1980, when 126 new stakes were created?

Most In One Month: November 1975 and May 1978 when 23 were created each month.

Most In One Day: Nov. 9, 1975 and Jan. 31, 1988, ten each.

Most In One Place: Ten – On Sept. 15, 1985, six stakes were formed in four days and a couple of weeks later four more stakes were formed over a weekend, all in Manila, Philippines. (CN 9/15/85)

Most Divided: the most stakes divided in a single weekend occurred Jan. 30-31, 1988, when 11 stakes became 18 in Lima, Peru.

The 1,000th Stake. The 1,000th stake in the Church was created in

Nauvoo, Illinois, on Feb 18, 1979. (Church Almanac 1989-90)

The 2,000th Stake. The 2,000th stake was created in Mexico City by President Hunter on Dec. 11, 1994. (Church Almanac 2001-02)

The First Non-English Speaking Stake. The Hague, Netherlands, Stake was created March 12, 1961, becoming the first non-English stake in the world and also the first Church stake on the European continent. (CN 3/9/86)

First Country Outside of the U.S. With 100 Stakes. Mexico organized its 100th stake, the Tecalco Mexico Stake, on June 25, 1989. (CN 7/1/89).

First Spanish Stake in the United States. Seven Spanish wards in Los Angeles were organized into the first Spanish stake in the United States, June 3, 1984, under the name Huntington Park West Stake. (LDS 6/23/84)

First Stake Behind the Iron Curtain. The first stake organized behind the so-called Iron Curtain (region of Europe dominated by the Soviet Union during the Cold War) was the Freiburg, German Democratic Republic, Stake, in the DDR (East Germany). It had 1,881 members when it was organized on Aug. 29, 1982. (LDS 9/ /82)

Last State to Get a Stake. With the dedication of the Fargo, North Dakota, Stake on Aug. 7, 1977, all 50 states in the United States had a stake center within its boundaries. The Fargo Stake was the 852nd to be organized in the Church. "This is a very historic day," Elder Boyd K. Packer said. "The tapestry is complete; the last piece is in place." (CN 8/12/77)

Longest Father-Son Succession in a Stake Presidency. The longest tenure of office as stake president by a father and son began Sept. 30, 1878, in the Eastern, Arizona, Stake when Jesse N. Smith was named stake president. He continued on in his calling, even after the stake was divided, for some 28 years until his death in June 8, 1906. He was succeeded by his son, Samuel F. Smith, who became stake president Feb. 11, 1907. Samuel served until July 2, 1939, a period of 32 years. In total, 60 years of service was rendered by the father and son. (CN 9/29/45)

Most Children – Stake Presidency. Can any stake presidency top this? The Union stake presidency of the Pendleton, Oregon, Stake boasted in 1954 that it had 26 children in the families of the presidency ranging in age from two months to 12 years. President Milan D. Smith had nine, First Counselor Vern L. Nebeker and Second Counselor Ernest C. Anderson each had six, and stake clerk Henry H. Stoddard had five. (CN 10/30/54)

First Stake President – East India. Gurcharan S. Gill, a native of Punjab in northern India and a BYU professor when called, is not only the first eastern Indian to be a stake president, but also the first to be so assigned without having served as bishop first. President Gill was called to head the BYU 6th Stake in 1976. (CN 10/30/78)

Oldest/Longest-Serving High Priest. Manasseh Julius Blackburn, 106 (in 1984), Vale 1st Ward, Nyssa, Oregon, Stake, could well have been the oldest and longest serving high priest in the Church. He was ordained a high priest in 1903 and held that priesthood for more than 81 years. (CN 1984)

Deseret Morning News file photo

Oldest and Youngest High Priests. The record for the youngest and oldest High Priests in the same stake was claimed by the Kolob, Utah, Stake in 1956 where Alma Jensen, 22, and James B. Burrows, 95, were members of the stake high priests' quorum – an age difference of 73 years. (CN 5/5/56)

An age difference of 73 years, the most in any stake?

WARDS & BISHOPS

A bishop's role in the LDS Church is to look after the physical and spiritual welfare of his ward. He is president of the ward's Aaronic priesthood members and provides organizational direction for all auxiliary groups. For a Church unit not yet a ward, a branch president or group leader is responsible for the same duties.

First Bishop. Edward Partridge, baptized by the Prophet Joseph Smith Dec. 11, 1830, was ordained an elder by Sidney Rigdon just days after his baptism. On Feb. 3, 1831, the prophet received a revelation directed to Edward Partridge: "And again, I have called my servant Edward Partridge, and I give a commandment that he should be appointed, by the voice of the Church, and ordained a bishop unto the Church. ..." (D&C 41:9). Broken in health from the trials he had endured from the mobs in Missouri, he died in Nauvoo May 27, 1840, at age 47. (CN 5/7/55)

All-Brother Bishopric. The only known all-family bishopric in the Church existed in the Montgomery family in 1950. Serving in various wards in Utah, the foursome made up a complete ward leadership quartet: Rollan was bishop of the Taylor Ward, Leland was first counselor in the Clinton Ward, and Anthon was second counselor in the Clearfield 1st Ward where younger brother Faunt served as assistant ward clerk. (CN 12/13/50)

Same-day Father-son Bishop Callings. Who can claim the first father-son bishop callings on the same day in the Church? On June 12, 1988, Eugene Brassfield was made bishop over the Buena Park 1st Ward, and on the same day his son, G. Gary Brassfield, was made bishop of the Buena Park 2nd Ward in the same stake as his father. The stake clerk almost went crazy because both men were known as Bishop G. Brassfield.

The First Blind Bishop. Was Ron Miyashiro, Nuuana Ward, Hawaii, Honolulu West Stake, the first blind bishop in the Church? He was called as bishop in 1988. He had been blind all his life, the result of an optic nerve that never developed. He was introduced to the Church in 1964 by Gail Kobayahi whom he met at the Church College of Hawaii, in what he describes as "a real blind date." They were subsequently married. Signing temple recommends was done using a template with cutouts over the signature areas. A gifted pianist, he played the organ in the Salt Lake Tabernacle and was in high demand for performances on the Hawaiian Islands. A tape of his patriotic music flew into space Jan. 24-27, 1985, aboard the space shuttle Discovery. (LDS 1989)

Same Wedding Date. The only bishopric in the Church known to share the same wedding anniversary was in the Lake Ridge 2nd Ward, Utah. On October 10, 1966, Bishop and Mrs. George J. Beagley observed their 20th anniversary; First Counselor Merle Wilkey and his wife observed their 21st anniversary; and Second Counselor Carl Crawford and his wife observed their 38th anniversary. The wives were all in the Relief Society presidency. (CN 11/5/66)

Oldest Bishop. Who is the oldest acting bishop in the Church? In 1976, it was 84-year-old Harold H. Cutler, 8th Ward, Salt Lake Liberty Stake. His first calling as bishop came in 1970. (CN 1/31/76)

Youngest Bishop. Who is the youngest bishop in the Church? In 1973, it was Almir S. Dutra, age 21, who was ordained bishop by Mark E. Peterson at the Sao Leopoldo Ward, Porto Alegre, Brazil, Stake. He had been a convert four years at the time. His ward's membership stood at about 300 when he was made bishop. (CN 5/12/73)

Longest Serving Bishop. Elijah Sheets, a native of Pennsylvania, a convert to the Church, and a laborer on the Nauvoo Temple, was the bishop of the 8th Ward in Salt Lake City for 48 years, the longest active bishop in the Church. Three weeks after his release on June 12, 1904, he died while visiting a son in Rexburg, Idaho. (CN 7/9/55)

Most Father-Son Bishops at Same Time. In 1970, Van Ness Wallentine was being released as bishop at about the same time that his three sons served as bishops in their respective wards: Max in the Salem 2nd Ward, Spanish Fork, Utah; Robert in the Mantua Ward, Box Elder, Utah; and C. Booth in the Des Moines, Iowa, Ward. (CN 11/21/70)

Most Brother Bishops at Same Time. In 1973, the four Hills boys were serving as bishops in their respective wards. Dennis L. was bishop in the Orem 6th Ward, North Orem, Utah, Stake. Garth A. was bishop in the Butler 5th Ward, Butler, Utah, Stake. Lee R. was bishop in the Spanish Fork 13th Ward, Spanish Fork, Utah, Stake. And Farrell J. was bishop in his Pleasant Green 3rd Ward, Oquirrh, Utah, Stake. (CN 2/17/73)

Deseret Morning News file photo

Brother Hua's admiring branch members called him the 90-year-old miracle.

Oldest Serving Branch President. Who was the oldest branch president in the Church? In 1993, it was 90-year-old President Huang Hsi Hua of the Pei Tou Branch in Taiwan. Baptized at age 70, President Huang's love for his branch had brought many inactive members back to regular and renewed activity in the Church. The resulting increase in membership required their branch meetinghouse to be enlarged. President Huang was the first to arrive at Church on Sunday and the last to leave. He was also a regular and faithful temple goer. (CN 2/20/93)

Longest Serving Branch President. In 1974, Godfrey Olson, Bergland Branch, Ontario, Canada, was released as branch president after serving 38 years. His prior calling was second counselor in the same branch, a position he held for 10 years. Brother Olson was one of the first members in the area and donated an acre of land and the timber to build the Bergland chapel. After 38 years in the same calling, Olson commented, "This was a period of time full of blessings that money can't buy." (CN 2/2/74)

Farthest Branch from Salt Lake City. The unit of the Church most distant from Salt Lake City is the Albany Branch, Manjimup, Western Australia, District, some 13,000 miles away as the wombat flies (they don't fly, except in airplanes). Resting on the southernmost tip of Western Australia, the branch sits on a peninsula bounded on three sides by the Antarctic Ocean. Founded in 1969, the branch had grown to about 100 active members by 1979. (CN 7/21/79)

Smallest Ward. In 1961, the smallest ward in the Church was the Lynn Ward, Raft River Utah, Stake, with only 32 members on the rolls when a new bishopric was called. (CN 10/14/61)

Highest Branch. In 1985, the highest regularly-meeting branch in the Church was in the high mountains of Potosi, Bolivia, at 14,714 feet above sea level. Another branch in Suriquina, Bolivia, wasn't much lower at 14,173 feet above sea level, had some 150 members, most of them Aymara Indians, who tended to their Church business at the nose-bleed height of 14,000 feet above sea level. Their village was 80 percent LDS. (CN 10/27/85)

Highest Chapel. Is the branch chapel built in the heart of the Andes Mountains in Hopuepala, Peru, in 1960 the highest in the Church at 9,000 feet above sea level? (CN 1/17/59)

Most Expansive Branch. In 1987, the Port Hedland Branch, Port Hedland, Australia, encompassed more than 266,000 square miles -- perhaps the largest region covered by a branch in the Church. (CN 8/22/87)

Coming in second place at 52,500 square miles is the Fort St. John Branch of the Canada, Calgary, Mission. Its boundaries extended 350 miles by 150 miles. Because of the distances involved, an elder 250 miles from the branch chapel was authorized to conduct Sunday services among members in that area. The branch president said that, when some boys in his branch were called on missions, they had to travel 130 miles for their pre-mission medical and dental exams. (CN 12/4/76)

In 1970, President John M. Lobley of the Australia West Gippsland Branch, Moe, Victoria, Australia, put more than 1,600 miles on his car each month to visit the remote ends of his branch that covered 6,000 square miles. (CN 3/21/70)

Most Awkward Trip to Church in the United States. Who has the toughest time going to stake conference? In the United States, the only known Church members who must travel through parts of three states and into another time zone to attend stake meetings live in the five wards in Mesquite and Bunkerville, Nevada. In 1988, the LDS in those two communities had to cut through Arizona into Utah and set their watches forward an hour. (LDS 11/12/88)

Most Difficult Trip to Regional Conference. In 1970, servicemen and their families in the Athens Branch, Athens, Greece, had to travel 1,000 miles to attend the annual LDS Servicemen's Conference in the German Alps. The long trip to Berchiesgarden, Germany, was a yearly pilgrimage for the 20 families in the Athens Branch. And after the conference, it was 1,000 miles back home. (CN11/7/90)

Most Mobile Ward. The only 100 percent mobile ward in the Church is the Kanesville 3rd Ward, Hooper, Utah, Stake. All ward members live in the Carol Estates Mobile Home Park near the Ogden airport, and are within ten minutes walking distance of each other. While the members meet in a stationary ward house, the bishop points out, "It's the only ward surrounded with a chain link fence and with the bishop living near the gate."

Illustration and photo courtesy of the Utah State Historical Society

The Salt Lake City First Ward building as it appeared in 1849 (above). It served as both a ward house and a school until 1854. The Salt Lake City Second Ward (right) was more typical of the earliest chapels built in the mid- to late-1800s.

Oldest Wards. The first wards organized in the Church that continue functioning are those Brigham Young set up in Salt Lake City in 1849. In February of that year, he divided the city into nine-block areas, declared each one a ward and numbered them from 1 to 19. Over time, the various wards were divided, renumbered or renamed. (CN 2/9/74)

Most Divided Ward. No, not "divided" as in angry with each other, but divided because of size! The Bear Lake Ward, Garden City, Utah, has the unique standing of being the most divided ward in the Church. Each summer, when huge vacation crowds swell Bear Lake Ward's ranks from less than 200 to more than 1,700, the ward is divided. Those vacationing on the north side of Bear Lake are asked to meet in Paris, Idaho, and those vacationing to the south meet at the Garden City chapel. Overflow is directed to nearby Laketown. (CN 6/26/82)

Longest Without a Meetinghouse? For 100 years, Horsefly, British Colombia, went without a church meetinghouse until LDS Church members finally built one in 1981. The isolated logging community of 500 had 42 members with a 95-percent activity rate when their new building was dedicated. Settled during the gold rush days in the 1870s and '80s, the community was first called Harper's Camp, but residents decided to rename it after the large and troublesome flies buzzing in the area. (CN 1981)

Church members in remote Horsefly, British Columbia ended a 100-year wait when they finally got their building in 1981.

Oldest Branch. In 1986, the Mahu Branch in Tahiti became the oldest in the Church that had not yet become a ward. It was organized by Addison Pratt in April 1844, and was also the first branch in the Pacific Islands. (CN 6/15/86)

Oldest Chapel – World. Built in 1687 in Hannoverisch, Munden, Germany, a 275-year-old building became the oldest LDS chapel in the world when it was dedicated in 1962. A sign over the door dated 1775 tells of a former occupant, George Grotfend, who was famous for being one of the original deciphering experts of ancient cuneiform script. (CN 12/8/62)

Oldest Chapel – United States. The Bountiful Tabernacle, dedicated March 14, 1863, is the oldest building in America that is still used by the Church as a regular meetinghouse. It underwent a $1 million restoration in 1976. (CN 11/29/75)

Oldest Chapel – Florida. The Oak Grove Branch was the first to build a permanent LDS meetinghouse in Florida. Organized in 1898, the branch moved around from schoolhouse to members' homes until the little Church building was finished in 1907. Though remodeled a couple of times, it still retains its turn-of-the-century character and look. (CN 3/6/76)

Oldest Chapel – Southeast United States. As of 1984, the oldest standing LDS meeting-house in the southeastern United States, outside of Florida, was the Northcutts Cove Chapel, Tennessee, dedicated Oct. 24, 1909. The building's interior is unchanged from the day it was dedicated – still heated by the original cast-iron wood stove that stands in the middle of the 20-by-40-foot room. Two large kerosene chandeliers and several small wall-hung kerosene lamps give the chapel its only lighting. Today the chapel is used only for special occasions. (CN 10/84)

Deseret Morning News file photo

LDS working on the first atomic bomb met for Church services at the residence of Eldred G. Smith.

Most Secretive Branch in the World. Until March 1949, the gates to America's atomic city at Oak Ridge, Tennessee, were closed to the public and special passes were required for admittance. Secrecy was necessary as this was the birth place for the atomic bombs invented during World War II. In nearly 1,000 days, a city of 75,000 people was built, the fifth largest in Tennessee. The city of 10,000 houses and apartments, 13,000 dormitory spaces, some 5,000 trailers and more than 16,000 barracks spaces, included several LDS. They met in the home of Eldred G. Smith, who became the first branch president when a branch was formed in April 1944. The branch flourished as new members and converts joined the ranks. As it grew in membership, LDS soon moved their meeting place to the Elm Grove School. When World War II ended, and many bomb specialists were released, the branch dwindled and became a Sunday School. Most of its members returned to their homes in other states. As the bomb effort was resumed at other locations, Oak Ridge dwindled in size and importance. (CN 1/29/50; CN 4/10/65; author's interview with Bro. Smith)

The Most Persistent. The "most persistent" unit in all the Church must be the village of Huacuyo, Bolivia, high in the Andes Mountains. In June 1976, a letter from Huacuyo arrived at the Bolivia, La Paz, Mission, signed with the thumb prints of 100 villagers. They wanted the missionaries to come and baptize them. Skeptical at first, the mission was slow to send elders on the six-hour four-wheel-drive trip into this obscure village. But a second letter arrived repeating the plea that missionaries be sent. As it turned out, the villagers had somehow obtained a copy of the Book of Mormon, had gained a testimony of it, and had built a chapel of adobe walls with a tin roof in which to worship. The missionaries finally arrived and spent their first two weeks teaching the standard missionary lessons. Then they baptized the first group of 36 in the icy waters of a nearby river. Two weeks later, 23 more were baptized, and by May of 1977, 96 had been baptized – every person who was eight or older. With only two baptismal outfits, members had to slide into the wet, cold clothing of the previous person, while the elders took turns thawing out during the three-hour baptismal sessions. (CN 7/30/77)

Garage Sale of the "Stars" When the Altoona Branch, Pennsylvania Mission, needed money for a new chapel in 1971, it turned to more than 100 celebrities for help with an auction. The branch presidency contacted celebrities ranging from Bob Hope to Chief of Naval Operations Elmo Zumwalt for personal contributions to the auction. The resulting list of celebrities who mailed "garage-sale" items for the branch's auction read like a who's who in America:

Gardner W. Ferguson and Timothy Kinser examine a trinket sent by Chinese statesman and military leader, Chiang Kai-shek.

- Mrs. Mamie Eisenhower donated her AM-FM radio with her signature card attached.
- Dr. Werner von Braun – a spaceship-shaped tie-tac.
- J. Edgar Hoover – an autographed book
- Dr. Benjamin Spock – an autographed book

Other items came from Arnold Palmer, Billy Graham, Jimmy Durante, Danny Thomas, Ed Sullivan, Sen. Barry Goldwater, George McGovern, Peter O'Toole, Frank Sinatra, and Chiang Kai-shek. (CN 11/27/71)

Most International Ward. The two wards in Geneva, Switzerland, the Petit Saconnex Ward and the Geneva Ward, together have representatives from 20 countries. The missionaries there use up to 50 translations of the Book of Mormon, and one elder stationed there for almost a year taught the gospel to people from 77 nations.

An example of this international flavor was found in 1987 when the Petit Ward had a bishop who was German, his wife was Austrian; the first counselor was British; the second counselor was Swiss; the executive secretary was American; the clerk was Iranian; the financial clerk was Japanese; the mission leader was from Mauritius; the young men's president was from the Philippines, and home and visiting teachers came from Chile, Cambodia, Italy, Portugal, Spain, Japan, Peru, West Indies, and Ghana. French is the official language, but Sunday School and Relief Society are also held in English. And one of the prayers in sacrament meeting is offered in any of the representative languages besides French. (CN 7/11/87)

First Radio Broadcast from a Chapel in the UK. In June 1977, the British Broadcasting Company (BBC) broadcast live from an LDS chapel in the British Isles a radio program patterned after the famous Tabernacle "Music and the Spoken Word" broadcasts out of Salt Lake City. (CN 7/9/77)

Last with an Outhouse? The last chapel in America with an outhouse was the Vernon Branch, Show Low, Arizona, Stake, which retained its outdoor accommodations beyond the birth of modern indoor facilities. In 1985, when construction on a replacement church building began, workers didn't need to venture far for the bathroom – it was out back. (LDS 5/4/85)

Chapel Topped With A Ship. When Ebenezer Bryce, after whom Utah's Bryce Can-yon is named, was summoned by Bishop Wi-lliam Snow to build the first chapel in Pine Valley, Utah, Ebenezer had only one problem – he had never built a building before. His trade was ship building. With the bishop's approval, Ebenezer constructed a sailing-ship keel upside down for the chapel roof and covered it so

Ebenezer Bryce was a shipbuilder by trade, and agreed to build the chapel only if he could do it his own way, using his shipbuilding expertise.

Utah State Historical Society

well from the outside that no one could tell the difference. With no nails available, Ebenezer made all of his connections with boring and pegging and rawhide thongs. The fruits of his labors could be seen in the attic: a maze of curving ribs, cross timbers, standing and interlacing braces, all made with the precise workmanship required for the keel of a ship – except it was upside down. Finished in 1868, it is still standing today, the oldest chapel in Utah. (CN 10/25/50)

Difficult to see in this photo, but the attic rafters are shaped like the bottom of a ship's keel flipped over.

Only Chapel With a Museum. When Renee S. Cushman passed away in 1981, she bequeathed to the local ward her priceless art collection of 63 pieces. In the collection: a pier table that won first place in the 1900 World's Fair; two etchings by Rembrandt; a Steinway grand piano believed to have belonged to Paderewski; two crystal decanters belonging to Napoleon, and other treasures dating back over 500 years. Mrs. Cushman was not LDS, but her friendship with local Stake President C. Bryant Whiting brought about the generous gift. Her only stipulation was that the ward must build a museum to properly house and display the collection. The ward was happy to comply and made the new museum a part of its Springerville, Arizona, Ward chapel. (LDS 6/7/82)

Any LDS Living in a Windmill? In 1974, Gerritt and Corri Kluit of Schiedam, The Netherlands, had the unusual distinction of calling home one of the tallest windmills in the country. Brother Kluit had lived in the area all his life and moved into the windmill with his wife in 1953. In those days, farmers brought the Kluits their wheat and other grains for milling into flour. As that process became automated, the Kluits turned to making cake mixes. Their home in the windmill is, like so much of the Netherlands, tidy and spotless. Up through the middle is the massive log beam that

An 87-foot-tall home that creaks in the wind.

turns the grinding stones beneath the windmill. Kluit said none of his family complains of the constant creaking when the wind blows the old mill into action. (CN 2/14/70; author's interview 1974)

WHERE THE SAINTS MEET - NORTH AND SOUTH

Northernmost

76:32:24 degrees North latitude – Airmen stationed at Thule Air Base, 790 miles from the North Pole, comprise the northernmost branch of the Church. Thule is on the west coast of Greenland, about halfway between the Arctic Circle and the North Pole. (CN 4/19/58)

Deseret Morning News file photo

Always a warm spirit when oil-field workers meet for Church with temperatures 60 degreees below zero.

71:19:38 degrees North latitude – In 1981, the northernmost LDS who regularly gathered as an informal group were those LDS oil-field workers on Alaska's North Slope. At the frigid area bordering the Arctic Ocean and the Beaufort Sea, some 40 members attended services about 600 miles north of Anchorage. The temperature never rises above 40 degrees F in the summer and dips to 60 below zero in the winter, and the wind chill can take the temperature to 180 below zero. Sacrament meeting was held at 8:30 p.m. each Sunday in a 10-foot-by-12-foot project room of an oil company. Home teaching meant bouncing in a truck over some 200 miles of tundra to remote drilling camps. (CN 3/16/81)

68:25 degrees North latitude – The Inuvik Branch, about 150 miles above the Arctic Circle, was organized March 22, 1964. All five families in the 20-member branch were on hand for the historic event because it was a warm day. It had heated up to 25 below zero F, from the prior day's high of 57 below zero. The branch was 1,800 miles from mission headquarters in Calgary, Alberta, Canada. (CN 4/4/64)

66:53:17 degrees North latitude – Thirty miles above the Arctic Circle in Kotzebue, Alaska, more than 30 members hold regular Church services, including early morning seminary. Temperatures fluctuate from minus 50 F in the winter to 100+ F in the summer when the sun shines 24 hours a day. (12/24/77)

64:50:14 degrees North latitude – The North Pole Ward, Santa's home ward when he's not traveling, is in Fairbanks, Alaska. During the winter,

Postmark from Santa's home town.

temperatures plunge to 60-70 below zero F (without the windchill factor) and, during Christmas, members get 2-3 hours of sunlight per day. Even the reindeer live farther south. (LDS 6/23/84)

63 degrees North latitude – The Trondheim, Norway, chapel, just below the Arctic Circle, is considered the Church's northernmost European chapel. Dedicated Feb. 14, 1965, it is about 200 miles below the Arctic Circle. (CN 3/6/65)

Photo: U.S. Naval Photographic Center

Latter-day Saints working in Antarctica hold regular church services at the "Chapel of the Snows" at McMurdo Station, seen at the middle top of this photo – at the top of "main street."

Southernmost

77:51 degrees South latitude – The group of LDS assigned to McMurdo Station, Antarctica, may well be the farthest south members of the Church who meet on a regular basis. Their home away from home for several months each year consists of 5-1/2 million square miles of frozen Antarctic territory. The group's membership will change as assignments change, but it is typically made up of civilian and military personnel. They meet in the "Chapel of the Snows," a multi-denominational chapel built out of surplus materials by Navy Seabees in 1955. (CN 1/8/77)

53 degrees South latitude – The Puntas Arenas Branch at the southern tip of Chile is in the southernmost city in the world. The branch was organized there in 1968 with about 25 members. (CN 5/4/68)

FIRST CHAPELS/WARDS/BRANCHES

Bahamas. The first meetinghouse built in the Bahamas was dedicated May 8, 1988, in Nassau, to serve some 80 English-speaking and 60 French Creole-speaking members.

China. It took a long time to finally get the first chapel dedicated in China. On April 16, 1967, Hugh B. Brown performed the dedication at Un Long in the Hong Kong zone. On Jan. 9, 1921, David O. McKay and Hugh J. Cannon formally dedicated China for the teaching of the gospel. (CN 4/29/67)

East Germany. On Sept. 11, 1949, a new chapel for members of the Hude Branch, East German Mission, was dedicated. It was built along the shore of River Eide, and 75 percent of the Hude's population attended the ceremonies. (CN 11/20/49)

The oldest LDS Chapel in the world was given to the Church when the building was only four years old.

England. Gadfield Elm Chapel, the oldest LDS chapel in England and in the world, was built in 1836 by the United Brethren. After 600 members of the religion joined the Church all about the same time, they gave the building to their new-found religion in 1840. In 1996, a rebuilding project began, and in 2002 it was rededicated. (Church Almanac)

Fiji Islands. During his tour of the Fiji Islands in January 1955, President David O. McKay selected a site for the first chapel to be built in that area. The chapel was constructed largely of concrete block manufactured by a Church-operated plant near the temple site in New Zealand, and the lumber was secured from Church-owned trees and finished in a Church-owned mill also in New Zealand. The anodized aluminum for the roofing came from England, and the acoustical tiles inside came from New Zealand. (CN 3/2/57)

Idaho. Franklin, Idaho, was first settled in the spring of 1860 by Church members from Salt Lake, Davis and Utah counties. The settlement was named Green Meadows, but was later changed to Franklin in honor of Franklin D. Richards of the Council of the Twelve. By April 1860, a branch was organized and when Brigham Young visited the settlement in June, a ward was organized. By 1874, it had became a boomtown as hundreds of wagons carried freight from the railroad station to the Montana mines. With the extension of the railroad to Pocatello, Franklin lost its commercial importance but continued to grow as an excellent rural community. (CN 12/3/55)

Japan. Sixty-one years after Heber J. Grant dedicated Japan for the preaching of the gospel, the first chapel was started in Tokyo in 1901. Lack of missionary success and subsequent war prompted the First Presidency to close the mission in 1920 and reopen it in 1948. The mission has flourished since. (CN 6/62)

South America. In 1931, missionaries and members of the Church in Santa Caterina, Brazil, erected a small but adequate chapel in Joinville. It was not only the first chapel in South America but had the first branch presidency in South America composed of local members. (CN 2/27/54)

Deseret Morning News file photo

Brazil: the first chapel.

Northwest. When Utahns David Eccles and Charles W. Nibley bought a large tract of timber land in Sumpter Valley, Oregon, the way was opened for the Church to be established in the Northwest. In 1893, the first branch was organized in Baker, Oregon, among Church members who had moved from Utah to work at the lumber yards. By 1901, the Baker Branch had become a ward when the Union Stake was organized. (CN 2/11/56)

Nauvoo. The first known settler in the Nauvoo area was Denis Julian, who moved there in 1805. Prior to that, the region was home and hunting grounds for the Sac and Fox Indians. In 1839, the Church bought four parcels of land to build its new city. The city grew so fast it was on its way to becoming the largest city in the state. But in 1846, after many tribulations and attacks, the Saints evacuated the city. It took more than 100 years until the Church was reestablished there with the formation of a new branch. With Charles R. Busard as branch president, members began holding regular meetings at the Bureau of Information on the old Temple Square in Nauvoo in March, 1956. (CN 3/17/56)

Peru. Ground-breaking for the first chapel in Lima, Peru, took place Aug. 19, 1962. Built for future expansion, the original design was for 1,200 people. (CN 9/62)

Poland. Ground was broken for the first meetinghouse in Poland on June 15, 1989. (CN 7/1/89).

It's a good beginning! This building is where the Tver, Russian Branch meets for services. Was this the very first Branch meeting place outside of embassy or other diplomatic facilities in Russia?

Rome. The first branch of the Church in Rome was organized Sept. 24, 1967. The city had been opened for missionary work just nine months earlier. There were 87 members by the time the branch officially started. (CN 10/14/67)

Spain. The first LDS meeting-house built in Spain was dedicated by Elder Charles A. Didier on July 10, 1977, in Madrid. More than 800 witnessed the event including 44 Spanish converts who had been baptized the day before. Twenty-nine media representatives attended the services and the story was carried in eight of Spain's nine newspapers. (CN 8/13/77)

Uruguay. Rocha, Uruguay, was the site for Uruguay's first chapel, dedicated in November 1950. At the time, the country already had 22 other branches of the Church. (CN 11/22/50)

AUXILIARY AND OTHER CALLINGS

Henry Perrett, 47 uninterrupted years!

Longest Serving Clerks. Is Henry Austin Perrett, Stirling 1st Ward, Raymond, Alberta, Stake, the longest serving clerk with 47 years of service? Perrett served as a ward, stake, or regional clerk from 1942 to 1991. (CN 4/6/91)

In 1963, Roy E. Francis completed 45 years as stake clerk of the Morgan, Utah, Stake. He was appointed in 1918. (CN 8/10/63)

Walter Rich McDonald of the Pocatello 4th Ward, Pocatello, Idaho, East Stake, was a dedicated ward or stake clerk for 38 years beginning in 1953. He served under seven bishops and three stake presidents. (CN 8/17/91)

F. Dennis Thatcher, Monument Park 4th Ward, Salt Lake Foothill Stake, served as ward clerk for 35 years, beginning his clerk job on the same day the ward was organized. (CN 9/23/89)

Oldest Financial Clerk. Louis W. Underwood may be the first officially appointed financial ward clerk in the Church. He was set apart for the job by Elder Harold B. Lee in November 1940, and finally retired in 1983 at age 85. Except for some short vacations and an absence due to a heart attack, he was on the job every Sunday for 43 years. (CN 5/22/83)

Longest Serving MIA Leader. In 1963, Mary Richards Tanner, Ogden, Utah, reached a milestone of 65 years service in the YMMIA. She began as stake secretary at age 17 in Parowan, Utah. She said she remembers working on the Mutual General Board when Salt Lake County was one stake. She served a mission to the central states and helped organize the first MIA in Jackson County, Missouri. Her brother was Alma Richards, Olympic gold medalist (see "Sports"). (CN 4/27/63)

In 1970, Grace Rowland completed 51 years as MIA secretary in her Springville 4th Ward. She was called in 1916 and served under 23 YWMIA presidents and 11 bishops. (CN 1/10/70)

Longest Serving Historian. Norma Bernice ZoBell, 80 (in 1992), served as historian of the Raymond 4th Ward and Raymond 1st Ward (after a boundary change) Magrath, Alberta, Stake, for a total of 38 years. As of February 1992, she was still serving as historian in the Raymond 1st Ward. She always went the extra mile in her work by recording all births, marriages, and deaths in the ward, and took pictures of the year's baptisms, primary graduates, high school graduates, missionaries, and changes in presidencies. She compiled the information in large scrapbooks that were frequently displayed in a glass cabinet in the chapel foyer. (CN 2/22/92)

First To Receive Aaronic Priesthood. On May 15, 1829, Joseph Smith and Oliver Cowdery received the Aaronic Priesthood from John the Baptist. They then baptized each other, as instructed. (Church Almanac 1989-90)

The Most Leadership – All In The Family. Of the eight children in the Clendon and Erma Gee family, all four boys were bishops and all four daughters were Relief Society presidents. (CN 6/20/87)

In 1988, Newell and Eleanor Foxall Packer of the Pocatello, Idaho, 32nd Ward, had four daughters serving as Relief Society presidents: Bonnie Stowell in the Bellevue, Washington, 6th Ward; Carol Miller in the Pocatello, Idaho, Tyhee 37th Ward; Marlene Packer in the Sacramento, California, Foothill Ward; and Janice Hunsaker in the Murray, Utah, 5th Ward. (CN 3/12/88)

Dorothy R. Hancock, Alma 8th Ward, Mesa, Arizona, West Stake, served as Young Women president in her own ward, and set the standard for all four of her daughters, Mildred, Mary, Sylvia, and Juneth, who by 1982 had served as Young Women presidents in their respective wards. (LDS 3/12/82)

For these brethren it was hard deciding on anything because their plans were always up in the air.   Photo: U.S. Air Force

Aerial Priesthood Meeting. The first known authorized aerial priesthood meetings held on a regular basis took place aboard a B-29 bomber in 1951. Eight of the aircraft's 11 crewmen were LDS, having been intentionally grouped together at the request of the crew's 28-year-old commander, Capt. Donald A. Funk of Salt Lake City. When not in the air, the elders met at the San Antonio, Texas, Branch. (CN 12/19/51)

Oldest Young Women President. Thelma Maloy from Safford, Arizona, was the oldest Young Women president in the Church at 80 years old in 1989. Thelma had three daughters, 14 grandchildren, 34 great-great-grandchildren, and three great-great-great grandchildren. Said Thelma in 1989, "I STILL enjoy camping out with the girls!" (LDS 5/31/89)

Oldest Teacher. It's one thing to divert the attention of rambunctious nine- and ten-year-olds from teasing and daydreaming to focus on a lesson during Sunday School. It's a whole 'nother thing to do it when you're 89 years old! In 1964, Bertha Kohler Chantry had been a teacher in Pioneer Stake's 35th Ward in Salt Lake City since 1909, some 55 years, and as she approached 90, she was still an interesting, wonderful and amazing teacher to the youth. (CN 9/5/64)

Youngest Superintendent. In 1963, John Dodson, Sydney Branch, Nova Scotia, Canada, became the youngest Sunday School superintendent in the Church at age 12. He was the son of Mr. and Mrs. William Dodson. (CN 6/8/63)

In 1951, Bengt Hoberg, a convert in the Norrokoping Branch of the Swedish Mission, was the youngest MIA superintendent in the Church at age 13. (CN 5/9/51)

Longest in Primary? When Eugene Dardall, Princeton Ward, Park, Utah, Stake, was ten months old, his mother took him to Primary while she served in the Primary presidency. From that Sunday on, he continued attending Primary each week, not missing a single activity or meeting. He kept a 100 percent attendance record until he graduated on his birthday at age 12. Is this string of 11 years two months in Primary a Mormon World Record? (CN 11/30/63)

Longest Fast Offering Collection Route. Is 30 miles round trip the longest route for a deacon to collect fast offerings? In 1962, Raymond and Roger Grow covered 30 miles on their bicycles in Klamath Agency, Oregon, to complete their monthly assignment. They visited 12 families scattered over ranch and Indian country from Fort Klamath to Chiloquin, Oregon. (CN 9/62)

Raymond (left) and Roger Grow put almost 400 miles on their bikes in a year.

Deseret Morning News file photo

Longest Continuously-Meeting Study Group. The longest continuously meeting study group may be that of some Dutch members who began studying together in 1947. These members of the Amsterdam Branch later migrated to the United States, and they continued to meet each Sunday for 40 years more. (CN 6/13/87)

Longest Continuously-meeting Beehives. A group of Beehive girls from Midvale, Utah, started meeting together when their class was formed in 1920. As of 1990, they had continued to meet at least once a year and most of the original 16 members were still alive and active in the group. (CN 7/26/80)

Longest-Serving Gospel Doctrine Teacher. Leland Call, Rigby 2nd Ward, Rigby, Idaho, taught the same gospel doctrine class for 50 years. He was released in the spring of 1975, having served the same class while the ward was divided and divided again under one mission president and 13 bishops. (CN 1/3/76)

Longest-Serving Sunday School Teacher. Bertha Kohler Chantry taught Sunday School continuously for 54 years at the 35th Ward, Pioneer, Utah, Stake. She retired in 1963 at age 87, having taught since 1909. (CN 7/27/63)

Most Generations Ordained in One Day. In the early '60s, three generations of deacons were ordained on the same day in the same ward. James C. Eakin, his son Edgar Leroy Eakin, and grandson Edgar Leroy Eakin Jr., were ordained deacons on July 22, 1962, in the Mesa 4th Ward, Maricopa, Arizona, Stake. (CN 8/4/62)

Youngest Organist and Oldest Conductor in Priesthood Meeting. Bishop Max J. Flake of the Price 4th Ward, Carbon Stake, Utah, reported in 1966 that his ward held the Church record for the "youngest-oldest" musician combination with 17-year-old Dennis Leonard as organist, and 85-year-old Nicholas P. Peterson as conductor – an age difference of 68 years. (CN 11/19/66)

RELIEF SOCIETY

Joseph Smith's Red Brick Store in Nauvoo, was the beginning place for the Relief Society in 1842. Twenty women, some still in their teens, attended the first meeting.

Largest Women's Organization in the World? Today, the LDS Relief Society numbers more than 3 million women in 165 countries. More than half of these are outside of the United States. The organization serves local Church members and communities with meals, clothing, quilts, hygiene kits and literacy training. Relief Society members visit one another (called visiting teaching) each month to offer assistance. Uniform lessons are taught each week worldwide. It promotes the development of leadership, teaching and homemaking skills towards the singularly important goal of raising strong, righteous families. (Author)

Longest Record of 100 percent Visiting Teaching – Ward. Which ward or branch Relief Society has the longest string of 100 percent visiting teaching? The Mesa 43rd Ward, Mesa Central Stake, went a full three years (1986-89) without spoiling their perfect record. Said Relief Society President Patty Darner Robison, "We decided there was no reason why we couldn't have 100 percent visiting teaching ... we did it from the first month on." (LDS 3/25/89)

A Church member teaches the Relief Society nursery in one of the first Branches in West Africa.

Longest Record of 100 percent Visiting Teaching – Individual. In 1974, Effie Stapley, Carlsbad, California, Stake, marked her 85th birthday and an amazing 67 years of 100 percent visiting teaching. (CN 8/17/74)

Largest Visiting-Teaching Route. Is 200 miles the largest regularly-run visiting route in the Church? Cheryl Lindner and Jenny Mahoney, of the Elizabeth Ward, Modbury, Australia, Stake, visited their six sisters in a nine-hour marathon that took them an entire day to complete. At the time (1987), the Elizabeth Ward covered an area 200 miles long. (CN 4/4/87)

The Power of the Boycott. It makes a formidable foe, the Relief Society, and the advertising world better watch out! In January 1986, Relief Society General President Barbara Winder called for a boycott (a first for the Relief Society?) of Continental Airlines due to the airlines' TV commercials showing a woman sitting in a bubble bath and saying: "Hi, I'm looking for some cheap frills, and someone gave me your number. ..." The ad was eventually replaced. (LDS 1/26/86)

Barbara Winder helped show the "power of good" with a boycott.

Non-LDS Relief Society Leader. In 1986, Margaret McPherson Keller, Mission Hills Ward, Granada Hills, California, Stake, became what was believed to be the first non-LDS to serve as director of Relief Society Social Services. (LDS 11/8/86)

YOUNG WOMEN

Largest Female-Teens' Organization in the World? The Church's Young Women's organization began on Nov. 18, 1869, as the Young Ladies' Department of the Cooperative Retrenchment Association. Brigham Young called together several of his daughters and their mothers in the parlor of the Lion House in Salt Lake City to formally organize the group. He encouraged them to "retrench in your dress, in your tables, in your speech, wherein you have been guilty of silly, extravagant speeches and light-mindedness of thought. Retrench in everything that is bad and worthless, and improve in everything that is good and beautiful." They were to be proper examples of Latter-day Saints, to not give in to rude or harsh frontier ways. Relief Society President and poet Eliza R. Snow became the supervisor of the new association, and Ella V. Empey, age twenty-three, was chosen as president. Their numbers now exceed 1 million, perhaps the largest young women's organization in the world. (Author)

First Telecast. The first General Young Women's fireside televised via satellite occurred Nov. 10, 1985, when the Young Women Values program was introduced to the Church. The fireside, the first general Church meeting following the funeral of President Spencer W. Kimball, was received by satellite at many stake centers across the United States (LDS 11/2/85)

Head Prefect. Kathryn Booth's excellent grades and leadership ability earned her the unique position as the first Mormon "Head Prefect" in the Catholic Holy Rosary Convent in Port Elizabeth, South Africa. She was the first non-Catholic girl to hold this position in 101 years since the school's founding in 1867. (CN 3/23/68)

SEMINARY

The First Seminary. In 1847, Church leaders encouraged the new pioneer stakes to establish schools. Religion classes were part of the new Church-sponsored school system. Fifty years later, Utah's school system was well established and the various academies were closed to support the public system. The first seminary was started in 1912 next door to Granite High School in Salt Lake City, and from there it spread throughout the Church. Today, almost one million young LDS men and women participate on a regular basis.

Most International. The Heerlen, Netherlands seminary meeting at the Heerlen Servicemen Branch welcomes Seminary students each day who must travel from three countries: Germany, The Netherlands, and Belgium. (CN 4/20/86)

Elvis Presley Attends Seminary. In the late 1960s and 1970s, world-renowned karate expert Ed Parker, Pasadena Ward, Pasadena, California, Stake, became close friends with Elvis Presley. Brother Parker was hired by Elvis to provide security at concerts and road trips. After one of his many concerts in Las Vegas, Elvis surprised Parker with a brand new Cadillac to show his appreciation. With Elvis' group members in his limo, and Elvis and Parker in the new Cadillac, the two vehicles drove in tandem through the night to reach Los Angeles. As morning broke, they approached Parker's neighborhood in southern Pasadena. He directed them to an old chapel that had been bought by the Church and converted into a seminary building. Parker's two daughters, Darlene and Beth, were in the building attending early morning seminary. "May I introduce you to my daughters?" he asked. "They'd love to meet you." Elvis was very happy to do so, and Parker went into the building to retrieve Darlene and Beth. Elvis greeted the girls with a hug and

Courtesy Leilani Parker

Elvis Presley (with Ed Parker) couldn't believe young people would rise so early each day to learn about Jesus Christ.

kiss, and then asked about their seminary classes. They explained it was a chance to learn the Gospel and about Jesus Christ, something they enjoyed as a way to begin their day. Elvis was so impressed, he asked, "Do you think the teacher would mind if I visited your class?" Arrangements were quickly made. Standing in front of a packed classroom, Elvis thanked the students for taking the time to learn about Jesus, and congratulated them for making good choices. He then bore his personal witness of Jesus, and gave them a warm good-bye. Word quickly spread, and it is said that there was nearly perfect attendance for years thereafter as rumors circulated of another surprise visit by Elvis. (Interview with Ed Parker, 1979)

First Seminary Teacher and Class. Thomas J. Yates opened the first seminary class in the Church in September 1912, in the new seminary building built by Granite Stake across from Granite High School in Salt Lake City. Among the first 40 students were Howard S. McDonald, later to become BYU's president, and Joseph F. Merrill, a future member of the Council of the Twelve. (CN 9/9/48)

Early Morning at the Mortuary. In 1968, doing work for the living among the dead was a unique daily exercise for seminary students in the San

Diego 5th, 10th, and 12th Wards. These were the only seminary students known to meet in a mortuary. Assembling at 6:30 a.m. in the mortuary of Charles L. Robines, a member of the Church, they had the usual scripture chase, lessons, testimony meeting, and a brief moment to rest from worldly cares. ... (CN 1/13/68)

LeRoi Bentley: Still teaching at age 95, to former Seminary students aged 87.

70 Years of Reunions. In 1995, a group of girls dubbed the "dizzy six" who graduated from Huntington, Utah, High School seminary in 1924, marked a milestone when they met for their 70th consecutive reunion. Three of the original six 87-year-old women were able to make the trip to see the teacher who inspired them in the beginning. LeRoi Bentley. He was living in Salt Lake City, and had turned 95 in time for the 70th reunion. The other two living ladies could not make the trip. For 70 years, the group had met to share stories, family and progress. They gave credit to Brother Bentley for teaching true values and pointing out how happiness only comes when doing what is right. The original Dizzy Six were Adeline Starr, Maudie Moffitt, Hilma Robertson, Eva Conover, Morrell Nielson, and Cecelia Coldesina (who passed away in 1979). (CN 10/21/95)

Farthest Traveled to Graduate. Is it worth the 2,400-mile round trip just to be at graduation ceremonies for seminary? For Colleen Ryan, 17, of the Hedland Branch, Australia, it was. She traveled 1,200 miles with her father to Perth so she could graduate. The Hedland branch is the farthest branch of any from the Perth mission headquarters. Colleen completed her seminary studies through home study. (CN 1/8/83)

Prison. The first graduates of seminary from prison were several dozen men at the Utah State Prison who completed the requirements in the summer of 1968. Many began study and instruction, but not all were able to graduate because of poor attendance or other problems. In June 1969, the second graduating class consisted of 31 men out of about 50 active in the Church program at the prison. (CN 6/21/69)

England's First Seminary Graduate. On May 14, 1982, Paul Smith, Leicester, England, 2nd Ward, became the first early morning seminary student in the British Isles to graduate. (CN 7/82)

First in Korea. With more than 1,300 seminary students looking for a place to meet, the first seminary building in Korea was a great boost to the program in that country. The 5,000-square-foot building helped relieve the need in Seoul, but across the country the need continued to grow at an amazing pace. (CN 7/12/75)

Deseret Morning News file

Paul Smith rode his bike three miles to early morning Seminary for four years.

HOME TEACHING

Home teaching is a direct outcome of D&C 20:42-54 where the saints are encouraged to "teach, expound, exhort, baptize, and watch over the church ... and visit the house of each member, and exhort them to pray." The practice of visiting families has undergone several name changes. Originally, the two priesthood-holding men knocking on the doors of fellow ward members were called "block teachers," a reference to the grid system by which Salt Lake City and other LDS communities were laid out. By 1909, the name changed to "acting teachers." In 1912, the name was formally changed to "ward teachers." This lasted until 1963 when it was changed to "home teachers." Each month, hundreds of thousands of home teachers contact as many LDS and sometimes non-LDS families as assigned.

Most Visited in Shortest Time. Delbart Barney, Jackson Branch, Gulf States Mission, holds the world's record for the most families home taught in the shortest amount of time. On Dec. 30, 1938, he was handed a list of 79 families to be visited before the end of the month – only two days away! Barney accepted the assignment, walked more than 60 miles, found everyone home, and working with five companions, completed the assignment without being offensive or terse in his messages. At 11 p.m. New Year's Eve, he bid good evening to his last family and returned to his home. (CN 6/16/56)

Longest 100 percent Home Teaching – Individual. In 1987, Marvin Ezra Clark, at age 96, ended a perfect record of 100 percent monthly home teaching lasting 85 years. And had it not been for the illness that prevented him from completing his monthly rounds, he would have kept his record intact well into the 1990s. At that advanced age he still managed to chop and cut wood for his wood-burning stove, and drove the 100 miles to the Logan Temple as many times as was necessary to meet his goal of 200 temple endowments a year. (Ensign 2/90)

In 1963, Dirk Evertsen, 9th Ward, Phoenix North Stake, completed 52 years of 100 percent monthly home teaching. A convert from Utrecht, The Netherlands, he emigrated to the United States in 1909. As a youth his arm was crippled in a factory accident, but this didn't stop him from using his good arm to make a living, sending his five boys on missions, and staying very active. (CN 6/1/63)

In 1956, Delbart Barney, Jackson Branch, Gulf States Mission, completed 20 years of 100 percent ward teaching. While this remarkable feat may not sound overly complicated for a person with one or two families, who in the Church could match Barney's 20-year average of 10.6 families visited per month? (CN 6/16/56)

Longest 100 percent Home Teaching – Companionship. As of September 1989, the longest period for the same companionship to have 100 percent home teaching was eight years two months by home teaching partners Rafael Salvioli, 90, and Francisco Vical Cunningham, 84, of the Mar del Plata 2nd Ward, in Clare, South Australia. (CN 8/13/88; CN 9/89)

Longest 100 percent Home Teaching – High Priests' Group. The high priests' group of the Mesa, Arizona, 53rd Ward completed five straight years of 100 percent home teaching in May 1986. They had 20-25 families to teach. (CN 6/15/86)

Longest 100 percent Home Teaching – Ward. Beginning in 1955, the Gunlock Ward, St. George, Utah, Stake, had an unbroken record of 100 percent home teaching for the entire ward for eight years. The record was maintained through three bishoprics. There was a close call when one ward family went to Salt Lake City for an extended period. The home teachers made a 600-mile round trip to deliver a message and check up on the family's needs. (CN 3/9/63)

In 1963, the Harper Ward in the North Box Elder, Utah, Stake, posted a record of five straight years of 100 percent home teaching. (CN 4/20/63)

Longest-Paired Companionship. Like thousands of other home-teaching companions, Ernest L. Snider, 72, and Edwin S. Brown, 71, went out every month to home teach their families in their Salt Lake City Poplar Grove Ward. Nothing too unusual about that except they had been doing it for 30 years, beginning in 1936, the longest companionship of any known in the Church. They watched the assignment undergo many name changes: block teaching, ward teaching, home teaching. Even when each took an eight-year turn as bishop, they remained companions. But they still have one point over which they constantly debate: "We're still arguing about who is senior and who is junior companion," they said. (CN 1966)

Longest Serving Home Teacher. In 1966, Robert P. Woodbury, Hurricane, Utah, celebrated his tenure of 70 years as a block teacher, ward teacher, and home teacher in the same ward. (CN 9/3/66)

Longest Home Teaching Route. In 1990, David A. Robinson, president of the Port Headland Branch in the Australia Perth Mission, traveled 10-1/2 hours each way to home teach the Paul and Karen Spicer family. He made the 1,000 mile round-trip visit each month and maintained a 100 percent home teaching record. Since the Spicers couldn't drive each Sunday to Church, they had permission to conduct services in their home. Their only contact with other branch members was through their home teacher. (CN 10/20/90)

ORDINANCES

The Endowment. The culmination of a Latter-day Saint's mortal life is to become worthy to enter into sacred covenants with God. This simple but beautiful ceremony is called the endowment, and it is performed in an LDS temple for both the living, and by proxy for the dead. The goal is to provide this great gift of the endowment to all worthy adults who so desire it.

100 Million Endowments. The number of proxy endowments completed reached the 100-million milestone in mid-August 1988. Two-thirds of these had been done since 1970. Elder William Grant

The Nauvoo Temple circa 1846-48, the second such building in which the saints could peacefully worship.

Bangerter of the presidency of the First Quorum of the Seventy and executive director of the Temple Department said the ratio of members to non-members worldwide has been about 1 in 1,000, and about the same ratio for ordinances for the dead. But things are improving, he said. Today, ordinances are being performed for about 1 in every 750 who have died. (CN 8/88)

Endowment Milestones

The first complete endowments were given in Nauvoo in the large meeting room on the second floor of Joseph Smith Jr.'s red-brick store. He had fitted the room with canvas partitions to represent the various stages of eternal progression.

At 4:25 p.m., Dec. 10, 1845, Brigham Young and Heber C. Kimball began administering the ordinances of the endowment in the Nauvoo Temple. The first to go through included many of the great names of the Church: Willard Richards, Heber C. Kimball, George A. Smith, Orson Hyde, John Smith, Newel K. Whitney, Brigham Young, William W. Phelps, Parley P. Pratt, Amasa M. Lyman, Hyrum Smith's widow, Mary Smith, and the widow of Don Carlos, Agnes Smith. The officiating continued until 3:30 a.m. Lucy Smith, mother of the prophet, went in with the second group. This remarkable woman, having lost her husband and four grown sons during five years in Nauvoo, remained anxious and determined to do what was required of her to gain eternal salvation. (CN 12/29/45)

During their last two months in Nauvoo, before being driven out, about 5,500 received their own endowments, including 107 on Christmas Day, 1845. (CN 8/27/88)

Deseret Morning News file photo

Alma R. Anderson

Most Endowments – Individual, Lifetime. By 1960, Alma R. Anderson, 17th Ward, Salt Lake Stake, had completed all of the temple endowment work for 17,021 of his direct ancestors. His effort required more than 40 years. And in the latter years of his life he did some 600 endowments annually. (CN 8/13/60; 3/1/58)

Most Endowments – Individual in One Year. Abner Monroe DeMille, 68, St. George 6th Ward, St. George East Stake, completed 1,553 endowment sessions in 1985. (LDS 8/87)

In 5-1/2 years (October 1964 to March 1970), Claude Simons completed 5,136 endowments. (CN 3/21/70)

Most Endowments – Stake. Which stake has the most endowments in a single day? In 1987, the Long Beach Stake completed 1,295 in one day at the Los Angeles Temple. Most participants were able to complete at least five sessions. (LDS 3/28/87)

Most Endowments – Ward. The most endowments by a ward in a one-year period is 18,000 by the St. George 7th Ward, St. George, Utah, East Stake, in 1988. (LDS 1989)

Endowment – Oldest. In December 1969, Maria Martinez, whose Zuni Indian name is Teoweluy Tetsa, left her village for the first time in her life to travel from Zuni, New Mexico, to the Arizona Temple in Mesa to receive her endowments at age 114. (CN 12/13/69)

Maria Martinez

Most Endowments – One Day, Salt Lake Temple. Thirty-six stakes from the Salt Lake Temple area came together in May 1967 to perform 4,718 endowments. According to Temple President Howard McDonald, that was the largest number of endowments ever done in one day at the temple up to that time. (CN 5/27/67)

The Old Endowment House. The old Endowment House that once stood on the northeast corner of Temple Square was the first edifice in Salt Lake City in which endowments were performed. About the time that polygamy was abandoned, the endowment house was used for additional polygamous sealings until it, too, was shut down for such purposes. It was torn down in November 1889. (CN 6/26/48)

The Old Endowment House on Temple Square as it appeared in the 1880s.

Most Difficult Trip to the Temple. Temple-recommend holders on Tonga's northernmost island of Vava'u traveled some 200 miles on rough seas for 24 hours one-way to reach the Nuku'alofa Tonga Temple. From their average annual incomes of $1,000, they spent $60 for each adult and $30 for each child on boat fare. They stayed in a Church-owned hotel for two to three weeks and, until 1987, brought along enough food to last the whole trip. The members' average total endowments per year was about 5,000. Typically, some 90 adults and 40 children made the trip twice a year. (CN 8/13/88)

First Non-English Endowment Session. On Nov. 6, 1945, the first non-English temple endowment session was given. Some 200 Mexicans from the United States and Mexico gathered in Mesa, Arizona, went through the Mesa Temple and attended a General Conference, all in Spanish. A special corps of temple workers trained under the direction of President Harry T. Payne was on hand for the three-day effort. (CN 11/10/45)

BAPTISM

The oldest first baptism

Bill Stuart, Deseret Morning News

Encarnacion Rampas

118: Encarnacion Banares Rampas of Cuzco, Peru, was baptized in October 1983 at age 118. Born in March 1865 in Anta, Peru, Sister Rampas told the missionaries during her first visit to a Church meeting, "I just like the feeling there." (CN 2/26/84)

116: Nicholas Santucho, Canada de Gomez, Argentina, was baptized in the fall of 1980 at the age of 116. His wife was baptized a week later at the age of 86. They had 17 children. "There is no secret to long life," Santucho said. "I have lived because God has wished it so." (CN 12/13/80)

Deseret Morning News file photo

Nicholas Santucho

106: William Cass Robertson, Ft. Bragg, California, was baptized in September 1971. He really liked the idea of an unpaid clergy and no collection plate. The Joseph Smith story didn't make any sense to him until a testimony came later through prayer. (CN 2/12/72)

105: Atanasia Villesenor was baptized April 12, 1975, just 20 days short of her 106th birthday, in San Diego, California. She had 17 children, and was born in Villa Madero, Michiacan, Mexico. (CN 7/12/75)

103: Maria Margarida de Souza was baptized at age 103 in Belem, Brazil. (CN 6/1/86)

103: Mrs. Concepcion Alvarez was baptized Aug. 18, 1971, in Mexico City, Mexico. (CN 11/13/71)

102: Santos Maria Acosta, of Portoviego, Ecuador, was at home one evening when Griselda Valarezo, a young woman doing a "mini-mission" with local missionaries, knocked on her door to introduce the gospel. As they became acquainted, they discovered to their mutual joy that Sister Valarezo was the great-granddaughter of 102-year-old Acosta. Sister Acosta accepted the gospel message from her great-granddaughter, and was baptized shortly thereafter. (CN 8/17/86)

FIRST CONVERTS

First Above Arctic Circle. The first known baptism above the Arctic Circle took place in December 1959 when servicemen Pete Davis and Larry Jensen were baptized in Thule, Greenland. Their baptismal font consisted of a tank filled with warm water from a steam connection into a water truck borrowed from an ordnance company. LDS Group Leader David Baker did the baptizing. (CN 1/9/60)

Bolivia. Long before missionary work began in earnest in Bolivia, Maria Van Gemeron became the first convert. She learned about the Church while a student at BYU. At the time, in 1963, Bolivia had a population of 3.5 million. (CN 10/12/63)

Corsica. Unless the Apostle Paul did some baptisms he didn't write home about, Ginette Caillard has the distinction of being the first person baptized into the Church in Corsica as of 1974. She joined two other members of the Church, Marie-Martene and Pierre Bertone, who had been baptized in another country before moving to Corsica. (CN 12/7/74)

Malaysia. Mr. and Mrs. K. Peter Chandran, Singapore, didn't understand other religions' concept of God. However, when told of Christ visiting the Americas, "We could see the truth that they were talking about," Peter said after their baptism in 1971. (CN 8/21/71)

Cambodia. Francis Cheung King Shaang was the first of her nation to join the Church when she was baptized in Hong Kong in January 1963. (CN 1/19/63)

Russia. Johan M. Lindlof and his wife, Alma, were dissatisfied with the Tsarist churches and one day stumbled on information about the Mormons. They wrote to the LDS Scandinavian Mission headquarters for more information and were promised a visit from President August J. Hoglund of the Goteborg Conference. In 1895, Elder Hoglund arrived in St. Petersburg. They sat in the parlor of the Lindlofs' home and spoke until the early morning hours. On June 11, 1895, the three hired a boat and rowed out into the Neva River to a quiet spot where the Lindlofs' were baptized. Occasional visits were made to the Lindlofs over the years, and on Aug. 6, 1903, Francis M. Lyman and three missionaries stood on the banks of the Neva to dedicate Russia for the preaching of the Gospel. They called upon God to "bless this great empire ... and endow its rulers with wisdom and virtue, that there may be peace and progress here, that darkness may flee and the voices of His servants may sound the glad tidings to the uttermost parts of this great land. ... " It was a prayerful plea that took more than 85 years to find fulfillment. (CN 6/10/67)

Deseret Morning News file photo

Srilaksana Gottsche

Thailand. Srilaksana Gottsche became the first Thai to join the Church on July 4, 1968, with two of her older children. She worked with the missionaries to begin translation of the Book of Mormon. Her other children were each baptized when they turned eight. (CN 10/20/79)

Siberia. On April 27, 1919, T. Earl Hunsaker performed the first baptism in Siberia, Russia. As an enlistee in the U.S. Army, Brother Hunsaker volunteered to join an expeditionary force that was being organized to go to Siberia to fight the Bolsheviks. They set up camp in Vladivostok in the spring of 1918 and began holding LDS meetings at the YMCA. Andrew Hasberg, an investigator, had attended the meetings and wanted to be baptized. The ordinance took place in the mountains near Vladivostok. (CN 7/22/67)

England. George Darling Watt had been bathing in the canal when other boys stole his clothes. He was naked and crying when a woman discovered him and led him to a workhouse to live. From there he attended school and, about a year later, became an apprentice to a shoemaker. After coming of age, he moved to Preston, where he married and settled down. He was in the congregation at Vauxhall Chapel on the Sunday the Mormon missionaries preached their first sermon. Convinced he was hearing the truth, he applied for baptism. On the all-important day he raced a fellow townsman to the riverbank for the privilege of being the first to be baptized in England. It was

July 30, 1837. He later emigrated to Nauvoo, received his endowments in the temple, crossed the plains to Utah, and died on his farm in Layton in 1881 at the age of 66. (CN 8/5/67)

Chile. Ricardo Garcia Orellrana, baptized Nov. 25, 1956, was the first of four baptized in Chile. Afterwards, he met with six others in his living room and legally incorporated the Church with Bill Fotheringham as the new branch president. Brother Orellrana recalled, "We had no idea the Church would grow so fast ... The missionaries asked us about that. We told them we didn't think many would join." (CN 10/4/80)

Spain. When David Wright was sent to Spain as the U.S. ambassador, little did he realize his future son-in-law would be waiting for him there. Jose Olivera fell in love with Brother Wright's daughter and courted her for seven years. She was anxious he embrace the gospel but after several talks with the missionaries, his investigation seemed to be going nowhere. She finally gave him a copy of The First 2000 Years (W. Cleon Skousen, Bookcraft). When Olivera read the essay on the atonement, he said, "I felt fire in me." His testimony then came quickly. He even started reading again the Book of Mormon because suddenly "God became a reality to me." He was soon baptized. Through his own efforts, more than 50 converts joined the Church (his relatives and friends), and he started the missionary program in Spain. Today he works as a movie producer. (Author)

Kosrae. The first to be baptized in Lelu, Kosrae, was Isidro Abraham, 22, on April 26, 1986. Part of the Micronesia-Guam Mission, the branch had an average attendance of 30. (CN 6/15/86)

Persian Gulf. Eight-year-old Janet Ann Holmes became the first person baptized a member of the Church in the Persian Gulf, just off the coast of Saudi Arabia, on June 1, 1951. Her father, Richard F. Holmes, was at the time employed by the Arabian American Oil Company. (CN 7/25/51)

Janet Holmes (second from left) spots the Persian Gulf with her family.

Newfoundland. Lavinia Webber Mercer became the first person baptized in Newfoundland on Aug. 13, 1950. It took two years and a week after the elders first arrived for Sister Mercer to finally join the Church. Many followed shortly thereafter. Said one of her nonmember friends, who witnessed the event with tears in her eyes, "I hope I can get up the courage to do that in the near future." (CN 9/13/50)

Bangladesh. Towhid-Ul-Alam, baptized while a student at BYU-Hawaii in 1981, hoped to help translate the Book of Mormon into Bengali. (CN 8/22/81)

Jamaica. In 1979, Victor Nugent became the first Jamaican to join the Church. He became district president in 1984. (CN 1/29/84)

First Mongol (of ancient Asian Mongols). On Jan. 13, 1973, Wu Rung Fu was baptized in the Taiwan Mission. He is believed to be the first Mongol to join the Church. He and his family had been living in Taiwan since the communist takeover of China. His father was a retired general from the Mongolian and Chinese armies. (CN 2/3/73)

First Moslem. On Jan. 6, 1973, Rahman Fatafitah, a student at American University in Beirut, Lebanon, was baptized. He is believed to be the first Moslem to join the Church. Other Arabs and Middle Easterners had joined, but they had come from a Christian or other non-Islamic background. Brother Fatafitah attended services in the Beirut Lebanon Branch. (CN 2/3/73)

First Arab Baptized in Jerusalem. In 1974, Sa'aik and Maher Fatafitah, 24 and 21 respectively, were baptized at 5 a.m. in the Pool of Siloam near the mouth of Hezekiah's tunnel in Jerusalem. Despite the early hour, meant to insure privacy before Arabs came to wash and take water, a half dozen little Arab boys witnessed the historic event. The branch president of the Jerusalem Branch, David Galbraith, performed the ordinance. (CN 8/10/74)

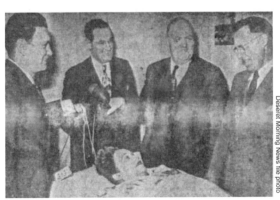

Deseret Morning News file photo

Sister Stanliff, strapped to her stretcher, visits with those who perfomed her baptism.

Baptized on a Stretcher. Mrs. Luett J. Stanliff, confined to a bed after a fall which injured her spine, was baptized in the Salt Lake Tabernacle baptistry on her stretcher in 1949. She was transported to Temple Square by ambulance, tied to her stretcher, immersed, and returned home where she was confirmed a member of the Church and given the sacrament. (CN Spring 1949)

First Baptized For The Dead. The first baptisms for the dead were performed in the Mississippi River near Nauvoo. At General Conference in October 1841, the Prophet Joseph declared, "There shall be no more baptisms for the dead until the ordinance can be attended to in the Lord's house and the Church shall not hold another General Conference until they can meet in said house for thus saith the Lord." The temple at this time had progressed far enough so that baptisms and meetings could be properly held in the very near future. (CN 6/12/49)

Most Ordinances – Individual. In 1988, G. Ronald Carter, 85, St. George 5th Ward, St. George, Utah, East Stake, was baptized for the one-millionth time in the baptistry of the St. George Temple Nov. 17, 1988. Brother Carter said he attended the temple five times a week for 11 years, and then had to cut back for a couple of years to just three times a week. "It's been a blessing to me," he said in 1988. "I've only got 996,000 more to get to my second million." (CN 12/24/88)

In 1983, Thomas Taylor Brower, 91, completed more than 1 million temple ordinances. A brief ceremony was held in his honor at the Mesa, Arizona, Temple. Brother Brower said he was able to accomplish this mostly in his retirement years when he could spend 8-10 hours a day five days a week in the Mesa Temple. (CN 9/83)

Most Baptisms by an Individual. Is the record for the most baptisms in the shortest time in modern times held by George Q. Cannon? As the first missionary to Hawaii in 1850, he baptized almost 3,000 people in three years. (CN 11/10/48)

Most Convert Baptisms in the Same Font. Which baptismal font or location is the busiest? In 1984, one of BYU's swimming pools was the setting for 2,054 baptisms. (LDS 5/18/85)

Most Convert Baptisms. Is 1990 the high-water mark year for the most convert baptisms in the Church, of 330,877? (Internet)

Most Baptisms by a Stake Missionary. Jacob Adolph, Big Horn Stake, Wyoming, may hold the record for baptizing the most converts as a stake missionary. More than 400 people within his stake boundaries had joined as of 1972. "If you think you can do this (teach investigators) on your own, you are mistaken," Brother Adolph said. "It doesn't matter how much education you have or what condition your pocketbook is in. This is the Lord's work and we have to depend on Him." (CN 10/28/72)

Oldest Married Couple Baptized. Are Mr. and Mrs. Robert A. Clark of Bromaderry, New South Wales, Australia, the oldest couple to be baptized into the Church on the same day? Brother Clark was 83 and his wife 80 at the time of their baptisms in 1959, a combined age of 163 years. (CN 7/25/59)

Oldest Mother-Daughter Baptized. Martha Bell, 97, and Mary Turnbull, 76, were both baptized on the same day in the Ashington Branch, Ashington, England, in January 1986. Their ages totaled 173 years. (CN 1/26/86)

On Feb. 17, 1973, Olive Jarvis, 64, and her mother, Hilda Knotts, 81, were baptized in Houston, Texas. Their ages totaled 145 years.

Most Generations at Once. The most generations of one family baptized on the same day is four. Members of the Pahrump Ward, Pahrump, Nevada, came together in January 1982 to witness the baptism of the Schuster family: Lura Schuster, 65, daughter Dixie Hines, 47, granddaughter Kathy Dillman, 30, and great-grandson John Dillman, 9. (CN 2/27/83)

Longest Investigation. Tough call on this one: Who has spent the most time investigating the Church? It took 53 years for Ted Wigglesworth to finally agree with his wife that he ought to join the Church. After first being introduced to the Church in 1934, Wigglesworth went through dozens and dozens of missionaries and fellowshipping friends before he finally asked to be baptized at his Brighton England Ward in 1987. (CN 6/6/87)

Lora Cox took 50 years. She first looked into the Church in 1933 and was finally baptized in 1983 at the age of 92. She resided in the Mission Viejo, California, Stake. (CN 3/6/83)

Taking Care of Business. On June 12, 1986, Chad Welch, Hyrum, Utah, 5th Ward, blessed his twin infants, Richard and Matthew. He then confirmed as members of the Church the family's other recently baptized twins, Jason and Justin. The Welchs had 11 children. (CN 9/7/86)

On Jan. 13, 1973, a proud dad stood in Church to bless his twin boys, Douglas and Darrell Trottier, three-months old, and afterwards ordained his twin daughters, Liena and Lisa Trottier, eight years old. They were members of the Winder Ward, Winder, Utah, Stake. (CN 1/13/73)

On a single Sunday in May, 1945, Bert Almond of the Downey Ward, Portneuf, Idaho, Stake, confirmed and ordained his four boys to their appropriate places in the Church: Grant, the youngest, was confirmed a member of the Church, Lyle was ordained a deacon, Dean a teacher, and Allen a priest. (CN 6/2/45)

Most Patriarchal Blessings in 21 Days. Patriarch Eduardo Balderas, accompanying Elder Spencer W. Kimball on a tour of South America in 1967, gave 250 patriarchal blessings in three weeks. As many as 30 blessings were given on some days. The blessings were tape recorded and transcriptions mailed to the recipients. When Brother Kimball and Brother Balderas left, three new patriarchs were in place to meet the needs of the remaining Saints. (CN 12/23/67)

First Patriarch in Missouri. After more than 110 years following the martyrdom of Joseph Smith Jr. and his brother Hyrum, a stake patriarch was called in Missouri. Thomas Few Crow of Liberty, Missouri, was sustained as patriarch for the Kansas City Stake on Nov. 15, 1959, the first since Joseph Smith Sr. (CN 7/27/63)

Largest Groups to Receive Sacrament. Sacrament was served in a 34-minute period to 9,900 young women and their adult leaders attending the 1984 Area Young Women Conference in Phoenix, Arizona. Three hundred bishops and their counselors passed the sacrament and used 180 disposable water trays that held 66 cups each. (LDS 8/84)

Sacrament was served in a 23-minute period to 7,200 LDS Boy Scouts and their adult leaders attending the 1982 LDS Scout Jamboree in Arizona. One hundred and twenty priests and 250 deacons were required to administer and pass the sacrament. This was also the only sacrament meeting on record where nine superficial knife wounds were sustained – by Scouts otherwise preoccupied with whittling during the talks. (LDS 8/20/82)

First Sacrament Served In Space. The first sacrament meeting conducted in space took place Sunday, May 5, 1985, when astronaut Don Lind knelt weightless on the ceiling of his sleeping berth aboard the space shuttle Challenger to bless the sacrament. His scriptures were packed away, so he read the sacrament prayers from personal notes he was allowed to take with him on the trip. Brother Lind made special note of the unique kneeling position he took in the shuttle. He

NASA photo

Don Lind, in orbit in 1985, could kneel in prayer upside down in the weightlessness of space.

was able to kneel and bow his head in proper respect, yet being weightless and kneeling upside down, he was actually facing "up," symbolic of where heaven is, something that can't be done on earth when we pray, he said. (LDS 5/18/85, LDS 5/25/85)

First Sacrament in Vietnam Since the War. The first sacrament meeting held by members of the Saigon Branch since the end of the Vietnam war occurred in December 1986 under the direction of Branch President Thach. The man who blessed the sacrament, Le Van Kha, had been partaking of the sacrament alone every Sunday for 11 years since the airlift in 1975. (LDS 1/31/87; LDS 1/24/87)

Airborne Sacrament Cup Delivery. When the Kangaroo Island Branch needed more sacrament cups, President Stef McCann requested several hundred from the Marion, Australia, Stake. Unfortunately, no boat could deliver the cups in time for the next Sunday's services, so stake executive secretary Michael Thorton volunteered to deliver them by air. Unfortunately, the Kangaroo Island airport was shut down by bad weather when Brother Thorton flew over, so he did the next best thing: he buzzed President McCann's home. After three fly-bys, McCann finally understood what the noise was all about and came out to receive the package as it dropped from the sky. He had planned to give fresh fish to the pilot to show thanks but said, "I couldn't throw that high." (CN 3/28/87)

Most Consistent Sacrament Bread Delivery. The most consistent delivery of bread for the sacrament is by J.C. Easter, Austin, Texas. For 22 years, he delivered the equivalent of two tons of bread to various Austin Wards, missing only once during that time. (CN 6/26/82)

FASTING

First. The first fast meetings in the Church were held in the Kirtland Temple, according to the journal of Eliza R. Snow. Writing during the winter of 1836-37, Sister Snow said that on the first Thursday of each month, the temple was crowded with Saints observing the day of "fasting and prayer." (CN 7/8/89)

Nationwide Fast. Nov. 24, 1985, a day set aside by Congress for Americans to fast and donate the cost of their skipped meal to a local charity, was actually promoted by Congressman Ronald C. Packer, a former bishop from San Diego. Rep. Packer said he got the idea at the April 1985 General Conference when Church leaders announced that a Church wide fast for the starving people of Ethiopia had raised $6.5 million. (LDS 11/30/85)

WELFARE SYSTEM

President Ronald Reagan Visits. Ronald Reagan twice had the chance to observe the Church's welfare program, once as governor and again as president. "(It's) far superior to anything the government has been able to manage ...with no disrespect intended, one can't help but wonder if government welfare would exist if all our churches had picked up on the task," he said. (LDS 3/25/82)

O. Wallace Kasteler , Deseret Morning News

Pres. Reagan praised the Church's Welfare program as a model for the nation.

Largest Canning Project in Shortest Time. Six northern Arizona stakes received the assignment to raise, pick, husk, silk, trim, transport and can 597 cases of corn. And more than 700 members did just that, harvesting and canning 14,328 cans of corn in five days using hand-operated equipment.

Tom Smart , Deseret Morning News

Thousands of Church members were excused from Sunday services to help bail out downtown Salt Lake City during the floods of 1983.

Largest Service Projects. Some 40,000 Latter-day Saints participated in the largest Church service project on record when they rushed to save Salt Lake City and environs during the spring flooding of 1983. When the danger grew beyond the capabilities of local emergency personnel, bishops up and down the Wasatch Front excused their flocks from Sunday services so they could converge on the flooding to fill and stack sandbags, relieve other crews, move people and their belongings from harm's way, and otherwise help. They are credited with saving $80 million in property damage and cleanup costs during the 10-day flood. In Bountiful, 20,000 volunteers sand-bagged in six-hour shifts, 24 hours a day for more than a week. (LDS 6/17/83)

For the 2002 Olympic Winter Games held in Salt Lake City and environs, Latter-day Saints numbering more than 24,000 stepped forward to volunteer their time and energies to make the games a success.

In 1999, Church members created more than 100,000 quilts for desperate refugees and the needy in Kosovar, Turkey, Mexico and elsewhere.

Largest Orchard Project. The Church's largest orchard project in the mid-1970s was the Woodcrest Citrus Project near Riverside, California. With the fruit of more than 95,000 trees, the harvest typically amounted to some 21 million pounds of oranges in the good years. Stakes in the area provided the 500-600 pickers on Saturdays who helped harvest the crop. (CN 1975)

No need to worry about scraping up green Jello spills on the cement steps of this giant stadium.

Largest Cleanup Job. In the mid-1970s, the largest stadium under a cleaning contract to members of the Church was the 70,000+ seat Oklahoma Sooners Memorial Stadium. It took at least 130 members from the local ward from 5 p.m. to midnight to scrub the place down. After each game they hauled out tons of litter from concessionaire goodies that were dumped under just about every seat. (CN 1/24/76)

Lowest Realistic Food Budget. For a family of seven children and two parents, $35 a week (in 1976) sounds like an impossibly low amount for a complete food budget. But Lorraine Tyler of Walnut Creek, California, man-aged to lower her food budget to that amount by cooking with wheat instead of more costly meats and bakery items. She created Phoney Baloney from wheat, among other things. Her experimenting ultimately resulted in a wheat cookbook in which she described how to buy, store and prepare wheat for easy consumption. (CN 1/17/76)

Largest for Animals. Is the two-year supply of food for cows in Cedar City, Utah, the largest animal "home-storage" project in the Church? In 1977, the Cedar City, Utah, West Stake built a concrete silage-storage structure for its stake farm cows. The project required more than 900 voluntary hours by stake members, plus 300 cubic yards of concrete and nearly two miles of half-inch rebar. (CN 2/12/77)

Most Valuable Find at DI. In 1982, a BYU student purchased from the Provo Deseret Industries used-book section an 1847 copy of the Millennial Star. But inside was the real treasure: 12 pamphlets, also 135 years old, containing reprints of the complete set of 12 letters written between Orson Spencer and Rev. W. Crowel. Until the find, there were only four complete copies of the pamphlets known to exist. (LDS 7/16/82; DU 3/19/82)

Cornelius Zappy, Deseret Morning News file photo

1947 – The gospel can heal all wounds. Two years after WWII, with Germany in ruins, the people were left starving. Efforts to help were brought to bear by Church members worldwide. Pictured above, Dutch LDS and missionaries load a truck with food and supplies to be delivered across the border to hungry Saints in Germany. These same Dutch citizens were victims of Germany's invasion and occupation, but they embraced the highest ideals of Christianity, and were able to forgive and send life-saving help to their neighbors.

Pinstripes for the Penguins? In 2000, Linda Parker, Salt Lake City, and Cherie Dennis, Cranbourne, Australia, were on a mission of sorts to help Australian penguins stay warm. A species of a relatively small penguin had come afoul of the oil tanker spills in the region. The oil temporarily destroyed the natural oil on the penguins' feathers making it impossible for the 20-inch-tall animals to stay warm or to swim. That's where Sister Parker and Sister Dennis come in. They knitted more than 100 sweaters, each tailored to fit snugly and safely on the penguins, providing warmth and protection until the animals could recover and return to the ocean. Any interested party was invited to contribute to the Penguin-sweater Project, and send away for a penguin pattern. (Internet)

Largest Apricots Project. Who processes the most apricots in one month? In 1977, it was the members of the Brentwood Ward, Stockton, California, Stake, who picked, cleaned, cut, dried and packaged 25 tons of apricots as part of their annual fund-raising activity. The one-month-long event prompted several ward members to have T-shirts printed saying, "I'd rather be cutting apricots." (CN 9/24/77)

Largest Grape Project. In 2002, the Church's 80-acre vineyard in Madera, California, produced its largest crop ever with 180 tons of grapes. The prior record of 142 tons was set in 2000. During harvest, as many as 10,000 Latter-day Saints from local wards and stakes descended on the farm and tended to the rows of grapes assigned to their individual wards. During the winter dormant season, another 2,000 local Saints returned to prune the vines in their assigned rows. The grapes were dried in the central San Joaquin Valley sun for three weeks before being delivered to nearby Sun Maid Raisin Co. The raisins were packaged in Deseret-label boxes and sent to the Bishop's Storehouse facilities in Salt Lake City for distribution through the Church's welfare system. (CN 9/7/02)

GENEALOGY

Largest Internet Presence. The world's largest online genealogy Internet service is the Church's, known to millions as FamilySearch.org. Put online in 1999, the site gave free access to more than one billion names to genealogy hobbyists around the world. By its first year anniversary, the site had been contacted more than 3 billion times. A year later, the number of "hits" or computer connections was rapidly approaching 5 billion. It typically gets more than 8.5 million hits a day and has more than 300,000 registered users – at least 20 percent of those outside the United States. The Church has more than 3,500 Family History Centers in more than 75 countries to help gather and extract information locally. (CN 1/20/01)

Most Names on Record. After 50 years of microfilming, the Church reached another milestone in 1988. It put its 2 billionth name on film and stored it away in the Granite Mountain Records Vault east of Salt Lake City. (LDS 12/10/88)

Largest LDS Genealogical Library. The Church's Family History Library, just west of Temple Square, features 136,000 square feet of space, 1.5 million catalogued reels of microfilm, and 160,000 printed volumes of family histories. It is the hub for the Church's network of branch libraries worldwide. (LDS 11/2/85)

Youngest Official Extractor. Lori Rose of the Magna, Utah, Stake, became the youngest name extractor in the Church when she was set apart for the work on July 31, 1988, at age 11. "It's fun to write down names and numbers from the microfilm," the sixth grader said. "It helps me to know that I'm helping other people who need their temple work done." (LDS 9/3/88)

Lori Rose, studying microfilm, was bit by the genealogy bug at age 11.

Most Names Extracted – Individual. The most names extracted by an individual: 43,000 by Mary Ordway Greco, 82, of the Taylor 3rd Ward, Taylor, Utah, Stake. Her project took her more than 30 years of work. By early 1989, she traced her family back 11 generations. "My most rewarding experience in doing this work was when I completed my 11th generation, which dates back to my Mayflower ancestors." (LDS 3/22/89).

Most Names Submitted – Individual. By 1968, Archibald D. Gardner, Salt Lake City, had submitted for temple work 50,000 names of proven relationship. He had another 260,000 names in his index file, 90 percent of which he believed were relatives. He had traced his family back to 1200 A.D. (CN 1/25/69)

By 1959, Myra Tolman Patterson, Salt Lake City, had found more than 200,000 names of ancestors in various family lines after 30 years of research. (CN 4/25/59)

By the time Lillian Millet, Mesa, Arizona, turned 90 in 1986, she had submitted more than 33,000 names for temple work. (LDS 6/14/86)

Best Free Advertising. In September 1989, the U.S. Post Office printed millions of family-tree charts, making them available at all neighborhood post offices. Listed as the best source for genealogical information was the LDS Church, and readers were urged to "visit a (Mormon) Church near you."

Youngest to Reach 5,000 Names. In 1964, Carolyn Diane Black, 12, Savannah 2nd Branch, Georgia, reached a milestone of identifying 5,000 of her ancestors. She also completed 524 family group sheets. She guessed she spent about 2,500 hours to reach the milestone and credited her mother for showing her how to get started. Some of the names she found date back to the 1400s. (CN 7/6/64)

World's Largest Permanent Genealogy Storage Center. Six huge vaults carved into a granite mountain are the culmination of the Church's effort to find a safe, permanent storage facility for microfilm. It is estimated that some 6 million rolls of film can be stored in the $1.7 million facility. At the facility's dedication on June 22, 1966, one vault was already half full with 440,000 rolls that had been microfilmed since 1938. Officials estimated it would take about 100 years to fill all six vaults. The Church owns enough acreage to build another eight vaults. A typical row of microfilm filing shelves or cabinets is 200 feet long with floor-to-ceiling cabinets on either size. (Church Almanac; Author)

Dave Conley, Deseret Morning News

An early photo showing the first vault partially filled with microfilm and computer-tape storage racks.

Name Extraction – Milestone. On June 6, 1989, the 100 millionth entry in the name extraction program was processed by the Church. (Ensign Oct 89)

The last card from the Family History Library's card catalog was entered onto computer July 15, 1987, ending some 1 million man hours of effort to make the central genealogy records electronically available to patrons around the world. (CN 7/87)

Most Name Extractions Completed – Stake. Name extraction workers of the Salt Lake Parley's Stake completed 100,000 names in the fall of 1989 after a five-year effort headed up by Perris Jensen, 87. He attributed the success to "a loyal bunch of workers." (CN 11/4/89)

Longest Documented Direct Family Line. Shum Hing-June, a returned Chinese missionary from Hong Kong, has a family record containing an unbroken genealogy from the time of the Chou Dynasty, about 1000 B.C., to the present. (CN 7/19/69)

James Murray, Auckland, New Zealand, Harbour Stake, has traced his family back 37 generations to when canoes left what is believed to be Hawaii and arrived in New Zealand about 1300 A.D. (CN 5/80)

FAMILY HOME EVENING

Photo courtesy Benson family

Family Home Evening at the Marriotts. President Eisenhower and his wife (left of center) join the Benson and Marriott families for a traditional LDS Family Home Evening.

First Family Home Evening with a U.S. President. It makes sense that America's First Family should have a first family home evening, and that happened in 1955. In February, President Dwight D. Eisenhower and his wife were hosted at the southern plantation home of President J. Willard Marriott of the Washington, D.C., Stake. Elder Ezra Taft Benson's family was invited to present a typical LDS home evening. The program included singing, story-telling, skits and readings. The Eisenhowers joined in with stories of their own. The evening came to an end with a song and prayer. (CN 2/12/55)

GENERAL CONFERENCE

The First General Conference was held June 9, 1830, in Fayette, New York.

Milestones
April 1978 – the first satellite broadcast; English only
October 1982 – Spanish was added to the broadcast.
October 1984 – French was added.
October 1988 – Tongan, Samoan, Portuguese, Korean, German, Laotian, Cambodian, Hmong, Vietnamese were added.
By October 1989, the latest technology allowed 16 languages to be simultaneously broadcast via satellite around the world. More have been added since then.
October 1999 – First conference broadcast over the Internet.

First Use Of A Microphone. The first electric microphone in the Salt Lake Tabernacle was used at the April 1924 sessions of General Conference. Prior to that time, the excellent acoustical properties of the Tabernacle, backed by strong lungs and quiet babies, was all the Saints had to rely on to enjoy conference sermons.

First Radio Broadcast. The first General Conference to be broadcast over radio occurred in October 1924.

Utah State Historical Society

First Televised. Setting up television cameras in the Salt Lake Tabernacle started out as a closed-circuit experiment by Salt Lake City television station KSL for the April 1948 sessions of conference. With eight television sets in the Assembly Hall and one in the Bureau of Information, thousands saw the conference proceedings as they were televised to buildings around Temple Square. It was the first time many people had ever seen a television in action. By conference end, it was estimated some 20,000 people had witnessed the innovation on Temple Square. (CN 4/10/48)

On Sept. 28, 1949, beginning with the Friday morning session, history was made as the six sessions of General Conference were telecast for the first time outside of Temple Square. The telecast was picked up by thousands in the Salt Lake Valley, including young listeners confined in Primary Children's Hospital who watched the proceedings on their brand-new television. (CN 10/5/49)

First Telecast Beyond North America. In 1989, General Conference was telecast for the first time to audiences overseas including 3,600 in San Jose, Costa Rica, 2,800 in Manchester, England, and 500 in Frankfurt, Germany. More than 200 men in England stayed up until 4 a.m. to view the telecast of the general priesthood session. The potential audience among those capable of receiving the signal was in excess of 1 billion. The broadcast was in addition to the customary telecast to North America and parts of Mexico.

Celebrating the 150th Anniversary. With broadcasting gear strung all over the newly restored Peter Whitmer farm in Fayette, New York, President Spencer W. Kimball inaugurated the first conference broadcast outside of the Salt Lake Tabernacle in 1980. The proceedings were part of the 150th anniversary celebration of the Church. President Kimball and his party were linked to the tabernacle by satellite.

There were several "firsts" during this particular conference. It was the first in post-pioneer times to be conducted from more than 2,000 miles outside of Salt Lake City. It was the first time the prophet's wife had joined her husband on the stand for General Conference. It was the first time a branch choir sang at General Conference; and the first time a chapel was dedicated during a General Conference. (Author; Ensign; CN 4/80)

First Broadcast Over The Internet. In 1999, the Church's Web site, www.lds.org, began offering an audio version of conference to listeners around the world using the Internet. For the Oct. 2-3 sessions, more than 100,000 people worldwide logged on, choosing from among 12 languages offered.

First on Water. For a change of venue that was quiet and separate from the trials of the times, the Church's leadership met on a ferry on the Big Blue River in Jackson County, Missouri, for their April 1833 General Conference.

First Cancellation. After a serious outbreak of influenza in September 1957, General Conference was cancelled for the first time in the history of the Church. The flu was easing off in Salt Lake City, but not in time for conference. The announcement, made "with deep regret," reached most conference visitors in time, but a few arrived in Salt Lake only to learn they had to turn around and return home. (CN 10/5/57)

First from a Temple. The first session of General Conference to be conducted in a temple occurred in April of 1893 at the dedication of the Salt Lake Temple.

First to Include a Presidential Nomination. Joseph Smith Jr. was officially nominated for President of the United States during the General Conference of the Church in April 1844.

First to Include a Sports Score. Though nobody would openly admit it, many of those attending the priesthood session of conference in October 1983 had to be torn away from a great BYU-UCLA football game that Saturday evening. President Gordon B. Hinckley was generous in his sympathies to the football fans and, towards the end of the meeting, announced over the pulpit that BYU had upset UCLA 37-35. Was this the first sports score announced during General Conference and probably the first in the Salt Lake Tabernacle? A faithful reader of *Mormon World Records* writes that President McKay might have once announced a World Series score.

Deseret Morning News file photo

Howard W. Hunter served as president of the Church from 1994-95.

First Conference Speech While Seated. The first-ever conference address given while seated was in October 1987 as President Howard W. Hunter was confined to his conference chair because of fragile health. His condition and sitting position, however, did not detract from an excellent sermon.

Last Conference in the Salt Lake Tabernacle. Oct. 3, 1999, was the last General Conference session held in the Salt Lake Tabernacle on Temple Square. From that point forward, conference has been held in the Conference Center. President Gordon B. Hinckley ended the tradition that dated back to 1867 by saying goodbye to "an old and wonderful friend." (Almanac 2001)

First from the Conference Center. April 1-2, 2000, saw the first sessions of General Conference in the new 21,000-seat Conference Center. More than 400,000 people petitioned for the free tickets that were offered to local LDS.

Shortest Sermon in General Conference. After President Gordon B. Hinckley's stirring denouncement of drugs in the October 1989 General Priesthood meeting, President Ezra Taft Benson approached the podium, stood next to President Hinckley and stated a firm: "Amen!"

The second shortest General Conference sermon on record was given by President Ezra Taft Benson during the April 1989 General Priesthood meeting. After receiving International Scouting's highest award, The Bronze Wolf, the prophet shook the hands of the Boy Scout representatives and said with a warm smile, "May the Lord bless you and the devil miss you!" And then he sat down. (CN 4/8/89)

Ezra Taft Benson, an advocate for great causes, was powerful, eloquent and to the point.

Dressing for Conference is an Art! The most unusual conference weather is just about every year, but it was especially unusual in October 1960. On the first day of conference – a Friday – the skies were sunny and the temperature warmed to 83 degrees by afternoon. Thunderstorms developed Friday night and it was cloudy and rainy Saturday with temperatures barely topping 60 degrees. By Sunday, the bottom had dropped out. And then it snowed. The high on Sunday was only 41 degrees.

Warmest Fall Conference. In 1979, conference-goers were treated to a high of 88 degrees.

Coldest Fall Conference. In 1890, the daytime temperature never rose above 30 degrees.

Youngest Speaker in General Conference. Michael Nicholas, 16, Dayton, Ohio, East Stake, spoke for six minutes at General Priesthood meeting during the 1982 October Conference. Michael said he rewrote his talk about six times, read it about 70 times, and after the terrifying experience was over, he vowed, "Next time they'll have to pay me." (LDS 10/29/82)

The First Power Outage During Conference. The only power outage during a modern-day General Conference occurred during the last half-hour of the Sunday afternoon session in April 1984. An automobile crashed into a power line in Salt Lake City, causing the lights to flicker and the sound in the Salt Lake Tabernacle to go off. Elder L. Tom Perry was just finishing his speech, and when the sound quit, his booming voice took over. Said one observer, "I could hear him better than with the sound system on!" Although power was restored seconds after the accident, satellite transmission could not be regained for 30 minutes, leaving more than 600 U.S. and Canadian Stake centers without audio or visual signals. (LDS 4/13/84)

MISSIONARY WORK

First Use of "Elder." The first official and sanctioned use of the title "Elder" came from the lips of an ancient prophet in the earliest days of the Church. Wrote Joseph Smith of that occasion, "The messenger who visited us on this occasion and conferred this Priesthood (Aaronic) upon us, said that his name was John, the same that is called John the Baptist in the New Testament, and that he acted under the direction of Peter, James and John, who held the keys of the Priesthood of Melchizedek, which Priesthood, he said, would in due time be conferred on us, and that I should be called the first Elder of the Church, and he (Oliver Cowdery) the second. It was on the fifteenth day of May, 1829, that we were ordained under the hand of this messenger, and baptized." (CN 7/26/47)

First Discourse. On Sunday, April 11, 1830, the missionary work of the Church was officially started. The first discourse was preached by Oliver Cowdery at the home of Peter Whitmer where the Church had been organized a few days earlier. A number of members and investigators were present, and after the meeting, several were baptized. (CN 3/9/49)

First Missionary. The Church's first formal missionary was Samuel H. Smith, a younger brother of the prophet. Sometime in June 1830, Joseph set apart Samuel to proselyte in neighboring villages. He headed out on June 30, 1830, marking the first missionary journey in the Church. (CN 6/7/80)

First Sister Missionaries. Since the early history of the Church, there are instances where the wife of a man called on a mission joined him, but not in an official capacity. The first sister missionary formally called and set apart as such was Amanda Inez Knight. She was set apart April 1, 1898, for a mission to Great Britain. In 1901, Lucy Grant and Fannie Wooley were called and set apart to serve in the new Colorado Mission. (CN 2/9/74)

First Handcart Missionaries. On April 23, 1857, a caravan of 28 hand-carts, all pulled by missionaries headed to missions in the United States and Europe, left Salt Lake City for Florence, Nebraska. After 48 days and 1,000 miles of walking, they arrived on June 10, sold their handcarts for $8-$12 apiece and then set out by riverboat, railroad and stagecoach to their various fields of labor. Such a west-to-east trek had never before been made by hand-cart. (CN 9/22/62)

First Foreign Mission. In 1833, three years after the Church was organized, missionaries began preaching in Canada, making it the first field of missionary labor outside of the United States. John Taylor was one of the distinguished converts to come from efforts in Canada. The first foreign branch was organized there as well. Although not formally organized as a mission until 1919, it was for many decades a productive field of labor. (CN 2/7/59)

First 'Calls' in Foreign Tongues. Beginning in early February 1967, the First Presidency began issuing mission calls in the native tongues of the prospective missionaries. The Church translation department put the calls into the elders' and sisters' native tongues, and sent them out over the signatures of the First Presidency. (CN 2/18/67)

Most Full-Time Missions. Who has fulfilled the most full-time missions for the Church? Orson Pratt, a member of the Council of Twelve from 1835 to 1881, served 19 full-time missions. His trips to and from the mission field included 16 crossings of the Atlantic Ocean by boat. (CN 6/13/48)

Most Missionaries – One Family. From grandparents to grandchildren, the Barson family had 10 family members serving full-time missions at the same time: H. John and Joan Barson (parents), Norm and Carol Gardner, Ruth Gardner, Kim Davis, Derilyn Larson, Julie Barson, Laura Call, Kyle Larson, Brent Barson, and Brandon Call. (CN 11/16/91)

On Feb. 19, 1945, eight members of the Moikeha family, Wailuku, Hawaii, were all released from their other Church assignments and called on part-time missions. (CN 2/45)

Five of the 11 children of the Osipo Somaray family, Catarman, Philippines, served missions simultaneously in 1987, including the family's set of triplets. (CN 11/7/87)

Five children of the Harold and Vera Stewart family, College Ward, Logan, Utah, served missions simultaneously in 1986, including their set of twins. (CN 2/16/86)

Sidney R. Henderson, mission president, and wife, Joyce Giles, plus three of their sons, Sidney B., Nathan, and Richard, all served simultaneously in 1991 (CN 11/30/91)

Missionaries – Most Brother-Sister Sets From One Ward. The Uintah 5th Ward, Ogden, Utah, Weber Stake reported in 1991 it had four sets of brothers and sisters serving missions simultaneously. Jacqie and Scott Newman, Triscia and Troy Christopulos, Diana and David Nellis, and Tausha and Shane Jessen were called to serve in missions ranging from Australia to the Philippines, Europe, Central and South America, and the United States. (CN 4/6/91)

Most Missionaries – Same Family, Same Time, Same Place. In 1895, the five sons of John C. Naegle were all serving in the Swiss-German Mission at the same time. (CN 8/1/48)

Most International Mission. In 1987, the most international mission in the Church was a small portion of the Hong Kong mission where missionaries from the United States, Philippines, Hong Kong, Sweden and Australia work in the congestion of an area 1/3rd the size of Rhode Island with 7,500,000 people. One district, five stakes, 28 wards and 10 branches were concentrated there. For lack of space, most of the teaching and contacting was done in the chapels, parks and public squares. (CN 1/31/87)

Youngest Missionary Couple. Who is the youngest full-time missionary couple in modern history? In 1983 it was Mark and Robin Hall, both 29. They were called to serve in the Los Angeles Mission and surrounding area. (LDS 9/28/83)

Highest Percentage – Ward. In 1963, the ward with the highest ratio of missionaries to families was the Tridell Ward, Ashley, Utah, Stake. Ten of the ward's 32 families were supporting 12 full-time missionaries. (CN 4/20/63)

First Heart Recipient. The first elder with a heart transplant to serve a full-time mission was Chad Ruesch, Las Vegas 42nd Ward, Paradise Stake. He was the University of Utah's 32nd heart- transplant recipient. A year after his surgery, he arrived at his assigned area in Salt Lake City in 1986. Laboring as a missionary was not easy as he had to maintain "upkeep" on his new heart. He required blood treatment every six weeks, a biopsy every 90 days, and a three-day angiogram procedure once a year. (LDS 8/1/87)

Struck by Lightning. The first elders known to have been struck by lightning were Elder John Dobyns of Denver, Colorado, and Elder Robert Asay of Billings, Montana. Thinking it wasn't proper for the American flag to be out during a thunderstorm, they were trying to lower it from the flagpole outside the Harrisburg, Pennsylvania, Ward building when the lightning bolt hit them. Said Elder Dobyns, "It was an aluminum pole, but I didn't think about that. All of a sudden I heard a crash and I saw lightning all around me. Then I saw Elder Asay hit the ground real heard and I was going down at the same time. I was out for maybe two seconds, then I came to and had this excruciating pain all over and in me. I couldn't see. I panicked. I thought I had lost my sight and I thought Elder Asay was dead." They both recovered from their injuries. (CN 9/11/76)

Most Frugal Americans. While LDS missionaries no longer embark on missions without purse or scrip, they remain the most frugal of all U.S. citizens traveling around the world. Prior to the missionary funding change in 1990, missionaries lived on 1/5th to less than a fiftieth of the minimum per-diem rates given to federal employees for travel or living allowances. A study made in 1990 showed that in Tampa, Florida, missionaries lived on only $13.48 a day, while government employees were allowed $78 a day. In Los Angeles, missionaries got by on $9.04 a day compared to the Fed's $114 a day allotment. For years, the lowest-cost mission in the Church was the Peru Trujillo Mission at $36 per month, and the highest was $568 in the England London South Mission. Today, the numbers are literally all over the map! (DN 2/9/90)

First Hearing-Impaired Missionaries. The first deaf missionaries for the Church were set apart March 9, 1952, in the Ogden, Utah, Stake Mission. The two elders and four sister missionaries labored in the 11 Ogden stakes, and in their first few months had already baptized two deaf converts. (CN 7/25/53)

The Only Bike-Riding Mission President. Elder Heinz Gundlach, president of the East German Mission in 1952, rode his bicycle 60 kilometers to hold Sunday services with his branch of 17 members. Afterwards, he pedaled the 60 kilometers back home. The round trip, the same as riding from Salt Lake City to Ogden and back every week, took more than three hours. (CN 10/4/52)

Deseret Morning News file photo

Elder Gundlach (left) put 4,370 miles on his bike during the first year of his calling.

Most Significant LDS Supreme Court Case? For parents of missionaries, the most significant Supreme Court case was handled by BYU President Rex Lee. He went before the U.S. Supreme Court on March 26, 1990, to argue that money sent to missionary sons and daughters of LDS members should be tax deductible. The IRS argued that such missionaries, if truly agents for the Church, should be supported by the Church, not their parents. The final ruling stated that money given to the Church for support of the missionaries was tax deductible – a

THE SKOUSEN BOOK OF MORMON WORLD RECORDS

ruling prompting the Church to adopt a uniform contribution program where all parents give the same amount regardless of where a son or daughter is serving a mission.

Temple Riders. It's not what most people expect to see riding up to an LDS Temple – middle-aged bikers dressed up in their leathers, riding their Harleys. But these are no Hells Angels. On their leather jackets or license-plate holders are the words "Temple Riders." These bike rid'n brothers and sisters are just your run-of-the-mill temple-worthy members of the Church, happily making the rounds. The group doesn't ride on Sundays and they take two cross-country trips a year, often stopping at local LDS temples along the way. The group sometimes can exceed 90 bikes at a time. Temple Riders was formed in 1987 in Salt Lake City, and though not sanctioned by the Church, the members do missionary work by passing out copies of the Book of Mormon at biker rallies or just being good examples. (LATimes 12/26/99)

President Writes a Missionary. U.S. Senator Jake Garn's son received an unusual letter of support and encouragement while preparing to leave for his mission to England. President Ronald Reagan wrote him, quoting a verse from the Book of Mormon, and offering words of admiration, respect and encouragement. Citing Alma 60: 11 ("...sitting on a throne ... do nothing ..." and be delivered by God), President Reagan said, "I have often thought about these words. They came back to me during the campaign, especially when it would be a long day and one that didn't go as well as we had hoped. I thought of them when I was in the hospital, and they have been on my mind since Jake told me that you would soon be leaving on your mission to England." (Sunstone 6/82)

Iron Curtain 'Firsts.' There are many "first missions" behind the Iron Curtain, the political and military barrier that cut off parts of Soviet eastern Europe from the West during the so-called Cold War. The first mission created in that part of Europe was in Czechoslovakia in 1929 and dissolved in 1950. The Yugoslavia Zagreb Mission existed in 1975-1976 and the East Germany (DDR) Dresden Mission in 1969-1978. The Germany Leipzig Mission was opened on July 1, 1989. (LDS 3/8/89)

The first missionaries into Poland after the Iron Curtain was raised were Stanley and Gwen Manzur, Fredonia, Arizona. They went to Poland in 1983 and brought 36 persons into the Church. (LDS 9/6/86)

First Missionaries to Newfoundland. In 1948, Elders A. Curtis Page Jr., Payson, Utah, and John Major Scowcroft, Ogden, Utah, arrived in Newfoundland as the first representatives of the Church. The local newspaper carried a large three-column photograph of the young men and a complimentary article on the Church and its teachings. (CN 9/1/48)

First Missionaries to Mexico. On Jan. 7, 1875, Elders Daniel W. Jones, Anthony W. Ivins, Wiley C. Jones, Helaman Pratt, and James Z. Stewart began in earnest the first missionary work in Ciudad Juarez, Mexico. (CN 5/16/48)

First Missionaries in the Pacific. After a seven-month voyage aboard a whaling vessel, during which time Elder Knowlton F. Hanks died of "consumption," Elder Addison Pratt, Benjamin F. Grouard and Noah Rogers made their way towards Tahiti. Elder Pratt left the ship at the island of Tuhuai in April 1844, where he preached to and baptized all but one of a group of American shipbuilders. They interpreted for him in preaching to the natives. Several of these investigators were soon baptized and the first branch in the Pacific was then organized. By 1852, active opposition against the white missionaries had become serious, forcing the French to banish the elders from the islands. Nevertheless, the foundation had been laid for the future establishment of missions in Samoa, Tonga and New Zealand. (CN 11/1/58)

First Missionaries in Fiji. By 1960, Gideon Dolo held a number of firsts:
- The first Fijian to be ordained an elder
- The first Fijian to receive his temple endowments
- The first Fijian to serve on a mission
- The first Fijian to enroll at BYU-Hawaii. (CN 11/5/60)

Two missionaries gave Church talks for the first time in the Fijian language when they addressed the district conference in Suva, Fiji, Sept. 23, 1962. The LDS hymn, "O My Father," was publicly sung in Fijian for the first time at the same conference. (CN 10/6/62)

First Missionary From Tonga. Duad Sahim, a native of the Fiji Islands, became the first Tongan ordained an elder at Suva, Fiji, on May 30, 1961. (CN 7/8/61)

First Missionaries in India. In 1851, a little nucleus of the Church began growing in Calcutta, India, thanks to the efforts of soldiers and sailors stationed there. The first baptisms occurred on June 22, 1851, when Captain James P. Meik, his wife, Major Matthew McCune and Maurice White were baptized. On Christmas Day that same year, the first full-time elder arrived. William Willes, a former resident of India, began in earnest to strengthen the little branch. By March of 1852, there were 32 members in Calcutta, and two months later, more than 150. However, the little branch did not last. The hundred poor Calcutta members rejoined their former Christian affiliates. "For a few rupees," Mission President Nathaniel V. Jones wrote in his journal, many offered to rejoin the LDS Church if they could be paid more than what they were earning at their jobs. With money a big issue, the missionary work began to unravel. It was finally decided to close the mission and pull out the missionaries. On May 2, 1856, the last Elder left for home. (CN 1/3/59)

Argentina Mission. Elder Melvin Joseph Ballard received a special assignment in October 1925. He was asked to open a mission for the Church in Buenos Aires, Argentina. With two companions, Rulon S. Wells and Ray L. Pratt, he arrived in the city on Dec. 7, 1925. After an extensive survey of the locale, he chose Christmas Day to dedicate the country and continent for the establishment of the Church. Before his return home, he helped in performing a number of baptisms and organized a branch at Buenos Aires. (CN 12/10/55)

First Missionaries to Brazil. In 1927, President Reinhold Stoof of the South American Mission and Waldo L. Stoddard went to Brazil to survey the country for missionary work. They found encouraging possibilities in Joinville and the surrounding areas. About a year later, the first missionaries, Elders William F. Heinz and Emil A. J. Schindler, returned to Joinville to begin proselyting. Their first baptisms were performed April 14, 1929, when Mrs. Bertha Sell and her four children joined the Church. (CN 4/25/59)

First Missionaries to France. The first missionary to France was William Howells, a convert to the Church and a former Baptist minister from Aberdare, South Wales. He arrived in Le Havre, France, in July 1849. With no French language skills, Brother Howells began his work in Le Havre in early July of 1849. He first began preaching to sailors on American ships and to local English people, and finally baptized his first convert, Augustus Saint d'Anna on July 30, 1849, in the ocean. On April 6, 1850, with six members, Howells organized the Boulogne-Sur-Mer Branch, the first in France. (CN 11/8/58)

First Missionaries to Great Britain. Heber C. Kimball led the first missionary efforts to England in 1837 to fulfill the commandment given him through Joseph Smith, "to go to England and open the door of salvation" to the people there. (CN 8/15/53)

First Missionary from Uruguay. Elder Francisco Guillermo Rial, from Rodo Sur, Uruguay, was the first missionary from Uruguay. He was called in 1967 to serve in the Italian Mission. (CN 2/11/67)

First Missionary from Peru. Wilfredo Rojas Hurtado, Huancayo, Peru, was that country's first missionary sent to a foreign country when he left March 7, 1967, for Santiago, Chile. He had been a member for about a year before his mission call came. (CN 4/15/67)

First Missionaries from the Philippines. On Feb. 8, 1965, the first two elders from the Philippines gave their farewell talks and departed for the Hawaiian mission. Elders Lino O. Brocka and Emiliano B. Antonio Jr. were early converts – Elder Brocka was the second Filipino ever baptized into the Church. Because of his loyalty to the Student Catholic Action at the University of the Philippines, he received what is perhaps the only farewell party to a departing Mormon missionary ever given by a Catholic organization. (CN 3/27/65)

First Missionary from Sri Lanka. The first missionary from Sri Lanka was Elder Bandu Sri Amarasekara, affectionately called "Elder A" by his companions, who served with him in Southern California in 1984-86. (LDS 3/1/86)

First Non white Missionary from South Africa. After only three years in the Church, Hilda Benans was called in 1986 to the Alabama Birmingham Mission. (LDS 5/3/86)

First Missionary from Swaziland. While looking for "a good job," Paulo Cipriano Zandamela met LDS missionaries in 1987, took the lessons and was baptized July 31, 1988. He became the first from his country called on a foreign mission when the letter from Salt Lake City arrived in January 1990 calling him to the Pennsylvania Philadelphia Mission. (CN 1/27/90)

First Missionaries from Bolivia. In 1968, Carlos Pedraja and Enrique Mansilla became the first native missionaries from their country when they were ordained at their home branch, the Cochabamba Branch, and sent into the countryside to preach full time for two years.

In 1973, lderse Benedicto Vega, Leon Caro, and Justo Cuentas became the first Aymara-speaking elders from Bolivia. (CN 10/5/68; CN 9/29/73)

First Missionaries from Japan. Two young Japanese elders, Toshio Murakami of the Meguro Branch and Yotaro Yoshino of the Tahasaki Branch of the Japanese Mission, were the first native Japanese to become full-time missionaries for the Church. They were called in 1951 and received financial assistance from their parents, none of whom were members of the Church. (CN 1/16/52)

ODD MISSIONARY TOOLS

Buck enjoys a sesame-seed bun.

Proselyting Hamster. "Buck" the hamster, a "member" of the Mesa, Arizona, 27th Ward, was sent among families in the ward to prompt them to do some type of missionary activity. The hamster lived in a member's home until that family fulfilled a missionary task such as handing out a copy of the Book of Mormon. They could then "pass the Buck" to another member's home. Explained ward Mission Leader Larry Tryon: "We've had him stay as long as a month at one house, but the wife usually gets tired of the mess and pushes the family into qualifying to get rid of him." (LDS 4/19/86)

Taxi Cab's Theater on the Air. Martin Kerper, Plainview 2nd Ward, Long Island, New York, Stake, played General Conference and dramatized Book of Mormon tapes in his cab while carrying fares around New York City in 1986. The most frequent question was, "Isn't that Nighttime Theater on the radio?" (CN 8/17/86)

In 1988, Bill Arnett, owner of Yellow Cab in Phoenix, became the first cab operator in the United States to offer non-smoking cabs to customers. (LDS 11/12/88)

Get me to the church on time – in the Grand Canyon.

Mules and Horses. Aside from the work animals that assisted the Saints across the plains, the first known horses called on a mission for the Church were a buckskin named "Relampago" (Lightning) and a palomino named "Palamo," both of Arizona. They were sent by their owners on a two-year mission to carry Church members eight miles down into the Grand Canyon to a Church branch in Supai, and then return them to the South Rim. The round trip took about five hours and was usually an overnighter for most visitors to the branch. (CN 7/82)

Helicopter. Named "Hereafter 727," a chopper was used in Vietnam to keep LDS members united, flying more than 250 hours ferrying local priesthood leaders to meetings, delivering scriptures and manuals for the organizing of servicemen's groups and bringing assistance when ordinance work was required. It was retired from its missionary work in December 1967. (CN 1/6/68)

Phantom Jet. An F-4C Phantom jet assigned to Major Loyal D. Hastings, the LDS group leader at Cam Ranh Bay, South Vietnam, had "TEMPLE SQUARE," painted in bold letters across its nose. It became one of the best Church advertisements in the air during the Vietnam war. (CN 3/22/69)

Brother Hasting's missionary message was loud and clear on his Phantom jet.

Boat. The good ship "Faifekau," which means "Missionary" in the Tongan tongue, was launched April 26, 1966. Built by local members of the Church, the 45-foot long, eight-ton sailing launch with an auxiliary motor, helped proselyting missionaries supervise operation of branches and districts in the many scattered islands of the Tongan mission. The boat builders were set apart for the task with a special priesthood blessing. They lived on the construction site and worked six days a week from September 1965 to April 24, 1966. (CN 5/14/66)

Yacht. The 50-ton Tahitian Mission yacht "Praita" (meaning Pratt in Tahitian) was bought to ferry missionaries around the 80 or so islands of Tahiti. The yacht was named in memory of Addison Pratt and his wife, Louisa Barnes Pratt, who were early missionaries to Tahiti and established the first branch there in April 1844. (CN 10/25/50)

In 1950, the Praita made the rounds in Tahiti.

Flags. In 1945, Ray N. Taylor was a soldier stationed at Camp Gilmore in Farragut, Idaho, for basic training, including the use of semaphore flags. One day, with no message to practice with, he pulled out a Church News article summarizing a speech by President Heber J. Grant. Brother Taylor proceeded to dictate the talk with the flags, unaware that some distance away a salty old chief was likewise unoccupied and sat down to read the semaphore message. It caught the chief's interest. He tracked down Taylor for more information and began taking missionary lessons. (CN 2/3/45)

Deseret Morning News file photo

The S.S. Flying Cloud was the main transport to starving Europe for Church-donated food that included tens of thousands of cases of corn, peas, milk, tomatoes, honey, jam, peaches, syrup, and more.

Ship. After World War II, when the Saints and others in Europe were in such desperate need of basic supplies, the Church donated thousands of tons of food, clothing and supplies. The S.S. Flying Cloud, owned by the Isbrandtsen Steamship Company, carried nearly all of these supplies to the needy in Europe and became known as the floating Mormon supply vessel. (CN 7/4/48)

Unusual Companionships. You'll always find cook and kitchen together, especially in the Washington, D.C. mission. Elder Roger Cook, Ogden, Utah, and Todd Kitchens, Norman, Oklahoma, were companions in the mission's African program in 1986. (CN 5/4/86)

Identical twin brothers Douglas J. and Jeffrey W. Cheney, San Bernardino, California, were not only called on their missions on the same day, but also to the same mission, and served their final months together as companions in Fairbanks, Alaska. (CN 7/27/86)

It was nice to see Elders Brigham Young and Smith together again! In 1970, Elder Brigham Young, the great-great-great-grandson of Brigham Young was teamed up with Craig Smith, a descendant of Joseph Smith Jr.'s grandfather (Asahel Smith) to serve in New Zealand. (CN 12/19/70)

STRUCTURES

LDS Temples

Largest. The Salt Lake Temple has the most usable floor space of any modern LDS temple with 253,015 square feet.

Busiest. Provo: Leading its closest contender, the Jordan River Temple, the Provo Temple has more than 350,000 endowments per year. The Provo and Jordan River temples account for approximately 20 percent of all the temple work conducted by the Saints worldwide. (Author)

Most Viewed. The Washington, D.C. Temple, seen by almost 200,000 motorists daily, attracts a great deal of attention. At its open house prior to its dedication in 1974, there were 758,328 persons who toured the building – the highest number in Church history. It cost $17 million to build, sits on a 57-acre site, and is the largest in overall dimension built by the Church.

The Washington, D.C. Temple offers a spectacular view to thousands of daily commuters traveling the beltway.

The Washington, D.C. temple also once held the distinction of being the most beautiful view along the nation's capitol beltway. According to a Washington Post Magazine article on the best and worst views in 1989, the Washington Temple received the "Best View on the Beltway" honor. The article said, "As you drive past Kensington at night along the Roller Coaster (the freeway stretch between Connecticut and Georgia avenues), the soaring spires and golden highlights of the Mormon Temple are always a thrill." And for the worst view, the magazine said: "Everything else." Dubbed "Oz" by some, a prankster once spray painted "RELEASE DOROTHY" on a nearby overpass. (CN 6/17/89)

Most Temples Dedicated in Shortest Time. On May 20-21, 2000, three temples were dedicated – Tampico, Mexico, Temple, Villahermosa, Mexico, Temple and the Nashville, Tennessee, Temple.

On April 23, 2000, two temples were dedicated – Reno, Nevada, Temple and the Memphis, Tennessee, Temple.

On June 4, 2000, two temples were dedicated – Montreal, Quebec, Temple, and the San Jose, Costa Rica, Temple.

The most temples dedicated during one international trip by members of the First Presidency is four, June 11-18, 2000 – Fukuoka, Japan, Temple, the Adelaide, Australia, Temple, the Melbourne, Australia, Temple, and the Suva, Fiji, Temple.

Deseret Morning News file photo by Markus Ringger

Freiberg, Germany: Joined by Thomas S. Monson (third from right), Elders Robert D. Hales (center) and F. Enzio Busche (second from right), participate in the official groundbreaking of the Church's 36th temple.

Deseret Morning News file photo

Freiberg: Gordon B. Hinckley dedicated the finished project.

First Behind the Iron Curtain. The first temple built and dedicated in a communist nation was the Freiberg, German Democratic Republic, Temple. It was dedicated by President Gordon B. Hinckley during seven dedicatory sessions June 29-30, 1985. (LDS 7/13/85)

Longest Wait Between Temples. The longest interval (so far) between the first and second temples built in a state is 139 years for the state of Illinois. The first temple, built in Nauvoo, was completed in 1846, and the next was the Chicago Temple in 1985. (LDS 8/24/85)

A Temple on Every Continent. The first temple in Africa, the Johannesburg, South Africa, Temple, was dedicated Aug. 24, 1985. This event marked the first time at which a temple was located on every inhabited continent on Earth — North America, South America, Asia, Europe, Australia and, finally, Africa. (LDS 9/7/85)

Gerry Avant, Deseret Morning News

The South Africa Temple completed a great circle of temples around the globe, bringing together many strangers into a common fold.

Farthest North Temple. The temple in Anchorage, Alaska, is the most northern in the Church. It was the second of the so-called "smaller temples" to be built in the world, and was dedicated by President Gordon B. Hinckley in 1999.

Asia. The Asian mainland finally received a temple when the Seoul, Korea, Temple was dedicated on Dec. 14-15, 1985. (CN 1/5/86)

First Temple in Europe. The Switzerland Temple, built seven miles from Bern in the beautiful little mountain town of Zollikofen, was dedicated by President David O. McKay on Sept. 11, 1955. It was the first LDS temple in Europe. President McKay called that moment of the dedication "probably the greatest event that has occurred in Europe since the gospel was brought here 118 years ago." (CN 9/17/55)

Most Temple Site Rejections. The most rejections of a temple site: 11 by the government of West Germany. The Church submitted 14 potential sites for the Frankfurt Temple, but 11 were rejected during a two-year struggle to find a suitable location. The temple was finally constructed on the five-acre site 20 miles outside of Frankfurt. (LDS 7/27/85)

Most Temples Built During One Administration. During President Gordon B. Hinckley's service as an apostle and president of the Church, he has dedicated 90 (and counting!) temples as of the dedication of the Manhattan New York Temple in June 2004. At that time there were 119 temples in operation with another 10 announced or under construction.

President Spencer W. Kimball saw 21 temples dedicated during his 12 years as Church president. There were another 11 under construction at the time of his death. (www.LDS.org)

First Wed In the Salt Lake Temple.

Deseret Morning News file photo

Can anyone identify these relatives? These are the first couples married in the Salt Lake Temple, shown here on their 50th wedding anniversaries, April 3, 1943.

Were James Cannon Lambert and Mary McAllister Waddell, married May 24, 1893, the first couple married in the Salt Lake Temple? They are listed first among several couples sealed in the temple on that day, some four weeks after the temple was dedicated on April 6-24, 1893. (CN 4/17/43)

From Hong Kong: Sheldon Poor and his wife, Eliza Lau, became the first couple from Hong Kong to be married in the Salt Lake Temple in August 1971. They saved for several years to pay for the trip. Brother Poor was serving as district president for the Church in Hong Kong. He said, "We feel this is the best way to set an example to our Chinese members in Hong Kong." (CN 8/14/71)

From Brazil: Elder and Mrs. Alfredo L. Vaz, both converts, became the first Brazilian couple to go through the Salt Lake Temple for their endowments in July 1949. A week before their civilian marriage, Vaz baptized his wife in their new Campinas, Brazil, LDS Chapel – a first for their new building, after which they made the trek to Salt Lake City. (CN 7/31/49)

Elder and Sister Alfredo L. Vaz.

From Uruguay. When Senor Carace Piedras and his wife, Irma, arrived at the Salt Lake Temple to be sealed as husband and wife, it was actually their third marriage. Before their trip to Salt Lake City in 1964, they were first married in a civil ceremony in Montevideo. Afterwards they had a church marriage at the Rodo Branch, also in Montevideo. At the Salt Lake Temple, Elder Spencer W. Kimball performed the sealing ceremony in Spanish, the first ever at that temple for a couple from Uruguay. Afterwards, the "thrice-newlyweds" left for California. (CN 10/17/64)

From Quito, Ecuador. Brother and Sister Tito Paez made their trek to the Salt Lake Temple in 1974, becoming the first from Quito to be so married. He was first counselor in the Quito, Ecuador, Branch, and his wife was the Relief Society president. (CN 7/27/74)

First Wed in Los Angeles Temple. In 1956, William and Bettycharles Shields became the first couple to be married in the Los Angeles Temple. They had five children, all of whom had temple marriages. As for being first, Brother Shields asked, "Do we get any extra credit for this?" (LDS 4/5/86)

First Wed in Swiss Temple. Mario Guggiari and his wife became the first couple to be sealed in the newly dedicated Swiss Temple on Nov. 1, 1959. (CN 2/21/70)

First (and only?) Baby Born in a Temple. During the 31 dedication ceremonies of the Salt Lake Temple on April 6-24, 1893, the April 7 evening session stands out as having a most unusual interruption. A Mr. and Mrs. Bennett of Provo, Utah, had made the long buggy ride to Salt Lake City to witness the historic dedication services. At the time, Mrs. Bennett was a little more than eight months pregnant and wasn't expecting her baby anytime soon. However, that evening, all expectations changed. When baby decided to come, Mrs. Bennett was quickly escorted to another room in the temple where she gave birth to a healthy baby boy. Juliana Smith, the wife of Joseph F. Smith, was an experienced midwife and helped Mrs. Bennett through the delivery. Several days later, the family returned to the room where the baby was born and President Smith blessed the baby, giving him the name "Joseph Temple Bennett." For 14 years thereafter, Mrs. Bennett and young Joseph returned each year for an anniversary visit. (CN 5/25/63)

Mark Ludwig, age 7, lends Pres. Hinckley a hand.

Deseret Morning News file photo

Youngest Participant in a Temple Ground-breaking. Mark Ludwig, 7, Greenwood Village Ward, Denver, Colorado, went over the heads of his parents and wrote President Gordon B. Hinckley asking if he could help with the ground-breaking for the Denver Temple. To the parents' astonishment, President Hinckley read Mark's letter at the ground-breaking ceremony and invited Mark to help, making him the youngest ever to break ground for a temple. (CN 5/27/84)

Most Ancient Language. The Andean language of Quechua, dating back to before A.D. 500, is thought to be the oldest language in which the temple ceremony has been given. Offered only in the Lima Peru Temple, the language is spoken by more than 2 million Peruvians who live primarily in Cuzco and other communities high in the Andes. Other languages used for the temple date to modern renditions of Germanic or the Romance languages that have been evolving since the fall of Rome and the decline of Latin. (LDS 3/26/88)

Attack on an LDS Temple. In 1848, the Nauvoo Temple was burned to the ground while the Saints were being driven from the east. In more recent times, the most destructive attack on a temple took place in the early morning hours of Nov. 14, 1962, when a plastic-explosive device attached to the doorknobs of the east doors of the Salt Lake Temple exploded. Eleven temple windows were shattered. While repairs were relatively easy to make,

Exterior: Priceless pioneer craftmanship was destroyed by the 1962 attack.

Photos: Deseret Morning News, J. M. Heslop and O. Wallace Kasteler

replacing the original pioneer-era hardware proved more difficult. FBI agents and U.S. Army explosive ordinance experts were given permission to examine the east end and interior of the temple. Salt Lake police were also curious about a white chalked "Viva Castro" written within a four-inch circle on a steel fence post immediately in front of the temple. No arrests were ever made. (CN 11/17/62)

Though not considered an overt attack, the Apia Samoa Temple was destroyed by fire on July 9, 2003. It was being renovated and was scheduled for rededicaton in October 2003. A week after the fire, the Brethren announced it would be rebuilt. Dedication of the new building is scheduled for mid-2005. (LDS.org)

OTHER STRUCTURES

Utah's First Structure. In 1989, BYU archaeologists uncovered what is believed to be the oldest structure yet found in Utah. A pit that dated back to 1800 B.C. was found at what researchers believe to be a prehistoric hunting camp near Salina Canyon. The basin-shaped depression was ringed with ancient post holes. (CN 12/31/89)

Photo courtesy J. Knollin Haws

Apia Samoa Temple -- Only the Angel Moroni statue was salvaged after the devastating fire. The Church bought additional land on which the new temple and a modern meeting house are under construction (see LDS.org).

A real mobile home ... but without the wheels, hookups or noisy dog.

Oldest House in Salt Lake City. Built in 1847, the oldest house in Salt Lake City has moved a lot since then. In 1849, it was moved from Pioneer Park to First North and West Temple. In 1912, it was placed in a museum on Richards Street near Temple Square. The Daughters of the Utah Pioneers had it placed on the southeast corner of Temple Square in 1915 where it stayed until the construction of a new visitors center in August 1976 forced its removal again. Today, it sits to the south of the Church History and Arts museum. (CN 8/14/76)

First Tabernacle. The first official tabernacle built in the Church was erected in 18 days at Kanesville, Iowa (now, Council Bluffs, Iowa). Bishop Henry W. Miller rallied about 200 men in two days and had them working in freezing winter weather to get the task done. The log building measured 40 feet by 60 feet, and could seat 1,000 people. It was dedicated on Dec. 24, 1847, by Orson Pratt during a general conference that had convened that day in the new building. At the same conference, Brigham Young was unanimously sustained as president of the Church with Heber C. Kimball and Willard Richards his counselors. A natural spring caused the bottom logs to rot over a 3-year period, and with the Saints having settled farther west, others salvaged the good logs and the building was lost to history. In 1996, an authentic replica was built and may be visited today. (CN 12/8/48; Internet)

Reconstructed Kanesville Tabernacle as it looked in 1847.

The Tabernacle and Its Amazing Dome. The most ambitious work of timber roof framing in the 1860s was that being done in Salt Lake City as the Saints built their Tabernacle. At a total cost of more than $300,000, the oval-shaped building of sandstone, lime and sand, required 1.6 million board feet of lumber and 350,000 large wood shingles to build its arching domed roof – an engineering marvel of its time. The roof's lattice-truss arch system was built without nails and is held together with dowels and wedges.

The Salt Lake Tabernacle was built between 1864 and 1867 immediately west of the Salt Lake Temple. Henry Grow supervised the construction, however Truman O. Angell was brought in to take care of problems with

The Salt Lake Tabernacle's massive dome remains an engineering marvel to this day.

the building's acoustics. Brother Angell added the gallery in 1870 to take care of the sound problem and helped give the building its worldwide reputation as a nearly acoustically perfect building.

The roof rests on 44 sandstone piers and the building can seat 8,000, including the gallery and choir seats.

Prior to the building's construction, Brigham Young and Church architect William H. Folsom sat in earnest conversation in the Beehive House parlor to plan it out. They got stuck on how to accommodate several thousand people in a single building with an unobstructed view for General Conference. Brigham

The Tabernacle's roof beams are held together with wooden pegs.

suddenly stood up, strode over to the doorway, picked up his big black umbrella and opened it. "This may give us a good idea for a roof and its support," he said. "Can you do it?" Folsom replied he would try, and by 1867, with the roof in place over the Tabernacle, the largest umbrella-inspired building in the Church had been finished. The first conference was conducted in October 1867, and the building was formally dedicated Oct. 9, 1875. (CN 3/20/65; various Internet sites)

Tabernacle Organ. The Tabernacle organ, which was expanded to its present size in 1915, has nearly 11,000 individual pipes. The combinations of tonal shadings and variations are calculated to number 36,000,000,000,000, 000,000,000,000,000,000,000,000,000,000,000,000,000,000,000,000,000 (36 followed by 66 zeros). (CN 12/8/79)

First Structural Change to Salt Lake Tabernacle. What greater reason could there be for making a major structural change to the great domed tabernacle than to add a crying room? In 1951, work began on the glassed-in, soundproof room for the care of small children during broadcasts and other events in the building. Sound engineers made exhaustive tests before the construction was begun to make sure the room – breaking as it does the ellipsoid shape of the Tabernacle interior – would not destroy the Tabernacle's world-famous acoustic excellence. This was the first structural change since the building's completion in 1895. (CN 8/22/51)

First Observatory. The Church's first observatory was a small adobe structure built by the federal government in 1869 on the southeast corner of Temple Square. Orson Pratt was the Church's first astronomer and mathematician and used the facility to "weigh the earth, compute distance in space, time the revolutions of distant suns, and chart the courses through space of planetary systems." (DN 11/23/35)

Highest Percentage of Homeowners. In 1991, Utah led the nation with the highest percentage of people, 75.1 percent, who owned the property they lived in. The average price of a home in the metropolitan area was $82,000. (DN 7/25/91)

BUSINESS AND REAL ESTATE

Is the Tokyo Temple site the most expensive real estate the Church owns?

Deseret Morning News file photo

Expensive Territory in Japan. Missionaries returning from Japan will relate the story of the Tokyo, Japan, Temple, and its place on the most expensive real estate the Church owns. According to local missionary lore, an aggressive push to gain new converts enlarged membership roles so high in that part of Japan that a temple seemed well justified. The Church bought property far from the busy city center and a temple, chapel, mission headquarters and parking area were constructed. Over the years, this part of the city became an important business center and property values shot through the roof. It was rumored that if you took a U.S. $1,000 bill and laid it anywhere on the Church-owned property when the temple was dedicated in 1980, the ground covered by that bill would be worth more than the face value of the currency. That little theory put the value of the half-acre temple site at more than $200 million. That figure sounds awfully high, but maybe not. For comparison, consider a much smaller lot. In 2003, 50 new cemetery lots were opened for sale at the Aoyama Cemetery in a ritzy Tokyo location. The cost for a 5 foot x 8 foot lot (40 square feet) was $86,000 – about one fourth of the rumored value of the prime real estate upon which the Tokyo Temple stands. (Author's interview; Associated Press; Internet)

Largest Parcel of Land Owned by the Church. The largest piece of land owned by the Church is its 300,000-acre ranch in Florida, not far from Disney World. The ranch is about half the size of Rhode Island and 10 times larger than Disney World. Local developers have estimated the water on the property is sufficient to sustain up to 50,000 residents. The Florida ranch makes the Church the largest single-proprietor landholder in Florida. In the late 1960s, the land was appraised for about $100 million. (LDS 7/26/89)

Most Expensive Real Estate. The New York skyscraper the Church built in the early 1960s sits on a prime piece of real estate. Situated just west of Fifth Avenue between 57th and 58th, and opposite the Hotel Plaza, the building was erected on a piece of property purchased in early 1962 for $1,250,000, or about $100 per square foot. (CN 1/13/62; CN 1/20/62)

Most Expensive Temple. The Washington, D.C. Temple, dedicated in 1974, cost more than $17 million to complete. Adjusting for inflation, that cost holds up against the construction expenses for subsequent temples. At the time, this was almost three times the cost of the Los Angeles Temple and the 13 acres upon which it sits in Westwood Village. In 1956, the Los Angeles Temple's land was valued at some $6 million. (CN 3/10/56)

Most Expensive Church Building. The largest Church-financed construction project built only for official Church work is the 28-story headquarters building in Salt Lake City. The $31.4 million building brought together Church employees from 13 buildings scattered around the city in 1972. The construction company winning the low bid was actually a joint venture by two Utah firms: Christensen Brothers, Inc., Salt Lake City, and W. W. Clyde and Co., Springville, Utah. (CN 7/26/69)

The new Church Office Building under construction in 1971.

Outbidding Billionaires. When the Church bid for 2,755 acres of prime tobacco land in 1980, it found itself up against some pretty heavy competition including those Texas oil billionaires, the Hunt brothers. But when the gavel fell, the Church had won the bid, beating out the Hunt brothers' best offer by $25,000. Incidentally, the land, located near Hopkinsville, Texas, is not being used for tobacco. (DU 9/18/80)

Settlements

Largest LDS city is Salt Lake City, population approaching 185,000, with 50 percent LDS, and 1.5 million across the Wasatch Front (Ogden through Provo) and closer to 70 percent LDS statewide.

Smallest LDS city is Orderville, Utah, population 596 (2000), the last to give up living the United Order.

The oldest community named after the Prophet Joseph Smith is Joseph City, Arizona (originally named Saint Joseph). It was one of Arizona's earliest Mormon settlements, established in March 1876. (LDS 3/23/85; Internet sources)

BUSINESS

Research Profits. In 2002, BYU was recognized as the best in the nation at taking research grants and turning them into profitable inventions. The Chronicle of Higher Education gave BYU top marks for its ability to earn income from research dollars. BYU's top-selling inventions earn the school $3 to $5 million each year. Half the money usually goes to the inventor and the other half is reinvested in further research. Such inventions include a drug to treat a rare form of leukemia, a digital hearing aid, water-modeling software, and a carbon-fiber structure that is lighter and 12 times stronger than steel. (CN 8/3/02)

Paul B. Skousen

The facade of the downtown Salt Lake City ZCMI ... not much different from the way it looked a century ago.

First Department Store. ZCMI (Zions Commercial Mercantile Institution) was the first department store in the United States. Established on March 1, 1869, the first ZCMI opened its doors with more than $50,000 in stock and merchandise. President Brigham Young made the first purchase. The chain was eventually sold to Meier and Frank Company in 1999. (Internet)

Utah's Smallest Post Office: The official post office at Axtell, Utah, about 135 miles from Salt Lake City, is almost too small to park a single car inside. Settled in 1870, the population of Axtell is guessed at around 150-200.  There are three stories about how it got its name, but nobody really knows. If you're writing somebody in Axtell, this (above) is where the letter will be dropped off. Many of the residents are employees at nearby Gunnison Prison.

ODDS AND ENDS

Largest Wooden Swing. Who in the Church can boast the largest homemade wooden swing? In the summer of 2002, a couple of returned missionaries with a lot of time on their hands created this monster swing with aspen, oak and pine trees that were felled during a windstorm in Provo Canyon. Joe and Ben Skousen, River Ridge Utah 3rd Ward, used logs that averaged 15 inches in diameter to create this family-sized swing. The bench is ten feet across and easily seats a family of 8 (or 5 couples on a group date!). It stands 9 feet tall and is 14 feet across. (Author)

Ben (left) and Joe Skousen built this massive wooden swing in 2002. Perfect for summer sunsets and lazy afternoons, the 14-foot creation posed an interesting and new obstacle for both the lawn-mower and the family dog.

Photo courtesy Joe and Ben Skousen

Philo Farnsworth (above), sports a moustache in a photo tagged for the patent lawsuit brought against him by RCA. Philo won.

The vision that filled Farnsworth's head when he worked the potato fields as a young man in Idaho was more than just that of endless furrows. He also envisioned a new concept for electronic communications: the world's first television. His great contribution was born of genius and creativity, but its utility extended far beyond anything he might have foreseen at that young age. Like millions of other Latter-day Saints, his faith embraced the creed that the glory of God is intelligence – and Philo knew such perfection only comes after a magnificant accumulation of *knowledge*.

Photo courtesy Kent Farnsworth

Knowledge

Mormon knowledge by the numbers.

1 — LDS National Geography Bee champion.
14 — Youngest age of student admitted to BYU.
600 — Rounds per minute fired by an LDS-designed rifle.
391,000 — Dollars paid for a rare LDS book.
2,009,950 — Points scored in under 7 minutes playing Nintendo.
1,000,000,000,000 — Places calculated for Pi thanks to a Mormon's discovery.

EDUCATION

First Schoolhouse in Utah. A military tent provided accommodations for Utah's first schoolhouse. It opened in October 1847, only three months after the first parties of Mormons arrived in the Great Basin. The first teacher, Mary J. Dilworth, a 17-year-old girl of Quaker descent, taught the class of 30 children of various ages. (CN 1/19/49)

First in the West. The University of Utah was the first university in the West. Founded on Feb. 28, 1850, it was initially known as the University of the State of Deseret. Classes met for the first time in the home of John Pack on the corner of West Temple and 100 North. (CN 1/11/58)

Secretary of Education. Terrence Bell was appointed Secretary of Education by President Ronald Reagan in 1980, the highest appointed education post in the United States

Perfect SAT and ACT Scores. Who among LDS youth have achieved perfect scores in the national college-entrance exams?

Ted Bell at his confirmation hearings in 1980.
AP/WIDE WORLD PHOTOS

2003 – 1600 on the SAT, Aaron Smith, 17, Boynton Beach Ward, Pompano Beach Florida Stake. (CN 11/8/03)

1993 – 1600 on the SAT and 36 on the ACT, Robert Ensign White, 18, Coppell Ward, Lewisville, Texas, Stake. (CN 11/27/93)

Youngest Honor Student. In 1993, Nathan Summers, 14, became the youngest honor student in Ball State University's 75-year history. He enrolled in the university's computer curriculum after scoring 1,130 on the SAT while still a freshman at Muncie Central High School. Brother Summers was a member of the Muncie 1st Ward, Indianapolis, Indiana, North Stake. (CN 11/6/93)

Youngest Graduate With Honors. In 1985, Alexandra Swann, Canutillo, Texas, completed a bachelor's degree from BYU through independent study at age 14. Sister Swann never attended public schools and gives credit to the home-schooling efforts of her mother for helping her read and write by age 5 and qualify for college work when barely in her teens. Her grades in BYU studies were excellent, putting her on the university's honor roll. (DU 1/31/86)

Ed Hoope, a quick study.

Quickest Graduation. Is 11 months the record for graduating with a straight-A average for 124 semester hours of undergraduate college work? In 1972, Edward W. Hoope, Detroit Stake, completed his psychology degree at the Mercy College of Detroit as a 29-year-old freshman, completing 57 credit hours of classroom work, passing 35 more by examination, and taking night classes for 32 more. Which part was the busiest? Probably his last semester when he took 33 credit hours. He enrolled at BYU for post-graduate work in 1972. (CN 1/8/72)

Youngest Graduate from California State University System. In May 1992, Scott J. Ferrell of Victoria Ward, Riverside, California, Stake, was recognized as the youngest student to graduate from the California State University system. Brother Scott, 19, attended San Diego State University and graduated with a bachelor's degree after spending less than two years in college. Advanced placement tests in high school gave Scott the start he needed to enter college as a sophomore. (CN 5/16/92)

Youngest College Student in Brazil. Jose Feitosa de Andrade Filbo, Areoporto Branch, Sao Paulo, Brazil, West Stake, was the youngest to qualify for college in Brazil in 1979. He not only passed the requirements to enter the university, but did it with the highest scores among the 117,000 competing for an opening. However, Jose had to delay his entrance to college – he was only 15 and still needed to finish middle school. (CN 2/3/79)

Most Outstanding Educator. Who is the most outstanding educator in the Church and the country? In 1984, it was Trish Whitney, Santa Ana, California, Stake, who was honored with the Outstanding Educator in America award for 1984. (LDS 3/30/84)

Kathleen Richards, a Brighton High School (Utah) business teacher, was honored as the outstanding business educator in the United States in April 1992. Each state nominates a teacher to compete for the honor. (DN 4/28/92)

Learning Disabled. Sharli Cartwright, Lewisville 1st Ward, Lewisville, Texas, Stake, was named the 1990 Outstanding Teacher of the Year by the National Council on Learning Disabilities. "I like to think in terms of learning difference rather than in learning disability," she told reporters. (CN 3/23/91)

First Blind Valedictorian. In 1964, Benjamin Lee, Alamogordo Ward, El Paso, Texas, Stake, was valedictorian for New Mexico High School. The totally blind Navajo was also elected president of his class. He had been blind all his life. Brother Lee was also on the honor roll, played the violin and sang in the school chorus. (CN 7/11/64)

First Female "Summe Cum Laude" from Harvard Law School. In 1997, Lisa Anne Grow became the first woman in Harvard Law School's 180-year history to graduate summe cum laude, and the first to graduate at the top of the class. She had perfect scores on her law school entrance exam and for two years in a row she was awarded the coveted Sears prize, awarded to Harvard's top two law students each year. Her grade-point average hovered between an A and A+. After graduation she clerked for the U.S.Court of Appeals (Fourth Circuit) and the U.S. Supreme Court. Today, she and her husband are busy parents in their Redwood City Ward, Menlo Park, Calif., Stake. (DN 6/5/97; author's interview)

Lisa Anne Grow, a first for Harvard.

THINKERS

JAMES WILLIAMS
WASHINGTON

Alex Trebek, host of the national Geography Bee, congratulates James Williams. "I had to study, study, study, study, study," James said. "I studied my brains out, but Sunday was never a study day. And I prayed a lot." By knowing that Goa in India was formerly a colony of Portugal, the home-schooled teen won the championship.

National Geographic Bee. On May 21, 2003, James M. Williams, 14, won the 15th National Geographic Bee held in Washington D.C., beating out 54 other competitors from each U.S. state and territory. Brother Williams, a member of the Salmon Creek Ward, Van-couver, Washington, West Stake, won a $25,000 prize for his college fund and went on a media tour to guest star on dozens of national television and international radio programs. He was featured as far away as Bangkok. Among the many questions he answered was the location of Lake Turkana, and the fact that Goa in India was a Portuguese colony until 1961. Was he scared? "I couldn't help being a little nervous," he told the Church News. To prepare, James said he had to "study, study, study, study, study." James was home schooled with his five younger siblings. His parents, Craig and Ann Williams didn't allow television, and the only computer game they could play was a geography game. (CN 6/28/03)

Best Spellers – Europe. Melinda Bassett, 10, took first place in the European spelling contest in 1984 by correctly spelling "rallentando." The contest, sponsored by Americans, was the last of a series of competitions involving more than 15,000 students from six countries. Although an American, Melinda represented the United Kingdom in the contest. (CN 8/26/84)

Tracy Seargeant, Heerlen Servicemen Ward, Utrecht Netherlands Stake, took first place in the annual Department of Defense Schools spelling bee held in Heidelberg, Germany in May 1992. Second place went to another LDS youth, Jonathan Jacobs, of the Karlsruhe Servicemen Branch, Stuttgart Germany Servicemen Stake. Tracy went on to represent the DOD schools at the national spelling bee in Washington, D.C.. (CN 5/16/92)

National Spelling Bee. Todd Wallace, 14, Groveland 2nd Ward, Blackfoot, Idaho, South Stake, placed second in the 65th annual National Spelling Bee held May 29, 1992, in Washington, D.C.. For four straight years, Todd had competed in the National Spelling Bee as a regional champion. In 1992, he made it to the 15th round before misspelling the word "pellagra," meaning a disease associated with a deficient diet, placing him second in the final round. "It's no good to know a language if you don't know how to spell," Todd told the Church News. (CN 6/7/92)

AP/WIDE WORLD PHOTOS

Todd Wallace (right) and other spelling bee finalists are greeted by Pres. George Bush, Sr., at the White House.

Keena Pack, 13, Nampa, Idaho, finished 11th out of the final 120 in the National Spelling Bee in 1981. She was eliminated in the second day after 7 rounds, on the word "turbot." She spelled it "turbit." (CN 6/81)

Kedra Haroldsen, 11, Blackfoot, Idaho, finished 24th in the National Spelling Bee in 1985. (CN 6/16/85)

World's Best Nintendo Player. For scoring 2,009,950 points in 6 minutes 21 seconds, 10-year-old Jeff Hansen of the Homestead Ward, Murray South, Utah, Stake, became the 1991 world champion Nintendo player for his age group. Jeff not only scored highest for anyone in his age group (11 and under),

Tom Smart, Deseret Morning News

Computer games paid off big for Jeff Hansen.

but also scored higher than the winner of the 18-and-over championship. For his expertise, he won a 1991 Geo LSI convertible (for his folks to drive, no doubt!), a $10,000 U.S. savings bond, a large-screen television set valued at $4,000, a Super Mario trophy, and a pair of Reebok "pump" shoes. (DN 12/12/90)

Champion Spellers, One Ward. In 1968, the Penryn, California, Elementary School held its annual spelling bee. As it turned out, the children from the nearby Loomis 1st Ward were pretty good spellers. The winner in each grade was from that ward: Amy Cisneros (4th grade), Brooke Wentzel (5th grade), Emily Stoddard (6th grade), Ryan Beal (7th grade), and Gary Beal (8th grade). (CN 7/13/86)

Henry Erying: "Einstein didn't know beans."

Chemistry. Henry Eyring, 1901-82, a chemist whose understanding of molecules and mathematics influenced more than a dozen branches of chemistry, was long recognized as one of the greatest minds in chemistry. A favorite speaker at firesides, Dr. Eyring loved to tell this anecdote: Once, during his 15 years at Princeton, Eyring walked with professor Albert Einstein through a garden. Eyring plucked a plant and asked Einstein if he knew what it was. Einstein didn't. The plant was a soybean, and Eyring later enjoyed telling people that Einstein "didn't know beans." (CN 6/82)

77-year-old Eyring sprints to 8th place in his annual Eyring Sweepstakes at the University of Utah. The winner was treated to a free lunch with Eyring.

Mathematics. In 2000, former BYU-mathematics professor Helaman Ferguson was honored for his discovery of an algorithm that permits the calculation of the infinitely-long decimal of pi. This amazing breakthrough also allows the calculating of any single digit of pi without calculating the entire number. Pi is the ratio of the circumference of a circle to its diameter, a never-repeating decimal that begins with 3.14159265 ... ad infinitum. The magazine "Computing in Science and Engineering" named the algorithm one of the top ten algorithms of the century in January 2000. Using

Ferguson's algorithm, personal computers can calculate pi to 1 million places in about 60 seconds. Mathematicians have since calculated pi out to more than one trillion places. (Lawrence Berkeley Labs Research News 1/20/00)

Software. David Buehler, 17, St. Paul Minnesota 2nd Ward, won $25,000 in 1983 from the Atari, Inc., in a contest for designing and writing programs. His program, called "Typo Attack," was designed to teach touch typing. (CN 3/6/83)

David Thaler, East Lansing University Ward, Lansing, Michigan, Stake, with two classmates, were ranked first in the United States and second in the world in the 1992 Association for Computing Machinery computer programming competition. The contest included more than 600 teams from universities throughout the world. David's team represented Michigan State University. (CN 9/12/92)

Physics. In 1991, Gary Stradling, White Rock Ward, Santa Fe, New Mexico, Stake, was awarded the Hubert Schardin Gold Medal from the German Physical Society during a ceremony at Cambridge University in England. Stradling was only the second American ever to receive the prestigious award. The award is given every two years by the German Physical Society to the top scientist in the field of high-speed physics and diagnostics. (CN 4/6/91)

First Software Patent. S. Pal Asija, Dallas 4th Ward, Richardson, Texas, Stake, was inducted into the Hall of Fame for Engineering Science and Technology in 1991 for obtaining the first software patent ever issued. Asija's software enabled novice computer users to communicate with computers in a human-like manner. (CN 3/23/91)

Soil. In 1984, Don Kirkham, Ames 2nd Ward, Ames, Iowa, a soils chemistry professor emeritus of Iowa State University, was co-recipient of the international $100,000 Israeli-based Wolf Prize in agriculture. He shared the prize with a researcher from Holland for his work in mathematical soils physics as applied to establishing a scientific basis for efficient land drainage systems and its impact on soil fertility and productivity. (CN 1/29/84)

Weeds. The first-ever Weed Science Society of America Outstanding Industry award was presented to Reed Gray, Saratoga 1st Ward, Saratoga, California, Stake, in recognition for his accomplishments that included 24 U.S. patents and more than 70 publications in scientific journals. (CN 7/8/89)

Agriculture. Homer M. LeBaron, patriarch in the Greensboro North Carolina Stake and counselor in the Charlotte, North Carolina, Mission presidency, received the Charles A. Black Award from the Council for Agricultural Science and Technology in 1991 in recognition of exceptional contributions to food and agricultural research. (CN 8/3/91)

Political Thinking. The only LDS to earn France's prestigious Montesquieu Prize, and only the second American to do so, was Ronald M. Peterson, Claremont 2nd Ward, La Verne, California, Stake. The award recognized his 50-page paper on Montesquieu's treatment of natural law in the 18th century. Montesquieu was one of France's leading 18th-century thinkers. (LDS 8/2/86)

Hawaiian Language. In 1963, Mary Kawena Pukui, Honolulu, Hawaii, published her 36th book, the English-Hawaiian Dictionary. It was the culmination of 30 years of effort. She was also very active in working to keep the ancient Hawaiian culture alive and was a strong promoter of the Polynesian Cultural Center. (CN 5/23/64)

EXECUTIVES

Kodak. Kay R. Whitmore, Rochester, New York, Palmyra Stake, served as Kodak's president beginning in 1983 and then its chief executive officer in 1990-93. During his service as a Kodak executive, he formally honored the Church for its microfilming efforts around the world that had cemented a long-standing association with Kodak. (Author)

Deseret Morning News file photo

Kay Whitmore, center, presents plaque to Elder Boyd K. Packer, Left, and Elder J. Richard Clarke, honoring the Church's use of Kodak products.

National Press Club Chairman. In 1986, Lee Roderick, Potomac South Ward, Washington, D.C. Stake, became the first LDS to be elected chairman of the board of the prestigious National Press Club. Founded in 1908, it is one of the world's premier journalistic organizations. (CN 2/16/86)

Black & Decker. Nolan D. Archibald, Potomac, Maryland, North Ward, was named chief executive officer of Black & Decker Corporation in 1986.

That year, Fortune magazine named him one of America's 10 most-wanted executives. (CN 6/22/86)

American Motors. George W. Romney was named chief executive of American Motors Corporation in October 1954 at age 47. (CN 10/16/54)

Marriott Corporation. From a humble soft-drink stand, J. Willard Marriott and his wife built one of the most respected hotel chains in the world, with several restaurant chains to match. Marriott's sons took over the business after his death and continue to provide quality rooms at affordable prices. The Marriott name now graces almost 2,600 properties offering more than 463,400 rooms in 50 states and 67 countries and territories, the world's largest food catering service, several major academic buildings. The multi-billion-dollar empire earns more than $10 billion a year. (LDS 8/24/85; www.mar-riott.com)

J. Willard Marriott (standing in the doorway) opens his first root beer "Hot Shoppe" in Washington, D.C. His first employee, Robert Smice, is shown in the window.

General Mills. Mark H. Willes, originally of Salt Lake City, took over the senior executive position at General Mills in 1985. He left Utah in 1961 to finish school, but never made it back. In a fireside talk to youth, he said, "You've got to virtually be better than everybody else at what you do. Find out what you do best, then focus on those things. Work hard. Have high standards. Be fair. Treat other people the way you'd like to be treated." (LDS 8/23/89)

PBS – Public Broadcasting System. In 1985, Bruce L. Christensen, Arlington Ward, Virginia, was president and CEO of PBS. He was formerly the director of broadcast services at BYU. (CN 4/28/85)

Courtesy Jon and Karen Huntsman

Jon and Karen Huntsman have donated hundreds of millions to build and support local community projects, cancer and medical research facilities, and various needs for or in support of communities and the Church worldwide.

Huntsman Corporation. Jon Huntsman, Salt Lake City, started his business while working for another company with the assignment to find a way to package eggs back in the 1960s. One day, as he and his team tried to develop some form of inexpensive plastic egg cartons, he got an idea to venture out with a container company of his own. It was a grand success. In 1974, his new Huntsman Container Corporation landed a major contract to create the famous "clamshell" container for McDonald's Big Mac. And so began a long and colorful expansion to become the largest privately held chemical company in the world. Originally known for pioneering innovations in packaging, and later, for rapid growth in petrochemicals, Brother Huntsman's companies today have annual revenues of approximately $8 billion, and employ more than 13,000 in more than 40 countries. His companies manufacture products for global industries involved with chemicals, plastics, automobiles, footwear, construction, paints and coatings, health care, detergent, personal care and packaging. In the middle of all that activity, Huntsman joined the Nixon Administration as associate administrator of the Department of Health, Education and Welfare and then special assistant to President Nixon. He later served as mission president in the Washington, D.C. mission in the mid-1980s.

(www.huntsman.com; author)

Mrs. Cavanaugh's Candies. Any candy connoisseur knows the taste of the world-famous Mrs. Cavanaugh's Candies. Part of the cost of building the business is wrapped in a wonderful quote from Cavanaugh, "It was an idea I started sixteen years and sixty pounds ago!"

Shortly after Marie and husband George Cavanaugh were married, they moved to his South Dakota ranch. She began experimenting with various chocolate candy recipes, and after more than 40 years and hundreds of tons of chocolate, her patience and hard work has paid off a million times over. Mrs. Cavanaugh's Candies are recognized by chocolate connoisseurs around the world. (Author; www.infomission.com/customize/53146/mrscavanaugh.html)

WordPerfect Corporation.

After several months in the boiler room of a Provo city building trying to develop a word-processing system for the city's new computers in the late 1970s, Alan Ashton and Bruce Bastian came upon a great idea. They would create a word processor that was just like the typewriter – a simple blank piece of "paper" displayed on the computer screen, simple commands, and an easy learning curve. In 1982, they brought their ideas together and went to market. In a few short years, WordPerfect became the world leader in the word processing industry. Sales of their products ran into hundreds of millions of dollars per year. Headquartered in Orem, Utah, the software company commanded the lead in its field in the United States and in many nations around the world during most of the 1980s and into the 1990s, and remains

Those were the days! In 1975, Dr. Alan C. Ashton, a computer professor at BYU, was teaching computers to play music. A half dozen years later, WordPerfect would take the world by storm. No word processing product has surpassed the ease, user-friendliness and power that was first visualized a quarter century ago.

the preferred word processor for many keyboarders who became acquainted with its user-friendly features. The company and its products were later sold to Corel Inc. (Author; WordPerfect Corp.)

Clorox. Robert A. Bolingborke, Danville, California, 1st Ward, was named president and chief executive officer of Clorox Company in 1990 after serving with the company for 28 years. He was selected from among three group vice presidents for the top position. (CN 10/20/90)

David Neeleman fills an important niche with his lower fairs and comparable or superior service.

JetBlue Airways. In 1999, David Neeleman, New Canaan, Connecticut, took his experiences with a couple of small start-up airlines, threw in an innate allotment of sheer determination and, with the backing of financiers, started JetBlue Airways. His family reluctantly followed him to New York as he began building his dream into a successful business. After the terror attacks of Sept. 11, 2001, Brother Neeleman worked hard to regain the flying public's trust. His was the first airline to install bulletproof doors in the cockpits, and he resisted the temptation to push the public to fly again. They need time to grieve, he told his staff, and he broadcast the message that when people were ready to fly again, "We'll be here." When the company went public in 2002, the opening day marked the best-received initial offering on Wall Street so far that year. JetBlue's stock soared 66 percent on that first day. The devout churchgoer, father of nine, and former missionary to Brazil was a college dropout but now heads one of the most successful small airlines in North America. (DN 4/16/02; http://www.nynma.org/events/neeleman.asp)

Sorenson Companies. James Sorenson has spent his lifetime building a large family empire that has provided thousands of jobs and created dozens of medical devices and other innovations that have helped millions. And with that fortune he has given to worthy causes that cross political, religious and state boundary lines. For example, he donated $30 million for the reconstruction of the Nauvoo Temple, $500,000 for the renovation of the Salt Lake City Cathedral of the Madeleine, medical research, college and university donations, and thousands more. His company's medical products can be found in hospitals around the world, and he holds 60 patents. Brother Sorenson started out by selling for Upjohn shortly after his mission. He took his extra funds and began investing into real estate. Over the years, income from those properties helped him finance research into inventions or developing medical innovations, another passion of his. He developed several products and formed a company called Sorsenson Research. In 1972, it was selling 500 different products and employed 1,700 people. Abbot Laboratories bought him out, and provided enough income that ultimately helped him launch more ventures and give away additional millions. Though he likes to keep out of the limelight, he and his wife, Beverley, and their eight children, have benefited the Church, medicine, and community causes in ways that will help hundreds of thousands for decades to come. In his early 80s, he continues putting in a full week at the office, and has no intention of stopping. (DN 9/7/03)

Swift Transportation. Jerry Moyes built the third-largest trucking company in the United States from a one-truck midnight express that hauled steel from Los Angeles to Phoenix in 1966. Over the years he bought or merged with smaller companies, making them efficient and profitable, and expanded his efforts into an operation worth more than $1.5 billion. He also owns other trucking companies and a Utah steel company; he's part owner of the Arizona Diamondbacks and the Phoenix Suns; and he played the key role in getting the new Arizona Cardinal stadium built in his hometown of Glendale, Arizona. Brother Moyes and his wife, Vickie, adopted nine children and have long shown great compassion for the less fortunate. They have spearheaded multi-million-dollar projects to help children in crisis and other community help programs. Ask local business leaders and associates what kind of man Moyes is and you'll often hear words like "humble," "unpretentious," "always charging ahead," "focused," "kind of guy who is the last to promote himself," "common touch." (Arizona Republic 9/1/02, www.arizonarepublic.com/special07/articles/0901Moyes01.html)

INVENTIONS

World's First Traffic Light. In 1912, the first electric red-green traffic light in the world was installed at the intersection of 2nd South and Main streets in Salt Lake City. A traffic cop named Lester Farnsworth Wire invented the 20-inch-square box that resembled a birdhouse. It stood on a pole in the intersection and was operated manually from the curb. (Assorted Internet sites)

World's First Television. Philo T. Farnsworth is the unheralded, humble LDS inventor who literally changed the world with his amazing creation, the television. As the story goes, the inspiration came when Farnsworth, only 14, was plowing an Idaho potato field with his horse-drawn harrow. The back-and-forth lines in the soil suddenly

Courtesy Melodie O'Carroll, Lester Farnsworth Wire Library

Lester Wire and some early stoplights. Red and green came first, and then yellow was added later ... with a degree of caution.

Deseret Morning News file photo

Philo Farnsworth held more than 300 U.S. and foreign patents and was one of four inventors honored with his portrait on a stamp issued in 1983 by the U.S. Postal Service.

painted an amazing image in his mind. Couldn't an electronic beam scan an image in the same way, back and forth, line by line, like reading a book? His genius exploded with questions and ideas, and he began his years-long quest to make his epiphany a functioning reality.

Fast-forward six years to Sept. 7, 1927. Farnsworth and his brother-in-law, Cliff Gardner, were joined in the lab by one of Farnsworth's financial backers. In the room was Farnsworth's newly-invented camera tube, a television receiver, and a bright carbon arc lamp. Farnsworth's first test of his television system would be a glass slide. A sheet of glass painted black with a scratch in the middle was placed so the arc lamp would project an image into the camera tube. The three watched a faint image emerge on the receiver as a blurry straight line. Cliff turned the glass on its side and they saw it move – the first electronic television transmission ever. In quiet subdued excitement, Farnsworth stated simply, "There you are, electronic television."

Today, there are more than 1 billion television sets in the world – or one for every six people walking the planet. In addition, the same television technology is used for millions more computer monitors and other electronic displays. Television enables images to be beamed from just about everywhere – from the top of Mount Everest to the bottom of the ocean; from inside an unborn infant's heart to the surface of the moon; and from the crumbling past of decaying movie film to new digital technology that allows space-borne cameras to return images of distant planets and stars. The furrows in Farnsworth's potato field continue to inspire and change the course of history as television entertains, educates and gives amazing remote power to an appreciative world of viewers now numbered in the billions. (Various on-line histories; LDS 10/28/83)

World's First Hearing Aid and Stereo Music.

It was BYU graduate Harvey Fletcher who developed the first hearing aid. He called it the Audiogram and had planned to use it to test people's hearing. He also worked under Nobel Prize winner Robert Milliken on the experiments that led to the development of the vacuum tube, and he played a central role in the development of stereophonic reproduction. His list of honors and accomplishments is long. He was the first Ph.D. summa cum laude at the University of Chicago (in physics), and returning to head BYU's physics department, he was at the time the only Ph.D.

Deseret Morning News archives

Before there was surroundsound, digital music and MP3, there was beautiful stereophonic sound, thanks to the creative genius of Harvey Fletcher.

on campus. He was the first Mormon to become a member of the National Academy of Sciences, and is noted around the world for his contributions in acoustics, electrical engineering, speech, medicine, music, atomic physics, sound pictures, and education. (DU 8/30/65; Internet)

World's First Man-made Diamonds.

In 1955, Dr. H. Tracy Hall, a native of Ogden, Utah, produced the first man-made diamonds. He was a researcher at the General Electric Research Laboratory in Schenectady, New York, when he developed the machine he called "the belt." According to a G.E. publication dated Feb. 15, 1955, "Man-made diamonds, the climax of a 125-year effort to duplicate nature's hardest and most glamorous substance, were displayed here today." The machine pro-

BYU – L. Tom Perry Special Collections

Several pistons exerted hundreds of tons of pressure on the target substance.

duced pressures greater than 1 1/2 million pounds per square inch at temperatures greater than 5,000 degrees Fahrenheit for long periods of time. The diamonds produced under these conditions are not "imitation" diamonds, or "diamond-like," but simply diamonds, the same as are taken from mines in the Belgian Congo or Brazil. Dr. Hall's diamonds were the first man-made substance to scratch other diamonds (chisels could split diamonds along their grain, but couldn't scratch them). His first version of "the belt" could produce up to 1/10th-carat diamonds. (CN 3/26/55; CN 12/17/77)

A common misunderstanding is that Dr. Hall's machine made artificial diamonds. It didn't. It made the real thing.

Father of the Pedal Steel Guitar. Alvino Rey's innovations in the 1920s and '30s led to the development of the electric guitar and pedal steel guitars widely used today. He was born Alvin McBurney on July 1, 1911, in Oakland, California, and married Luise King of the King Sisters. He gained a huge following during the big band era. (Internet)

Northwest Kidney Foundation

Artificial kidney pioneers (l-r): Albert Babb, Belding Scribner, and Wayne Quinton in 1993, posing by a new miniaturized version of a kidney or dialysis machine.

Home Dialysis Breakthrough. The first kidney machines could not be widely used for one important obstacle: the body would not tolerate the permanent placement of a tube allowing access to a patient's blood.

In 1943, Dr. Wilhelm Kolff's new kidney machine would do the blood-cleaning job, but how could it be hooked up to patients? It was a major hurdle that had to be crossed. That's when Wayne E. Quinton, Seattle 1st Ward, Seattle, Washington, Stake, came on the scene. As a biomedical instrument builder, Brother Quinton was asked to engineer a solution to this problem. With the availability of new materials the body would not reject, and a design that was well engineered, Quinton went to work and built a U-shaped tube that suddenly made kidney dialysis possible for millions worldwide. The tube was known as the Schribner shunt. It was permanently installed between a patient's vein and an artery and protruded from the skin. This gave a patient the ability to open the tube, hook up to a kidney machine, lie back and wait while blood flowed out of the body and through a cleansing membrane, and back into the body. Thanks to his great contribution, Quinton is among the great pioneers in the field of artificial kidney dialysis. (CN 2/9/63; www.washington.edu; author)

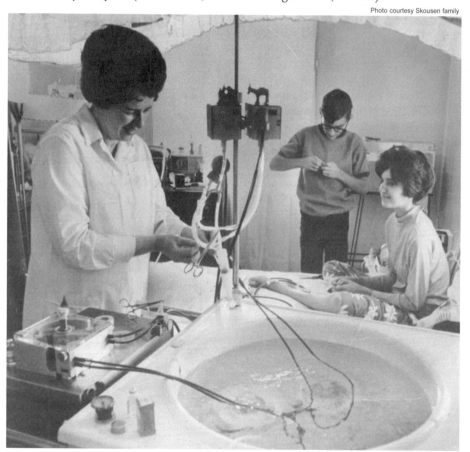

Photo courtesy Skousen family

Wayne Quinton's research led to home dialysis, a breakthrough that has saved millions of lives. Pictured here, Jewel Skousen, Parley's 1st Ward, Salt Lake City, helps her daughter, Kathleen, use an early model of the artificial kidney machine in 1969. Kathleen's brother Brent (center) assembled the dialysis filters (coils) right at home, saving the family thousands in costs.

Melvin Cook's ground-breaking research into explosives was honored with the Nitro-Nobel Gold Medallion, presented to him in Stockholm, Sweden, in 1968.

World's First Slurry Explosives.

In 1956, Melvin A. Cook invented the first-ever "slurry" explosives – a unique combination of ammonium nitrate, aluminum powder and water that out-produced dynamite for safety, application, storage and explosive power. This simple combination of ingredients revolutionized the commercial explosives industry. Mining and excavation firms around the world embraced the improved explosive and quickly moved away from "dangerous dynamite" to "safe slurry." The ingredients for slurry explosives were safe by themselves and did not have to be premixed. Pump trucks could deliver the ingredients where mixing could occur on site. Brother Cook is respected as a leading innovator in explosives research and had more than 100 patents in his name, as well as numerous national and international awards for his works. ("More Bangs for the Buck," David Hampshire 2002; various Internet sources)

World's Best Guns.

John Moses Browning, son of the talented gunsmith Jonathan Browning of Nauvoo fame, is the greatest inventor and designer of firearms ever. Born in 1855, he grew up in Ogden and served a two-year mission to Georgia in 1887. His skill and inventiveness changed the world forever. Although the Browning name isn't on many of his most famous designs, they nevertheless are his patented creations. He sold manufacturing rights to such notables as Winchester, Fabrique Nationale, Remington, Colt, and Savage.

First Lever-Action Repeater. In 1883, Winchester bought Browning's newly-invented rifle that facilitated easy ejection of a used cartridge with one flip of a lever and the loading a new one with another flip. This began Winchester's 50-year

Model 1894

domination of the firearms industry.

Models 1886 and 1894. These two Browning inventions won worldwide acclaim. Of the Model 1886, Theodore Roosevelt said, "It is the best gun I ever had." The famous Winchester 30-30 carbine (Model 1894) is the most popular rifle ever, with more than 6 million sold after a century of production.

Shotguns. Browning sold more than 40 gun designs to Winchester including pump-action rifles and shotguns, a

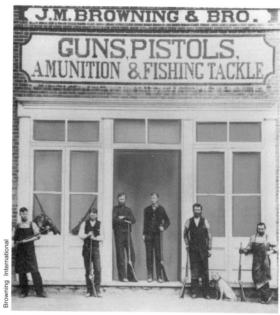

Browning – maker of the best guns in the world!

lever-action shotgun and a bolt-action rifle. The Remington Model 11 Automatic and Browning Automatic-5 were the most popular shotguns for 50 years.

Automatic Repeaters. Shortly after Brother Browning's mission, he devised a way to harness the expanding gas from a firing bullet to push out the used cartridge and load another, the world's first automatic. In 1890, he offered his invention to Colt Firearms. It was developed as the famous Colt Model 95, and could unleash 1,800 rounds in three minutes. This gun made the famous Gatling gun obsolete in six years, and gained the nickname, "The Peacemaker."

Famous Battles. When Teddy Roosevelt's famous Rough Riders were storming San Juan Hill during the Spanish-American war, Browning's automatic machine gun kept the enemy pinned so that the hill could be taken. During the Boxer rebellion in China, the "Peacemaker" empowered 400 United States troops to fend off multiple assaults by the Chinese for an entire month until reinforcements arrived.

Changing Warfare. Browning's inventions changed the way armies fought each other. Instead of the cavalry charge or the open-field standoff of gunfire exchange, warring

A 1918 B.A.R.

troops moved to trench fighting during World War I, where they could find protection from the more deadly and accurate weapons. The new Browning Automatic Rifle (known by millions as the B.A.R.) was an 18-pound automatic that could shoot 500 rounds per minute at a range of 600 yards. Soldiers from World War I to Vietnam all benefited from this, the most effective infantry weapon of all times.

When Browning died in 1926 at age 71, U.S. Secretary of War Dwight F. Davis said at the funeral, "It is a fact to be recorded that no design of Mr. Browning's has ever proved a failure, nor has any model been discontinued. ... It is not thought that any other individual has contributed so much to the national security of this country as Mr. Browning in the development of our machine guns and our automatic weapons to a state of military efficiency surpassing that of all nations." (Various Internet sources)

First Cardiac-Testing Treadmill. In 1953, Wayne E. Quinton, Seattle 1st Ward, Seattle, Washington, Stake, started a company, Quinton Inc., to build the first treadmills specifically designed for cardiac testing. It was a field of cardiology research and testing that others had failed to explore up to the time. His expertise in biomedical instruments pushed the company to world renown. It was bought out in 1984 but remains to this day highly respected for the quality and durability of its products. (www.quinton.com)

World's First Disposable Diapers. Carlyle Harmon, originally of Sugar City, Idaho, was the innovative scientist who helped newborns around the world break free of safety pins, rubber pants and reusable cloth diapers. Thanks to his discovery of a highly absorbent material, disposable diapers and other non-woven fiber fabrics were created and the world was forever changed. His 39 patents covered items that today are used in diapers, gowns, wipes, surgical/dental napkin covers, hygiene products and sheets used in homes and hospitals everywhere. Brother Harmon's inspiration came from the study of single-cell amoeba. He observed that the amoeba had a remarkable capacity for absorbing liquids. Further research brought him the breakthroughs for which billions of babies, and their parents, owe him a great debt of thanks – about 4-5 times a day, at least! Harmon worked for Johnson and Johnson, taught at BYU and founded the Eyring Research Institute. He died in 1997 at age 92. (DN 3/27/97)

World's First Computer Games. When the history of computers is written, Nolan Bushnell, Salt Lake City, Utah, will probably find a place in the books as the "father of video games." After moving to California to study at Stanford University, he got an idea one day for a game. He set up shop in his daughter's bedroom and spread out computer equipment so he could write a space-adventure game. Finding it too difficult for people to play, he dumbed it down and called it "Pong." The year was 1972, the same year he founded Atari, and introduced the Atari 2600 home video-game system, a huge success that launched the video-game industry. (SLTrib 10/21/01)

Wagon Odometer. When the Mormon pioneers began their trek across the plains to the Rocky Mountains, the troop needed a way to measure distance. The assignment fell to William Clayton who figured out a counting device that could be attached to a wagon's

Courtesy Church History Museum

Hand carved wooden gears helped pioneers track with surprising accuracy the distance traveled while crossing the plains.

wheel. His idea went to Orson Pratt who drew up a workable design, and to Appleton Milo Harmon, who set to work building it. The wooden device worked wonderfully and helped advance wagon parties map out stopping places for those that followed. A replica can be seen at the Museum of Church History in Salt Lake City. (Church archives)

Wheelo. One of the best-selling toys in the world during the 1950s was the Wheelo, a looped wire track with a spinning wheel on a magnetic shaft. The popular toy was invented by Harvey Job Matusow, Ascutney Ward, Vermont. Brother Matusow called his new gadget the "stringless yo-yo." It continues to sell by the thousands, even today. (Assorted Internet sites)

Chromium and Stainless Steel. Dr. Marvin J. Udy, Niagara Falls, New York, won international acclaim for his achievements which led to the establishment of several multi-million dollar businesses dealing with ores processing. He patented a process for cadmium plating, and developed "Chrom-X," an exothermic ferro-chromium produced from low-grade chromite ores. To the layman, that

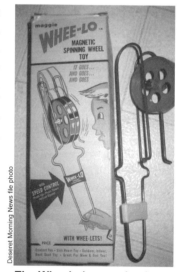
Deseret Morning News file photo

The Wheelo has evolved into an assortment of variations. It was the second-best selling toy in the 1950s.

means he came up with a way to make iron, steel and nonferrous metals harder and more resistant to corrosion and oxidation. He died in April 1959. (CN 4/25/59)

Talking Mannequins. The LDS Church was awarded a patent for its talking mannequins once used at the various visitor centers. The mannequin has a head, neck and torso. A film with sound track projected onto the mannequin's face gave the illusion of facial motions on the otherwise smooth plastic face. (CN 10/16/76)

TD Nickel. TD nickel is the super-strength metal that made possible many engine and body components in jet aircraft. The formula for TD nickel was one of the 33 patents filed by Guy B. Alexander, formerly of the Philadelphia stake presidency. During World War II, his innovations helped fellow scientists working on the Manhattan Project in Ohio create the world's first atomic bomb. (CN 4/10/65)

Anti-Lock Brake System. Andrew K. Watt, Lansing Ward, Lansing, Michigan, Stake, was named with a co-worker as the inventor/developer of an anti-skid brake device. His original ideas were developed over the years as the forerunner of today's anti-skid brakes found on nearly all newer automobiles. This was Brother Watt's fifth patent. He also first perceived the idea of a front-wheel drive full-size automobile after test-driving a 1958 Citroen. (CN 10/14/67)

Skinfolds Measurement. The first person to effectively estimate a person's body-fat percentage was John Lemperle, using a simple technique of measuring the thickness of skin in certain areas of the body. His technique has been duplicated around the world as a means of determining if a person has too much or too little fat. (BYU)

Saving Infants with SIDS Monitor. Paris Wiley developed a device in 1983 to prevent SIDS (Sudden Infant Death Syndrome) among infants who are prone to stop breathing in their sleep. The device detects when breathing stops and sounds an alarm. Every year it saves hundreds of lives. (Author)

T-Square. A revolutionary attachment to the table saw, invented by Bill Beisemeyer, Mesa 47th Ward, Mesa, Arizona, Central Stake, won the Challenger's Award at the International Woodworking Fair in 1982. Called the T-square Saw Fence System, it allows the user to quickly set up an accurate width on his table saw. (LDS 11/26/82)

WordPerfect Software. Once the most popular word-processing software in the world, the various versions of WordPerfect commanded anywhere from a 30 percent share in its smallest market to 92 percent of the DOS market in North America. The company was founded by Alan Ashton (see page 305) and Bruce Bastian in a basement and grew into the largest privately held software company in the world. In the 1980s, it was worth more than $2 billion. With the advent of the Microsoft Windows operating environment, WordPerfect eventually lost popularity and was later sold. (Author)

Best Invention – Age 9. Third-grader Brennon Jack Butler, Castle Dale 3rd Ward, Castle Dale, Utah, was named best inventor in the nation in his age group by Invent America in 1991. He invented "Dog Gone Garbage Bags," to discourage dogs from getting into garbage cans by treating garbage bags with a chemical used to keep pets out of shrubs. He and his three brothers, also Invent America winners for the state of Utah, have appeared on "Home Show," "Late Night with David Letterman," and other TV shows. (CN 1/4/92)

Most Expensive Invention. Charles Davidson, Fort Bridger, Wyoming, sold an invention to the IBM company in 1947 for $5 million just before leaving for his mission to Denmark. He received payments at the rate of $250,000 a year for 20 years. His invention, he explained, was a device capable of projecting one of 100,000 tiny films onto a screen merely by typing the description on a keyboard. (CN 11/10/48; CN 3/15/47)

Best Invention – Age 12. In 1990, Samuel Aaron Routson, 12, became the sixth grade winner in Virginia for his "licking bubbles" invention. His invention, for those who don't like to lick and seal envelopes, was a small bubble wrap filled with water and fastened to the seal of an envelope. When the flap is closed, the bubbles break and the water moistens the glue. Samuel was a member of the Herndon Ward, Oakton, Virginia, Stake. (CN 12/1/90)

BYU FACTS & FEATS

Largest Church-sponsored University – U.S. In 1953, Brigham Young University began its reign as the largest church-related university in the U.S. Raymond Walters, president of the University of Cincinnati calculated the enrollment figures across the United States and placed BYU first among the 14 major church-related universities and colleges with 6,605 full-time students. By autumn quarter 1955, BYU still ranked first with 7,639 students taking 12 or more hours of class work. BYU ranked 4th for total enrollment and 12th in the list of all private schools. Today, BYU remains the largest church-sponsored private university in the U.S., with an average enrollment of more than 28,000. (CN 1/21/56, 10/31/53; various Internet sources, 2003)

First Use of "BYU." With the awarding of five degrees and a special certificate of music at its annual commencement in 1904, Brigham Young Academy stepped into the world of "universities" as that class became the first to have "Brigham Young University" inscribed on its sheepskins. (CN 6/5/54)

Oldest Graduate. Laird Snelgrove graduated from BYU at age 91, on Feb. 13, 2003. He started at BYU in 1930, but a mission, the family ice-cream business, and the demands of life consumed his years until 1979 when he decided to work at his degree again. After more than 20 years, he was awarded his bachelor's degree (Spanish) in 2003 by BYU President Merrill J. Bateman and Elders M. Russell Ballard and Henry B. Eyring. The popular Snelgrove-brand ice cream is sold nationwide. (DN 2/13/03)

Lyle M. McDonald graduated from BYU at age 84, on Aug. 17, 1984, making him the oldest graduate from BYU at that time. The World War I vet received his bachelor's degree in elementary education. (CN 8/26/84)

Marjorie H. Holbrook, Wells Ward, Elko, Nevada, Stake, was awarded a bachelor's in education at age 80, on Aug. 15, 1986, making her the oldest woman to graduate from BYU. (CN 8/24/86)

Jeffrey D. Allred, Deseret Morning News

Laird Snelgrove receives his bachelors degree from BYU president Merrill J. Bateman in 2003 at age 91, becoming the oldest BYU graduate ever.

Youngest Graduate. Who is the youngest BYU graduate? Amy Bryson graduated in 2-1/2 years in April 1985 at age 18. Denise Woodbury graduated in 2-1/3 years in April 1983 at age 18 1/2. (LDS 5/18/85; LDS 6/3/83)

BYU's Oldest Alumnus. In June 1982, Rosetta B. Robinson, 95, was honored as BYU's oldest living graduate at an Emeritus Club luncheon. She was also honored as the oldest living graduate of St. John High School in Kansas where she graduated in 1905 as valedictorian. (CN 7/89)

Largest Mountain Emblem. BYU's massive block-letter "Y" is thought to be the largest such emblem in the world. It measures 465 feet tall by 168 feet at the widest point, with an area of about 32,847 square feet. It was originally made of lime, sand and whitewashed rocks. Designing the block "Y" created some perspective problems. Ernest Partridge and three of his students, Elmer Jacobs, Clarence Jacobs, and Harvey Fletcher, surveyed the three letters, "B," "Y," and "U" with enough foresight to realize special perspectives had to be controlled. Had the "Y" been made to scale, it would have appeared squatty and too short from the oblique angle given to viewers on the valley floor. The potential problem was avoided by making the block "Y" elongated to appear normal to the average viewer. When the whole student body showed up in 1906 to hand-carry supplies to make the mountain emblem, they tired after spending the entire day just creating the "Y." It was enough. The students returned to campus to be rewarded with a spectacular

Utah State Historical Society

1906: Students labor in rocks and whitewash to create the largest mountain emblem in the world.

emblem of pride and school spirit, and the rest of the emblem was never completed. (Brigham Young University, A School of Destiny, Ernest L. Wilkinson, W. Cleon Skousen)

Photo courtesy Dr. Eric N. Skousen

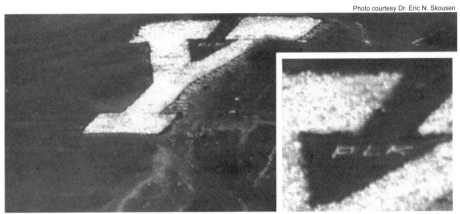

Block Y: The finished product became a world-renowned symbol for quality education and deeply supported traditional values ... and sometimes a billboard for love-struck students. Inset: PLK = Paul Loves Kathy.

Youngest Admitted. Amy Hovenden, Orem, Utah, was admitted to BYU at age 14. She was the oldest of nine children and passed all the entrance exams with flying colors after being home-taught. (LDS 2/3/84)

Youngest at BYU-Hawaii. With an IQ over 200, 11-year-old Arnold Sasaki became the youngest student ever enrolled at BYU-Hawaii in 1985. Arnold could read and write by age 2, took up chess by age 6 and was ranked among the world's top 50 chess players in the 13-and-under age group. (DU 2/6/85)

BYU – L. Tom Perry Special Collections

Alice Louise Reynolds

First Female Professor at BYU. In 1894, Alice Louise Reynolds became the first female professor to be hired at Brigham Young Academy. During her 44-year career at the "Y," she taught an estimated 5,000 students in 20 different English courses. She was also only the second woman in Utah to become a full professor. Thanks to her efforts, more than 10,000 books were collected for BYU's first library. (LDS 1988; Internet)

First Female Student-Body President. In 1991, Amy Baird, Edgemont 17th Ward, Provo, Utah, Edgemont South Stake, became BYU's first female student-body president when she was elected with 61 percent of the vote. In BYU's 100-year history, only one other woman had served in that capacity. However, she was not elected but appointed to the post when the student-body president was drafted during World War II in 1943. (CN 3/2/91)

First Female Student-Body President at BYU-Idaho (Ricks College). The first female president of Ricks College (now BYU-Idaho) was LaRue Cottle Murray. During the war years, Sister Murray served as president in 1943-44, followed by Ruth Thomas Dowdle in 1944-45. Not until 1992 did the school see its next female student-body president when Kris Shelley of the College 8th Ward, Ricks College 1st Stake, was elected. (CN 5/16/92)

BYU Cougars. The name "Cougars" was given to the athletic teams of BYU in the early 1900s by Eugene L. Roberts, athletic director and head coach at BYU. He used the name "Cougars" in sports articles he did as a contributor to the Deseret News. Brother Roberts thought the name aptly described the vigor and ability of his alma mater. Before long, the cougar became the official mascot at BYU. Roberts will also be long remembered for his beloved campfire legend, "Utahna and Red Eagle," a tale about Mt. Timpanogos. (CN 12/27/75)

First Debate Champs. BYU won its first national debate championship in 1981 at the National Cross-Examination Debate Association Tournament at the University of Nevada, Reno, April 4-6, 1981. The BYU team set two records in the process, becoming the first school ever to have two pairs of debaters end up as finalists and being designated co-winners. They also amassed the largest point total ever by a single university in one year. (CN 4/25/81)

The longest run as national debate champs belongs to the Ricks College debate team, which won its third straight national championship at the National Junior College Debate Tournament in Concord, California, in 1989. Ricks had to compete against 89 other colleges for the honor. (CN 4/29/89)

Best College Dance Team. Beginning in 1996, the BYU Cougarettes dance team won the National College Dance Team title four out of five years. Some 5,000 college students from more than 180 colleges and universities across the country compete for the title each year. (CN 5/30/01)

First Touch-tone Registration. Already acclaimed for its computerized admissions and records system, in 1984, BYU became the first university in the United States to develop and use a touch-tone telephone registration system. A $125,000 computer system donated by Perception Technology of Massachusetts made the program possible. The computer could handle 32 phone calls at a time. It wasn't long before the idea swept the country. By 1984 more than 300 schools had sent representatives to BYU to examine its system. Several schools copied BYU exactly. (CN 9/16/84; 12/14/86)

LIVING WORLD

TREES

Deseret Morning News file photo

All that remained of the Lone Cedar Tree until it, too, fell prey to vandals in 1958.

Desert Shade. On 6th East just south of 3rd South in Salt Lake City, a Utah red cedar tree once stood along side the road, remembered now by only a stump and a plaque erected in its honor. Over this road the pioneers first entered the valley in 1847, and paused beneath the tree's shade.

Songs were sung and prayers of gratitude were offered up, children played beneath its shade, lovers made it a trysting place, and townspeople and loggers found it a convenient spot to gather. When the tree was accidentally felled, the Daughters of the Utah Pioneers dedicated the site to the memory of these early men and women with a plaque erected in its honor. (CN 9/1/48)

Deseret Morning News file photo

Daughters of Utah Pioneers on hand in 1960 for the placement of a plaque marking the stump of the Lone Cedar Tree.

Oldest Tree. Perhaps the oldest tree on modern LDS Church property is a 500-year-old 21-foot-circumference oak in London, named after President David O. McKay. The tree was first seen by President McKay in 1953 when he was inspecting the new London Temple property. He took a special interest in the old giant and asked that whatever was necessary be done so it could be preserved. Workmen were sent to trim out the dead wood, patch old wounds and support some of the ancient and heavy limbs with steel cable. When President McKay arrived to dedicate the London Temple in 1958, the Saints showed him a bronze plaque they had placed on the trunk. The tree was dedicated with

Pres. McKay sizes up the 500-year old oak in 1954.

a beautiful inscription as "The David O. McKay Oak." Pres. McKay thanked them for their kindness and generosity but asked that his name be removed from the plaque so that the inscription would instead be a fitting tribute to the sturdy oak that had been growing since Columbus's discovery of America. (CN 9/13/58; CN 10/31/59)

The DAVID O. McKAY OAK
(QUERCUS PEDUNCULATA)

LIVING BEAUTY AND INSPIRATION
GREAT STRENGTH AND STABILITY
REACHING TOWARD HEAVEN
RESPONSIVE TO GOD'S SUNLIGHT
SERVICE FOR MANY GENERATIONS
CASTING FRIENDLY AND COMFORTING SHADE
GENTLE IN ITS CONTRIBUTION TO MANKIND
UNMOVED BY DISTURBING WINDS

TO BE REMEMBERED

Deseret Morning News file photo

A quarter century ago, this Russian Olive was the largest in the world and stood at 65 feet.

Largest Russian Olive Tree. In 1980, a beautiful 65-foot-tall Russian olive tree was recognized as the largest known specimen of its kind in the United States by the American Forestry Association. It was listed in the National Register of Big Trees. The tree was located beside Carlson Hall on the University of Utah campus. The tree measured 9 feet 10 inches around its trunk, had a crown spread of 35 feet, and stood 65 feet tall. (DN 11/13/80)

"Mormon" Desert Tree. When members of the Mormon Battalion were returning to Utah, they observed a desert tree that reminded them of Joshua of the Old Testament with his arms outstretched in prayer to God. They named it "The Joshua Tree," the name it carries today. (Internet California firsts by LDS)

Most Trees Planted. In August 1982, 7,200 young men at an LDS Boy Scout Jamboree in Arizona planted 24,000 trees in one hour. The trees were all three years old or older. (LDS 8/20/82)

Oldest Log Cabin. The oldest cabin in Utah was built by Miles Goodyear with cottonwood logs in 1844 or 1845. It was relocated to Ogden's Tabernacle Park. (CN 2/9/49)

Violin Trees. Engelmann spruce trees from Utah may replace the Norway spruce as the best wood in the world from which violins and other stringed instruments are made. In 1983, researchers sought 45 Engelmann spruce trees that were growing at an elevation of 9,000 feet or higher and at a latitude of about 39 degrees. They had to be large, mature and with few limbs, straight grain and evenly spaced rings. The U.S. Department of Agriculture directed the researchers to Utah's Dixie National Forest where trees matching these stringent requirements were found and harvested. The trees were shipped to Baltimore where they were cut, split and dried for 10 years before they were used by violin makers. (DU 1/17/84)

FLOWERS

Most Beautiful Gardens. The world-famous gardens on Temple Square and at Church Headquarters are frequent recipients of awards and recognitions. In 1999, the gardens were honored with a "once-in-a-century" medallion, and in 2003, they were voted among the top ten gardens in the world. The landscaping typically includes more than 165,000 flowers of 460 varieties. (www.bellaonline.com/articles/art9080.asp)

Hybrid Rose. The new hybrid "Mia Maid" rose was christened on Temple Square at a sunrise ceremony June 13, 1953. Initial plans were to plant a "Mia Maid" rosebush on the grounds of every ward and branch chapel in the Church. Three years of experimentation were needed to produce the new rose. It is a cross between the famous "Charlotte Armstrong" and "Signora" roses, and is the same cross that produced the world-famed "Sutter's Gold" rose. (CN 6/30/53)

The "Mia Maid" rose is an ever-blooming rose with two main blooming seasons.

Most Important Plant. The sego lily (mariposa lily) often stood between the pioneers and death by starvation, and thereby became an important part of early pioneer history and heritage. The sego lily, Utah's state flower, grows in desolate areas from Canada to Guatemala and was used as food by American Indians. The small bulbs are extremely sweet and can be eaten raw, roasted, boiled (they taste much like potatoes), or pounded into flour for bread or porridge. Almost harvested to extinction in the 1800s, the sego lily is now being saved by the efforts of the Mariposa Foundation for Conservation. (CN 7/22/84)

Youngest To Win All-American Rose. In 1981, Jack E. Christensen, 33, Ontario, California, 1st Ward, became the youngest ever to be credited with an all-American Rose Selections winner. After the honor was bestowed, he flew to Washington to personally present his new hybrid, "First Lady Nancy," to the flower's namesake, U.S. President Ronald Reagan's wife, Nancy Reagan. (CN 1/9/82)

This sunflower giant grew an average of two inches a day.

Deseret Morning News file photo

Tallest Sunflower. In August 1959, James McAfee, Salt Lake City, found himself at the base of a sunflower plant that skyrocketed to 15 feet above the ground after just three months of hot-summer growth. (DN 8/12/59)

Tulips. The "Marriott" tulip, named after LDS hotel magnate, J. Willard Marriott Jr., president of the Marriott Corporation, was presented to him by the Royal General Bulb Growers Association in 1980. The association cited the Marriott family's contributions to the hospitality industry and setting a standard of excellence in landscaping at Marriott facilities. (CN 5/24/80)

The "Joseph Smith" tulip was planted for the first time in America in the gardens of Temple Square in 1953. It was named by its developers, M. Van Waveren and Sons, Inc., of Hillegom, Holland, one of the foremost bulb hybridists in The Netherlands. It was the custom of Dutch tulip growers to name new varieties of flowers after prominent world figures. (CN 12/5/53)

Oldest Shrubs. Perhaps the shrubs of greatest significance to LDS are those transplanted onto Temple Square in 1968. They had been growing locally since the pioneers arrived in the mid-1800s, and were so mature at transplanting time they almost looked like trees. The shrubs are of the Honeysuckle or Lonicera family, and are rated the finest living example of this kind of shrub in America or Japan, where this type of plant is used extensively. Each shrub with its ball of dirt weighed 3 1/2 tons. (CN 11/23/68)

JUDICIAL

U.S. Solicitor General. Former BYU Law School Dean Rex Lee was Solicitor General during Ronald Reagan's first term in the early 1980s, and argued before the Supreme Court nearly 50 times. He later became president of BYU after miraculously recovering from a serious bout with cancer. A recurrence of the disease later took his life. (LDS 7/26/86)

Oldest Practicing Attorney. Who holds the record for being the oldest practicing attorney in the Church? In 1987, the oldest was Marion Earl of the Las Vegas, Nevada, 1st Ward. Specializing in wills, trusts, probate, and adoptions, Earl turned 89 in April 1987, having outlived the two doctors who told him to stop working or he'd die. "I fooled them both," he says. "I got well again." (CN 4/4/87)

Largest Fine Paid With Food Storage. The largest fine ever paid with food storage was $200 by a 45-year-old Provo man, James Quanda. After a debate with Brother Quanda over the constitutional definition of legal tender, Judge E. Patrick McGuire finally said, in so many words, "You can pay in gold, silver or wheat, but the fine is $200!" The next morning, the Provo man dumped 1,350 pounds of wheat in the hallway outside the judge's chambers. (LDS 2/3/84; DU 1/13/84)

Wheat – worth its weight in pennies.

Shortest Jail Sentence. When Missourians finally caught Orrin Porter Rockwell in St. Louis, they took him to trial for the attempted assassination of ex-governor Lilburn W. Boggs. Lawyers got a change of venue to Independence, where Rockwell sat in jail for several weeks before a jury found him innocent of the shooting but guilty of another crime – jailbreak! The judge sentenced him to five minutes in jail. (CN 11/10/62)

Arrest on Sea of Galilee. W. Cleon Skousen has the distinction of being the first and only LDS person ever arrested on the Sea of Galilee. In 1986, he was on tour in Israel with cameramen from Living Scriptures to produce a documentary on the life of the Savior. During filming, Brother Skousen was positioned in a small boat far from shore, telling of Jesus' ministry and His experiences in the area during a storm on the Sea of Galilee. Suddenly, an Israeli coast-guard boat swept down on the little entourage, put the boat's occupants under arrest and towed their little craft to shore. It turned out that the rented boats were not licensed. Despite the company's official filming permits, the coast guard hauled the Americans off to an Israeli jail. Only after intervention by a friend in the Israeli Knesset were they freed. Two weeks prior, a sudden storm had capsized a similar unlicensed craft, drowning all aboard and sparking a more careful patrol of Galilee. (Author)

MORMONS WHO PUT MEN ON THE MOON

NASA photo

Many Mormons helped build and support the largest launch vehicle in the world.

Slurped in Space. On Christmas Day, 1968, history was made for U.S. astronauts thanks to Bishop Clayton S. Huber. Huber had hidden on board Apollo 8 a complete turkey dinner in flexible bags to be eaten with a spoon (photo on page 330). This ended years of slurping liquid meals through straws. This unauthorized experiment proved that decent meals could be prepared and eaten without the danger of food particles escaping into the space compartment and damaging equipment. After the success of Huber's experiment, NASA assigned him to perfect the process. (DU 10/16/85)

Engineer. Craig E. McCreary, Titusville, Florida, had a closer seat at the moon launches than anyone else except the astronauts. Seated only two miles away from the launch pad, he monitored various systems as the rockets launched. One of his major assignments following the Apollo program was to design the landing gear and the aerodynamic seal for flight controls on the space shuttle. (CN spring 1977)

Tooling. Manfred H. Erekson, Oroville 1st Ward, Chico, California, Stake, was in charge of the tooling project for the first Saturn rocket. The 32-foot-diameter 320-foot-tall rocket had never been built before and no tools existed to do it. His team developed a plastic-explosive technique to blow the materials into underwater molds. He also developed and holds the patent on a teleoptics device to survey the work and ensure various stages were aligned properly as the Saturn was built. (CN spring 1977)

Deseret Morning News file photo

Manfred Erikson, demonstrating Apollo's trip to the moon, helped engineer the rocket that sent it there.

Photo: RockeDyne

Saturn second stage: This massive piece of engineering had never before been constructed. Manfred Erikson led the team that figured out a way: water!

Food. Bishop Clayton S. Huber, Alvin Ward, Houston, Texas, East Stake, was director of the food-research program for America's manned-space flights. In their first report from space, a happy and well-fed Apollo 15 crew praised the food prepared by Huber and his staff. Huber tried to match the

James Lovell performs experiments aboard Apollo 8. The smile is thanks to Brother Huber for the unauthorized turkey dinner.

menus with astronauts' favorite menus by interviewing them and their wives. Huber says the astronauts' wives were more candid about what their husbands liked. He then went about making the food items space worthy. He was on the forefront of enriching foods with vitamins, minerals and other nutrients, and using soybeans and other plants as a basis for manufactured synthetic foods and food products. (CN 1/8/72)

First LDS to Head NASA.

Former University of Utah President James C. Fletcher, who headed the U.S. space agency in 1971-77, took the post again on Jan. 28, 1986, following the tragic Challenger space shuttle explosion. Brother Fletcher died of cancer on Dec. 22, 1991. (LDS 5/17/86; CN 5/25/86)

NASA photo

At the Oval Office: President Nixon looks on as James Fletcher is sworn in as the head of NASA in 1971. Looking on is Sister Fletcher and Judge James Belson.

Flight Surgeon. Dr. Norman W. Pincock, Melbourne Ward, Orlando, Florida, Stake, was the astronaut's flight surgeon in the mid- to late-1960s. He was assigned to give pre-launch physicals and physiological testing and to be responsible for their safety and comfort. He was assigned to the Launch Site Medical Operations Office in July 1965. (CN 8/27/66)

First to Hear Sputnik. David C. Skousen, Salt Lake City, was the first Mormon to intercept the transmission signal of the Soviets' "Sputnik," the first satellite put into orbit around the earth. Using amateur ham-radio equipment from his room in the basement of his parent's home, Skousen, 17, intercepted the tell-tale signal on Oct 6, 1957, two days after

Photo courtesy David C. and Eric N. Skousen

David Skousen first heard Sputnik using this early tube-powered ham radio equipment.

the satellite was launched. The 184-pound sphere traveled around the earth every 96 minutes, crossing over the United States seven times a day for about three months. It was 500 miles high and traveled 18,000 miles an hour. "The satellite was very unstable, so its signal varied greatly as it spun," Brother Skousen said. "It made a regular 'beep-beep-beep' tone, 132 beeps per minute." A local television station interviewed him and played a tape of the noise for the rest of Utah to hear. And the world was never the same. (Author's interview)

SCIENCE

World-Renowned Black Hole Expert. Kip Thorne, a research scientist at Cambridge University, is best known as a leading expert in the field of black holes. A black hole is an object whose mass is so great that even light cannot escape, hence its nickname. (www.ldsfilm.com/bio/bioT.html)

ARCHEOLOGY

Last Surviving Nauvoo Star Stone? The only known complete star stone located since the destruction of the Nauvoo Temple was given to the Church by Elizabeth Bauer, Keokuk, Ill., in 1962. When Mrs. Bauer heard of plans to restore Nauvoo, she recalled that her grandfather had brought such a stone home many years before and located it in her attic. The original temple, started in 1841, was decorated with 30 star stones, 30 moon stones and 30 sun stones. Three moon stones and two sun stones are known to exist. Mobs burned the temple in 1848. (CN 10/6/62)

J. M. Heslop, Deseret Morning News

Dr. Atiya shows missing papyri to N. Elden Tanner.

Papyri Of Greatest Significance. A few of the papyrus manuscripts that played an important role in early Church history, and thought lost in the great Chicago fire of 1871, were found and presented to the Church in 1967. The papyrus manuscripts included the item known as Facsimile No. 1 in the Book of Abraham in the Pearl of Great Price. The 11 pieces included a letter signed by Emma Smith Bidamon (widow of the prophet) and the Prophet's son, Joseph Smith III. The papyri were located by Dr. Aziz S. Atiya while browsing through the papyri collection at the New York Metropolitan Museum of Art. He couldn't believe his eyes. "I was electrified," he said. "I recognized immediately the original of Facsimile No. 1 in the Pearl of Great Price. Although it had been damaged some, I knew it was the one Joseph Smith had." The papyri were sent to BYU for further study. (CN 12/2/67)

Deseret Morning News file photo

Facsimile 1 was thought to have been destroyed in the Great Chicago Fire of 1871, but was discovered in great condition in New York library.

The Mummy! The most beautifully preserved mummy to emerge from the sandstone hills of the Egypt, just 90 miles south of Cairo, is unquestionably that found by BYU Professor C. Wilfred Griggs in 1989. Brother Griggs estimated that the woman preserved in a 7-foot-long hardwood coffin, was buried between 100 B.C. and A.D. 100. "This is, by every opinion I've been able to get, the finest preserved mummy from the later, pre-Christian period of Egyptian history," Griggs says. Hieroglyphics at one end of the coffin indicate the woman was of "sweet disposition" who was "loved by everybody," according to Hugh Nibley, professor emeritus of ancient scripture at BYU. (LDS 5/17/89)

This woman's fingernail covering was real gold leaf, a stylish addition to any woman's wardrobe for that special night out on the town.

Treasure from Pit Tomb 33. Around 1830, Antonio Lebolo was in Thebes, Egypt, digging for ancient burial pits when he discovered what was later catalogued as Pit Tomb 33. About 300 mummies were inside, 11 still in good shape. In two of them were found two Egyptian papyri scrolls. One began, "... I, Abraham ..." and the other appeared to be written by Joseph, the great-grandson of Abraham (about 1700 B.C.). Portions of the Abraham scroll translated by Joseph Smith are included in the Pearl of Great Price as The Book of Abraham. (Author)

The bricked-up entry way to Pit Tomb 33, visible at lower left, near Thebes, Egypt. Inset: A piece of stone from Pit Tomb 33 showing a few of the Egyptian hieroglyphics carved into the tomb's rock walls.

Photos: Bartonian Institute of Technology

SCIENCE/ENGINEERING

"The Skylab is Falling!" Keeping an eye on the heavens was a full-time job for 1st Lt. Howard Stewart in 1979. As an "orbital analyst" for the Air Force, his job in the deep inner-mountain confines of NORAD was to help track more than 7,000 individual items in orbit around the earth. One of the largest items, the U.S. Skylab, had been up for years until its orbit began to decay. Stewart says he spotted the orbital changes in 1977 and began plotting Skylab's eventual fall to the earth. "There was no system for predicting decay (reentry) of satellites as far out as Skylab, so we developed a program that simulated orbital parameters and the influence of sunspot activity." On July 11, 1979, the bulk of Skylab plunged into the Indian Ocean, with pieces scattering into Australia. For his careful analysis and watchful care, Stewart received the meritorious service award from the Air Force. (CN 7/14/79)

First Radio Broadcast. The first radio broadcast in Salt Lake City took place at 8 p.m. on May 6, 1922. Nate Fullmer, business manager at the Deseret News, took the mike to speak the historic first words, and called out into the night, "Hello, hello, hello! This is KZN. KZN, the Deseret News, Salt Lake City calling. KZN calling! Greetings!" He then turned the mike over to LDS President Heber J. Grant who recited a scripture and shared a gospel message with listeners. Bringing radio to Utah was no easy task.

Deseret News announces that radio has come to Salt Lake City in 1922.

American Telephone and Telegraph had a monopoly on radio transmitters and was charging $25,000 per machine. President Grant refused to finance the cost so a transmitter was built from scratch on the roof of the Deseret News building. It took a year and a lot of experiments to complete the project. After that initial 30-minute broadcast, President Grant was uncomfortable with the broadcast booth's temperature and, thinking he was off air, said, "Turn off the heat." Curious listeners wrote to the Deseret News wondering just what their prophet was trying to say. In 1930, President Grant was again speaking over the radio while giving his conference address in the Salt Lake Tabernacle when suddenly sounds of the World Series started playing on the speakers. For an embarrassing eight long minutes, conference goers were treated to an animated sportscaster calling the game! Presiding Bishop Sylvester Q. Cannon raced to the radio station, then into the Union Pacific Building, to alert engineers to the problem. Everyone had a good laugh afterwards. In 1924, the call letters were changed to KSL, the 50,000-watt powerhouse station that is still in operation today. (CN 1/12/80; Internet)

World's First Intercontinental Satellite Broadcast. The first satellite television broadcast beamed from Telstar featured a concert by the Mormon Tabernacle Choir. On July 23, 1962, a 15-minute telecast was scheduled to include the choir singing patriotic hymns beneath majestic Mt. Rushmore. The brief satellite experiment also included a news conference by President Kennedy and action from a major-league baseball game. This marked the first time the entire choir had flown to a concert assignment. (CN 7/28/62; CN 1/12/80)

World's First Long-Distance Stereo Broadcast. On Easter Sunday, 1966, long-distance stereo broadcast history was made when the Mormon Tabernacle Choir broadcast was transmitted in binaural sound to an FM station in New York City (WRFM). Despite failed efforts by others in the past, cooperation with American Telephone and Telegraph and a lot of hard work resulted in what one WRFM official called "beautiful music" and a major breakthrough in the application of stereo to long-distance broadcasting. (CN 4/23/66)

First Airship. Was the 225-foot-long by 50-foot-wide giant craft created by Clarence W. Conrad and his son Darwin in 1975 the first dirigible airship built by Mormons? The duo began assembling the craft near Williams Air Force Base just outside of Chandler, Ariz. With engineering help from Arizona State University and money from the Air Force and other interested parties, the Conrads made rapid progress. The craft had 10 separate helium cells covered with nylon-laminated plastic material and three aluminum-block motors to give it direction once airborne. The 425th Tactical Fighter Training Squad at Williams Air Force Base presented the Conrads with a plaque commending them for their spirit of daring, plus $150 to help with construction costs. (CN 11/15/75)

Elder Pratt's telescope was used from this observatory (lower right) on Temple Square (notice the removable partitions on the shack's roof).

Utah State Historical Society

Earliest LDS Telescope. Elder Orson Pratt, a skilled mathematician, was the astronomer and scientist for the Mormon pioneers as the vanguard company tried to chart a trail westward from Winter Quarters. Using a telescope bought in England by John Taylor, Pratt took regular measurements of latitude and longitude as the company traveled west. The telescope had arrived in Winter Quarters just three days before the first group left for the Rockies. It came complete with a five-foot wooden tripod and attachments to aid in making very precise measurements. It is on display at the Church's Museum of Church History and Art. (CN 3/24/90)

The Only Man to Stop Niagara Falls. Col. Amos L. Wright, Cumorah Stake, gained the unique distinction of being "The Man Who Stopped the Niagara Falls" in June 1969. The water stoppage was to permit scientists to

When the American Falls were reduced to a trickle on June 12, 1969, scientists could collect sample rocks to look for weaknesses contributing to constant collapse. The flow was restored on Nov. 25, 1969.

Deseret Morning News file photo

study the eroding crest of the falls and learn how to stop the damaging rock slides at the cliff where the falls make their descent. Wright, district engineer for the Buffalo District of the Army Corps of Engineers, was in charge of diverting the Niagara River for the five-month study. The falls had never before been stopped by man. On March 29, 1848, and Feb. 22, 1936, great blocks of ice plugged the river, bringing the falls to a trickle – but these were both acts of nature. (CN 7/5/69)

Strongest Balsa Bridge, Junior Division. Drew Higbee, 9, and his teammates built a balsa bridge that supported 880 pounds before collapsing, to win the 1998 Odyssey of the Mind World Championship. More than 5,400 students representing 30 countries took part in the world competition in Lake Buena Vista, Fla. He is a member of the Plano 9th Ward, Plano, Texas, Stake. (CN 9/5/98)

The strongest balsa bridge weighing under 20 grams and entered in a regular contest was that of Benjamin Lungren, 10, Carrollton, Texas, Ward, and his five teammates. They won the 1987 Odyssey of the Mind world finals when their 15-gram bridge withstood 405 pounds before collapsing. The 11-inch bridge beat out competing bridges from 48 states, Canada and Mexico. (CN 6/20/87)

Strongest Balsa Bridge, Age 18. The strongest balsa bridge weighing under 100 grams entered in a regular contest held 3,464 pounds before collapsing. It was designed and built by Ken Mickelson, 18, Greenwood Village, Colorado, Ward. He won the national bridge-building contest sponsored by the U.S. Bureau of Reclamation in 1986. (LDS 5/17/86)

Balsa wood bridge contests are popular across the country. Here, Robert Riedel sets up a test during a contest held at BYU. BYU - L. Tom Perry Special Collections

337

MEDICINE

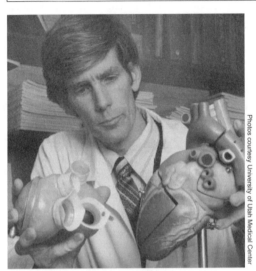

Dr. William DeVries compares the "Jarvik 7" artificial heart (left) with an enlarged model of the human heart (right).

The First Artificial Heart. The first permanent artificial heart was implanted by LDS surgeon Dr. William DeVries, Monument Park, Utah, Stake, on Dec. 2, 1982, at the University of Utah Medical Center. At the time, he was chief of cardiac surgery at the University of Utah Medical Center. He had been intensely researching artificial-heart technology for several years when the "Jarvik 7" became available, thanks to the dedicated research by Dr. Robert K. Jarvik.

The recipient of the artificial heart was LDS dentist Dr. Barney Clark, Federal Way 1st Ward, Federal Way, Washington, Stake. Brother Clark had suffered minor kidney failure and already had surgery to correct lung leaks and failure in one of his heart valves. After the implanting of the artificial heart, he was tethered permanently to an equipment package (the size of a small desk) via two six-foot long drive lines connected to

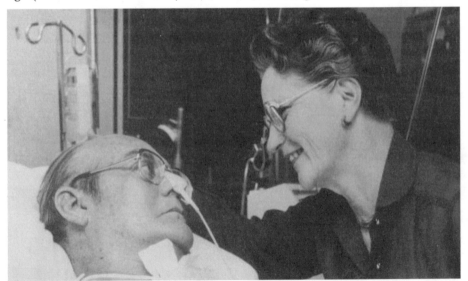

Dr. Barney and Una Loy Clark rejoice for time with one another that otherwise might not have happened. Their extended time together lasted 16 weeks.

Courtesy University of Utah Medical Center

Dr. Robert K. Jarvik, LDS inventor of the "Jarvik 7." Before his artificial heart was used on Dr. Clark, an identical model had kept a 330-pound holstein calf alive for 268 days.

the artificial heart in his chest. Clark made medical history by living on the machine for 112 days. He died March 23, 1983. (CN 1/23/83; phone interview with Dr. DeVries)

Longest Running Artificial Heart Valve. One of the first artificial heart valves ever placed in a human being made medical history when, in March 1983, it became the longest running valve of its type, exceeding 18 years. Sister Randy Crum, 75 at the time, of Mesa 1st Ward, Mesa, Arizona, North Stake, received the stainless-steel silicone ball-socket valve in her heart in January 1965, and was all smiles for the press for the 18th anniversary. (LDS 4/8/89)

First Heart Transplants Among Family. The first exchange of hearts in the world between immediate family members occurred when the heart of Jonathan Simper, 16, was placed in his grandfather, Albert Nielson, 63. Jonathan was fatally injured in a car-train crash in Brigham City, Utah, March 3, 1987. His grandfather had been on the waiting list for a heart transplant, and doctors succeeded in keeping Jonathan's heart alive long enough to perform the heart-to-heart transplant. (CN 3/14/87)

"Firsts" and "Onlys" Among LDS Kidney Recipients. U.S. Senator Jake Garn caught the nation's attention and empathy when he underwent surgery to donate a kidney to his 27-year-old daughter, Susan Horn, in 1986. (8/16/86)

May Charles, 22, Lexington, South Carolina, 2nd Ward, made medical history following her second kidney transplant in 1986. The first transplant came when she was four years old. But her case was the first cadaver transplant involving removal of both kidneys. In 1986, she became the longest surviving cadaver transplant recipient ever. (CN 6/15/86)

Susan Jessop, 30, Paul, Idaho, became the first woman in history to retain a transplanted kidney and pancreas after delivering a baby on Jan. 3, 1990. She is the fourth woman in history to deliver a baby after this kind of transplant surgery. She gave birth by caesarean section to a two-pound 11-ounce daughter, Misti. Doctors had warned Susan that a pregnancy would probably force her body to reject the transplanted organs, so she went on the pill. When she got pregnant anyway, doctors advised her to get an abortion. Susan replied, "That (abortion) is totally against my beliefs. I told doctors that we would just take it a day at a time. ... I think there is a reason that I was supposed to have this baby or I wouldn't have gotten pregnant." (DN 1/9/90)

Producing Penicillin in a Pinch. What can you do if you have no penicillin and no means of procuring any in the near future? The next best thing is to make your own. Dr. Eldredge Wayne Stratford Sr., Portland, Oregon, is credited with being the first Navy doctor to culture and produce his own penicillin on board a battleship to supplement scarce medical supplies during World War II. (CN 8/3/57)

THE WORD OF WISDOM VERSUS CANCER

Cancer studies continue to prove that the healthy life style of LDS who live the Word of Wisdom help them avoid cancers of nearly all types. Compared to the national averages, active LDS are 85 percent less likely to contract lung cancer, 29 percent less likely to contract any of the kidney cancers, and 40 percent less likely to contract cancer in general. (LDS 5/3/89)

Non-LDS versus Inactive LDS: Statistics on the population in Utah show that a person's chances of avoiding most forms of cancer are better if he or she is non-LDS rather than being an inactive Mormon. From a study in the 1980s by Dr. Joseph Lyon of the University of Utah Medical Center, non-LDS in Utah are 26 percent less likely to contract lung cancer, while inactive LDS are only 17 percent less likely. And while non-LDS in Utah are 30 percent less likely to get kidney cancer, inactive LDS are 64 percent MORE likely to get kidney cancer. Some have speculated that inactive LDS may have poorer health than non-LDS for reasons of anger or bitterness. Some who abandon the Church tend to go overboard in various vices to prove they no longer adhere to Church teachings. (LDS 5/3/89)

Nuclear Bomb Testing. While the Word of Wisdom makes Mormons a healthier people, it's not a cure-all in the face of nuclear weapons. A study released in 1984 showed that Mormons living downwind of atmospheric nuclear tests in the 1950s had increased cancer rates despite their healthy lifestyles. Church members suffered five times more cases of leukemia than expected between 1958 and 1966, and higher rates of thyroid, gastrointestinal, brain, bone and other cancers. The high rates persisted and, in certain cancer types, increased through 1980. The 1984 report concluded, "The excess incidence of cancer (among the southwest Utah Mormons) is actually caused by the exposures to radioactive fallout." (DU 1/16/84)

Skin and Lip Cancer. Even though Utah and its predominantly Mormon population have fewer cases of cancer connected with drinking and smoking than any other state, the same group has higher rates of lip and skin cancer. Studies indicate this is primarily due to the higher altitude and Utah's 90+ percent white population (lighter-skinned populations are more prone to such problems than darker-skinned populations). (DU 9/25/79)

American Cancer Society Concurs ... In 1995, Dr. Harmon J. Eyre, deputy executive vice president for medical affairs and research for the American Cancer Society, delivered a paper on "Mormons and Cancer" at the American Cancer Society's Futures Project on Cancer in the 21st Century in Atlanta, Georgia. He noted: "Mormons who are active have a much lower chance of dying from cancer than do all other Americans combined." He explained that active Mormons are about 35 percent as likely to contract or die from cancer as the general population. In his paper, Dr. Eyre observed that Utah, which was 68 percent LDS at the time of the study, had the lowest mortality rate for all causes of cancer in all 50 states since records have been kept. If the U.S. mortality rate were defined at 100, then the mortality rate for all Mormons would be 47, while that for religiously active Mormon men would be 34. On the same scale, the mortality rates for men for cardiovascular diseases is 52 for all Mormons, but drops to 14 for religiously active Mormons.

DENTISTRY

First Male Dentist. The first dentist to practice in the Territory of Deseret was Alexander Nebaur, a German immigrant to the United States in 1841. He seldom received money for his services that included cleaning and plugging teeth, as well as making and repairing false teeth. His pay came in the form of cornmeal, molasses, pigweed greens, or whatever the Saints could offer during those impoverished early years in Utah. (DN 2/11/91)

First Female Dentist. Utah's first woman dentist was Rose Ellen Valentine, who held a license from 1903 until 1960. (DN 2/11/91)

No More Rinse And Spit. The next time you're at the dentist and the assistant puts that suction tube in your mouth, you can thank Utah dentist Elbert O. Thompson, who invented the idea. After years of leaning over patients and subsequently developing a back problem, Dr. Thompson decided there had to be a better way. The practice used for prior decades was to have patients seated in an upright position so they could spit in the spittoon. His "washed field" technique allows the dentist to sit upright and work over a reclining patient. This technique revolutionized the entire dentistry profession. (DN 2/11/91)

Paul Barker, Deseret Morning News

Dr. Elbert Thompson revolutionized dentistry when he found a way to better position patients – and do away with the famous porcelain spitoon.

OTHER MORMONS & MEDICINE

First Pre-natal Surgery on a Baby. Seventeen weeks before Amy Spencer was born, a doctor discovered a rare and 100 percent fatal cyst called cystic adenomatoid malformation. It was preventing the natural development of Amy's heart and lungs. Dr. Steven Clark, Orem, Utah 27th Ward, tried to save Amy by operating on her while she was still in her mother's womb. He made an incision into the womb and then inserted a shunt into infant Amy's chest to drain fluid away from the deadly cyst. Some 17 weeks later, Dr. Dennis Vatale, BYU 4th Stake, operated to remove the shunt. Amy survived the surgery and beat the life-threatening cyst. When news of the life-saving surgery became public, the medical team was swamped with information requests from doctors around the world. The grateful parents were Darwin and Susan Spencer, Pleasant Grove, Utah, 3rd Ward. (CN 5/11/86)

First Head-Conjoined Twins Among Mormons. In a history-making operation, 21-month-old twins Elisa and Lisa Hansen, Ogden, Utah, were separated after being born connected at the upper portion of their heads. The 16-hour operation on May 29, 1979, involved 20 people in the operating room. Six weeks later, the twins went home. The genetic odds of head-conjoined twins such as the Hansens are less than one in 2.5 million, and the odds of successful separation are close to zero. (CN 7/28/79)

March of Dimes National Poster Child. Timothy Fass, Whittier, California, a four-year-old-Mormon boy (in 1967), was selected the 1968 National March of Dimes Child for the organization's 30th anniversary campaign. As 1968 poster child, Timmy toured the country to meet dignitaries and leaders, and promote funding for research towards cures of various and life-threatening diseases. (CN 11/18/67)

Most Mormon-Sponsored Injections. On June 25, 1988, the Church paid for 1 million polio immunizations for young people in Kenya and the Ivory Coast. The $250,000 contribution went to the Rotary International PolioPlus program. (Church Almanac 1989-90)

Youngest Medical Student. Not only did Norman Loayza of the Miraflores Ward, Lima, Peru, Stake, pass the medical-school exam and rank fourth among 3,000 applicants for the 61 openings, but he was only 15 at the time, becoming the youngest ever admitted to Lima's Ceyetano Heredia University Medical School. (CN 1980)

Norman Loayza, qualified for medical school at age 15. He placed fourth among 3,000 applicants.

Most Persistent Burn Victim. RaNelle Wallace, Bakersfield 1st Ward, Bakersfield, California, East Stake, miraculously survived a fiery plane crash. While convalescing at home with serious burns, she saw her neighbor's home on fire. Wanting to save them from the same painful ordeal she was having to endure, she raced to warn them, but became trapped in their burning garage. She lived to tell about her ordeal and, in 1986, was listed in Newsweek's special edition, "100 New American Heroes." (LDS 5/10/86)

PLACES OF HISTORICAL SIGNIFICANCE

An unidentified nerd (left) models the latest in 1970s-era pre-mission clothing next to his more smartly attired brother, Dr. Eric N. Skousen, at Mt. Joseph Smith, a.k.a., Mt. Palomar, home for what had been for a long time the world's largest telescope.

Mt. Palomar This famous mountaintop telescope observatory in Southern California is home to the 200-inch Hale telescope, for many years the largest telescope in the world. The mountain was originally named Mount Joseph Smith by early Mormon settlers in the area. (LDS 7/21/84)

San Bernardino, California. Founded in 1851 by Mormon settlers. (LDS 7/21/84)

Las Vegas. Brigham Young sent the first settlers to Las Vegas under the leadership of William Bringhurst in June 1855. On June 14 they erected a shelter and a fort. Brother Bringhurst sent word back to President Young that he had found two springs and "a patch of nice grass, about half a mile wide and two or three miles long." "Las Vegas," Spanish for "meadow," takes its name from this spot. A way station, small colony and a lead mine were started but lasted only two years, until the so-called Utah War began. Church members returned later to establish ranches. By 1905, the area was growing and LDS settlers were moving in. In 1924, the first ward was organized, and today there is a temple. (CN 12/23/89)

Island. "Mormon Island" in the Los Angeles harbor was so named because a former Mormon Battalion member and his son were the island's only occupants for many years. They made their living by fishing. (CN 12/12/48)

Most Flooded. The most flooded Mormon settlement has to be Woodruff, Arizona. The river that supplies this community with life-giving water also rises to flood levels on a regular basis to choke the life out of the town. In a 60 year period (1879-1939), the community rebuilt the dam 13 times. (CN 3/27/83)

ROCKS AND THE EARTH

Only Gem Discovered by a Mormon. The only known gem to have been discovered and named by a member of the Church is lavulite, a rare, lavender-colored gem-quality stone. It was discovered and named in 1985 by Randy Polk, of Tempe, Arizona. A "highest grade" sample was once displayed in the Smithsonian Institute. (LDS 9/7/85)

Largest Arch Located by Mormons. A survey crew from BYU in August 1983 established Kolob Arch as the world's largest natural span, at more than 300 feet. The previous record holder was Arches National Park's Landscape Arch at 291 feet. The arch's discovery date is unknown, although visits to it were recorded as early as the 1920s. It didn't appear on most maps until the 1950s, and the park service left it nameless for years. (DU 8/2/83)

Most Significant Hole. At the dedication of the Hill Cumorah Monument on July 21, 1935, President Heber J. Grant was photographed standing on the side of the Hill Cumorah pointing to a large depression, all that remained of the hole from which Joseph Smith retrieved the golden plates. When a search was made some years later to again locate the hole, an old farmer took Church investigators to the site, saying it was easy to find because of the old oak standing just a few feet from it. When they

1935: After Pres. Grant pointed out the place where the golden plates had been buried, Rita Skousen, San Bernardino, California, stepped into view to point out the same hole for this photograph. Notice the new monument over her left shoulder.

arrived, the oak could not be found. After some searching, they found the oak's rotted trunk lying on its side, and the depression nearby. The stones lining the box from which the golden plates were removed had for years lain at the bottom of the hill, unearthed by scavengers digging for more treasure. Unfortunately, the stones have since disappeared, probably removed by local residents. (CN 7/21/35; author)

Most Significant Stone. Alert missionaries in Stirling, Scotland, rescued in 1965 the stone that may well be of greatest significance to LDS. For gen-

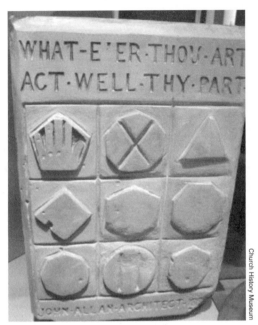

David O McKay gained inspiration from this stone and shared its slogan throughout the Church.

erations, Church members have heard repeated President David O. McKay's missionary motto, "What E'er Thou Art, Act Well Thy Part." President McKay said he first saw those words chiseled into a stone on the face of a then-unfinished building in Stirling, Scotland, in 1898 while he was serving his mission. When the building was razed in 1965, the local missionaries rescued the stone, which eventually wound up on display in the Church History Museum. Said President McKay in 1955, "This message came to me, not only in stone, but as if it came from One in whose service we (missionaries) were engaged: 'What E'er Thou Art, Act Well Thy Part.'" (CN 3/76)

Historical LDS Cave. Cache Cave, a small, forgotten hole in the sandstone near Castle Rock, Summit County, Utah, was for years one of the West's important landmarks to an untold number of passing travelers. It was used as a shelter by many trappers, explorers, and Utah pioneers. The 30-foot-long, 15-foot wide and 20-foot high cavern has carved on its walls the names of 150 people dating back to 1820. (CN 8/29/48)

The world's second-longest "soda straw" hangs among hunderds at Kartchner Cave.

Secret Cave. An LDS family of 100 did the almost impossible by keeping secret for 14 years the existence of a large and magnificent cave discovered on their property in 1974. To avoid vandalism until a deal could be worked out with the state of Arizona, the Kartchner family of Benson, Arizona, kept the cave's existence secret until they finally sold it for $1,625,000 in the fall of 1988. The cave is home to formations considered to be the best of their kind in the world. Now known as Kartchner Caverns State Park, it is home to:

- The longest soda straw formation in America, and second longest in the world, measuring 21 feet 2 inches (see it in the Throne Room)
- The tallest and most massive column in Arizona: Kubla Khan, measuring 58 feet tall (Throne Room)
- The world's most extensive formation of brushite moonmilk (Big Room)
- The first reported occurrence of "turnip" shields (Big Room)
- The first cave occurrence of "birds nest" needle quartz formations

And many other unusual formations such as shields, totems, helictites and rimstone dams.

Latter Day Sentinel file photo

A huge 50-foot column drawfs a human (visible in circle) at its base.

When first exploring the cave, paleontologists discovered the skeleton of an 80,000-year-old Shasta ground sloth, a 34,000-year-old horse, and an 11,000-year-old bear, among many other animals and creatures. They also found about 1,000 female cave myotis bats that use the cave to give birth each summer. Their waste supports an amazing food chain that keeps other life forms in the cave alive year around. The bats provide the only link between these life forms and the outside world. The creatures, insects and bacteria consume the bat's waste almost completely, and are able to survive until the bats return the following summer.

The Kartchner Cave is a popular site in Arizona, now with a visitors center, regular tours, and nearby camping. (LDS 10/22/88; Internet)

Historical Site – Adam-ondi-Ahman. The summit of Spring Hill, Missouri, was pointed out by the Prophet Joseph Smith as Adam-ondi-Ahman, a place where Adam and "his posterity offered up sacrifices to the Lord and where Adam will return in the last days to preside at a grand council." In 1944, the Church purchased the 30-acre site that included Spring Hill. For years LDS tourists have made a pilgrimage to Adam-ondi-Ahman. Somewhere along the line, they began hearing of an ancient Nephite altar or the altar of Adam, and a sign was posted to identify a pile of rocks as the altar's ancient remains. Some years later it came to light that a local farmer had been dumping rocks in that spot. "Each year I'd dump a load, and each year it would disappear," he said in regard to the tourists who took away souvenirs. The exact location of the altar has long been lost, but myths and rumors continue to circulate. For its past and future historical significance, the site remains a good stop on any Church history tour. (CN 3/4/44)

DINOSAURS

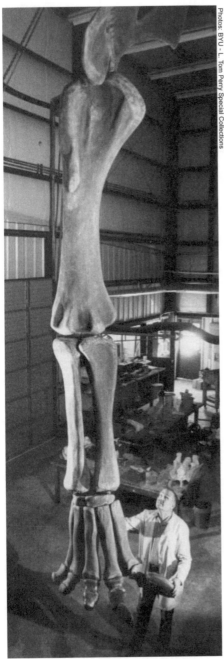

Photos: BYU - L. Tom Perry Special Collections

Jim Jensen working on the world's smallest dinosaur, another of his many discoveries.

"Dinosaur Jim" Jensen was world-renowned for his expertise in excavating dinosaur remains. Among his finds were many of the world's superlatives when it comes to dinosaurs. At the time of their discovery, he had unearthed the world's smallest dinosaur, the oldest bird bones, and a quarry that had produced more fossil animal species than any other quarry in the world. He gained additional fame from his work at the Dry Mesa dinosaur quarry in Colorado, where he excavated the giant sauropods "Ultrasaurus" and "Supersaurus," and the large megalosaurid theropod Torvosaurus. Many of the dinosaur references in this section come thanks to his decades of untiring research and study into this amazing science.

Jim Jensen is dwarfed by the 26-foot-long front leg of the Ultrasaurus he discovered near Delta, Colorado.

World's Largest Dinosaur. The largest dinosaur ever found, the 80-foot-tall Ultrasaurus, was discovered by BYU paleontologist "Dinosaur" Jim Jensen in 1979. The Ultrasaurus would be able to peer into the window of a seven- or eight-story building. The leg of the beast stretched 26 feet from toenail to scapula (shoulder blade). Brother Jensen estimated the neck to be at least 40 feet long, and calculated that the giant sauropod probably weighed about 100 tons. (LDS 9/24/88; DU 2/17/83)

Jim Jensen, 6 foot 3 inches tall, stretches out along side the 9-foot tall scapula of the Ultrasaurus.

In 1972, Dinosaur Jim discov-ered the Supersaurus, whose scapula was eight feet long. (DU 9/22/80)

World's Biggest Pelvic Bones. In 1988, "Dinosaur Jim" Jensen led a team of BYU researchers to uncover the largest pelvic bones in the world. Researchers matched the petrified remains to the Supersaurus, an animal estimated to stand some 60-80 feet. tall.

Largest Dinosaur Bone Collection in the World? Could the 100 tons of bones stored beneath the new LaVell Edwards Stadium seats at BYU be the largest such collection in the world? "Dinosaur" Jim Jensen said in 1980 that the collection had been valued at $27 million, and has probably grown in value to ten times that amount. "You can't put a monetary value on something like that," Jensen said. Included in the collection are fossils that throw some curious monkey wrenches into the various theories on the origin of man. (DU 3/29/82)

First Discovery of Cancer in Dinosaurs. Researchers have confirmed that cancer did afflict dinosaurs, based on evidence among several specimens in BYU's dinosaur-bone collection. Signs of bone cancer prove the disease is as old, literally, as the hills. (Author)

Gerald W. Silver, Deseret Morning News

President Tanner kept models of his namesake on his desk at Church headquarters.

Only Dinosaur Named After Apostle. "Dinosaur Jim" Jensen named one of his newly discovered dinosaurs after President Nathan Eldon Tanner in 1981. The "Torvosaurus tanneri" was estimated to be about 148 million years old. The first and only specimen went on display at BYU in 2000, but two small models had earlier adorned President Tanner's desk at Church headquarters. Said President Tanner, "I hope Jim didn't have some hidden meaning in naming the creature that." (LDS 7/16/82)

Best Ancient Omelet, er, Dinosaur Egg. The 150-million-year-old fossilized egg with a premature embryo found by BYU researchers in 1988 may be the most complete egg ever found from the Jurassic period (middle age of the dinosaurs). The find brought international attention to BYU. When news of the remarkable egg spread around the world, grocery store tabloids blasted across their front covers, "American Scientists Unearth BABY 75 MILLION YEARS OLD." "Top Scientist predicts ... Dinosaur AGE WILL RETURN! Hundreds of dormant eggs could hatch and attack American cities." (LDS 4/9/88; LDS 9/24/88)

This squashed allosaurus egg was the only one of its kind when discovered by BYU researchers in 1988.

Deseret Morning News file photos

BYU's 152-million-year-old allosaurus egg undergos a CAT scan at American Fork Hospital. An embryo was discovered inside.

Dinosaur Mascots. If being the majority in the state of Utah means being LDS, then the Allosaurus, also found in great abundance in Utah, became the official Utah state fossil in 1988. The petrified bones of more than 20 of the beasts have been found in Utah, more than anywhere else in the United States. Measuring some 40 feet in length, the meat-eating animals stomped all over the Wasatch Front towards the end of the dinosaur period. (BYU; DU 9/19/79; Internet)

The first fossil remains ever unearthed in Antarctica, along with two other fossils discovered in South America in 1979, were named after "Dinosaur Jim" Jensen of BYU. (DU 9/18/79)

Oldest Footprints in Utah and Idaho. Some 200 million years ago in the sands of southern Utah, dinosaurs left behind their footprints. Dinosaur tracks discovered there in 1982 are the only prints of their kind in North America. Researchers estimate the prints were made by three separate dinosaurs ranging from 8 to 20 feet in size. (DU 10/8/82)

Ravell Call, Deseret Morning News

Following in another's footsteps ... millions of years later.

What were horses doing in Idaho 1 million years ago? Scientists examining footprints protruding from the ceiling of a Malad Gorge, Idaho, cave attribute the tracks to an extinct North American horse similar in size and shape to today's equines. The horses apparently were fleeing flowing lava as they stumbled through a marsh. The lava filled the footprints and, over time, the softer rock beneath eroded away, exposing the underside of the hardened mold of the horse tracks. (DN 12/23/90)

OTHER HISTORIC ITEMS

First American Irrigation. The Mormons were the first non-American Indians in the United States to use irrigation. Visitors from the east who saw irrigation canals high up on the hillsides fed by runoff from the canyons insisted that the Mormons had learned to make water run uphill. (CN 8/29/48)

Most Important Wooden Cane. In 1948, Thomas Sessions identified to the Church News an old cane that had been in his family for many decades. It was carted across the plains with the early pioneers to Salt Lake City by his father, one of the Prophet Joseph Smith's bodyguards. "The cane is hardwood and it is made from the wood of the same tree the planks for the prophet's coffin was made from," Brother Sessions said. "If it could talk, it could tell things that mortal men forget as time passes." (CN 10/20/48)

1962: A. William Lund, assistant Church Historian, examines bricks from demolished Vauxhall Chapel.

Deseret Morning News file photo

Historic Bricks. A couple of old bricks delivered to the Church in 1962 brought to America an important piece of early Church history. The two clay bricks came from the Vauxhall Chapel in Preston, England, where LDS missionaries taught in England for the first time in 1837. On July 22, Apostles Heber C. Kimball and Orson Hyde, with five missionaries, were invited to speak in the chapel and tell of the restored gospel. The brother of one of the LDS missionaries was the pastor in Vauxhall Chapel. On Aug. 6, 1837, the first branch in England was organized in Preston. (CN 9/62)

The Mormons at Sutter's Mill. The great California gold rush of 1848-49 was actually started when members of the Mormon Battalion found gold at Sutter's Mill. The battalion had just completed the longest march in U.S. military history (2,000 miles) when six of the soldiers went looking for work. They found a job with James W. Marshall at Sutter's Mill in Coloma, California. On Jan. 24, 1848, while cleaning out the tail race works for a mill, one of them spied something yellow and shiny. They took time to collect several pieces. Henry Bigler, one of those who made the discovery, wrote in his jour-

Utah State Historical Society

Sculpter Avard Fairbanks poses with the statue he created honoring the discovery of gold at Sutter's Mill by members of the Mormon Battalion.

nal, "Monday, 24 – This day some kind of metal was found in the tail race that looks like gold." When word spread that gold had been discovered, another Church member, Samuel Brannan, announced it to residents of the San Francisco Bay area. The rush was on. Several LDS opened up a gold-mining operation on what is now called Mormon Island. Diggings there later yielded fortunes in gold. As for the original Mormon men, they completed their work contract, washed gold for a few days, and then cast away the "gold fever spell" and returned to Utah to till the sage lands of the valleys and build lives for their families. (CN 1/31/48)

First Fired-Clay Bricks in California. For dozens of decades, structures in California were made with rough, sun-dried bricks. When the Mormon Battalion arrived in California, they introduced fired-clay bricks, the first such bricks ever manufactured there. Members of the Mormon Battalion produced some 40,000 bricks for the courthouse and school in San Diego in 1847. During the work, Lydia Hunter, the wife of Battalion member Jesse Hunter, gave birth to a son named Diego Hunter, the first American born in San Diego. Sister Hunter died within a week of the birth of her only child. (LDS 7/21/84; Internet)

Secret Trash! The only remnants of what historically could be the most important trash in the world – Oliver North's Iran-Contra shredded secrets from the White House – were spared an undignified fate at a local Virginia dump in 1986 by Paul B. Skousen, Fair Oaks Ward, Fairfax, Virginia, Stake. Brother Skousen was an employee at the White House Situation Room during the Iran-Contra affair. When Ollie North's office shredder jammed on the weekend of Nov. 22-23, 1986, North took his secret documents to the Situation Room, and said, "My shredder broke, can I borrow yours?" The resulting shred — considered declassified garbage by the National Security Agency — was on its way to the trash truck parked outside the White House when Skousen decided to save it for posterity. (Author)

Photo courtesy of the Skousen family dog, Annie

Paul Skousen displays sack of shredded paper removed from the White House after Ollie North's busy weekend of shredding during the so-called Iran-Contra affair in 1986.

Utah State Historical Society

Children play near the remains of the old Mormon Wall, 6-miles in total length, that was built in 1853, and meant to give early pioneers protection from American Indians. Small portions of the wall can still be found today behind buildings and parking lots.

Largest Mormon Wall. In 1853, the Saints decided to build a Spanish-style wall around Salt Lake City. The six-mile-long wall served as both a make-work project for Salt Lake residents and as protection against the Indians. Very few specifics about the wall were recorded. The adobe-and-rock wall was 12 feet high, 6 feet thick at the base, and tapered to 2 feet 6 inches thick at 6 feet above the ground. During the mid 1900s, portions of the wall were unearthed during renovation and construction projects in the down-town Salt Lake City area. (CN 8/29/53)

Longest Continuous Time Capsule. In 1899, a Sunday School time capsule was created to commemorate the first Sunday School that was organized by Richard Ballantyne on Dec. 9, 1849. The 1899 capsule contained memorabilia and records of the first 50 years of Sunday School. In 1949, a new time capsule was created called the "Centennial Box." This capsule was made of wood shipped to Salt Lake City from all over the world. Included among the wood samples was stink wood from Africa, cypress from Florida, walnut from Independence County, Mo., and olive wood from Palestine. The box was loaded up with histories and records of the second 50 years of Sunday School. In 1999, President Gordon B. Hinckley opened the Centennial Box at a special ceremony in the lobby of the Joseph Smith Memorial Building. At the April 1999 General Conference, the next edition of the Sunday School time capsule was sealed up. This one was high tech – a polished sphere of titanium about 28 inches in diameter loaded with old and new Church documents, histories and memorabilia, and stored away at Church headquarters for another 50 years. (CN 9/18/49; CN 6/26/49; Internet)

COLLECTIBLES

Rarest Book. The rarest edition of the Book of Mormon, according to professional book collectors, is a first edition in Hawaiian.

The rarest LDS book is a first edition (1835) hymn book, the collection of hymns selected by Emma Smith. Only eight copies are known to exist.

Most Paid for an LDS Book. The most paid for an LDS book was $391,000 in 2001 for an 1833 copy of The Book of Commandments. It was sold at the famed Christie's auction house in New York City. The first printing of the Book of Commandments was just being start-

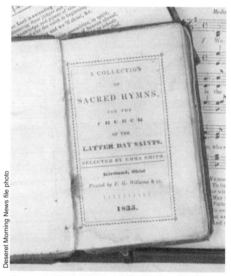

Rarest: One of eight hymn books containing hymns collected by Emma Smith.

ed when a mob destroyed the new Mormon press on July 20, 1833. Pages that were blowing in the streets were rescued and used to assemble at least 20 copies, most of them in homemade bindings. A copy sold in 1987 for $32,000, but the value of this extremely rare book increases each year. Another copy

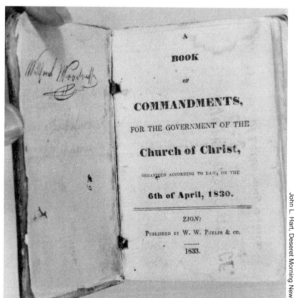

Wilford Woodruff's personal copy of the Book of Commandments.

of the book was traded by the RLDS Church (Reorganized LDS) for the purported blessing proving Joseph the prophet blessed his son, Joseph III, to become the next leader of the LDS Church. The bles-sing turned out to be a forgery by convicted murderer Mark Hofmann, and the Church returned the copy of the Book of Commandments to the RLDS Church. (CN 11/3/01)

An English first edition of the Book of Mormon in excellent condition now sells for more than $60,000.

Signatures. The rarest signatures among Church members are those of the women in early Church history. The wives of the brethren were rarely involved in any official business, and their signatures are found almost exclusively in personal correspondence.

Signatures of Joseph and Brigham pale in value compared to those of their wives and other early sisters in the Church.

The wax seal used by Joseph Smith for official Church business.

Seal of the Prophet Joseph Smith. The only known wax seal used by the Prophet Joseph Smith was discovered in the Church historian's library in 1966. Though many envelopes are on file with indications that a seal was once attached, only one was sufficiently preserved to show what the seal looked like. Showing a side view of the Prophet Joseph's face looking left, the seal looks remarkably similar to the profile painting by Maudsley of Joseph Smith as shown on an 1842 map of Nauvoo in the Church historian's office. (CN 8/13/66)

The Prophet's Finger Ring. The only known piece of personal jewelry of the Prophet Joseph Smith still in existence is his finger ring, prominently shown in the well-known oil paintings done of him. The Smith family still retains the ring, a whopping size 11-1/2, which was appropriately large for the 6 foot 2 inch, 215-pound Joseph Smith. (Author's interview)

Liberty's Lock and Key. Liberty Jail in Missouri was the scene of a terrible endurance test for the Prophet Joseph Smith and his companions in 1839. From this period of incarceration and suffering came sections 121, 122 and 123 of the Doctrine and Covenants. Years later the old jail was torn down and the lock was preserved by an anonymous interested party. It sat around at the Liberty Tribune newspaper offices until 1927 when it was given to LDS Bishop W. J. Gough of Glendale, California. In 1944 it was presented to the Church, complete with its original key. (CN 8/19/44)

Most Prominent Sculpture. The Smithsonian Institute paid $100,000 for one of the two sunstones that survived the sacking of the Nauvoo Temple in the late 1840s. Joel Scarborough, president of the historical society for Quincy and Adams counties, Illinois, said the stone was first offered to the Church, but the asking price was too high. It was important to get the stone out of the weather, Scarborough said, because vandalism and weathering was slowly destroying the classic artifact. The 2-1/2 ton stone was placed inside the Smithsonian's Museum of American History in November 1989. It sat atop an eight-foot pedestal just a few

A sunstone on display at the Smithsonian Insitution in Washington, D.C. The stone is one of 30 that was carved for the Nauvoo Temple. It stands 4 feet high, 6 feet wide, 18 inches thick, and weighs 2 1/2 tons.

feet to the side of the original score of the Star Spangled Banner. The Nauvoo Temple, completed in 1845, originally had 30 sunstones. Limestone pilasters—or square columns—around the exterior of the temple had moonstones decorating their bases and were capped by sunstones. Starstones were carved above the sunstones. (DN 11/28/89)

Most Expensive Mormon Gold Piece. Mormon gold pieces are fetching huge sums. In the 1980s, a Mormon $10 gold piece sold for $135,000, while the $20 gold coins typically sold for around $40,000. The $5 gold piece typically sold for $3,000. After the Saints settled Salt Lake Valley, Brigham Young ordered dies so the Saints could mint their own gold coins. After receiving the dies, the brethren witnessed the first $10 coins to be stamped out, but the die broke after only 46 coins were impressed. The new die that was subsequently ordered was less expensive to make and had fewer details carved into it, making the original impressions extremely rare and valuable. Recent market activity puts them at around $75,000 per coin. (Internet)

Mormon $5 gold coin minted in 1850. The reverse side shows clasped hands of friendship, the date "1850," and the initials, GSLCPG (Great Salt Lake City, Pure Gold). Gold was valued at $16-18 per ounce in those days.

Most Expensive Clothing. The most offered for articles of clothing once belonging to early members of the Church was $500,000 for items worn by Hyrum Smith after his martyrdom at Carthage Jail in 1844. The clothing remains in private hands. (Author)

Joseph Smith's Pistols. When the Prophet Joseph Smith was Lieutenant General of the Nauvoo Legion in 1841, he was was the highest ranking officer in the U.S. He couldn't lead regular Army forces, but with 2,000 men under his command, his Legion was stronger than most local militias. By this time, cap and ball pistols were available, but many soldiers were still issued these flintlock weapons.

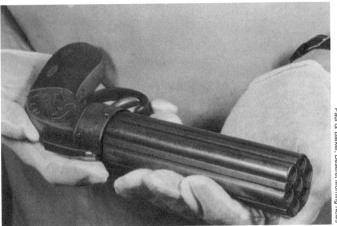

The Church museum also has in its possession this six shooter (left) once belonging to Joseph Smith, Jr. (from photo captions)

ODDS AND ENDS

World's Best Bodyguards. When film and aviation tycoon Howard Hughes sought to surround himself with the very best, he turned to the Mormons. Nearly all of his young assistants and bodyguards were members of the Church. According to an article in Look magazine (1954), Hughes wanted LDS people because they tended to be men of integrity who devoted themselves slavishly to their jobs. They neither drank, smoked, nor gambled. "This is exactly what Hughes requires amid the temptations of Las Vegas," the article stated. "These assistants work 24 hours a day, and if there were another hour they would be at work then." Look further explained the young men were asked to do anything: "deliver flowers to a sick friend; reach by telephone someone who has not been heard from since 1936; see that some beautiful young lady has the best table at the liveliest local night club, and keep the wolves away." And if anyone wanted to see America's richest man, they first had to talk to one of his Mormon assistants. Hughes' wife, Terry Moore, who was LDS, may have had something to do with the Mormon connection. (CN 1/30/54)

Library of Congress

Howard Hughes' LDS wife, Terry Moore, probably influenced his demand that he be surrounded with a contingent of body guards who were active in the Church.

Best Telephone Number? The very best phone number in the Church was in the Washington, D.C. Temple Visitor's Center. For the 17 million tourists visiting the nation's capital during the Bicentennial celebrations in 1976, visitors could dial 667-6667 for help and scheduling times to visit the Washington, D.C. Temple. So what's so great about 667-6667? It spells M-O-R-M-O-N-S. (CN 2/7/76)

Utah State Historical Society

When did the first airplane land among the saints in Utah? In 1911, this "Wright flier" made a visit to Willard, Utah. Who then could have guessed that only 50 years later aircraft would be moving missionaries to nations around the world – anywhere in just *hours*!

Deseret Morning News file photo

At a national track meet, Creed Haymond refused wine and tea, and the following day, he broke the world's record in the 220 yard dash. His story, along with those of many other LDS athletes, inspire and challenge Saints around the world to "lengthen your stride" in all endeavors, including *Sports*.

Sports

Mormon Sports by the Numbers

1— Heisman trophy won by a Mormon

13— Consecutive years a former BYU player has been on a Super Bowl team

35— Highest-place finish by a Mormon in the Anchorage-to-Nome dog-sled race.

106— Days needed by LDS cyclists to circle the globe.

4,800— Feet above sea level for for the 2002 Winter Olympic games

24,000— People who watched Alma Richards pray before winning the 1912 Olympic high jump.

From basketball to karate to the high jump, LDS athletes from around the world have indeed taken to heart Spencer W. Kimball's admonition to "lengthen your stride." And with every record set, there comes another athlete, a dozen, or a thousand striving to out-perform and find their place in history. Here are a few of those.

LDS Kid Clobbers the Siberian Bear

For many, it was the most thrilling highlight of the entire 2000 Olympic Summer Games in Sydney, Australia. A Mormon kid from Afton, Wyoming, Rulon Gardner, was facing the three-time Olympic gold medalist, Alexander Kareline, in the final round of Greco-Roman wrestling. Everyone expected the Russian to walk off with his fourth gold medal. Everyone, that is, except

Ravell Call, Deseret Morning News

Rulon Gardner. For 12 years the Siberian Bear had won every match at every tournament he had entered. When the two met on the mat, "it was like pushing around a cow," Brother Gardner said afterwards regarding Kareline's world-renowned strength. But with Gardner holding a one-point lead, the clock ticked down to zero and the Siberian Bear turned his back and walked away. In front of a stunned audience of millions, Gardner was declared the champion and gold-medal winner. At 6 feet 3 inches, 281 pounds, Gardner did a perfect cartwheel, embraced family and circled the arena waving an American flag. The world was frozen in time but thawed out seconds later in thunderous applause as shock turned to realization. History had been made by the kid from Wyoming. (DN 9/27/2000)

Most on Championship Teams. Only one college in America, Brigham Young University, could boast having a former player on the world championship-winning teams in all three major sports in 1986: Jim McMahon (football, Super Bowl champions, 1986), Danny Ainge and Greg Kite (basketball, Boston Celtics, NBA national champions, 1986), and Dane Iorg (baseball, Kansas City Royals, World Series champions). (LDS 1/87)

Longest String of Participants on Championship Super Bowl. Only one college in America, Brigham Young University, could boast of having an alumnus playing on each of the NFL teams that won the Super Bowl over the five-year span of 1982-86. And for 13 straight seasons, 1980-1993, a BYU alumnus played on either the winning or losing side (sometimes both) in the Super Bowl. (LDS 9/3/86; DN 1/21/93)

Alma Richards said he became a good jumper by chasing jackrabbits at his home in Parawon, Utah.

First Gold Olympic Medal (Summer Games). In 1912, Alma Richards represented the United States at the Stockholm, Sweden, Summer Olympics. When his talent for high jumping was first discovered, he was still in high school playing basketball. A BYU coach invited him to try the high jump. As Richards slipped over the bar with ease—a bar that was set just two inches short of the school record—the coach went pale. He had found a natural-born high jumper. Richards was steered into the high jump and excelled at every track meet. Richards's adventure took him to Chicago and then Sweden for the 1912 Summer Olympic Games. Wearing his lucky gray floppy hat, he sprinted to the bar time and again as other world-class jumpers were eliminated one by one. He out-jumped Jim Thorpe and other United States contenders. In the end, it was Richards alone going head to head with the German champion, Hans Liesche. With the bar raised to 6 feet 4 inches, it was Richards's turn next. He eyed the bar and then walked over to a spot on the infield grass, knelt down in the presence of the sold-out crowd of 24,000, removed his hat, and offered prayer. "God give me strength," he pleaded. He ended his prayer, stood, and took his run at the bar. His teammates watched in wonder as Richards cleared the bar by a good two inches. The crowd exploded in cheers. The distraught German missed on his next three tries, and Richards was declared the gold medal winner. (Internet)

First Silver Olympic Medal (Summer Games). Is Paula Meyers Pope, United States, the first LDS to win an Olympic silver medal? In 1952, she was the second best in the world in diving.

First Bronze Olympic Medal (Summer Games). Is Jane Sears, United States, the first LDS to win an Olympic bronze medal? In 1952, she was the third best in the world in swimming.

Richards won 245 medals in track and field events.

Two Gold Medals (Summer Games). In 1984, Peter Vidmar won two gold medals and one silver for gymnastics.

In 1988, Troy Dalbey, U.S., won two gold medals in swimming.

First (and Only) to Win All Three Olympic Medals (Summer Games). The first LDS to win all three Olympic medals was Kresimir Cosic, in basketball: silver in 1968 and 1976; bronze in 1972; and gold in 1980.

As team captain, Peter Vidmar led the 1984 U.S. Men's Gymnastics Team to America's first team gold medal, upsetting defending world champ, China. He also scored a perfect 10 on the pommel horse.

Most Olympic medals (Summer Games). Paula Meyers Pope, United States, won a total of four Olympic medals in diving: 1952, silver; 1956, silver and bronze; 1960, silver.

Once again, Kresimir Cosic, Yugoslavia, won a total of four Olympic medals in basketball: 1968, silver; 1972, bronze; 1976, silver; 1980, gold.

2002 Olympic Winter Games. Athletes participating in the 2002 Olympic Winter Games made history as they performed at the highest altitude every selected for the Winter Games. Every event was held at least 4,300 feet, or about .8 miles, above sea level.

With more than 9,000 journalists covering the Winter Games, the Salt Lake post office had to give them their very own ZIP code.

All the medals awarded at the 2002 Winter Games, each weighing 1.25 pounds, consisted entirely of metal mined in Utah.

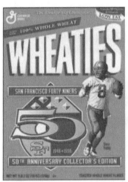 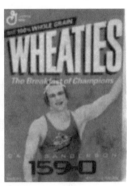

Wheaties Box Heroes. Calling itself, "The Breakfast of Champions," the breakfast cereal "Wheaties" has long featured athletes on its boxes. Many of the world's best have become familiar at the breakfast table to millions around the world, including:

Steve Young, BYU star quarterback and backbone of the San Francisco 49ers – featured on Wheaties in 1986 (above left), and Cael Sanderson, undefeated collegiate wrestler at Iowa State – featured on Wheaties in 2002 (above right). Are there other LDS athletes who have been featured?

TRACK

Fastest 100-Meter Dash. In 1971, Canagasabai Kunalan, Singapore Branch in the Southeast Asia Mission, was being billed as Southeast Asia's fastest man alive with a 100-meter time of 10.3 seconds, just 4/10ths of a second off the world record and a Singapore national record. He became Singapore's Athlete of the Year for the second consecutive year. Later in his life he was inducted into Singapore's athlete hall of fame. (CN5/2/70)

The First World Record (1919 World Record). At the annual meet of the Intercollegiate Association of Amateur Athletes of America in 1919, Creed Haymond set the world record in the 220-yard dash with a time of 21.00 seconds – a record not broken until Jesse Owens raced for Gold at the

On the back of this old photo was written: "1920 race at Utah State in Logan. Creed Haymond about to break tape to set a world's record in the 220 yard run. He didn't find out about having broken the world's record until 2 years after the event. W. Creed Haymond." Photo: Utah State Historical Society

1936 Olympics. Prior to his world-record race, his teammates wanted to take some sherry wine, thought in those days to help harden muscles. Haymond refused to take the wine and went to bed. The next morning, Haymond's University of Pennsylvania teammates were sicker than dogs and missed the track meet or performed very poorly. Haymond, the only healthy runner, won the 100-yard dash and smashed the world-record mark for the 220-yard dash. Haymond went on to participate in the 1920 Olympics but came away without any medals due to a torn hamstring muscle. He held the high-school world record for the 100-yard dash in 1913. (CN 6/19/99; Internet)

Fastest 100-Yard Dash – Men Over 70. In 1983, Homer Leman, Phoenix 36th Ward, Glendale Stake, ran the 100-yard dash in 12.5 seconds at age 75. When in his youthful prime, he ran a blazing fast 9.5 seconds. (LDS 9/2/83)

Fastest 100-Meter Dash – Women Over 70. Who is the fastest sprinter among women 70 years and older? In 1986, Lily McLead Bell, Santiago, Chili, 70, she ran the 100-meter dash in 19 seconds. She also is reported to have set the South American record for the 200-meter dash in her age group. (CN 8/3/86)

400-METER DASH

Fastest LDS in Fiji – 400-Meter Dash. In 1971, Saimoni Tamani, Longview 1st Ward, Longview, Washington, Stake, set the Oceania 400 indoor record of 47.0 seconds. He won Fiji's first medal in track and field at the 1970 Commonwealth Games, and competed in the 1970 Olympic Games, where he won a bronze medal in the 400-meter race. (CN 1/18/92)

Canagasabi Kunalan

Besides the 400 meter record, Kunalan also set Singapore's 100-meter dash record at 10.3 seconds in 1968.

Fastest LDS in Singapore. In 1971, Canagasabi Kunalan, first counselor in his Singapore branch presidency, set the Singapore national record for the 400-meter event at 46.9 seconds, only 3.1 seconds off the world mark. (CN 1/71)

Fastest Female 55-Meter Hurdler in the World (1997 World Record). Tiffany Lott of the Leeds Ward, St. George, Utah, Pine View Stake, was the fastest woman short-distance hurdler in 1997 when she set a new American and world record for the 55-meter hurdles in 7.30 seconds. (Internet)

Fastest Male 55-Meter High Hurdler. In 1985, Chad Burnett, Southglenn 1st Ward, Littleton, Colorado, Stake, set a new high school indoor record in the 55-meter high hurdles with a time of 7.30 seconds. The old United States record set in 1978 was 7.40 seconds. (CN 7/21/85)

Fastest 440-Yard Intermediate Hurdler in the World (1970 World Record). In 1970, Ralph Mann set a new world record in the 440-yard intermediate hurdles in a blazing time of 48.74 seconds. He was the NCAA champion three times during his years at BYU. He was also three-time All American and won the silver medal at the 1972 Olympic Games. (Internet)

Fastest 440-Yard Run – 12-13, Girls. In 1974, Lezla Peterson, Santa Cruz Ward, Saratoga, California, Stake, set a new AAU record for girls age 12-13 in the 440-yard run with a time of 57.5 seconds. (CN 6/15/74)

Fastest 400-Meter Hurdles – Women. Who is the fastest LDS woman hurdler? In 1993, UCLA Bruins sprinter Erin Blunt set a personal best in the 400-meter hurdles of 57.68 seconds. (Internet)

800-METER/880-YARD RUN

Fastest LDS – 880-Yard Run. Wade Bell set a new AAWU (Athletic Association of Western Universities) record for the 880-yard run in 1967 with a time of 1:46.1, the third fastest in history.

Fastest 800-Meter Run, High School, Women. Who is the fastest LDS female high schooler in this event? In 1992 it was Shawna Halford, a freshman at Cottonwood High, Salt Lake City. She set a new school record in the 800 at 2:09.00. (DN 4/20/92)

1,600-METER RELAY

First LDS Gold Medal – 1,600-Meter Relay (1960 World Record). In 1960, Lt. Jack Yerman, Berkeley, California, helped his team win the Olympic gold medal after his blazing first-leg sprint of 46.14 seconds. The team's total of 3:02.2 was a new world record. (CN 7/62; Internet)

Jack Yerman's relay team set a world record.

ONE MILE RUN

First LDS to Break Four-Minute Mark. The first LDS to break the four minute mile was Wade Bell, who reached that goal in 1966 with a time of 3:59.8. He was the 71st person ever to run a four-minute mile.

Best Under-Four-Minute-Mile Time. Doug Padilla set his best mile time on May 6, 1989, with a time of 3:54.2. His first under-four mile came six years earlier on May 21, 1983, setting a new Utah record with a time of 3:57.23. The world's number-one world ranked steeplechase runner, Henry Marsh, ran two laps with Padilla at that meet, helping to set a fast pace. Padilla ran his last lap before a standing, cheering crowd in 56 seconds. (DU 5/24/83; Henry Marsh e-mail)

In 1996, Jason Pyrah set a new personal best in the mile during a track meet at Eugene, Oregon, when he ran a 3:55.14 mile.

Wade Bell was the 17th American to beat the 4-minute mile. He also won both the NCAA and AAU title for the 880 yard run in 1967.

In 1974, Paul Cummings set his fastest under-four-minute mile with a time of 3:56.4 in Tempe, Arizona. He had the fastest mile in the NCAA that year. His record time also was a BYU record that has stood ever since.

Best Mile Run – Women. In 1994, Liz Lynch of Ricks College, set a new event record for the indoor mile with a time of 5:00:50 at the Junior College Athletic Association indoor finals.

TWO MILE RUN

Deseret Morning News archives, Tom Smart

Best Two-Mile Runner – Indoor. Doug Padilla set a new United States record in the indoor two mile on Feb. 16, 1990, with a time of 8:15.02. Running at the Los Angeles Times-Eagle Indoor Games, Padilla missed the world record by just two seconds. (DN 2/17/90)

1,000/1,500/3,000-METER RUN

Fastest 1,000-Meter. Wade Bell became the fastest LDS 1,000-meter runner in 1967 when he set a new American record with a time of 2:18.7.

Fastest 1,500-Meter Run – Women. Cindy Reeder, College 18th Ward, Rexburg, Idaho, College 3rd Stake, won the 1,500-meter run at the National Junior College track meet in Odessa, Texas, in August 1990. She also placed fifth in the 3,000 meters, both earning her All-American honors. In 1989 she led the Ricks College cross country team to its second consecutive national championship. (CN 9/8/90)

1982: Doug Padilla races to set the first under-four-minute mile in Utah. The following year he set a personal best and a new Utah record in the mile.

Deseret Morning News, Garry Bryant

For the 1984 Olympics in Los Angeles, Paul Cummings had the fastest qualifying time on the U.S. team.

Fastest 1,500-Meter Run – Men. In 1979, Paul Cummings set an American indoor record for the 1,500 meters at a track meet in Long Beach, California, with a time of 3:37.6.

In 1992, BYU sophomore Jason Pyrah ran the 1,500 meter in 3:38.66 at the Mt. San Antonio College Relays. (DN 4/20/92; Internet)

Most Prolific United States Distance Runner. As stated at Henry Marsh's Web site, he is "the most prolific distance runner in U.S.A. history." In other words, he accumulated more world - ranking

points than any other American distance runner in history. In 1988, Brother Marsh, now of Bountiful, Utah, became the second male runner to make four United States Olympic teams ('76, '80, '84, '88), and was rated number one in the world in 1981, 1982 and 1985. He culminated his career with 13 straight years as one of the top ten 3,000-meter steeplechase runners in the world. This is the longest period of time that a distance runner has been consecutively world ranked in the top ten. He has held the American record for an unprecedented 23 years and counting. In November 2001 he was inducted into the U.S.A. Track & Field Hall of Fame along with former teammate Carl Lewis. He currently holds the American record for the 3,000-meter steeplechase with a 8:09.17 (a record he set in 1985, breaking his own record held since

Henry Marsh

"It's easy to stay the course and fight the fight when you're on top, when you're winning, but what of those times when everywhere you look you see nothing but hurdles, obstacles, roadblocks, barricades, detours and swamps? That is when you find out who you are."
– Henry Marsh

Photo courtesy Henry Marsh

Henry Marsh, an Olympic torch bearer in 2002, is now a popular motivational speaker.

1980.) He reached a childhood goal at age 31 when he broke the four-minute mile (the oldest athlete to do it for the first time) with a time of 3:59.31 in Bern, Switzerland, on August 16, 1985. He did it again at age 34 in Seoul, South Korea. (henrymarsh.com; runnersworld.com; LDS 3/8/89; author)

Best 3,000-Meter Run – Men. Doug Padilla set a new American record for the outdoor 3,000-meter run in 1991 with a time of 7:35.84. (DN 11/18/91)

Best 3,000-Meter Run – Women. Who is the fastest female 3,000-meter runner? BYU's Nicole Birk ran the 3,000-meter in 9:13.2 in April 1992. (DN 4/20/92)

Fastest 3,000-Meter Steeplechase – Women. In 2002, BYU's Michaela Mannova set a new NCAA Championship record of 9:45.94. (BYU Today Fall 2002)

In 2001, BYU's Elizabeth Jackson set a new United States record for the 3,000-meter steeplechase with a time of 9:49.73. She also became only the seventh woman ever to break ten minutes. (CN 6/16/01)

Best 3,000-Meter Run – Girls, Age 13-14. Sheri Lanesen, Granada Hills, California, won the Athletic Congress National Championship in the 3,000-meter race on July 4, 1983, making her the fastest runner for that distance and her age group. (LDS 9/23/83)

Best Distance Runner – Boys, Age 11-12. In 1983, Craig Laneson emerged champ in all three events (3,000m, 1,500m, 800m) in the midget division in the Track and Field Association National Age Group Championship, making him the fastest LDS for those distances in his age group. (LDS 9/23/89)

3,000-Meter Run, Boys Age 11-12. In 1994, 12-year-old Joshua Rohatinsky of the Provo, Utah, North Stake ran the second-best time ever for the 3,000-meter run at the U.S.A. Junior Olympic Track and Field Championships at Gainesville, Florida. He finished the race in 9:50.00 in the Midget Boys division (11-12 year olds). (CN 8/20/94)

Best 3,200-Meter Run, Boys Age 17-18. In 1996, Ryan Bowman Andrus, a priest in the Timpview 6th Ward, Orem, Utah, Timpview Stake, beat runners from seven western states in the 3,200-meter run with a time of nine minutes 11 seconds. (CN 7/27/96)

5,000/10,000-METER RUN

New United States Record. In 1990, Doug Padilla set a United States record for the 5-kilometer road race with a time of 13:29.50. He also held the indoor record with a time of 13:20.55. (DN 11/18/91)

First Runner in Decades to Win Both 5,000- and 10,000-Meter Races. In 1985, BYU star Ed Eyestone became the first runner in nearly two decades to win both the 5,000 and 10,000-meter runs at the NCAA track-and-field championship. (LDS 6/15/85)

World's Record at Altitude (1982 World Record). Ed Eyestone broke the Utah record for the 10,000-meter run during the Days of '47 races held July 24, 1986, with a time of 27:39.5. It may also be a world's record for the 10,000-meter at such a high altitude (4,800 feet). In 1992, Eyestone had the fastest 10,000-meter time in the world (that year) with a time of 27:53.58. (CN 8/3/86; DN 6/17/93)

10,000-Meter Women. Who is the fastest female 10,000-meter runner? In 1992, BYU's Leanne Whitesides ran the 10,000-meter with a time of 34:06.8. (DN 4/20/92)

In 1984, Ed Eyestone won every collegiate cross country race he entered and was only one of three "triple crown" champs in history to win the national title in the 5,000, 10,000 and cross country race in the same year.

Most Wins in Same Marathon (1987 World Record). Demetrio Cabanillas, Magna 10th Ward, Magna, Utah, held the world's record for winning the same marathon the most times. He won his ninth consecutive Days of '47 marathon (26.2 miles) on July 24, 1987. (CN 8/1/87)

Fastest Runner at Days of '47 Marathon. In 1982, Demetrio Cabanillas set the course record for the traditional Pioneer Days Parade marathon with a time of 2:16:57. (CN 7/28/85)

Best Distance Runner – 50-60 Age Group. In 1987, Gaylon Jorgensen, 57, Provo, Utah, was ranked #1 in the nation for the 55-59 age group by

Running Times. He has set national age-group records in several distance races. (CN 9/5/87)

24-hour Marathon (1990 World Record). Dick Rozier, Fresno, California, 8th Ward, set a world endurance record by covering 139 miles and 400 yards in the Sri Chinmoy 24-Hour Race in Oakland, California, in 1989. Rozier, 59, had run in 12 Boston Marathons but had participated in only one other 24-hour race. (CN 1/13/90)

Best Marathon, Age 10 – Boys. In 1973, 10-year-old Regie Heywood, Mesa 29th Ward Mesa, Arizona, Stake, was just six minutes shy of the world record for boys his age in the 26-mile 388-yard marathon. He ran an amazing time of 3:25:25 at the annual Days of '47 marathon in Salt Lake City. The world record for his age at that time was 3:19:18. (CN 6/23/73)

HIGH JUMP/LONG JUMP

First World Record (1917 World Record). Clint Larsen set a world record in 1917 with a jump of 1.9 meters (6 feet 3 inches), and reportedly became National AAU Champion that same year.

First Gold Medal. The first LDS to win a gold medal at the Olympics was Alma W. Richards who high jumped 6 feet 4 inches during the 1912 Sweden Olympics. (LDS 7/21/84)

Highest by an LDS Man. (2001 World Record). Weber State University's Charlie Clinger, Lorin Farr 4th Ward, Ogden, Utah, Lorin Farr Stake, set the world high-jump record in 2001 with a leap of 7 feet 8 1/2 inches. (CN 6/16/01)

First NCAA Champion. In 1970, Kenneth Lundmark, Skelleftea, Sweden, became the first LDS NCAA indoor high jump champion when he cleared 7 feet 2 inches. (CN 1/16/71)

Best High Jump in Argentina. Cal Clark, an LDS missionary in Argentina, set a new high jump record for that country with a leap of 6 feet 5 inches in an athletic contest in 1950. He broke the all-time Argentina record, set in 1943, by two inches. (CN 1/17/51)

High Jump – Boys, Age 18. In 1992, Tory Bailey, 18, of the Heyburn 1st Ward, Rupert, Idaho, West Stake high-jumped 7 feet 1 inch. (CN 5/29/93)

High Jump – Girls, Age 15. In 1995, Kristin McQuade won the United States national high-jump title for her age group when she cleared 5 feet 10 inches. The same year she set a national heptathlon (seven events) high jump record of 5 feet 11 1/2 inches. She was a member of the Casper 4th Ward, Casper, Wyoming, Stake. (CN 7/8/95)

High Jump – Girls, Age 13. Lori Mertes, 13, Chatsworth, California, 2nd Ward, won two national high jump age-group championships with leaps of 5 feet 5 inches, and 5 feet 6 inches at the national amateur and junior Olympics competitions in 1986. (CN 9/21/86)

Highest Jump By a Hearing Impaired Person. In 1984, while still a high school student, Steven Walker, Glendora, California, 4th Ward, posted a high-jump record that was one inch short of the world's record mark set by a hearing impaired man with a leap of 6 feet 6-1/4 inches. (CN 1984)

Standing Long Jump (Unofficial World Record). Ab Jenkins was not only an amazing race car driver, he also had an amazing standing long jump. On one occasion he leapt 10 feet 11 inches from a standing position.

Long Jump – Men and Boys Division. In 1993, Jared Hansen, Colorado Springs, Colorado, North Stake, set the United States national high school indoor long-jump record with a leap of 25 feet 2 inches. He also set a new Idaho state record for the triple-jump with 46 feet 6-1/2 inches. (CN 10/16/93)

In 1991, Shu-Hwa Wang set the Taiwan long-jump record with a leap of 21 feet 1-1/4 inches, at the World University Games in Sheffield, England. (DN 8/27/91)

In 1998, Jared Passmor, 9, of the Manila 4th Ward, Pleasant Grove, Utah, Manila Stake, set the United States record in his age group at 7 feet 9 3/4 inches to beat the old record by 2 1/2 inches. (CN 3/12/98)

Long Jump – Women and Girls. In 1993, Melanie Bemis, 15, became the first girl at Canby Union High School in Oregon since 1973 to win a state track and field event. She won the long-jump with a leap of 17 feet 2-3/4 inches. She was a member of the Canby 2nd Ward, Oregon, City Stake. (CN 8/7/93)

Triple Jump – Women and Girls. Who has the longest triple-jump? In 1993, it was Meagan Gable, 15, Buckeye 2nd Ward, Buckeye, Arizona, Stake, who triple-jumped 34 feet 8-1/2 inches. (CN 8/28/93)

OTHER FIELD EVENTS

Pole Vault. Does Jeff Hansen, who jumped 17 feet 11 inches in 1999, hold the record for the highest pole vault in the Church?

For decades, Jay Silvester was the world's leading discus thrower.

Discus Throw – Men (1968 World Record). By 1968, the longest discus throw by an LDS man was a world-record 224 feet 6 inches by Jay Silvester, Orem, Utah, BYU 32nd Ward. He had previously set a world record in Frankfurt, Germany, in 1961, with a throw of 199 feet 7 inches. He was also the first in the world to throw 220 feet and 230 feet. He exceeded his personal best in 1971 with a throw of 230 feet 11 inches. Silvester won five national titles and was a member of 16 national teams. He competed in four Olympics and won silver and bronze medals. He remained competitive until he was 39 years old. He was inducted into the National Track and Field Hall of Fame in 1998. (CN 11/7/98)

Discus Throw – Women. Lorna Griffin, Corvallis Ward, Missoula, Montana, Stake, set a United States women's discus record in April 1979 with a throw of 187 feet 8 inches, exceeding the previous record by 6 feet. She went on to break the record again with a throw of 191 feet 2 inches. (CN 4/28/79)

Nik Arrhenius set a world record at age 17.

Discus Throw – High School Boys (2001 World Record). On April 14, 2001, Nik Arrhen-ius set a new high school discus record with a huge throw of 234 feet 3 inches at the Arcadia Invitational in Arcadia Califor-nia. He was a priest in the Lakeridge 4th Ward, Orem, Utah, Lakeridge Stake. (CN 9/22/01; USA Today Sports 6/19/01)

Javelin Throw – Adult. In 1963, Krege B. Christensen, Yale 2nd Ward, Bonneville Stake, representing the

University of Utah, threw the Javelin 250 feet 5-1/2 inches during a track meet at Albuquerque, New Mexico. Today, BYU's record for the "old javelin" throw is 284 feet 1 inch by Jari Keihas in 1982. The "new javelin" record at BYU is 247 feet 6 inches by Soren Tallhem in 1986. (Internet)

Javelin Throw – High School Boys (1969 World Record). Richard George set the world record for 15 year olds in 1969 with a throw of 224 feet. In 1976, he set a BYU record that stood for 6 years with a throw of 275 feet 4 inches. (Internet)

Shot Put – Men. In 1985, BYU's Soren Tallhem threw the shot 69 feet 8-1/2 inches. (Internet)

Shot Put – Women. Lorna Griffin of Corvallis, Montana, made the second-longest women's-shot put throw in the United States, as of the 1984 Olympics, at 58 feet 7 inches. (Almanac)

Shot Put – High School Boys. In 2003, Leif Arrhenius, Orem, Utah, threw a 25-pound shot put 76 feet 1.75 inches. He and his brothers, sons of BYU shot put champ Anders Arrhenius, have been regularly ranked top in the nation in shot put, weight throw, and the discus. (Internet)

Hammer Throw – Women. Jana Tucker, Ricks College 20th Ward, Ricks College Idaho 2nd Stake, threw the hammer 142 feet 5 inches, setting a record for the National Junior College Track & Field Meet held in Odessa, Texas in 1991. This was the first year women competed in the hammer throw, making Jana the first national champ and national meet record holder. (CN 8/3/91)

Decathlon Champions. In 1915, Alma Richards smashed Jim Thorpe's Olympic decathlon score by more than 1,000 points.

Robert R. Gent, a seventy in the Grangeville Ward, Lewiston, Idaho, Stake, was the 1976 National AAU decathlon champion in the 30-34 age group. (CN 8/76)

Triathlon Champion – Senior Men. In New Zealand, in 1985, Max Burdick, 62, took first place for men over 60 in New Zealand's Ironman Triathlon. Brother Burdick swam two miles, biked for more than eight hours, and ran for 20 miles to complete the competition in 14 hours 43 minutes. He was a member of the Cottonwood 14th Ward, Salt Lake Big Cottonwood Stake. (CN 4/28/85)

Triathlon Champion – Bantam Girls (9-10 years old). In 1995, Amy Menlove, 10, won the U.S.A. Track and Field Association Junior Olympics

Region 10 triathlon championship. Her total of 1,030 points tied the region record and broke the Utah state record. Triathlon events include the 200-meter dash, high jump and shot put. She was a member of the Eastridge 4th Ward, Draper, Utah, Eastridge Stake. (CN 8/12/95)

Fastest Walk Across the United States (1968 World Record). For a Mormon who doesn't walk on Sundays, Bryon D. Young's record for walking across the United States in 64 days 14 hours was a remarkable feat. In 1968, it was a new world record. But considering he had rested on Sundays, his trip actually took the equivalent of 55 days 14 hours. Brother Young, a member of the Sparks, Nevada, West Ward, walked from San Francisco's Golden Gate Bridge to the George Washington Bridge in New York City, breaking the old record of 66 days set in 1960. He averaged 58 miles a day. For the first 1,000 miles, he said, shin splints made walking painful, so he slowed his pace until they went away. (Imp.Era 1/69; CN 2/14/70)

50-Kilometer Walk. In 1984, Bo Gustafsson, Sweden, won a silver medal for the 50-kilometer walk at the Olympic Summer Games with a time of 3:53.19. At the following Olympics in 1988, he bettered his previous Olympic time by almost 9 seconds, but came in seventh with a time of 3:44.49. During the 1980s he was ranked among the top eight distance walkers in the world. (www.sporting-heroes.net)

Most All American Honors in Track and Field – Women. In 1995, Tiffany Lott of the Leeds Ward, St. George, Utah, Pine View Stake, became the first BYU woman to win three all-American awards. At the NCAA Track and Field Championships at Knoxville, Tennessee, Tiffany took fifth in the javelin throw (166 feet 7 inches), sixth in the heptathlon (5,589 points) and eighth in the 100-meter hurdles (13.64 seconds). (CN 7/22/95)

BYU - L. Tom Perry Special Collections

PARALYMPICS

Javelin and Slalom. Mike Johnson (left) was the first LDS to hold both the national and Olympic championships for wheelchair javelin throwing and slalom. In 1978, he won gold medals in the javelin, slalom, and four-man 100-yard relay, holding national records in each of those events.

Long-Distance Wheelchair Racer (1978 World Record). In 1978, Curt Brinkman held the long-distance wheelchair marathon record by going 275 miles (Cedar City to Salt Lake City) without stopping—at the time a world record. In the 1980 "Disabled Olympics" in Holland, Brinkman took home four gold medals for speed and distance racing. (Internet)

Basketball. Michael Schlappi, Tempe, Arizona, 8th Ward, and a member of the United States wheelchair basketball team, won a gold after his team went undefeated in the 1988 Paralympics in Seoul, South Korea. (CN 11/5/88)

1978: Brinkman at the start of his 275-mile, record-setting trip.

Boston Marathon – Wheelchair Division.

Curt Brinkman won the Boston Marathon, Wheelchair Division, setting a new course record on April 21, 1980, of 1:55:00, breaking the previous record by 30 minutes. He also beat fabled Bill Rodgers by 17 minutes to become the first wheelchair entrant ever to outpace the able-bodied running winner. Brinkman also set a new national record in the 1,500-meter wheelchair race. (CN 4/26/80; DU 10/27/80)

Kenneth Archer won the Boston Marathon in 1979 – Wheelchair Division, covering the 26-mile, 385-yard course in a time of 2:38:59, beating the previous year's winner, George Murray of Tampa, Florida. (CN 4/28/79)

Brinkman became the first wheelchair racer to win the Boston Marathon in 1980, setting a new course record in the process. Ten years later (1990) he chomped a half hour from that time and set a new course record of 1:23:30.

Short-Distance Wheelchair Racing. At the 2000 Paralympics in Sidney, Australia, Troy Davis of the Sunrise Ward, Tucson, Arizona, Stake, won a bronze medal as a member of the United States 4x100 (one lap, four racers) relay team. Troy has the fastest start in the world. In 1998 he was on a team that set a United States record in the 4x100 with a time of 56.22 seconds. (CN 12/9/00; www.wsusa.org)

Marathon – Wheelchair Division. John C. Brewer, Garden Park, Salt Lake City, 1st Ward won a gold medal in the marathon and silver medals in the 800- and 1,500-meter races during the 1988 Paralympics, wheelchair division, in Seoul, South Korea. (CN 11/5/88)

FOOTBALL

First NFL Head Coach. When Mike Holmgren took the reins of the Green Bay Packers in 1991, he became the first LDS head coach of a team in the National Football League. Holmgren coached for Seattle, Green Bay, and assistant coach for San Francisco. His teams have posted a 177-93-1 (.655) record, hit double digits in the win column 10 times, made the postseason 12 times. (BYU Sports Information)

Deseret Morning News file photo

So far, Mike Holmgren's teams have won three Super Bowls (XXXI, XXIV, XXIII) and reached another (Super Bowl XXXII).

BYU - L. Tom Perry Special Collections

BYU's Lavell Edwards, one of the three most-winning college coaches in the U.S.

Winning College Coach. BYU head football coach Lavell Edwards entered his 29th season in 2000 with a 257-101-3 record, and setting an NCAA record of continuous scoring games of 324. His win-loss record placed him third behind Joe Paterno (Penn State) and Bobby Bowden

Celebrating a hard-fought win over Michigan in 1984, Lavell's team was perfect that year, winning its fourth Holiday Bowl game, and the national championship.

Photo: Tom Smart, Deseret Morning News

(Florida State) with the most wins among active coaches. On the all-time list he ranks sixth on the NCAA's victories list. His teams played 22 bowl games and won or tied 21 conference championships. He led his team to one national championship in 1984, he was National Coach of the Year twice, and he was inducted into the College Football Hall of Fame in 2004.

• Seven of his quarterbacks were among the top 25 ranked passers in NCAA history.

• His teams were nationally ranked number one in passing eight times, and in total offense five times.

• He coached some nationally ranked champion players: one Heisman Trophy winner, two Outland Trophy winners, four Davey O'Brien Award winners, 32 first team all-Americans and at least 100 NFL players. Other star players included the top runner, the top punter, the top kick returner, the top receiver, and the top passer (five times) among all U.S. colleges.

• He beat powerhouse teams such as Notre Dame, Michigan, Miami, Penn State, Texas A&M, UCLA, Arizona State, Arizona, Colorado, Texas Washington, and Oklahoma.

• Edward's teams finished the season in the top 25 thirteen times and in the top 10 four times.

• He coached his teams in the Cotton Bowl, the Holiday Bowl, the Citrus Bowl, the Tangerine Bowl, the Aloha Bowl, the Freedom Bowl, the Copper Bowl, the All American Bowl, the Fiesta Bowl, the Motor City Bowl and the Silk Bowl. (CN 8/26/00; Internet)

First Professional Quarterback. Danny White, who retired from the Dallas Cowboys in July 1989, was the first LDS quarterback to make it into professional football. Said Danny on the day of his retirement, "I'm grateful to the Cowboys for the opportunity they've given me to play football. But more than that, for the opportunity to have an effect on people's lives. That's the thing I'm going to remember most." (LDS 7/26/89)

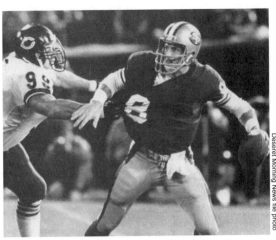

Deseret Morning News file photo

Steve Young was great at getting the ball away when sure destruction loomed eminent.

Best NFL Quarterback?

Steve Young has been a good sport in more ways than one. Living in the shadow of his famous ancestor, Brigham Young, he endured the relentless teasing of friends and associates about being single. In a cameo appearance in the 2002 film, "Singles Ward," he admonished singles, quoting his great-great-great grandfather, "If you're 25 years old and unmarried, you're a menace to society." And so he was until, at age 38, he and Barbara Graham, 31, married in the new Kailua-Kona Temple in Hawaii on March 14, 2000.

Young's rise to football fame began at BYU where he led the team to winning seasons, capping off his last season in 1984 with a Holiday Bowl win. Those who knew Young were familiar with his famous junker car, a blue 1965 Oldsmobile he dubbed the "Young-mobile." It carried him more than 270,000 miles during 23 years, even when he was a multimillionaire professional football player. When that car finally died, he picked up a Jeep demonstrator floor model—it was cheaper than a new one, he said.

During his college career, he was a consensus All-American, an Academic all-American, and a runner-up in the balloting for the Heisman Trophy.
- At BYU (1981-83), he completed 592 of 907 pass attempts.
- He threw for 7,733 yards and 56 touchdowns.
- He has been inducted into the College Football Hall of Fame.

Young's professional career began with the newly formed USFL (United States Football League) Los Angeles Express, where his contract in 1984 was reportedly close to $44 million. The league went belly up and Young moved around until he finally found a home with the San Francisco 49ers in 1987.

During a professional football career that spanned 15 years, Young racked up some amazing firsts, feats and NFL (National Football League) records.

• He is to date the highest-rated quarterback in NFL history.
• He was the NFL's MVP (Most Valuable Player) in 1992 and 1994, and the MVP of Super Bowl XXIX (1994).
• He made NFL history with the highest career pass completion percentage (64.3 percent), highest career passer rating (96.8), most seasons leading the league in touchdown passes (4), and most consecutive seasons leading the league in passer rating (4; 1991-1994).
• He also holds the NFL record for the most consecutive games with 300 or more yards passing (6), and the NFL single-season record for the highest passer rating (112.8 in 1994).
• He holds the single-game record for the most touchdown passes in a Super Bowl game (6 in 1995), and the most consecutive attempted passes without an interception (36 in 1995).
• He and receiver Jerry Rice broke the record for most touchdowns by a quarterback-receiver duo; he became the NFL's leading quarterback for rushing touchdowns when he exceeded 40; he passed more than 30,000 yards (that's more than 17 miles!); and he was the second NFL quarterback in history to rush for more than 4,000 yards.

In the midst of his career, Young finished up his law degree at BYU in 1994. After some serious personal injuries and a desire to get on with life, he retired from professional football in 2000. Young, his wife Barbara, and their two boys live in Park City, Utah. He works for an investment firm, and as a studio analyst for ESPN. (LDS 2/22/89; DN 6/27/03; Internet)

Steve Young also goes on the speakers' circuit to share his experiences with others under the title, "Success From the School of Hard Knocks."

First Canadian Football League Championship. The first national championship game won in Canada with an LDS quarterback occurred Nov. 29, 1988. Sean Salisbury, 25, led his 9-wins 9-losses Winnipeg Blue Bombers to a 22-21 win over the British Columbia Lions for the coveted Grey Cup. In the locker rooms after the game, champagne was pouring everywhere, except into Sean's glass. A reporter from the Winnipeg Sun asked Sean why. "I'm a Mormon," Sean said, "I don't drink." Sean and his wife, Kimberly, were members of the Winnipeg 1st Ward. (CN 12/24/88)

First National College Football Championship. Brigham Young University reached the pinnacle of performance in 1984 when the Cougars were crowned national college football champs. After an undefeated season of 13 games, the Cougars wrapped up their perfect season by winning the post-season Holiday Bowl over a strong Michigan team. Robbie Bosco's supreme effort to win the game came while he hobbled around the field with a strained knee, torn ligaments and bruised ribs. Disbelievers: NBC's Bryant Gumbel and Oklahoma Coach Barry Switzer. Believers: the rest of the world. (LDS 1/25/85)

Stuart W. Johnson, Deseret Morning News

Ty Detmer receives the key to the city from Provo Mayer Joe Jenkins during "Utah County Ty Detmer Day" in 1990. More thann 4,000 crowded into the Cougar Stadium parking lot to share in the celebration of his Heisman Trophy.

First Heisman Trophy. In 1990, Ty Detmer, BYU's quarterback from 1988-1991, became the first athlete from not only an LDS Church-owned school but also the Western Athletic Conference to win the coveted Heisman Trophy. Detmer finished the season with 52 NCAA records, was named first-team All-American by AP, UPI, Football Writers Association, Water Camp, Football News and Scripps Howard. He won the Maxwell Trophy and was named player of the year by Football News, Scripps Howard and the WAC.

Ty was baptized into the Church Feb. 6, 1991, at the Lindon Stake Center by Frank Herbert, the father of Ty's fiancée Kim. Said one observer at the baptismal service, "It was so crowded, only those nearest the font, and Shawn Bradley, could see it happen." (Shawn Bradley was BYU's towering 7-foot 6-inch BYU basketball player.)

Most NCAA Records Set. BYU's Ty Detmer broke some 52 NCAA records and tied five on his way to becoming the first Heisman Trophy winner ever in the Church, BYU, and the Western Athletic Conference. Though not a member when the award was given, he had been taking the lessons and was baptized later that spring (1991). Below are the NCAA records set or tied by Ty (updated to end of 1990-91 season). He also became the first player in its 11-year history to win back-to-back Davey O'Brien Trophies, given to the nation's outstanding quarterback. (BYU Today Jan 1992; BYU.Sports)

Total Offense (21 records)
Plays (two years): 1,132
Yards (two years): 9,455
Yards (3 years): 10,644
Yards/Game (two years): 393.9
Yards by a sophomore.: 4,433
Yards/game by sophomore: 369.4
Games with 300+ yards (season): 12
Games with 300+ yards (career): 24
Consecutive 300-yard games (season): 12
Consecutive 300-yard games (career): 19
Games with 400+ yards (career): 11
Consecutive 400-yard games (season): 5
Consecutive 400-yard games (career): 5
TDs (3 years): 96
TDs (4 years): 96
TDs, average/game (3 years): 2.82
Points responsible (two years): 504
Points responsible (3 years): 582
Points responsible (career): 582
Points responsible/game (3 years): 17.1
High average/play: 8.92

Passing (21 records)
Attempts (two years): 974
Completions (two years): 626
Completions/game (two years): 26.1
Yards (season): 5,188
Yards (two years): 9,748
Yards (3 years): 11,000
Yards/game (two years): 406.2
Yards/game (3 years): 323.5
Consecutive games 300+ yards (career): 24

TD passes (3 years): 86
TD passes (career): 86
Consecutive games with TD Pass: 23
Yards by a Sophomore: 4,560
Games 300 yards (season): 12 twice
Consecutive games 300-yard (season): 12
Consecutive games 200-yard (career): 27
Games, 300 yards (career): 25 - Old: 17
Consecutive games, 300-yard (career): 24
Yards gained/attempt (min. 237 atts): 11.07
TDs freshman and sophomore seasons: 45 (13 & 32)

Total Offense Tied (3 records)
Seasons gaining 3,000 yards: two (many players hold this record)
Games 400+ yards (season): 8 – Ties David Klingler, Houston, 1990
TD responsible (two years): 83 – Ties Jim McMahon, BYU, 1980-81

Passing Tied (2 records)
Consecutive games 200 yards (season): 12 twice - Ties Robbie Bosco, BYU, 84-85
Games 200 yards (season): 12 twice – Ties Robbie Bosco, BYU, 1984-85

1990 Honors
Heisman Trophy Winner
Maxwell Trophy Winner
Davey O'Brien award
First team All-America, Associated Press

Continued next page

Continued from previous page

First team All-America, UPI
First team All-America, Football Writers
First team All-America, Walter Camp
First team All-America, Football News
First team All-America, The Sporting News
UPI Player of the Year
CBS Player of the Year
Football News Player of the Year
First team All-America, Scripps Howard
Scripps Howard Players of the Year
Western Athletic Conference Player of the Year
First-team All-WAC, unanimous
WAC Offensive Player of the Week (vs. Miami)
CNN Player of the Week (vs. Miami)
Football News Player of the Week (vs. Miami)
Athlon Player of the Week (vs. Miami)
WAC Offensive Player of the Week (vs. San Diego State)
Chevrolet Player of the Game (vs. San Diego State)
CBS Toyota Leadership award (vs. San Diego State)
WAC Offensive Player of the Week (vs. Air Force)
Amateur Athlete of the Year by U.S. Sports Academy (vs. Alabama)
Amateur Athlete of September by U.S. Sports Academy (vs. Alabama)
Athlete of the month for September, Deseret News

First Outland Trophy. Merlin Olsen, Utah State University's star lineman, was the first LDS to capture the Outland Trophy, considered the Heisman Trophy for college lineman. One of nine children, he attended the Logan 11th Ward. (CN 5/13/61)

In 1986, Jason Buck, BYU's All-American defensive lineman, became the first BYU player to receive the Outland trophy. (LDS 12/13/86)

New Bowl-Game Records. Ty Detmer's passing for BYU against Penn State in the 1989 Holiday Bowl broke two unofficial records for all-time bowl performances. His 576 yards passing and 594 yards total offense in the thrilling up-and-down game surpassed the marks achieved by players in all other bowl games in the country. The old passing record was 467 yards by Steve Clarkson (San Jose State) in the 1981 California Bowl. Buster O'Brien of Richmond held the total offense record of 468 yards set in the 1968 Tangerine (Florida Citrus) Bowl. (DN 1/11/90)

Most Touchdown Passes In a Season. In 1985, Robbie Bosco, BYU, set a college record for the most touchdown passes in a season with 47. (BYU Sports)

First All-Army MVP to a Lineman. In 1954, Hal Mitchell became the first lineman ever to win both the Most Valuable Player and All-Army Tackle awards. He was, at the time, stationed with his family at Ft. Lee, Virginia. He was also one of the very few tackles at that time to be honored in any kind of national football poll. The California native played for the New York Giants for a year before entering the military. (CN 1/1/55)

Tom Smart, Deseret Morning News

(l-r) President Ronald Reagan, U.S. Senator Orrin Hatch, and BYU Head Football Coach Lavell Edwards, reflect on the first-ever national football championship for an LDS university. The signed football given to Reagan was displayed with other of his treasured momentos in the president's private study.

Highest Profile LDS Football. Following BYU's national football championship in 1984, Coach Lavell Edwards visited President Ronald Reagan at the White House in January 1985. The coach presented Reagan with a football signed by all the players. The ball remained prominently displayed on a shelf in the president's personal study, just off the Oval Office, where only the personal and powerful friends of the president ever got close enough to see it. (DU 1/15/85; author)

Powerful Kicker! University of Utah's Marv Bateman had one powerful leg. He may hold the record for the longest field goal by an LDS player with a 59-yard boot in 1971, and the longest punt of 89 yards.

National Junior College Player of the Year. In 2000, Marc Dunn, BYU-Idaho, was named Offensive Player of the Year by the National Junior College Athletics Association. Brother Dunn broke eight school records, including most passing yards in a season 4,351, an average of 395.5 yards per game. His season of 60+ percent pass completion and 42 touchdowns led his team to an 8-3 record, a victory in the Real Dairy Bowl and a top-10 ranking. (CN 12/30/00)

RUGBY

Greatest Player in New Zealand. The greatest rugby halfback in New Zealand and, by some accounts, the whole world, was Sid Going, of Maromaku, New Zealand. Dominating the world of rugby in his native land and leading New Zealand's national rugby team, the All Blacks, to numerous championships and victories in international play, Sid fast became a folk hero. After a long 17-year stretch of professional play, he retired in 1978. (CN 9/16/78)

Sid Going in 1970.

Oldest Surviving Professional Player. In 2002, Tori Reid, 89, a four-time bishop in Hastings, New Zealand, was honored on his country's national television as the oldest surviving player on the Ranfurly Shield rugby team of 1934. He was on the Maori All Blacks and New Zealand's traveling teams that played in England, South Africa, Ireland, Scotland, France and Australia. He was devout and prayed before each game. At one game in England, he had just knelt to pray when he was interrupted to meet the king of England. He never did finish his prayer and suffered his only serious injury in his career, requiring that he be carried off the field. He later told family and friends that prayer was always the most important, even more important than the king of England. (CN 9/7/02)

United States National Champs. The first national United States rugby champions were from the Church College of Hawaii, who finished the 1966-67 season unbeaten in 13 games. The United States Rugby Log named them national champs out of all 241 member clubs. (CN 9/9/67)

BASKETBALL

Three-Time All American. In 1929, John Thompson of Dixie, Utah, led his Montana State College teammates to a national championship in 1929. As one of America's top players, his college team amassed a 72-4 record over two seasons. He averaged 15.4 points a game when the national team average was 40 points per game. In three seasons, he scored an astonishing 1,539 points. (www.hoophall.com)

Most LDS on One Pro Team. When Danny Ainge, Greg Kite and Fred Roberts all played for the Boston Celtics in 1986-87, some people dubbed the Celtics the "BYU of the East." Eventually, however, all three were traded to other teams. (LDS 6/28/86)

Most 3-Pointers (1989 World Record). Danny Ainge shot 148 three-pointers in a season for the Boston Celtics in 1988, setting a new world's record. (Author)

First Returned Missionary in the NBA. Was Devin Durrant, the former BYU basketball star, the first returned missionary to play in the National Basketball Association? In 1984, he signed with the Indiana Pacers and later joined the Phoenix Suns. His career led him overseas where he played pro basketball in Spain. (LDS 10/19/85)

First Returned Missionary in the ABA. Was Dick Nemelka, star of the 1966 BYU basketball team that won the National Invitational Tournament, the first returned missionary to play for the American Basketball Association? After his sterling basketball career at BYU, he served a mission and eventually signed with the Utah Stars in the ABA.

Ravell Call, Deseret Morning News

Ainge became the second NBA player to shoot more than 900 three-pointers, and the fourth to reach 1,000. He was a starter on the Boston Celtics two NBA championship teams (1984, 1986).

Longest Nonstop Basketball (1988 World Record). The world record for the most hours of nonstop basketball was set by nine BYU students in August 1988, when they played for 120 hours straight on an outdoor court. The play began Monday afternoon and finished Saturday morning. The players took the allowed five-minute break every hour and the allowed 90-minute break every night. (LDS 9/17/89)

Longest Nonstop Basketball (1975 World Record). In 1975, the longest continuous basketball play was 48 hours and two minutes, by 10 members of the Temple View 1st Ward, Temple View, New Zealand, Stake. They had five minutes of rest each hour. (CN 4/26/75)

Best College Basketball Player in Canada? Richard Bohne was known as "that Mormon basketball player" from the University of Calgary. And what an amazing player he was. In the 1993 season he sank a bucket from the center line in the final second to break an 83-83 tie and send his team into the national playoffs. Brother Bohne's shot made national news. In 1995, he scored 64 points in one game, setting a university record and winning a write-up in Sports Illustrated. In addition, his 684-point total for the 1994-95 season set a new national record, breaking the old record set in 1981-82 by Karl Tilleman, another LDS athlete who played for the University of Calgary. Bohne grew up in Raymond, Alberta, where he was a star player in high school. He once sank 11 3-pointers and scored 69 points in one game. He served a mission in Brazil. (CN 4/15/95)

First LDS Team to Win the NIT. BYU won the National Invitational Tournament in basketball for the first time in 1951 in Madison Square Garden. Its second win came in 1966. (CN 3/66)

World's Largest Basketball League. In 1948, the world's largest basketball league was the Church's — Men's Basketball League. There were more than 1,000 teams from Canada, Mexico, the United States, and Hawaii, with players from several nationalities and races. With teams numbering 5-10 players each, the total number of LDS boys in the league totaled almost 12,000 – more than any other basketball league in the world. (CN 9/22/48)

Most Basketball Records – Woman. In 1984, Tina Gunn held the most basketball records made by one LDS woman. She set a record in almost every basketball category on the books. Today, she still holds nine records at BYU including the most points in a game (56). During her BYU career she was first in the nation in scoring (31.2 points per game in 1984), first in total points (967), fourth in rebounding (14.9 rebounds per game), 14th in field goal percentage (59 percent). She was named to the Kodak All-American First Team, the American Women's Sports Federation First Team and Player of the Year, and to the National Scouting Association All-American Team (twice). She was a Wade Trophy finalist two times. (BYU Sports)

Highest Scoring Average. Karl Tilleman set a Canadian Inter-university Athletic Union basketball record by scoring an average 32.9 points per game in 1982.

Most Rebounds in One Tournament. In 1994, Becky Hunt, Mesa 45th Ward, Mesa, Arizona, South Stake, set a National Junior College Athletic Association basketball tournament record when she pulled down 47 rebounds. (CN 7/16/94)

Best Hoopster Under 10 – Boy. In 1987, Kristopher G. Katseanes, 9, won first place in Boy's 8-9 year-old division at the Elks Club National Hoop

Shoot in Indianapolis, Indiana. A member of the Thomas 2nd Ward, Blackfoot, Idaho, West Stake, Kristopher hit 23 of 25 free throws to win the national competition. (CN 5/23/87)

Best Hoopster Under 13 – Girl. Jennifer Johnson, a Beehive in the Phoenix 2nd Ward, won the National Basketball Association's Hotshot basket shooting competition on April 18, 1982. She shot her winning 88 points during halftime of the Phoenix Suns vs. Los Angeles Lakers game. In three one-minute rounds, she scored 41, 18, and 29 points to become the national champion in the 9-12 year-old girls' division. She beat the Eastern champion who came from a state that had produced five national Hotshot champions in the past. (LDS 4/23/82)

BASEBALL/SOFTBALL

First Mormon in the Big Leagues. Spencer Adams, born in Layton, Utah, in 1898, was the first LDS to play in the major leagues. He began his short-lived baseball career with the Pittsburgh Pirates, and played four years on four different teams. (www.baseball-almanac.com)

Home Runs Champs. Harmon Killebrew, the only Minnesota Twins player in the Hall of Fame in 1989, was selected as the American League's Most Valuable Player in 1969. He holds the American League record for homers by a right-handed hitter, and he hit more home runs in the 1960s than any other player including even Aaron, and Mays. A great role model and credit to the game. Some highlights listed on his Web site:

BYU - L. Tom Perry Special Collections

- He was signed by the Washington Senators at the age of 17.
- He became an everyday player six years later in 1959.
- After he became an everyday player, he won 5 home run titles, led the league in RBI three times and slugging twice.

The longest home run ever hit at the Twins' Metropolitan Stadium was blasted by Harmon Killebrew on June 3, 1967. The ball landed in the second deck of the bleachers.

- He hit more than 40 home runs 8 times in his career.
- He won the MVP in 1969 when he hit 49 home runs, drove in 140 runs, and walked 145 times (all were league leading totals).
- His career total of 573 home runs was fifth on the all time list.
- He had seven seasons with over 100 walks.
- He is tenth on the all time walks list with 1559.
- He was elected to the Hall of Fame in 1984.

In May 1988, Dale Murphy hit his 336th homer, the most by any member of the Braves since the team moved from Milwaukee to Atlanta. He finished his 18-year career with 398 home runs, 1,299 RBI and more than 2,000 hits. He was a great role model on and off the field, and was known as a player with real class. In almost 2,200 games covering 18 seasons (mostly for the Braves), he was a seven-time All-Star, and five-time Gold Glove winner. On Nov. 8, 1983, he was again honored as the National League Most Valuable Player, becoming only the fourth man in history to receive back-to-back MVP awards. (DN 8/29/89; LDS 6/28/89; www.baseball-reference.com)

Top Rookie in Major Leagues. In 1986, Wally Joyner, first baseman for the California Angels and a former BYU slugger, became the first LDS and one of the few rookies in the history of baseball to be named a starter for an all-star team. He later finished a close second in the Rookie of the Year balloting to star slugger Jose Canseco. (LDS 7/12/86)

Baseball's Best. Want to make the perfect baseball team? Take all of the LDS stars in 1984, line 'em up, and look at who's on first:

- **First Base:**   Dane Iorg, Kansas City Royals
- **Third Base:**   Garth Iorg, Toronto Blue Jays
- **Shortstop:**   Vance Law, Chicago White Sox
- **Catcher:**   Alan Ashby, Houston Astros
- **Pitcher:**   Bruce Hurst, Boston Red Sox
    Jim Gott, Toronto Blue Jays
    Jack Morris, Detroit Tigers
- **Outfielder:**   Dale Murphy, Atlanta Braves; Barry Bonnell, Seattle Mariners (CN 6/24/84)

Most Mormon Homers in One Day. On April 27, 1980, "Mormon homers" each brought wins to their respective teams:

- Ray Knight, Cincinnati third baseman; two-run homer to win over San Francisco Giants 3-1.
- Dale Murphy, Atlanta Braves catcher; homer to help win over Montreal, 6-3.

• Alan Ashby, catcher for Houston Astros; a homer to help win over the Mets, 4-3.

• Barry Bonnell, Toronto Blue Jays right fielder; homer to clinch win over Milwaukee, 8-2. (CN 5/3/80)

First No-hitter. Former BYU great Jack Morris was the first LDS major-league baseball pitcher to pitch a no-hitter. He starting pitching for the Detroit Tigers in 1977. At a game in Chicago on April 7, 1984, he pitched his first no-hitter. Final score: Detroit 4, Chicago 0. (www.baseball-almanac.com/pitching/pinohit1.shtml)

First Father-Son All-Stars. Who were the first father and son all-stars in the Church? Vernon and Vance Law were the first and possibly the only LDS all-stars where son followed father for the honor.

There is a story that while Vernon Law was on the bench during a particular baseball game, his teammates in the dugout booed and hissed the umpire using offensive language. Knowing of Law and his personal convictions, the umpire approached him and said he didn't belong in the company of those men that day. And for that, he got tossed from the game.

BYU - L. Tom Perry Special Collections

Vernon Law was called "The Preacher" or "The Deacon" by his teammates because of his strong religious beliefs.

First Inducted Into Hall of Fame. The first LDS to be inducted into Baseball's Hall of Fame was Harmon Killebrew who hit 573 home runs in his career. He was inducted in 1984.

LITTLE LEAGUE SOFTBALL

World's First Over-the-Wall Homer. Jennifer Ann Dalton, 15, Glendale, California, 3rd Ward, set a Little League Softball World Series record when she became the first player ever to hit a home run over the fence in the World Series finals (held in Kalamazoo, Michigan) in 1989. Her team placed second in the senior division. (CN 1/13/90)

Best Hit in Little League Baseball. Jeremy Hess, 12, Long Beach, California, 5th Ward, drove in the winning run to give his team the Little League World Series championship in August 1993. With two out in the bottom of the last inning and the score tied 2-2, the coach sent in Jeremy to pinch hit with the bases loaded against their opponent, Panama. Jeremy hit out a single to right field to drive in the winning run. (CN 10/16/93)

BOXING

Library of Congress

Above, the historic photograph by the New York News' Henry Olen, captured the aftermath of Luis Angel Firpo's powerful right that knocked Dempsey out of the ring. Dempsey was so angry, he roared back in the second round and knocked Firpo out cold. It was September 14, 1923, one of the most historic and famous fights from the golden era of boxing.

Heavyweight Champion. Jack Dempsey of Mannassa, Colorado, was the world heavyweight boxing champion in 1919-26. He won the crown in 1919 when he knocked out Jess Willard. Nicknamed "the Mannassa Mauler," but also known as "Jack," allegedly because he was a "Jack Mormon," Dempsey lost the crown to Gene Tunney in 1926. He died May 31, 1983, at the age of 87 years, 341 days — the longest lived heavyweight champion ever. He was not active in the Church, but he prayed before each fight, and three to four more times a day, he said. He lost to Tunney after the infamous "long count" fight. He was inducted into the World Boxing Hall of Fame in 1980, and the

1975: President Spencer W. Kimball and Jack Dempsey exchange a laugh at the open house of the Church's new Visitors Center in New York City.

International Boxing Hall of Fame in 1990. He also appeared in 16 movies, most often starring as himself. (CN 6/5/83)

Most Knockouts (1960 World Record). The world record holder for the most knockouts is Lamar Clark, who administered his 44th consecutive KO at Las Vegas on Jan. 11, 1960. He KO-ed six in one evening, five of those in the first round, in Bingham Canyon, Utah, Dec. 1, 1958. (Author)

Middleweight Champion. Gene Fullmer beat Sugar Ray Robinson Jan. 2, 1957, to become the first LDS world middleweight champion. He defended the title in 12 additional fights, losing it to Sugar Ray Robinson on May 1, 1957, and then regaining it on Oct. 28, 1959. Nigeria's Dick Tiger finally took the title from Fullmer in 15 rounds on Oct. 23, 1962. Fullmer retired to Utah and is a member of the West Jordan 54th Ward, West Jordan Stake, Utah. (Author's interview)

Junior Middleweight Champion. Ron Amundsen, Chicago 1st Ward, Illinois, and known in boxing circles as the "Stormin' Mormon," won the United States Boxing Association Junior Middle-weight title in Reno, Nevada, in December 1990. Ron was 29. (CN 1/12/91)

Fullmer beat Spider Webb in 1959 to retain his NBA middleweight crown.

Welterweight Champion. In 1992, Dumisane Polo won the gold medal in East London, South Africa, in the welterweight boxing division of the Olympic Trials. Polo, 19, was a member of the Mdantsane Branch, South Africa Cape Town Mission, and had been boxing for five years prior to the Olympic tryouts. He represented his country in the 1992 Olympics in Barcelona, Spain. (CN 8/1/92)

Featherweight Champion. Danny Lopez beat Dave Kotey in Ghana in 1976, after 15 rounds, to become the first LDS to win the world feather-weight title. He retained his title in a March 1979 fight by knocking out Roberto Castanon, a Spaniard who had a professional record of 29 wins and no losses prior to the fight. He held the title for four years, losing it to Salvador Sanchez in 1980. (CN 3/79; Internet)

Golden Gloves and Everlast. B.J. Flores, who grew up in Missouri, astonished boxing enthusiasts when he stepped away from a promising box-ing career after winning the 1997 Golden Gloves boxing tournament in his weight category to serve a mission in Mexico. But the two-year hiatus served him well. He returned to win his weight class in the Everlast U.S. boxing tournament in 2001 and 2002. Also in 2002, he won the Four Nations Tournament in Paris that included fighters from France, Australia and Germany. (CN 7/27/02)

VOLLEYBALL

Jason Olson, Deseret Morning News

Kristin Richards shows her classic spike during a game in 2002.

National Volleyball Player of the Year. In 2003, Kristin Richards, Timpanogos High, Orem, Utah, and a member of the Heatheridge 5th Ward, Orem, Utah, Heatheridge Stake, was honored as the best volley-ball player in the U.S. In 2002, she logged 248 kills (spiking the ball past defenders), led her school to four state champi-onships, is a two-time All American, and has been a mem-ber of the U.S. junior national teams. Despite all of her accom-plishments and fame in volley-ball, she told the Church News, "The Church is the most important thing in my life. I wouldn't give up my standards to win a game of volleyball." CN 2/22/03)

Kristin Richards is awarded the Gatorade National Volleyball Player of the Year Award from representatives from Gatorade.

First NCAA Champions. BYU's men's volleyball team won its first NCAA championship on May 8, 1999, after the Cougars' fantastic 30-1 season record. Their victory against the Long Beach 49ers was even more satisfying because the 49ers were the only team to spoil the Cougars' otherwise perfect season record. The Cougars have won the NCAA volleyball championship four times in the past six years, beating LA for the title again in May 2004. (DN 5/9/04)

Women Volleyball Champions. There are many LDS women playing world-class volleyball. For six years in a row (1986-92), the Eastern, Arizona, College women's volleyball team was ranked number one or two in the United States. Coach Gerald Hekekia (Thatcher 1st Ward) said his 1992 women's national volleyball championship team included five LDS girls out of the twelve team members. (CN 4/18/92)

SWIMMING/DIVING

Fastest Relay Swimmer (1988 World Record). Troy Dalbey of Tempe, Arizona, and his teammates, set two world records in the 400-meter (3:16.53) and 800-meter (7:12.51) relay swimming races at the 1988 Summer Olympics in Seoul, South Korea. The team won gold medals for both efforts. (World Almanac)

Dalbey joined the Church before competing in the 1988 Olympics.

Fastest 100-Meter Freestyle (1984 World Record). At the 1984 Olympic Games in Los Angeles, Ambrose "Rowdy" Gaines IV topped his astonishing swimming career by winning three gold medals and setting two world records. He set a new Olympic record for the 100-meter freestyle, finishing shy of his own world record by only .45 seconds. His second gold was as the anchor for the 4x100-meter freestyle relay. His third gold came when he swam the anchor for 4x100 meter medley relay, setting a new world record. "Rowdy" was baptized in Birmingham, Alabama, in 1998, and attended the Hoover Ward. (Internet)

100-Meter Backstroke – Boys, 14. Kris Fisher, 14, Richmond Hill Ward, Brampton, Ontario, Stake, set a national age-group record of 58.98 seconds in the 100-meter backstroke in 1991. The previous record of 59.58 seconds had been set by Olympic swimmer Mark Tewksbury in 1983. (CN 4/18/92)

500-Meter Freestyle. Alma Olly Saunders, Kendall Park, New Jersey, won a gold medal at age 74 in 1976 in the 500-meter freestyle at the annual East Coast Masters Invitational Swim Meet. In 1975 she won a gold medal and set a national record in her age group, finishing the 1,650-yard freestyle in 45 minutes and 34 seconds. (CN 8/21/76)

200-Meter Breaststroke – Women. In 1995, Staci Malin, Dayton Second Branch, McMinnville, Oregon, Stake, set the seventh school record of her career at Linfield College, Oregon. She swam the 200-meter breaststroke in 2:24.22 at the NAIA Division III national swimming championships. She made the all-American team for the third year and academic all-America team for the second time. (CN 5/20/95)

At the World Masters Championships in Montreal in 1994, Dea Ann Joslin, 35, of the Rafael, California, Stake, set a new United States record for the 200-meter breaststroke in her age group with a time of 2:52.40. This was just a half second shy of the world record at the time. The mother of four also won the 50- and 100-meter races. The championships were well attended with 3,500 swimmers from 45 countries. (CN 8/20/94)

100-Meter Breaststroke – Women. In 1995, Staci Malin of the Dayton 2nd Branch, McMinnville, Oregon, Stake, set a new NAIA record of 1:05.38 for the 100-meter breaststroke. (CN 5/20/95)

100-yard Breaststroke – Girls, 13. In 1998, Tamber Marie Covington, a Laurel in the Oak Ridge Ward, El Dorado, California, Stake, set a new Northern California Junior Varsity record for the 100-yard breaststroke with a time of 1:05.30. (CN 1/9/99)

Sandi Kimball, at age 14, set a new SPAAU 100-meter breaststroke record in 1959, with a time of 1:31.8. She was 7/10ths of a second off the existing national record for her age group that year. (CN 9/5/59)

Breaststroke – Boys, 8. Craig Grebe of the Bay City Ward, Bay City, Texas, Stake, won the gold medal in the 25-meter breaststroke at the 1994 Texas State Games at Texas A&M University in College Station. Seeded No. 2 in the 8-year-olds' division, Craig had a time of 22.26, half a second faster than the swimmer who was the No. 1 seed. Then, anchoring his 100-meter relay team, he passed two swimmers to boost his team to the silver medal. (CN 12/3/94)

Best Swimmer – Senior Women. Shirley Rannells of the Basin Ward, Worland, Wyoming, Stake, won four gold medals in swimming at the 1993 Montana Senior Olympics, competing in the 70-74 age group. She took first place in the 50-meter backstroke with a time of 1:28.01, as well as in the 100- (2:51.71), 200- (6:21.95) and 500-meter (15:28.91) freestyle races. She also claimed a silver medal in the 100 backstroke. The swimming competition was held in an outdoor pool in Kalispell, Montana, with temperatures in the 40s. (CN 9/18/93)

Butterfly – Boys, 11-12. Bart Bowen, Pacific Beach Ward, San Diego Stake, set two national swimming records for 11-12 year olds in the 50-yard butterfly (34.5 seconds) and for the 75-yard individual medley event (51.7 seconds) in 1953. (CN 7/18/53)

Best Speed-Swimmer in 220- and 440-Yard Freestyle. Budd Shields was America's premier short-distance swimmer in the late 1920s, and was the first swimmer ever to break three national records in one night.

In 1927, he beat Johnny Weismuller's 220-yard freestyle time, and improved the following year to set an American and NCAA record. His best 220 was 2:19.2, and his best 440 in 1929 was 4:57.8.

Springboard Dive – Girls, 15 (1987 World Record). Venessa Bergman, 15, Los Altos, California, 3rd Ward, held the world's record for her age group for the 1-meter springboard dive in 1987. She is also believed to be the first United States girl under 18 to do a forward 3-1/2 tuck on the 3-meter board. (CN 11/7/87)

Highest Dive – Women. (Unknown Year – World Record). Lucy Wardle holds the women's world record for the highest dive at 120 feet 9 inches. (/s64.emuunlim.com/manuals/internationalsportschallenge.htm)

Most Records? Michael J. Burton was a pioneer of the "mega-mileage" training regime and swam 4,000 meters a day to increase his endurance. As a result, he was the first to swim 1,650 yards in less than 16 minutes. He also was the first to break the 8-1/2 minute barrier in the 800-meter freestyle. He is the only man to win the Olympic 1,500-meter freestyle twice (1968 and 1972). (www.hickoksports.com/biograph/burtonmi.shtml)

Best Bodyboarder. Peter Avery, 17, San Luis Obispo, California, 2nd Ward, became the United States National Junior Bodyboarding Champion when he placed first in the United States Surfing Federation finals held in the summer of 1993 in Oceanside, California (CN 10/16/93)

Deseret Morning News file photo

Bob Cooper standing on a wave? Cooper was one of the first "purists" from the U.S. to escape the hectic California surf scene and find fantastic waves in Australia. He became a world expert on surfboard manufacturing and performance.

World-renowned Surfer. Bob Cooper, a high councilor in Nambour, Australia, is considered one of the founding fathers of the sport of surfing. He was raised in California and was one of the first to adopt the new sport of surfing in the late 1940s. A decade later, he had become one of the world's greatest surfers and traveled around the globe to star in surfing movies. He met his wife in Queensland, and after living in several countries, they settled on Australia's east coast. In 1969, they helped establish the Coffs Harbour Branch. Dropping out of professional surfing because finals were always on Sunday, Brother Cooper started making surf boards and over time built up the largest surf shop in Australia. (CN 10/19/02)

SCHOOL SPIRIT

First Female Cheerleader at Auburn University. Miki Bozeman, 21, Auburn University Branch, and a gymnast, was selected head cheerleader for the 1983-84 year, the first female to be cheerleader in the history of Auburn University. Sister Bozeman served as a primary teacher in her Branch. (CN 1983)

Best Drill Team in the U.S. The Skyline High School (Salt Lake City) drill team of 20 girls, 18 of whom were LDS, won the national championship at the 1981 Miss Drill Team competition in Los Angeles. The team captured the best "prop precision" title, plus dance, military, and novelty precision championship awards, and the prestigious "Producers Award." (CN 2/1981)

Best drill team in the country in 1981.

Best in the U.S.! Amy McBride (Sandy, Utah, Granite Stake), Sharissa Gardner (Sandy, Utah, Hillcrest Stake), Shelby Jackson (Utah Midvalley Fort Union South Stake), Allison Welchers and Tricia Tueller (Sandy, Utah, Cottonwood Creek Stake), and Gina Hale (Sandy, Utah, North Stake). Deseret Morning News file photo

Best Cheerleaders in the U.S. Six LDS young women at Hillcrest High School won the 1990 United Spirit Association National Cheerleader title. The six girls were each active in their respective wards. (CN 9/8/90)

Another group of LDS young women won the National Cheerleading Association Championship in Dallas, Texas, in 1991. Maria Taitano, Midwest City, Oklahoma, 1st Ward, and Jennifer Wagner, Midwest City, Oklahoma, 2nd Ward, and their teammates swept the 57-team field of cheerleaders from across the United States. Teresa Wilkerson, sponsor of the group and a member of the Midwest City, Oklahoma, 1st Ward, led the group to the championship. (CN 4/18/92)

Best Baton Twirler in the U.S. Mark Nash, 14, Lake Prot Ward, Ukiah, California, Stake, won the U.S. National Open boys' baton-twirling championship in 1983. He also won the 2-baton division. (CN 3/27/83)

GYMNASTICS

Fresh from the Olympics, gold-medal gymnast Peter Vidmar with his wife, Donna, attended the 1984 October General Conference.

Best Gymnast – Men. Peter Vidmar, representing the United States, won two gold medals in gymnastics at the 1984 Summer Olympics. He was the first Mormon to receive the coveted Nissen award, the gymnasts' equivalent of the Heisman Trophy. He was also the first American to win a medal in an Olympic gymnastics, and was at the time the highest scoring male gymnast in the history of the Olympics. (Church Almanac 1989; CN 11/30/91)

First World Games' Champion. Wayne Young took first place in gymnastics for the United States at the World Games in Bulgaria in 1974.

World Tumbling Champions. In 1990, Ryan Weston, Chubbuck, Idaho, 4th Ward, clinched the world title for tumbling at the World Games in Dillenburg, Germany. He qualified for the games by winning fourth place at the American National Tumbling and Trampoline Association meet earlier in Rockford, Illinois. In 1992, Brother Weston, then 12, won the World Championship Trophy in power tumbling at the World Age Group Championships in Trampoline and Tumbling. Ryan traveled to Auckland, New Zealand, for the finals. This was Ryan's second world championship trophy in the event.(CN 1/12/91; CN 1/9/93)

In 2003, Krista Mahoney, 17, won the U.S. national power tumbling championship in the senior elite level. The competition was held in Sacramento,

California. She was a Laurel in the MIll Road Ward, Heber City, Utah, East Stake.

Becki Hamblin was United States national tumbling champion in 1973, 1975, and 1978 at ages of 10, 12, and 15.

WRESTLING

Pro Wrestling

At 6 feet 6 inches, 225 pounds, Don Leo Jonathan (real name Don Heaton) of British Columbia was the most prominent professional wrestler in the Church. His wrestling career spanned 30 years, beginning in 1949. In one of the most famous main events in Montreal history, the battle of the giants pitted Don with Giant Jean Ferre (Andre the Giant) in May 1972. Don won by disqualification when Andre the Giant would not break a choke. Don defeated Yvon Robert for the International title in Montreal, but later lost the belt to Killer Kowalski. (From *Wrestling As You Like It*, Nov. 20, 1954)

Photo courtesy of Terry Dart

Don Leo Jonathan, one of the "Giants."

Steven Gatorwolfe, a 6 foot 5 inch, 300 pound half-Cherokee, is the only known pro-wrestler who is part American Indian. He lives with his wife and 3 children in Salt Lake City. (LDS 3/28/87)

Greco-Roman Wrestling. In 1989, Oleg Konyushenko, 22, was the wrestling champion in his weight class for the entire Soviet Union. He went on to become the 1993 Ukrainian champion and won the 1995 Ukrainian National Greco-Roman Wrestling Championship in the 52-kilogram weight class. At the time he was second counselor in the Topol branch presidency, Ukraine Donetsk Mission. (CN 11/18/95)

For information about Rulon Gardner, see the introduction page for Sports.

Undefeated College Champion. Cael Sanderson, originally of Heber, Utah, achieved the remarkable record of going undefeated during his career at Iowa State University. He stepped onto the mat 159 times, and stepped off a winner every time, including four national championship matches. He was the first college wrestler ever to win four NCAA titles with an undefeated record. Nicknamed "The Heber Creamer," he was featured in Sports Illustrated and on ESPN. He was honored with an ESPY, and was named NCAA Most Outstanding Wrestler four times. He even had a Congressional resolution written in his honor, and later received a congratulatory handshake from the president of the United States. (CN 3/30/02)

Best Heavyweight Wrestler – Boys, 17. William Butler Yates, 17, Hopkinsville 1st Ward, Hopkinsville, Kentucky Stake, won the 1991 AAU/U.S.A. Elite Heavyweight Wrestling Championship in the freestyle category. (CN 11/2/91)

Best 130-pound Division Wrestler – Boys, 13. In 1995, Ashton Buswell, 13, won first place in the 130-pound School Boy division at the National AAU Wrestling Championships in St. Louis, Missouri. He was a two-time Kansas state champion and a member of the Topeka 3rd Ward, Topeka, Kansas, Stake. (CN 7/8/95)

Best 70-pound Division Wrestler – Boys, 12. Robert Ho, 12, Meridian, Idaho, 6th Ward, won the national U.S.A. Wrestling Federation championship in the 70-pound division for the second consecutive year in 1984. He had not been defeated for two years. (CN 8/19/84)

Best Middleweight Arm/Wrist Wrestler – Women. Laura Lee Edgson, Prince George Branch in the Canada Vancouver Mission, won the 1991 middleweight right arm title at the World Wrist Wrestling Championship held in Petaluma, California. She placed second in the left arm competition. (CN 3/2/91)

MARTIAL ARTS

Most Ice Cracked with Hand or Head (1988 World Record). In 1988, Sam Alama Kuoha, 41, Alpine Ward, El Cajon, California, Stake, was the youngest karate grandmaster in the world. He held a 10th degree black belt in Chinese Kempo style karate, and held world records for ice breaking:

(1978 World Record). In April 1978, Brother Kuoha broke 4,200 pounds of ice with one hand, setting a new world record.

(1979 World Record). In May 1979, he broke 4,950 pounds with one hand (consisting of 33 blocks of 150 pounds each, stacked 4 stories high), setting a new world record.

(1979 World Record). In November 1979, he broke 1,500 pounds with his forehead, setting another new world record. (LDS 7/30/88)

"Karate King." Ed Parker, long-time karate instructor, might well be the "Karate King" in the Church for his participation and contribution to the sport. He helped develop the belt system students use to gauge their progress, choreographed most martial arts scenes in the "Pink Panther" movies, introduced Bruce Lee to Hollywood and helped build him into a star, and was Elvis Presley's trainer and part-time bodyguard. Additionally, his father was the first Polynesian patriarch in the Church. (LDS 2/17/84)

Karate Champion – Boys, 14-16. In 1991, the karate champion in the 14-16 age group for boys was Mark Osborne, 15, of the South Jordan 18th Ward, South Jordan, Utah, East Stake. He was declared the champion of the 1991 Karate Championship National Finals in New York City. This wasn't Mark's first major championship. He also took first place in the International Karate Competition in November 1990 in Palm Beach, California. (CN 3/23/91)

Photo courtesy of Leilani Parker

Ed Parker guest stars in The Lucy Show, with Lucille Ball, about to be flipped by Ethel (Vivian Vance).

In 1987, Mark Buckwalter, Las Vegas 72nd Ward, Green Valley Stake, won the World Karate Championship in the 14-16 year-old red belt category. (LDS 1/16/88)

Youngest Black Belt? In 1985, the youngest member of the Church to earn a first-degree black belt was Justin Balog, 10, Albany Ward, Albany, New York, Stake. He studied with the World Seido Karate Organization, and was declared the youngest ever to reach the coveted level in that organization, and one of only a handful of 10-year-old youth around the world to win the award. (CN 12/29/85)

Photo courtesy Camille and Dennis DeLoach

Camille DeLoach started karate at age 32.

World Karate Champ, Women. As of 2003, Camille De Loach, Willow Creek 7th Ward, Willow Creek Utah Stake, was a nine-time world champion in karate. A typical championship fight took place at the 2003 International Women's Taekwondo Open Championships, where she beat two women from Japan and one from China to win two gold medals and one silver. All routine sounding for a world champ, right? Except for one thing: Sister DeLoach was 44, with six kids ages 6-19. She also stands 5-foot-1 and weighs 110 pounds. Her grueling daily training schedule includes getting up at 6 to do a four-mile run, then off to a kenpo karate class or weight training, home to do house work, off to a Taekwondo class, then a tumbling class, pick up the kids from school, and then off to teach her own class of karate students. Then comes dinner, and the evening is spent sparring in the family room. The joke around her home, she told Doug Robinson of the Deseret News, is that when she needs a sparring partner, her kids have to tell friends, "I can't talk now, I gotta fight my mom." (CN 9/15/03)

Best Kata Champion – Girls, 9. Susan Covalt, 9, Hawaii Kai 2nd Ward, Honolulu, Hawaii, Stake, became the 1991 champion in team kata in her age group by taking first place in the International Karate Federation Tournament held in Honolulu. (CN 3/2/91)

Best Kung Fu Fighter. Phil Ennis, 25, Hyde Park Ward, London, England, Hyde Park Stake, beat hundreds of competitors at Kuala Lumpur, Malaysia, in 1980 to win the world kung fu championship, middleweight division. (CN 5/21/81)

Best Judo Champions. Katherine Beaton, 17, Las Vegas 37th Ward, East Stake, won the National Judo Championship in the 17-20 age division among 2,000 participants in San Diego July 2-4, 1987. The sport cost her parents about $10,000 a year for tournament fees, doctor bills and traveling expenses, something none in the family regrets, according to her dad. (LDS 8/29/87)

Heidi Rhodes, 10, Columbia Falls Ward, Kalispell, Montana, Stake, won her third Junior National Judo Championship in 1991. She won her first at age 8 and her second a year later. (CN 11/16/91)

Levi Colburn, 7, a CRT-B in the Kea'au Ward, Hilo Hawaii Stake, placed second in the 1992 U. S. Judo Federation National Tournament in California, compating against other 7-year-olds 65 pounds or heavier. (CN 9/12/92)

CYCLING

Fastest Bicycle Trip Around the World (1984 World Record). Matt DeWaal and Jay Aldous, both of Salt Lake City, pedaled 14,290 miles around the world in 106 days to set a new record. They left "This is the Place" monument in Salt Lake on April 2, 1984, rode to New York City, flew to Madrid, Spain, biked up through France, Switzer-land and Germany, cycled around to Austria, Italy and into Yugoslavia and Greece. They flew to Cairo, Egypt, biked over the Sinai Desert to Israel, then flew to Bombay, India, rode the length of that country, and then flew from Calcutta to Bangkok, Thailand, and pedaled on through Malaysia. They flew to Perth, Australia, and pedaled across that country, left Sydney, Australia, and flew to Hawaii to pedal across the islands, then flew to Anchorage, Alaska, where they pedaled down through Canada and into Montana, Idaho, and finally back to Salt Lake City. They were frostbitten in the Austrian Alps and dehydrated while struggling through 114 humid degrees in India, but they persevered to the end. (CN 7/22/84)

Owen Stayner, Deseret Morning News

At the end: Approaching the "This is the Place" monument, the start and finish for the world-record race.

Deseret Morning News file photo

Salt Lake cyclists Jay Aldous and Matt DeWaal congratulate each other on making it home safely.

Fastest Cross-Country Bicycle Trip in the United States. Who holds the record for the fastest cross-country bicycle trip across the United States? In 1966, Craig Nelson, Washington, D.C., pedaled his bike from the nation's capitol to Salt Lake City in 80 days. During the 2,200 mile trip, he stopped at Church sites and slept in a sleeping bag or at members' homes. (CN 8/13/66)

In 1997, Leon Bergant, a Sunday school teacher in his branch in Ljubljana, Slovenia, won the Bicycle Racing National Championship of Slovenia in Nova Gorica. He interrupted his cycling career to serve a two-year mission. (CN 11/29/97)

Longest Bicycle Trip to Church. In 1963, Pvt. A. Ralph Coleman, originally from Englewood Ward, Denver Stake, found himself stationed in Germany with no place to go for Sunday services. He learned there was an LDS branch some 30 miles away in Karlsrhue. So, he found himself a good bicycle and for more than a year made the 60-mile round trip to Church each Sunday. (CN 10/19/63)

Best Long-Distant Competition. In 1985, Russell C. Scott, 18, Sandy 10th Ward, Sandy, Utah, Hillcrest Stake, was among the top 25 finishers of the 75-mile World Junior Cycling Championships in Stuttgart, West Germany. Brother Scott was the only representative on the six-man United States team to finish the race. He won a place on the team after competing against 60 top racers from across America. (CN 9/1/85)

Best BMX Cyclist – Girls, 13. Julee Lindsay, 13, Layton, Utah, 10th Ward, won the grand national BMX bicycle race in Tulsa, Oklahoma, in 1984. The win established her as the second rated MBX racer among United States girls. She had won more than 600 trophies for racing. (CN 2/19/84)

Most Miles Pedaled on a Stationary Bike. Luella Bybee Hansen, Rosecrest Ward, Salt Lake Canyon Rim Stake, pedaled 10,000 miles in 25 months at the age of 70. During her two-year "trip," she lost 18 pounds and read all of the standard works except the last half of the Bible while seated on her bicycle. (CN 7/82)

GOLF

First NCAA Champions. BYU's golf team won the school's first NCAA championship in 1981 by edging out Oral Roberts University. The win left 13-time NCAA champion Houston struggling in third place. (CN 1981)

1984 at Jeremy Ranch, Utah, Johnny Miller shows the form that made him one of the world's best.

Largest Cash Prize. Until 1982, the largest cash prize won by a professional golfer did not exceed the $500,000 won by Johnny Miller, Napa Ward, Napa, California, Stake. He took the prize in golf's richest tournament, the Sun City Golf Challenge at Sun City, Bophuthataswana. That tournament was golf's first-ever million-dollar tourney. Brother Miller also won the British Open. (CN 1/9/82)

Lowest Score (1989 World Record). The lowest score for 18 holes in the United States open is 63 by Johnny Miller, Napa Ward, Napa, California, Stake, on the 6,921-yard, par-71 Oakmont, Pennsylvania, course on June 17, 1973. This represented 8 under par. Brother Miller's great game was part of his overall score of 5 under par, 279 total, for 72 holes to win the $35,000 first prize. (CN 6/23/73)

First LDS Woman in the LPGA. The first known LDS woman to be a member of the Ladies Professional Golf Association is Terri Carter, Duncan Stake, Arizona, who toured with the LPGA in 1984. (LDS 5/84)

Johnny Miller was the first player elected to the PGA Tour Hall of Fame, part of the World Golf Hall of Fame, in 1996.

Youngest Golf Champs – Boys, 10. Jayson Manuia, a Valiant B in the Ainaola, Hawaii, Ward, was the 1986 Optimist Junior World Golf Champion for the 10 and under age group. He beat out 800 players from the United States and 30 foreign countries for the title. He had played golf a total of 18 months before entering the contest. (CN 9/7/86)

TENNIS

First LDS in Wimbledon. Brad Pearce, second-ranked junior in the United States, was also ranked No. 5 in the world after reaching the semifinals at the 1984 Junior Wimbledon. He was back at Wimbledon in 1990 in a quarterfinal singles appearance on center court. He lost to the No. 1 player in the world, Ivan Lendl, in four sets. His highest career ranking was 71 in singles and 23 in doubles. (www.byucougars.com/tennis)

First Coach to Win Championships. In 2002, David Porter, tennis coach at BYU-Hawaii, became the first coach in history to win the NCAA Division II championships for both his women's and men's tennis teams. Brother Porter's women's team won the national championship in 1997, 1998, 1999, and 2000. By 2002, his women's teams had a cumulative record of 132 wins and 1 loss. His men's teams had a record of 386 wins and 88 losses. He has been named the National Coach of the Year four times since 1988. (BYU Today Fall 2002)

Coach Porter led his women's teams to national top-five finishes for six years in a row.

SKIING/SNOW

Longest Forward Somersault in the World (1973 World Record). On April 30, 1973, Darol Wagstaff, Canyon Estates Ward, Bountiful, Utah, North Canyon Stake, completed the longest single front somersault ever on skis, for a record-breaking distance of 164 feet. The jump was performed during the Most Spectacular Event portion of the Inter-national Gelande Contest, held at Alta, Utah. The official name of his jump is a "single front lay-out somersault." At the peak of the jump, he was approximately 60 feet off the ground and flying through the air at about 50 miles per hour. He out-jumped

At the peak of his jump, Wagstaff worried he would plant his face into the hard-packed snow at 50 miles an hour. And then he felt that his forward rotation miraculously slowed down enabling him to land safely. "I believe Heavenly Father was watching over me," he said.

the landing hill and landed on the "flats" at the base of the mountain. Today, Brother Wagstaff is president of Youth Motivation Institute and shares this adventure, along with hundreds of others he's had, to millions of people across North America. (www.a-motive.com; author's interview).

Darol Wagstaff

Best Skier, Women. In 1984, the most world championships held by any LDS woman in skiing was five by Jan Bucher in freestyle skiing. (Author)

First Black Woman Luger in Olympics. In 2002, Dinah Browne, St. Croix, Virgin Islands, was the first black woman to compete in the Olympic luge event. The 32-year-old English teacher didn't even sit on a luge sled until she was 29. At the Salt Lake City 2002 Olympic Winter Games, she came in 28th out of a field of 28. However, her combined time of 2:59.745 was only 7.281 seconds behind the gold-medal winner. Coaches and observers believe she could be a powerhouse competitor by 2006.

Oldest Luger in the Olympics. At age 39, Werner W. K. Hoeger was the oldest male to compete in the Olympic luge event at the Salt Lake City 2002 Olympic Winter Games. He was joined by his son, Chris, 17, both of Boise, Idaho, making them the first father-son athletes to compete in the same Olympics. They both entered the luge event representing Venezuela. Out of 50 competitors, Werner finished 40th and Chris finished 31st. (BYU Magazine Fall 2002; Internet)

Dinah Browne loved the luge. "I had a vague notion of what the sport was," she said. "Then they gave me a helmet, and I was like, 'Oh, you need a helmet?' It was a real natural feeling."

Best Skiers, Girls, 5. Wendy Shingleton, Castle Rock, Colorado, Ward, was ranked third among all 5-6 year olds in Colorado in 1989. Is this the highest state ranking of any skier in that age group in the Church? (CN 1/13/90)

National Championships. For the first time ever, the BYU ski team captured the National Collegiate Ski Association Championship in the winter of 1982-83. (LDS 4/8/89)

Best Blind Skier. Mike Holman, Billings, Montana, Stake, became the first blind LDS on the United States Ski Team in 1982. He qualified after winning three medals in Michigan, a silver medal for his second-place finish in the 5-kilometer cross-country race and two bronzes for his third-place finishes in the giant alpine slalom and the 10-kilometer cross-country race. He had been an alpine skier before becoming blind in 1972. (CN 3/6/82)

Photo courtesy Nels Anderson family

Dr. Nels Anderson stopped to give medical aid to injured racers, hampering his own ranking, but scoring first in the hearts of those he helped.

Highest Finish in a Dog Sled Race. The highest finish by a member of the Church in the grueling Alaskan Anchorage-to-Nome dog-sled race was 35th by Dr. John Nels Anderson of the Soldotna, Alaska, Ward, in the winter of 1987. Of the 63 who entered, many did not finish the 1,157-mile race. Dr. Anderson would have finished closer to the top of the pack, but had brought along his medical bag and stopped to treat injured racers along the way. (CN 6/20/87)

Longest Barefoot Water Skiing (1961 World Record). Jerry Dabbs, 17, Omaha 1st Ward, Winter Quarters Stake, shattered the world record for barefoot water skiing in 1961 by remaining upright for 11 minutes 27 seconds. The old record was five minutes 37 seconds. (CN 10/28/61)

World Water Speed Records (1988 World Record). Blake Esank, Las Vegas 31st Ward, Las Vegas Stake, set three world water speed records while winning a seven-hour marathon speedboat race in 1987. Winning the national championship on the Kankakee River required Esank to travel in excess of 150 miles per hour over water. (LDS 7/88)

Longest Endurance Water-skiing. Is Ron Cartwright the champion Utahn for the longest nonstop skiing at Lake Powell, Utah, with a run of 12 hours straight? (Cartwright family)

SKATEBOARDING

First World Champion Skateboarder. The first LDS World Champion Skateboarder is George Orton, Santa Fe Springs Ward, Cerritos, California, Stake. He was highlighted by CBS Sports Spectacular in December 1978, and again in February 1979. (CN 2/10/79)

MOUNTAIN CLIMBING

Deseret News file photo

Ron Cartwright takes the pounding for 12 solid hours.

First to Climb Mount Everest. The first LDS to climb Mount Everest is Larry Nielson, Olympia, Washington, 4th Ward, reaching the summit on May 7, 1983. He also was the first American to reach the top without the aid of oxygen. This is no small feat. At about 25,000 feet, the so-called "Death Zone," the body begins to shut down as it tries to adopt to a lack of oxygen. Although some people will adapt better than others, it can cause hypoxia, brain swelling and death. Brother Nielson is one of only 90 or so climbers to make the summit without oxygen and live to tell

Larry Nielson

Larry Nielson has also climbed Kangchenjunga, LaPerouse, Peak Lenin, McKinley and Rainer 180 times.

Jack Monson, Deseret Morning News

about it. He was also the first to successfully transmit a live television signal from the top of Everest. He was assisted on the climb by three fellow Americans, plus one guide. (LDS 5/20/83; CN 5/15/83)

The second LDS to scale Everest is George H. Lowe III, 39, an inactive priest who described himself as a "cultural Mormon." He conquered the east face of Mount Everest on Oct. 8, 1983, the second Mormon to conquer Everest that year. (CN 11/13/83)

Kristan Jacobsen, Deseret Morning News

Aaron Shamy took out two years for his mission to Italy, a departure that shocked the climbing-sports world. His two years away were so satisfying that climbing "didn't even compare."

Fastest Speed Climber (1999 World Record). In 1999, Aaron Shamy shattered the world record in the 60-foot World Extreme Speed Climbing Championship in San Francisco, with a time of 12.61 seconds. Aaron was an 18-year-old priest from the Holladay 24th Ward, Holladay, Utah, North Stake. He has been ranked number one in the world. (CN 8/21/99)

HIKING

Oldest Mass Hike. Since 1912, BYU and various clubs and organizations have sponsored the annual Timpanogos Hike. The two-day event is the oldest mass hike in the United States. The late E. L. Roberts, a BYU physical-education professor, started the mass trek up the 12,000-foot peak. Roberts was the creator of the legend of Timpanogos, the love story of Red Eagle and Utahna, who was sacrificed on the rugged mountain. He began relating his tale to hikers at the bonfire on the first night of the hike. Early the next morning, hikers began the long, all-day trek up and back. Roberts' legend remains a favorite among LDS. (DU 7/8/69)

Oldest Hiker. Lori Lund, 86, of Williams, Oregon, was understandably upset when the police and her bishop interrupted her 900-mile hike from Oregon to Salt Lake City in the dead of winter and forced her to finish the trip by bus. After all, she had hiked the Pacific Coast trail from Mexico to

Alaska several times, and this particular hike was, in her words, "a drop in the bucket ... I've walked in colder weather than this. I wish they would leave me alone." The police said she was dressed and prepared for the hike and was of sound mind and very sound body. (DU 11/27/85)

JUMP ROPE

Best Jump-Rope Champion. The most decorated jump-rope champion in the world in 2000 was Kyle Hair of Bellevue, Washington. The five-time world and five-time national champion won his fifth gold medal in June 2000 at the national championships in Orlando, Florida. The most decorated male jump roper in the world has the distinction of also winning speed and freestyle titles while performing with a broken foot. He has won almost every national and world title since 1994. (SLT 9/20/00)

STRENGTH – MEN

Strongest – Man. Jerry Irvine, Mesa, Arizona, who is a world-class weightlifter, has dead lifted (lifting barbells from the floor to the waist) more than 800 pounds. (LDS 4/19/86)

David Y. Chiu, BYU 147th Ward, BYU 11th Stake, won three gold medals for weightlifting — snatch, clean and jerk, and total, at the 1990 Collegiate National Championships. He holds seven Utah state records and has captured three Utah championships in his division. (CN 7/28/90)

After jumping rope for 13 of his 18 years, Kyle Hair retired his world famous rope to serve a 2-year mission.

Strongest Man – Denmark. In 1974, Egon Auerbach won his ninth national weightlifting championship for Denmark. He and his wife, Karen, attended Church at their home ward in Copenhagen, Denmark. (CN 11/9/74)

STRONGEST POWERLIFTERS

1,900 pounds. Steve Denison, Laurelglen Ward, Bakersfield, California Stake, has lifted in the 275 weight class a 705 pound squat, 507 pound bench, and 688 deadlift for a total of 1,900 pounds. He has competed at the Men's

Photo courtesy Steve and Lisa Denison

Steve Denison has deadlifted 688 pounds.

National Powerlifting Championships three times from 1993-95. He also took second at the 1995 nationals held in Baton Rouge, LA. Brother Denison is the California State Chairman for the U.S. Powerlifting Federation, and is a national referee. He and his wife host the Central California Powerlifting Championships each year in Bakersfield. (CN 1/4/92; email)

1,780 pounds. In 2004, David C. Oyler, Arlington Heights 1st Ward, Schaumburg, Illinois, Stake, took first place for the *14th time* in the Natural National Power-lifting Champion-ships in 2004. He set records for the U.S. and the world in his class (age 40 and above) with 716 pounds in the deep squat, a 424-pound bench press, and a 640-pound dead lift for a 1,780-pound total. (CN 3/13/04)

1,480 pounds. Kenneth Lucas Vehikite, 18, placed first in the heavy-weight division of the Indiana State Powerlifting competition. He lifted 550 pounds in the squat, 400 pounds in the bench press, and 530 pounds in the dead lift for a total of 1,480 pounds. He was a member of the Elwood Branch, Indianapolis, Indiana, North Stake. (CN 6/12/93)

1,254 pounds. Glen Crockett, Salem Ward, Roanoke, Virginia, Stake, won the national and world master powerlifting championships during competition in San Bernardino in November 1980. He had a 479.5 pound dead lift and lifted 480 pounds in the squat. He also had a 294.5-pound bench press for a total lift of 1,254 pounds. (CN 11/80)

793 pounds. Harrison Benner, 72, a high priest in the San Diego 8th Ward, San Diego, California, Stake, set four new national records and took first place in the 148 3/4-pound weight class for 70-year-olds and older at the Masters National Drug Free Powerlifting Meet. He set a national squat record at 259 pounds, bench press at 203 1/2 pounds and dead lift at 330 1/2 pounds. His total weight was 793 pounds. The records allowed Brenner to qualify as a national team member and gave him the opportunity to attend the World Master Championships in Sydney, Australia, in 1993. (CN 1/23/93)

Best Bench Press – Senior Men (1991 World Record). Bishop Alfred L. Gonzales, Hawaii, set a world record in 1991 at the 15th Annual Dash World Record Breakers Powerlifting Competition when he bench pressed 231.5 pounds in the 198-pound masters 70-74 age group. He was also the Hawaii State Power lifting champion for his weight and age group. (CN 7/27/91)

Best Weightlifting 114-, 119- and 130-Pound Class. LeGrand Sakamaki, Kilauea 2nd Ward, Hilo Hawaii Stake, won the National Junior Weightlifting Championship in his weight class two years in a row in 1992 and 1993. LeGrand's total in 1992 was 379-1/2, and included a 214-1/4 pound clean and jerk, which won him the title. The following year he scored 438 including a snap of 192 pounds and a clean-and-jerk of 236 pounds.

At the 1995 National Junior Weightlifting Championship in Savannah, Georgia, Brother Sakamaki set a new Junior National record of 242 pounds in the snatch, and cleaned and jerked 292 pounds. The total of 534 pounds was also a national record for the 20-and-under age group. By this time, Sakamaki was in the Ainaola Ward, Hilo, Hawaii, Stake. (CN 4/18/92; CN 7/24/93; CN 4/1/95)

Best Dead Lift – Boys, 17. Seventeen-year-old Quinn Millington, Blackfoot, Idaho, High School, won the national high school powerlifting competition when he dead lifted 545 pounds. (CN 6/5/83)

STRENGTH – WOMEN

Only American to Lift Twice Her Own Weight. In 1999, Melanie Kosoff, Sumner, Washington, was the only American woman who could lift twice her own weight with the clean-and-jerk maneuver. She could thrust 250 pounds. In two years, Melanie had set the American record in the clean and jerk (250 pounds) and the snatch and clean-and-jerk total (424 pounds) in the 117-pound class.

Strongest Female – Dead Lift (1980 World Record). On Jan. 27, 1980, Lorna Griffin broke the world record in the dead lift for the 182 weight class at a competition in Culver City, California, when she lifted 418 pounds.

Photo courtesy Steve and Lisa Denison

Lisa Denison set a world record in the deadlift by picking up 407 pounds off the floor.

Strongest Female – (2003 World Record). In 2003, Lisa Denison, Laurelglen Ward, Bakersfield, California Stake, set three World and U.S. records for the 165 weight class at the Amateur World Powerlifting Congress in Maine. She posted a 440 squat (world record), 192 bench, and 407 deadlift (world record) for a total of 1,039 pounds (world record). (Author's interview)

In 1997, Claire Ashton Heckathorn set new records for the bench press and dead lift at the World Association of Bench Press and Dead Lift Championships in Portland, Oregon. She was also named top woman lifter in the Masters Division. A new grandmother, she is very active in missionary work in the Bothell, Washington, Stake. (CN 2/7/98)

Johanna Workman, Deseret Morning News

Effie Nielson sets a world record for the deadlift by a 90-year-old woman with this 135 pound deadlift. She later appeared on the David Letterman show and did pushups to the standing ovation of Letterman's studio audience.

Strongest Female – 90 Years Old (2002 World Record). On Sept. 21, 2002, Effie Nielson, Wilford 2nd Ward, Salt Lake City, broke three world records at the Nevada Powerlifting Championships in Elko, Nevada. As a 90-year-old, she set age-group world records for the dead lift (135 pounds), squat (80 pounds) and bench press (50 pounds). The 105-pound Effie credits her amazing strength to a life of good clean living, eating her own veggies, drinking a lot of water and chugging down some secret brew of honey and vinegar every day. Aside from being a power lifting world record holder, Sister Nielson is heavily involved with genealogy work and has extracted more than 10,000 names. (CN 9/22/02)

Best Female Athletes – Senior Division.

Betty Vickers, Canyon View, Orem, Utah, 1st Ward, had numerous success at the December 1990 Huntsman World Senior Games in St. George, Utah. Of the 17 events she entered, she won a record 16 medals. Her 17th event, golf, awarded no medals. She won five gold medals in swimming, two gold in tennis, three gold in track, one gold and one silver in racquetball, one silver and one bronze in bowling, and one silver and one bronze in track. (CN 1/12/91)

Laura Downum, Commerce Branch, Joplin, Missouri, Stake, won eight medals at the 1991 Oklahoma Senior Olympics: four gold, three silver, and one bronze. She participated in swimming, horseshoe pitching, bowling, discus, javelin and shot-put in the 60-64 age group. She is also the Oklahoma state powerlifting champion for her age group, and a national masters power lifter. (CN 2/22/92)

RODEO/EQUESTRIAN/JOCKEY

Best Calf Roper.
In 1978, Jim Gladstone won the World's Champion Calf Roping title at the National Finals Rodeo in Oklahoma City. He was one of 15 finalists competing for the title. Over the years, he has won 30 saddles, 30 belt buckles and hundreds of trophies. (CN 3/4/78)

In 1974, Lance Robinson, Farmington 3rd Ward, Farmington, Utah, Stake, was the top calf-roper in the nation when he took first place among 789 competitors from across the United States (CN 9/14/74)

Best Calf Roping, High School.
Edward Kip Bowler, St. George, Utah, 16th Ward, became the National High School Calf Roping Champion in Shawnee, Oklahoma, in January 1991. He competed with 155 calf ropers representing every state in the United States and several provinces of Canada. (CN 1/12/91)

Most Money Won at One Rodeo.
Lewis Feild, Elk Ridge, Nevada, 2nd Ward, won first place in the all-around category at the National Finals Rodeo in 1987, receiving a prize of $140,000.

Brother Feild also set two records in cowboy earnings in 1986 as he won his second Pro Rodeo Cowboys' Association

Just another day at the office for Lewis Feild, one of the most winning riders ever.

Deseret Morning News file photo

Lewis Feild

All-Around Championship and his second World Bareback Championship. His earnings for 1986 totaled $166,042. He won $130,364 in 1985, and won both championships that year as well. (LDS/NV 3/12/88; CN 12/28/86)

Best Bareback Rider. Gary Brogan, Boise, Idaho, 12th Ward, was the national champion in bareback riding at the National Intercollegiate Rodeo Association Finals in 1986. (CN 9/7/86)

Best Horse Jockey. In 1976, George Woolf, Alberta, Canada, was inducted into Canada's horse-racing hall of fame. And with good reason. Woolf won 97 major United States stakes races, including four American classics three times each – the Belmont Futurity, Hollywood Gold Cup, Havre de Grace Handicap and American Derby. He was unsuccessful in nine attempts to win the Kentucky Derby. However,

AP/WIDE WORLD PHOTOS

Historical moment: George Woolf on Seabiscuit (in the lead) races to an upset victory over War Admiral at Pimlico in 1938.

he did win the Preakness, Santa Anita Handicap, Jockey Club Gold Cup, Lawrence Realization, Hopeful Stakes, Hollywood Derby, Hawthorne Gold Cup, Dixie Handicap, and scores more of the top races of his day. The biggest ride of his life came aboard Seabiscuit when he upset Triple Crown winner War Admiral at Pimlico in 1938. He was in such demand that he could get $1,000 in advance plus 10 percent of the purse to ride in stakes races during the Depression years. His mounts included such immortals as Whirlaway, Alsab, Devil Diver, Occupy, Pavot, Kayak 2nd, Stand Pat, Challedon, Bold Venture, Bymeabond, Askmenow, and his favorite mount of all, Seabiscuit. By 1942 he was the leading money-winning jockey in North America. Unfortunately his career and life were cut short when

George Woolf statue at the Santa Anita, Califorinia, racetrack where he died in an accident in 1946.

he was killed while riding Please Me in the fourth race at Santa Anita on Jan. 3, 1946. Weakened from diabetes, he fell from the horse, striking his head and died. A bronze statue honors him at the California track. The George Woolf Memorial award is presented each year to the jockey who best combines riding ability with personal qualities that made Woolf a giant in his profession. (Internet)

Best Cowgirl – Girls, 12. Amy Kathryn McGee, 12, Choctaw Ward, Oklahoma City South Stake, was named all-around cowgirl in the 12-and-under age group of the Miniature Rodeo Cowgirl Association in 1983. She earned the title after performing in 44 rodeos. She won a saddle, a two-horse trailer and three belt buckles. (CN 1983)

Oldest Rodeo Clown in the World (1995 World Record). In 1995, Earl W. Bascom, an 89-year-old high priest in the Apple Valley 4th Ward, Victorville, California, Stake, was honored as the oldest rodeo clown and bull fighter in the world. The organizers of the Rodeo Clown Reunion in Colorado Springs, Colo., presented him with a commemorative belt buckle to honor his distinctive role in the sport. Earl began his clowning in 1931, but started competing in rodeos in 1916.

Brother Bascom was also the first rodeo cowboy inducted into the Sports Hall of Fame at Raymond, Alberta, Canada. His induction came in 1987. In his prime, he was the Bareback and All Around Champion in 1934, setting world records at national and world championships. (CN 10/28/95; LDS 1/88)

Best Equestrian Jumper. Rob Call, 16, Fort Worth 5th Ward, Fort Worth, Texas, Stake, won the world championship in the jumping event at the 1991 American Quarter Horse Association Youth World Show in Tulsa, Oklahoma. He also won the Reserve World Championship in the Hunter Hack event. (CN 1/4/92

Oldest Active Jockey. Thousands of harness-racing enthusiasts know Clarence Hansen as the "Mormon Miler." At 76 years of age (in 1971), Hansen continued to race in about 200 events a year. His largest purse was $15,000. Said Hansen, of the Banning Ward, Palm Springs, California, Stake, "I've won hundreds of races ... if I were 20 years younger and winning races like I used to, I'd be a millionaire!" (CN 1 /2/71)

Horseshoe Toss – Junior Boys Class. Richard Haynes, a teacher in the Raymond 1st Ward, Magrath, Alberta, Stake, became Canada's horseshoe champion for his age group in 1992. He won both the Alberta title and then first place in the Canadian finals. (CN 8/15/92)

Best-Known Farriers. The most well-known LDS horseshoe expert, or "farrier" as they are professionally known, is Lee Green, Yucaipa 3rd Ward, San Bernardino East Stake. In the 1980s, Lee and members of his family traveled some 50,000 miles a year giving seminars, judging and entering contests. Even the Korean Olympic organizers invited the Greens to take care of the horses used in the Games and parades of the Summer Olympics. (LDS 11/23/85)

BOWLING

Perfect 300s – Both Hands. Wally Studer, a dairyman from Rupert, Idaho, in 1984 became only the fourth person in American Bowling Congress records to bowl perfect 300 games with his right and left hands. He is also the only LDS we know of to accomplish this remarkable feat. He bowled a 300 with his right hand prior to an accident that prevented him from using it. He later bowled a 300 with his left hand. (CN 3/25/84)

AUTOMOTIVE/MOTORCYCLES

Most Durable Car (1990 World Record). A 1957 Mercedes-Benz 180D sedan had, by 1990, clocked 1,198,000 miles that have been documented by Mercedes-Benz of North America, a world endurance record. The car has had six or seven owners. Randal K. Aagaard of Salt Lake City obtained the car from Mark S. Glade, also a Utahn who bought the car from a man in Shelton, Washington. It was first recognized as a "long hauler" in 1964 when it became the first car in North America to surpass the million-kilometer mark (about 640,000 miles). (DN 2/21/92)

World Land Speed Records (1950 World Records) Ab Jenkins, born David Abbott "Ab" Jenkins II, in Spanish Fork, Utah, in 1883, has set dozens of world land speed records. In 1927, he set a world record by driving from New York to San Francisco in 76 hours. Eleven times he drove a race car for 24 hours straight without getting out of

Ab Jenkins' famous "Mormon Meteor" set hundreds of records. Pictured here, Ab takes the famous car for a last "spin" before putting it on display at the Utah State capitol.

Photo: Utah State Historical Society

a sitting position. One of his most memorable races was in 1940 when he was mayor of Salt Lake City. Driving his newly designed Mormon Meteor III, he broke all of the world circular records from one to 3,868.14 miles in a 24-hour race. His record for driving one hour was 182.51 mph, and for the 24-hour period he average 161.18 mph. The rest of the world's car makers took more than 50 years to break Brother Jenkins 24-hour average record.

1956: Ab Jenkins takes a glass of milk to celebrate breaking every Class C stock car record up to 24 hours. It was a hot day on the Bonneville Salt Flats – 122 degrees.

On Labor Day, 1950, Jenkins lapped a circular track at 199 miles an hour, breaking 34 more American and world records. The records Jenkins set covered distances from 10 to 10,000 miles. He embarked on his racing career at age 15 (in 1898) when he began racing on his bicycle. He started racing automobiles in 1912, and just kept going. By age 73, Jenkins had broken every American unlimited and Class C endurance record up to 24 hours. Jenkins' Duesenberg cars were built especially for him. Mormon Meteor I set records with its original engine. Mormon Meteor II had a Curtis Conqueror airplane engine for more record-breaking performance. In 1938, Augie Duesenberg designed the Mormon Meteor III, the last car built by the famous auto engineer. The airplane engine was moved to this car, and it went on to become one of the most successful race cars ever. Its last record run was in 1950. (CN 11/15/50; DN 3/16/90; DN 8/29/00)

1938: Roy Faulkner (left), president of Ford Motor Corporation, and Capt. Eddie Rickenbacker (center) present a silver cup to Ab Jenkins to honor his 1933 record-setting 24-hour race on the Salt Flats.

Best Motocross Racer – Woman. Delores "Lorie" Watson, a happily married mother of three and a member of the Tustin 3rd Ward, Orange, California, Stake, won the 1975 national women's motocross championship for 125cc motorcycles. She was ranked an expert in national competition but hadn't amassed more titles because so many races were held on Sunday.

In 1984, Sister Watson, then of the Huntington Beach 4th Ward, Huntington Beach, California, North Stake, won the Women's National Championship in dirt biking in Carlsbad, California, at the age of 37. Proving that age doesn't matter, Watson competed against more than 300 young women, most of whom were aged 18-21 years old, from all over the country. (CN 12/20/75; LDS 3/30/84)

Best Motocross Racer – Boys, 7. In 2000, 7-year-old Tanner Krahenbuhl of the Legacy Ward, Las Vegas, Nevada, Green Valley Stake, became the grand national champion motocross rider in his age group. He won his title on a 51cc motorcycle and recorded the fastest time in the Amateur Motocross Association National Championship Finals at Loretta Lynn's Ranch in Hurricane Mills, Tenn. The competition included racers from across the United States and other countries. Tanner has been racing since he was three years old. (CN 10/7/00)

ROWING

Photo courtesy Richard Jones

Longest Rowing Trip. Richard Jones, a high priest in Sandy, Utah, rowed solo across the Atlantic Ocean in 2000-2001, completing his trip of 4,579 miles on Feb. 20, 2001. At age 57, Brother Jones' 133-day trip also put him into the record books as the oldest man ever to row across an ocean, and the first American to row the entire Atlantic. Jones actually rowed farther than Columbus sailed on his first voyage to the Americas. For more details on his trip, see his entry under "Courage." (www.oceanrowing.com/richard_jones)

Best Rower. Robert Detweiler, Orem 89th Ward, was captain of the Navy's rowing team that went undefeated in the 1952 Helsinki, Finland, Olympics to win the gold medal. He was told about the Church through a team interpreter and, after some 24 years of investigation, was baptized in 1976. (LDS 7/21/84)

CHESS

Best Chess Player – High School Level. In 1995, David James Buck, 17, Normal 1st Ward, Peoria, Illinois, Stake, helped his Illinois Math and Science Academy chess team win first place in a national competition at Chicago. His team won the Illinois state championship a week earlier. (CN 5/20/95)

Highest Ranked United States Chess Champion – Youth Level. Brian Ray Harrow, 12, Willow Creek 5th Ward, Sandy, Utah, was ranked 12th in his age group in 1992. To earn that ranking, Brother Harrow won a string of chess championships that are impressive by any standard. In 1992, he participated in the United States Amateur Chess Team Championship East, where his team won top team 1800-1899 (a ranking scale). He holds three Utah state titles, including 1991 State Elementary Chess Champion, 1991 State Junior High Chess Champion (he won in the sixth grade), and 1991 Utah Scholastic Co-Champion. He was also a runner-up for the 1991 All-American Chess Team. (CN 4/18/92)

Deseret Morning News file photo

Brian Harrow, chess champion

YO-YO

Best Yo-Yo Performer. The best LDS Yo-Yo performer in 1993 was Heather Stoneman, 15. She finished first in the Northwest Regional Yo-Yo Competition, Advanced Division, in Seattle. Not only was Heather the only female competitor, she was also the only person to earn a perfect score. Her prize? A new Yo-Yo. Sister Stoneman was a member of the Spokane 11th Ward, Spokane, Washington, Stake. (CN 12/18/93)

In 2000, Roger Pimentel, Florida, placed 11th in the World Yo-Yo Championship. (CN3/13/04)

LAST MINUTE RECORDS & ENTRIES

David Oyler sets a world record, in his class, by deep squating 716 pounds.

Strongest Father-Son Powerlifting Team. (See page 414) Champion powerlifter David Oyler and his son Michael, both members of the Schaumburg Illinois Stake, became the strongst father-son team in February 2004, after winning a national championship. They earned first place at the Natural Athletes Strength Association where a strict drug-free training program is enforced. This was the 14th time that David has won first place, and the second championship for Michael. In the process of winning, David also set new American and World Master class records for competitors age 40 and above. David lifted 716 pounds in the deep squat, 424 pounds in the bench press, and 640 pounds in the deadlift, for a total of 1,780 pounds. Michael curled 61 pounds, benched 115 pounds, and deadlifted 203 pounds to take first place in the youth division. (CN 3/13/04)

Michael Oyler deadlifted 203 pounds as a competitor in the youth division, taking first place.

24-Hour Marathon. (See page 372) On Feb. 28, 2004, Brazilian runner Sebastian Ferreira da Guia Neta, Rio de Janeiro Andarai Brazil Stake, raced on foot for 121 miles to take first place in the Ultramarathon 24-hour race. Brother Ferreira beat the second-place finisher by more than eight miles. He is a world-class competitor and has traveled the Earth to compete against the world's best. He is a high councilor in his stake. (CN 3/13/04)

Top Ranked in Brazil. (See other "top ranked" musical artists beginning on page 169) Liriel Domiciano, San Paulo, Brazil, at age 22 is one of Brazil's most famous pop artists ever. With a singing voice that brought one conductor to kiss her feet following an exceptionally powerful performance, Sister Domiciano's greatest wish was to perform with the Tabernacle Choir. Her wish came true at April conference in 2004. And she loved it. Back home in San Paulo, her fame spreads. She was on Brazil's version of "American Idol" for eight months, singing offers flood her home constantly, baby girls are named after her, autograph hounds follow her everywhere, talk of a Liriel doll is bantered about, and the two CDs she recorded have sold in the millions. Liriel joined the Church as a teenager, thanks to the persistence of an LDS friend. Her mother and other family members also joined. In an interview with the Church News, she said her life was centered on Christ when she found the Church. "I could see that the only way I would be protected from the things of the world that I didn't

Liriel Domiciano, a popular Brizailian soprano, began singing at age 5, and is world-renowned today.

approve of was to follow His path and to keep His commandments," she said through interpreter Jeanette Oaks. And evidence of that commitment is her Young Women's medallion that she hangs from every necklace that she wears. Fans are noticing and ask, "where can I get such a medallion?" (CN 3/27/04)

Squash Champion – Women. (See page 407 for other LDS racket-sports champions) Leilani Marsh Rorani, Invercargill 1st Branch, Invercargill, New Zealand, became the best LDS women's squash player when she was ranked No. 1 in the world, and went on to prove it (after healing from an injury that year) to win double gold medals for her home country of New Zealand at the 2002 Commonwealth Games in Manchester England. She was competing against players from 72 other nations. Squash is similar to racquetball, and is a very rigorous, tiring game. She and her husband Blair are the parents of a son, Joseph, and she serves in the Primary presidency of her home ward. (CN 3/27/04)

Ranked No. 1 squash player in the world, Leilani Rorani won gold medals in the women's and mixed doubles events.

ABOUT THE AUTHOR

Paul B. Skousen has been slaughtering the English language for 25 years at firms and agencies in New York, Washington, D.C., and downtown Lindon, Utah. His writings have confused corporate executives, senators, congressmen, the CIA, FBI, Ronald Reagan, and George Bush, Sr. – but usually in a good way. He also speaks fluent three-year-old.

He invented a mathematical formula to get something for nothing, published a joke in Reader's Digest, and delivered two babies on purpose.

He holds the record for the longest paper-airplane flight in a BYU ballroom, he built a solar bread baker, he set a 100-yard-dash record in high school, he played the tenor sax in Reno, he made roof trusses by hand, he started a rumor that was published in Time Magazine, he asked Gerald Ford two

Preparing to measure Lee Redmond's world record-setting collection of fingernails in 2003.

loaded questions, he enjoyed a first-name friendship with Ollie North, and he was the subject of Paul Harvey's "The Rest of the Story." He once broke his dog's tail.

He has stood between the paws of the Sphinx, crept inside the Great Pyramids, swam in the Dead Sea, climbed the hill of Calvary, snorkeled in the Caribbean, toured a loaded missile silo, stepped in poo outside of Luxor, walked right past Toronto's Hockey Hall of Fame, got sunburned in Maui, changed the orbit of a spy satellite, mortally wounded a yapping dog in Belgium, got seasick in St. Thomas, test-fired a captured AK-47, wailed at the Wailing Wall, jay-walked in Rome, watched a midnight storm at Nagshead, yelled at a drug smuggler in Tijuana, changed a diaper atop the

White House photos

Paul B. Skousen

"Your secret is safe with me, Mr. President."

"And so is yours, Mr. Bush ...."

"I can beat your rap, Ollie, but it will cost you. Ever hear of the Mormon Church?"

U.S. Senate photo

Comparing sideburns and power ties with U.S. Senator Orrin Hatch in 1979.

World Trade Center, passed a kidney stone, was stung raising honey bees, flew in the President's seat aboard Marine One, ate fondue in Lucerne, peeled off a piece of foil from Apollo 11, climbed inside a smuggled Soviet MiG 21, got caught smooching in Parley's Canyon, confessed to it on live radio, and witnessed his wife writing the first check at the new Nauvoo Temple clothing desk. He once measured the speed of light.

He has shoveled the walks for President Ezra Taft Benson, collected fast offerings from Marvin J. Ashton, and shook the hands of President David O. McKay, Harold B. Lee, Spencer W. Kimball, Ezra T. Benson, Gordon B. Hinckley, and Miss Universe 1984. None will admit having ever met Mr. Skousen.

He and his wife, Kathy Bradshaw Skousen, are the parents of 10 children – all boys except for six girls. For genealogical purposes, she is his fourth cousin twice removed. He was educated at BYU and Georgetown University, is managing editor of Studies Weekly newspapers, and is a high priest trying to do whatever the Bishop asks of him in his South Jordan, Utah, River Ridge 3rd ward.

No hobbies.

Richard Jones holds water-ruined scriptures and tells of his near-drowning during his solo ocean row (shown in back, Jones' yellow, 27-foot, torpedo-shaped boat).

Photos by Paul B. Skousen

The whole gang in 2004 (front, l-r): Joshua, Maryann, Elisabeth; (row 2) Wendy, Julie, Annie; (row 3) Michelle Kennedy, Joe, Boo, Heidi Poulsen Skousen; (row 4) Peter Kennedy, Christian Kennedy, Patricia, Jen Jorgensen Skousen; (top) Benjamin, Jessica Marie, Brittany Wallick Skousen, Paul and Kathy, Jacob.

PHOTO CREDITS

Our sincerest gratitude to these many people for their photographic talents, donations, courtesy and cooperation.

Note: We have endeavored to be as accurate as possible in giving proper credit for all photographs. Please contact us immediately (see preface pages) if a photo was not credited accurately or if there is some other mistake or oversight.

Photos are courtesy of the Associated Press; Ace Anderson; Nate Anderson; Lee Benson; Brigham Young University, Church of Jesus Christ of Latter-day Saints; Church Museum of History; Church News; Brian Crane; Terry Dart; Dennis and Camille DeLoach; Steve and Lisa Denison; Deseret Morning News; Lestor Wire Farnsworth Library, Richard Jones and Theodore Rezvoy; John Goddard; Chris Hicks; Jon and Karen Huntsman; Jerry King; Henry Marsh; Gerald R. Molen, NASA; Lee Nelson, Olson twins; Lialani Parker; Lee Redmond; Crystale Richardson, Dr. Eric N. Skousen; Paul B. Skousen; W. Cleon Skousen; U.S. Library of Congress; University of Utah Medical Center; Utah State Historical Society; Darol Wagstaff; Jack Yerman; The White House; Lestor Farnsworth Wire Museum, and many others.

Index by Name, Achievement or Topic

A

Aaron, April 209
ABA 387
Abel, Elijah 63
A-Bomb 79
Abraham, Isidro 253
Ace, most decorated 74
Acord, Lawrence "Rusty" 21
Acosta, Santos Maria 251
Acuna, Lydia 122
Adams, Katie 122
Adams, Spencer 389
Adolf, Gustaf VI 159
Adolph, Jacob 255
Advertisement, beer 144
Age, over 100 48
Age, over 65 47
Age, over 85 47
Ainge, Danny 386-387
Air Force, best tow 75
Airplane, the first? 359
Airship 335
Alaska, North Slope 232
Aldous, Jay 405
Alexander, Guy B. 316
Ali, Muhammad 154
Allen, Claudia and Steven 55
Allen, Tera Michele 122
Allosaurus 351
Allred, Alma 43
Almond, Bert, Grant, Lyle, Dean, Allen 256
Alo, Ke Aloha May Cody 121
Alquist, John T. 85
Alvarez, Mrs. Concepcion 251
Amarasekara, Bandu Sri 277
Ambassador, Mickey Mouse 139
Ambassador, NATO 132
Ambassador, youngest 132
America's Perfect Couple 125
American Royal Live-stock, Rodeo and Horse
          Show Queen 124
American Young Mother 119
Amundsen, Ron 393
Anderson, Ace 141
Anderson, Alma R. 248
Anderson, Deryk 11
Anderson, Jack 164
Anderson, John Nels 410

Anderson, Joseph 213
Anderson, Nate J. 11
Andre, Dorothy 116
Andrus, Matilda 220
Andrus, Ryan Bowman 370
Animation, Book of Mormon 114
Animation, Mickey Mouse artist 113
Animation, most prolific artist 114
Antonio Jr., Emiliano B. 277
Arave, Helen 58
Archeology 331
    Mummy 333
    Papyri 332
    Pit Tomb 33 333
    Star Stone 331
Archer, Kenneth 377
Archibald, Nolan D. 302
Archivist of the United States 136
Ardmore, Ricky 21
Argentina, Canada de Gomez 46
Argentina, parliament 134
Armenian, oldest 47
Armstrong, Kevin 86
Arnett, Bill 278
Arrhenius, Anders 375
Arrhenius, Nik 374-375
Arrington, Leonard and Harriet 42
Arsenault, Michael 86
Artists, comic books and cartoons 188
    Crane, Brian 189
    Estrada, Ric 188
    Leishman, Ron 189
    Velluto, Sal 190
Asay, Robert 272
Asbell, Scott and Robbie 130
Ashby, Alan 390-391
Ashton, Alan 305, 317
Asija, S. Pal 301
Asper, Frank W. 180
Astronaut, first 199
Astronaut, first in space 199
Athlete of the Year, first Indian 67
Atomic Bomb Testing 80
Atomic bomb, first 79
atomic city 228
Attorney, oldest practicing 327
Audience of Viewers 17
Auerbach, Egon 413
Avery, Peter 398
Ayllon, Raul 23
Azevedo, Lex de 114

B

Babies, first twin test-tube 55
Babies, most in one delivery 51
Baby, first born in Congress 134
Baby, first test-tube 55
Baby, heaviest 49
Bachman, Randy 174
Bagger, fastest groceries 32
Bailey, Tory 372
Bainson, Samuel Eko 64
Baird, Amy 321
Baker, Tiffani 122
Balderas, Eduardo 257
Ballantyne, Richard 90
Ballard, Melvin Joseph 276
Ballard, Suzanne 119
Ballard, Suzanne Webb 120
Balloon, fastest 30
Balloon, highest flight 19
Balloon, largest release 14
Balloon, most inflated 22
Balog, Justin 403
Baptism 250
  oldest 250
Baptisms, 251
  Above Arctic Circle 251
  Bangladesh 254
  Bolivia 251
  Cambodia 251
  Chile 253
  Convert Baptisms 255
  Corsica 251
  England 252
  First Arab Baptized in Jerusalem 254
  First Mongol (of ancient Asian Mongols) 254
  First Moslem 254
  For the dead 255
  Jamaica 254
  Kosrae 253
  Longest Investigation 256
  Malaysia 251
  Most by an Individual 255
  Most Generations 256
  Most Ordinances – Individual 255
  Mother-Daughter 256
  Newfoundland 253
  Oldest Married Couple 256
  Persian Gulf 253
  Russia 251
  Same Font 255
  Siberia 252
  Spain 253
  Stake Missionary 255
  Stretcher, baptized on a 254
  Thailand 252
Baptist, John the 270
Baptized, first Cherokee 67
Baptized, oldest Indians 66
Barker, E. Wiley 35
Barker, Ryan and Merilee 112
Barkley, Vice President Alben W. 161
Barnes, Suzanne 110
Barney, Delbart 245-246
Barson, Brent 271
Barson, H. John and Joan 271
Barson, Julie 271
Barty, Billy 48, 106
Bascom, Earl W. 419
Baseball, major leagues 389
Basketball, largest league 388
Basketball, nonstop game 387
Bassett, Melinda 298
Bastian, Bruce 305, 317
Bataan Death March 73
Bateman, Marv 385
Bates, Kent 85
Baton Twirler 400
Battalion, Mormon 77
Baxter, Tiffani 122
Baxter, Laura 123
Beagley, Bithen C. 177
Beagley, George J. 223
Beaton, Katherine 404
Beck, Glenn 196
Beehives, longest continuously-meeting 239
Beesley, Evengeline Thomas 180
Begay, Nora 121
Beisemeyer, Bill 316
Bell, Lily McLead 365
Bell, Martha 256
Bell, Terrence 295
Bell, Wade 366-368
Bement, Linda 98, 118, 120
Bemis, Melanie 373
Benans, Hilda 63, 277
Benner, Harrison 414
Bennett, William H. 218
Benson, Ezra Taft 29, 83, 130, 217, 265, 269
Benson, Reed 156
Bergant, Leon 406
Bergeson, F. W. (Bill) 118
Bergman, Venessa 397
Bestor, John 374
Beuhner, Alice 119
Bice, Mike 126
Bicycle, BMX 406
Bicycle, longest trip to church 406
Bicycle, stationary 406

Bicycle, trip across the U.S. 406
Bicycle, trip around the world 405
Bigler, Henry 352
Bigney, Hugh 130
Bill, oldest paid - medical 28
Bill, oldest paid - transportation 28
Binks, Amanda 47
Bird, most important 95
Birds, most popular 43
Birk, Nicole 370
Births, arithmetic progresson 54
Births, most multi-generational 55
Bishop 222
  All-Brother Bishopric 222
  Blind 223
  Father-son 223
  First 222
  Longest Serving 224
  Most Brothers 224
  Most Father-Son 224
  Oldest 223
  Same Wedding Date 223
  Youngest 223
Bishop, first Indian 66
Black Belt 403
Black Hole 331
Black Panther 65
Black, Carolyn Diane 263
Blackburn, Manasseh Julius 222
Blackwell, Sandy 124
Blake, Brian 174
BLM Director 133
Blocker, Dan 108
Blunt, Erin 366
Bluth, Don 114
Bodyguards, world's best 358
Bohne, Richard 387
Bolingborke, Robert A. 305
Bomber, the Candy 72
Bonnell, Barry 390-391
Bonneville Productions 195
Book of Commandments 355
Book of Mormon 142, 145, 148
  Advertisement 149
  Blank Paper 151
  Book of the Month Club 145
  Broadcast 149
  Family-to-Family Placement 146
  Greatest Number Distributed 146
  In Space 147
  Japanese, in Braille 148
  Marathon Reading 149
  Modern Mormon Alphabet 150
  Most Influential Books 146
  Printings 145
  Quickest Read 149
  Quote on a Stamp 149
  Titanic, aboard the 147
  Typesetter 149
  World Trade Center 148
Book of Mormon, Copies to Famous People 152
  Adolf, Gustaf VI (King of Sweden) 159
  Barkley, Alben W. (U.S. vice president) 161
  Buthelezi, Mangosuthu G. (Zulu leader) 160
  Churchill, Winston (British statesman) 157
  Edinburgh, Duke of (England) 161
  Fleming, Peggy (ice skater) 160
  Frederik IX (King of Denmark) 162
  Jackson, Jesse (Civil rights leader) 160
  Kennedy, John F. (U.S. president) 155
  Kennedy, Ted (U.S. senator) 153
  Khrushchev, Nikita (Soviet Union premier) 156
  King, Coretta Scott (Mrs. Martin Luther King) 159
  Lincoln, Abraham (U.S. president) 152
  Oldest Living Person 154
  Paul II, Pope John (Catholic Pope) 154
  Peron, Juan D. (Argentina president) 161
  Pius XII, Pope (Catholic Pope) 154
  President, first U.S. 152
  Presley, Elvis ("King" of Rock and Roll) 158
  Queen Elizabeth (England) 157
  Queen Juliana (Netherlands) 161
  Queen Salote (Tonga) 162
  Queen Sirikit (Thailand) 157
  Queen Sophia (Spain) 160
  Queen Victoria (England) 153
  Reagan, Ronald (U.S. president) 153
  Schweitzer, Dr. Albert (famous humanitarian) 160
  Thatcher, Margaret (England prime minister) 157
  Tolstoy, Leo (Russian novelist) 158
  Trueba, Andres Martinex (Uruguay) 161
  Twain, Mark (American humorist) 155
  York, Sgt. Alvin C. (WWI hero) 159
Book of Mormon, Hawaiian 355
Book Signings 144
Book, fastest selling 32
Boone, James R. 84
Booth, Kathryn 242
Borglum, John Gutzon 191
Bosco, Robbie 382, 384
Bountiful Tabernacle 227
Bow hunt 37
Bowen, Bart 397
Bowen, Marsha 123
Bowler, Edward Kip 417
Bowling 420
Box, cereal 190
Boxing, featherweight 394
Boxing, Golden Gloves and Everlast 394
Boxing, heavyweight 392
Boxing, junior middleweight 393
Boxing, middleweight 393

Boxing, most knockouts 393
Boxing, welterweight 394
Boy Scouts 257
Boycott 113, 241
Bozeman, Miki 398
Bradey, Glen L. 196
Bradley, Annette 49
Bradley, Shawn 48-49
Brady, Pat and Julee 125
Brady, Rodney H. 86
Braithwaite, Brett 84
Branch President, longest serving 224
Branch President, oldest 224
Branch, expansive 225
Branch, highest 225
Branch, oldest 227
Branch, secret 228
Branch, West Point 73
Brannan, Sam 89, 353
Brassfield, Eugene and G. Gary 223
Braun, Wernher von 117
Brazil, congressman 135
Brewer, John C. 378
Bricks 352
Bricks, fired-clay 353
Bridge, balsa wood 337
Bridger, Jim 90
Bringhurst, William 344
Brinkman, Curt 377
Brocka, Lino O. 277
Brogan, Gary 418
Brothers, shortest 49
Brower, Thomas Taylor 255
Brown, Charles family 118
Brown, Eddie F. 65
Brown, Edwin S. 246
Brown, James E. 42
Brown, Jennifer 42
Brown, Susan 120
Browne, Dinah 409
Browning, John Moses 312
Browning, Jonathan 312
Brunson Burners 175
Brunson, Arlon, Deron, Geynor and Raland 175
Bryson, Amy 319
Buchanan, Bay 133
Bucher, Jan 409
Buck, David James 423
Buckwalter, Mark 403
Bud, Janet K. 119
Buehler, David 301
Bug Collection 12
Burdick, Max 375
Burnett, Chad 366
Burns, Violet Gibson 33
Burtenshaw, Frances Davis 120

Burton, Michael J. 398
Bus Trip, longest 34
Bushnell, Nolan 314
Business, First Department Store 292
Business, research profits 292
Buswell, Ashton 402
Buthelezi, Mangosuthu G. 160
Butler, Audria 41
Butler, Brennon Jack 317
Butler, Jodi 110
BYU 318
    Admitted, youngest 320
    Alumnus, oldest 319
    Cougars 321
    Dance Team, best college 321
    Dancers 15
    Debate Champs, first 321
    Facts & Feats 317
    Graduate, oldest 318
    Graduate, youngest 319
    Mountain emblem, largest 319
    Professor, first female 320
    Registration, first touch-tone 322
    Student-Body President, first female 321
BYU-Idaho 321

C

Cabanillas, Demetrio 371
Caillard, Ginette 251
Call, Brandon 271
Call, Laura 271
Call, Leland 240
Call, Ora O. and family 118
Call, Rob 419
Camp Floyd 78
Campbell, Tracy 30
Canada, cabinet minister 134
Candy Bars 40
Cane, most important wooden 351
Cannon, George Q. 255
Cannon, Hugh J. 214
Cannon, John K. 69
Captain Canuck (comic book) 189
Car Dealership 16
Car, most durable 420
Card, Largest Christmas 217
Card, Orson Scott 105, 114, 144
Cards, most birthday 23
Cards, most hand-delivered 24
Carlile, Jessie 41
Carlisle, Robert 33
Carson, Craig 85
Carter, G. Ronald 255

Carter, Terri 407
Carter, William 89
Cartoon Collection 16
Cartwright, Ron 411
Cartwright, Sharli 297
Casper, Mrs. Billy 120
Cat, heaviest 43
Catmull, Edwin 115
Cavanaugh, Marie and George 304
Cave, Cache 346
Cave, Kartchner Caverns State Park 346
Cederlog, Tammy 122
Census, 2000, of Utah 45
Chandran, Mr. and Mrs. K. Peter 251
Chantry, Bertha Kohler 240
Chapel, first Indian 66
Chapel, highest altitude 225
Chapel, last with an outhouse, U.S. 230
Chapel, oldest Florida 227
Chapel, oldest in U.S. 227
Chapel, oldest Southeast U.S. 228
Chapel, ship for a roof 230
Chapel, with a museum 231
Chapels/Wards/Branches, first in 234
    Bahamas 234
    China 234
    East Germany 234
    England 234
    Fiji Islands 234
    Idaho 234
    Japan 235
    Nauvoo 235
    Northwest, U.S. 235
    Peru 235
    Poland 235
    Rome 236
    South America 235
    Spain 236
    Tver, Russia 236
    Uruguay 236
Chaplain, first Navy 76
Chaplain, first VFW 75
Cheerleader, 398
Cheney, Christy Ann 123
Cheney, Douglas J. and Jeffrey W. 280
Chess 423
Chess, longest non-stop game 33
Chicken, largest 42
Children, most in one family 56
Chiu, David Y. 413
Choir, Mormon Tabernacle 175
Choir, Vienna Boys 176
Chorister, longest serving 177
Chorister, youngest 176
Christensen, Bruce L. 303
Christensen, James C. 187

Christensen, Krege B. 374
Christensen, Lyda G. 177
Christensen, Von E. 30
Christmas, first 96
Church College of Hawaii 386
Church, Flora M. 177
Church, The LDS 211
    Auxiliary and Other Roles 236
    Baptism 250
    Busiest Church 212
    Business and Real Estate 290
    Chapels 227
    Converts, first in ... 251
    Family Home Evening 265
    Fasting 258
    Frequency, people joining 211
    Genealogy 262
    General Conference 266
    Home Teaching 245
    International Roots 211
    LDS Temples 281
    Membership 211
    Membership worldwide 212
    Membership, fastest growing area 212
    Membership, U.S. 212
    Missionary tools 278
    Missionary work 270
    Ordinances 247
    Prophets, General Authorities 213
    Relief Society 240
    Religion, newest major 212
    Seminary 242
    Stakes 220
    Structures 281
    Structures, other 287
    Wards & Bishops 222
    Welfare System 259
    Where the Saints Meet 232
    Young Women 242
Churchill, Sir Winston 157
Cinema, Best Picture 101
Cinematographer 101
City, youngest population 50
Clark, Addison 35
Clark, Barney and Una Loy 338
Clark, Cal 372
Clark, Lamar 393
Clark, Marvin Ezra 245
Clark, Mr. and Mrs. Robert A. 256
Clark, Russell 29
Clark, Steven 342
Clarke, Cam 115
Clarke, Kathleen Burton 133
Clarke, Robert 102
Clawson, Dal 101
Clayson, Jane 111

Clayton, William 315
Cleaver, Eldredge 65
Clegg, Milton C. 75
Clemmer, Janice White 67
Clerk, oldest financial 237
Clerks 236
    Francis, Roy E., long serving 236
    McDonald, Rich, long serving 236
    Perrett, Henry Austin, long serving 236
    Thatcher, F. Dennis 237
Climber, speed 412
Clinger, Charlie 372
Clock, oldest 29
Clothing, modest prom dresses 126
Coburn, Richard 56
Colburn, Levi 404
Cole, Tina 108
Coleman, A. Ralph 406
Collectibles 355
    Book, most paid for 355
    Book, rarest 355
    Clothing, most expensive 358
    Gold Piece (coin) 357
    Pistols, Joseph Smith's 358
    Ring, Joseph Smith's finger 356
    Sculpture 357
    Seal, wax 356
    Signatures 356
Combs, Ray 110
Comely, Richard 189
Comic Books and Artists 188
Commute, longest 35
Condie, Richard P. 179
Conductor, youngest and oldest 240
Congress, most LDS 131
Connors, James 176
Conrad, Clarence W. and Darwin 335
Conveyor Belt, Human 12
Cook, Melvin A. 13, 312
Cook, Roger 280
Cookbooks, best selling 40
Cookie, largest 37
Cookies, most 38
Cookies, puzzle 41
Coolbrith, Ina 144
Cooper, Bob 398
Corbett, Irene Colvin 147
Cornucopia 17
Correa, Ley 178
Cosic, Kresimir 135, 363-364
Cougarettes, BYU 321
County, youngest population 50
Couple, longest wed 46
Courage 199
    Adventuresome 201
    Astronaut, closest call 200

Astronaut, first 199
Astronaut, first in space 199
Bravest Man 206
Drowned, longest 208
Fatal Disability 208
Forgiveness 209
Lifesaving Youths 207
Row the Atlantic 203
Space Shuttle commander 200
Wilderness Survival 207
Covalt, Susan 404
Covington, Tamber Marie 396
Cow, largest 42
Cowdery, Oliver 237, 270
Cowgirl 419
Cowley, Samuel P. 206
Cox, Lora 256
Cracker Jacks 40
Crane, Brian 189
Crapo, Micah 32
Crawford, Carl 223
Cricket, Mormon 95
Criers, Town 138
Crockett, Glen 414
Cross, Denise and John 52
Crow, Thomas Few 257
Crozler, Kate 66
Crum, Sister Randy 339
Cruz, Roberto A. 134
Cummings, Paul 367, 369
Cunningham, Francisco Vical 246
Curtis, Keene 117
Curtis, Reuben E. 70
Cushman, Renee S. 231
Cutler, Harold H. 223

D

D'Arc, James 103
Dabbs, Jerry 410
Daines, Gladys D. 137
Dalbey, Troy 363, 395
Dalton, Clark Golden 176
Dalton, Jennifer Ann 391
Dance Festival 128
Dance, "Star Search" champion 25
Dance, Ballroom 129
Dance, Ballroom – senior division 129
Dance, Clogging 130
Dance, Disco 129
Dance, Highland 130
Dardall, Eugene 239
Dash, 100-meter 365
Dash, 100-yard 365

Dash, 400-meter 365
Daut, Michael and Laura 54
Davidson, Charles 317
Davidson, Margaret Olson 47
Davis, Kim 271
Davis, Pete 251
Davis, Troy 378
Day, Laraine 101
Daynes, Joseph J. 179
Decathlon 375
DeLoach, Camille 404
DeMille, Abner Monroe 248
Demille, Cecil B. 104
Dempsey, Jack 392
Denison, Lisa 416
Denison, Steve 413
Dennis, Neleh 112
Dental, military 75
Dentistry 341
    Dentist, first female 341
    Dentist, first male 341
    Rinse And Spit, abolished! 341
Derby, national soap box 31
Deseret Industries 20
Detmer, Ty 382
Detweiler, Robert 422
Devine, Paul 125
DeVoto, Bernard 143
DeVries, William 338
DeWaal, Matt 405
Diamonds, world's first man-made 309
Dickson, Carol Lyn 122
Didra, Adam H. 43
Dilworth, Mary J. 295
Dinosaurs 348
    "Dinosaur Jim" Jensen 348
    Bone Collection, largest in the world 349
    Cancer 349
    Egg 350
    Footprints, oldest 351
    Largest in the world 349
    Mascot 351
    Named after an Apostle 350
    Pelvic bones, biggest in the world 349
Discus Throw 374
Distance, traveled at sea 36
Dittemore, Ron 201
Doan, Phuong-Anh 124
Dobyns, John 272
Dodd, April Aaron 209
Dodge, Delos 53
Dodge, Delos Allred and Allice Ann Allred 56
Dodson, John 239
Dog Tags 75
Dog-sled race 410
Dolo, Gideon 275

Domiciano, Liriel 425
Done, Richard and Eva 11
Downum, Laura 417
Drabble (comic strip) 189
Drawings 21
Drill Team 399
Drowning Survivor 208
Dunn, Marc 385
Durham, L. Marsdan 72
Durrant, Devin 387
Dutra, Almir S. 223
Dutson, Deborah 123

E

Eakin, James C., Edgar Leroy, Edgar Leroy Jr. 240
Earl, Marion 327
Earnest, Sandra 119
East, Franklin T. 73
Easter, J.C. 258
Edgson, Laura Lee 402
Edinburgh, Duke of 161
Education 295
    Educator, outstanding 297
    Graduate, youngest in CSU 296
    Graduate, youngest with honors 296
    Graduation, quickest 296
    Honor Student, youngest 296
    Learning Disabled, outstanding teacher of 297
    Perfect SAT and ACT Scores. 295
    Schoolhouse, first 295
    Secretary of Education 295
    Student, youngest in Brazil 297
    Summe Cum Laude, first female at Harvard
        Law 297
    Valedictorian, first blind 297
Edwards, Lavell 378
Edwards, Lavell, with Ronald Reagan 385
Eisenhower, Dwight D. 265
Elder, first black 63
Elector, youngest 131
Eliason, Karine 40
Elizabeth, Queen 157
Emmy 116
Endowment 247
    100 Million 247
    Milestones 248
    Most, individual 248
    Most, one day at SLC Temple 249
    Most, one year 248
    Most, Stake 248
    Most, Ward 249
    Non-English 250
    Old Endowment House 249
    Oldest 249

Engineering, first Indian woman graduate 67
Ennis, Phil 404
Erekson, Manfred H. 329
Erickson, Orlando 47
Esank, Blake 410
Estrada, Ric 188
Evans, Brent R. 190
Evans, Richard L. 180
Evertsen, Dirk 246
Executives 302
    American Motors 303
    Black & Decker 302
    Clorox 305
    General Mills 303
    Huntsman Corporation 304
    JetBlue Airways 306
    Kodak 302
    Marriott Corporation 303
    Mrs. Cavanaugh's Candies 304
    National Press Club Chairman 302
    PBS – Public Broadcasting System 303
    Sorensen Companies 306
    Swift Transportation 307
    WordPerfect Corporation 305
Explosion, largest 13
Explosives, inventor of slurry 312
Extermination Order 139
Eyestone, Ed 371
Eyring, Henry 300

F

Facsimile No. 1 332
Factories, first sugar beet 94
Fagan, Kevin 189
Faifekau 279
Fairbanks, Avard 192
Falkner, Rees A. 83
Fall, farthest 37
Families, most 49
Family, education and size 50
Family, largest combined 57
Family, largest living 54
FamilySearch.org. 262
Fan, fanatical football 24
Farm, Peter Whitmer 267
Farnsworth, Philo T. 193, 307
Farrell, Mike 117
Farriers 420
Fass, Timothy 343
Fast meeting 258
    First 258
    Nationwide 258
Fast Offering, longest collection route 239
Fatafitah, Rahman 254

Fatafitah, Sa'aik and Maher 254
Faylor, Nichole and Nathan 51
Feild, Lewis 417
Fence, fastest construction 32
Ferguson, Helaman 300
Ferrell, Scott J. 296
Fichtner, Christy 121
Filbo, Jose Feitosa de Andrade 297
Finch, Art 85
Fingernails, longest 60
Firearms 312
Firefighter, U.S. administrator 137
Fish 11
Fish, largest 43
Fisher, Kris 396
Fisher, Steve 82
Flag, Arizona 28
Flag, highest 25
Flag, highest flying 27
Flag, largest 27
Flag, largest display 26
Flag, Los Angeles. 28
Flag, most recognized 25
Flag, most recognized proxy 26
Fleming, Peggy 160
Fleming, Rhonda 106
Fletcher, Harvey 309, 319
Fletcher, James C. 330
Fletcher, Lorena Chipman 121
Flier, fastest civilian 31
Flier, highest 19
Flooded, most 344
Flores, B.J. 394
Flu 267
Fong, Shirley 122
Food storage, largest fine paid with 327
Football League, Canadian 381
Ford, President Gerald R. 42, 154
Forsey, Paul 144
Forsyth, Janene 123
Fowers, David 131
Fraughton, Edward J. 191
Frederik IX 162
Freeman, Joseph Jr. 64
Freestone, George Elton 81
French Horn 176
Frustaci, Samuel and Patti Oragenson 51
Fu, Wu Rung 254
Fugal, Lavina 121
Fullmer, Gene 393
Fullmer, Nate 334
Funk, Donald A. 238
Funk, Michelle 208
Furniss, Mike 33
Future Homemakers of America 123

G

Gable, Meagan 373
Gaines, Ambrose "Rowdy", IV 396
Galilee, arrest on Sea of 327
Game Show 110
   First LDS announcer 110
   First LDS host 110
   Most money won 110
Garage Sale 229
Gardner, Archibald D. 263
Gardner, Norm and Carol 271
Gardner, Rulon 361
Gardner, Ruth 271
Garn, Daniel 139
Garn, Jake 147, 199, 274
Garner, Mary Field 219
Garth, Vic 138
Gates, Carole B. 119
Gathering, largest 13
Gatorwolfe, Steven 401
Geary, Anthony 116
Gee, Clendon and Erma 237
Gemeron, Maria Van 251
Genealogy 262
   Advertising, best 263
   Extractor, youngest 263
   Family Line, longest 265
   Internet, largest on the 262
   Library, largest 263
   Name Extracted, most - stake 265
   Name Extraction – Milestone 264
   Names Extracted, most - individual 263
   Names Submitted, most - individual 263
   Names, most on record 262
   Names, youngest to reach 5,000 names 263
   Storage vault, largest 264
General Authority, first Asian 62
General Authority, first Black 63
General Authority, first hijacked 218
General Authority, first Indian 66
General Authority, first to fly 218
General Conference 266
   Cancellation, first 267
   First 266
   First from Conference Center 268
   Internet 267
   Last in Tabernacle 268
   Microphone, first 266
   Milestones 266
   Nomination, first presidential 268
   Power Outage 270
   Radio Broadcast, first 266
   Sermon, shortest 269
   Speaker, youngest 269
   Speech While Seated 268
   Telecast Beyond North America 267
   Televised, first 266
   Temple, from a 268
   Warmest and coldest 269
   Water, first on 267
   Weather 269
General Conference Talk, foreign language 216
General Conference, in Russian 216
General Conference, sports score 268
Gent, Robert R. 375
Geographic Bee, National 298
George, Richard 375
Gerrard, Connie 136
Gibbons, Dianna Lyn 20
Gilbert, John 102
Gilbert, Kent 62
Gill, Gurcharan S. 222
Gladstone, Jim 417
Glider, farthest soar 35
Goddard, John 12, 19, 31, 201
Going, Sid 386
Gold rush 352
Golf 406
   Cash Prize, largest 407
   Champs, youngest 407
   LPGA, first LDS woman 407
   NCAA Champions 406
   Score, lowest 407
Gomez, Nicholas Santucho, Canada de 250
Gonzales, Alfred L. 415
Goodman, Robert 75
Goodyear, Miles 324
Gospel Doctrine teacher, longest serving 240
Gott, Jim 390
Gottfredson, Floyd 113
Gottsche, Srilaksana 252
Granite Mountain Records Vault 262
Grant, Heber J. 59, 218
Grant, Heber J. (first radio broadcast) 195
Grant, Heber J. at the Hill Cumorah 345
Grant, Lucy 270
Graves, WWII, most dedicated 73
Gray, Reed 301
Grebe, Craig 397
Greco, Mary Ordway 263
Green, Lee 420
Greeting, Largest Happy Birthday 217
Griffin, Lorna 374-375, 415
Griggs, C. Wilfred 333
Grigsby, E. Peter and family 118
Gritz, Bo 76
Grover, Wayne C. 136
Grow, Lisa 297

Grow, Raymond and Roger 239
Guitar, electric 311
Gundlach, Heinz 273
Gunn, Tina 388
Gustafsson, Bo 376

H

Haeder, Judy Gerrard 136
Hair, Kyle 413
Hair, longest 58
Hair, most cut 22
Hakala, Eddie 67
Hale Center Theaters 128
Hale, Ruth and Nathan 128
Halford, Shawna 367
Hall, Helen John 67
Hall, Mark and Robin 272
Hall, Tracy 309
Halliday, Bryan and Ryan 54
Halvorsen, Gail 72
Hamblin, Becki 401
Hamburgers, most consumed 20
Hamilton, Keith 63
Hammer Throw 375
Hancock, Dorothy R., Mildred, Mary, Sylvia,
     Juneth 238
Hands Across America 96
Handwriting 58
Hang Glider Pilot 25
Hanks, Corinne 57
Hansen, Clarence 419
Hansen, Elisa and Lisa 342
Hansen, Florence 168
Hansen, Jared 373
Hansen, Jeff 299
Hansen, Kellie 124
Hansen, Laurie and John 52
Hansen, Leah Christiansen 186
Hansen, Luella Bybee 406
Harding, Edith B. 177
Harding, Rep. Ralph R. 155
Harmon, Appleton Milo 315
Harmon, Carlyle 314
Haroldsen, Kedra 299
Harper, Brittany Lynn 124
Harrow, Brian Ray 423
Hart, C. Monroe 69
Harvard Law School 67
Harvey, Kristine Rayola 121
Harward, Nevada 40
Hasberg, Andrew 252
Hastings, Loyal D. 279
Hatch, Senator Orrin 153

Hawkes, Sharlene Wells (see: Wells, Sharlene) 26
Hawkins, Paula and Gene 137
Haycock, D. Arthur 215
Haymond, Creed 360, 364
Haynes, Richard 419
Health, best in U.S. 61
Hearing aid, world's first 309
Heckathorn, Claire Ashton 416
Heidenreich, David 86
Heinz, William F. 276
Heisman Trophy 382
Hemi, Vicki 121
Henderson, Jesika 122
Henderson, Nathan and Richard 54
Henderson, Sidney R. and Joyce 271
Hess, Jeremy 392
Heywood, Jim 25
Heywood, Regie 372
Hickman, Tracy 145
Higbee, Drew 337
High jump 372
High Jump, best in Argentina 372
High jump, by a hearing impaired person 373
High Priest, oldest/longest 222
High Priests, oldest and youngest 222
Hiking, oldest 412
Hill Cumorah 345
Hills, Dennis L., Garth A., Lee R., Farrell J. 224
Hilton, Bob 110
Hinckley, Gordon B. 217
Hing-June, Shum 265
Hinton, Kirsten and Rob 52
Historian, longest serving 237
Hitchcock, Alfred 103
Hitchhiker 24
Ho, Robert 402
Hoberg, Bengt 239
Hoeger, Chris 409
Hoeger, Werner W. K. 409
Holbrook, Marjorie H. 318
Holidays, Pioneer 95
Hollingsworth, Becky 123
Holman, Mike 410
Holmes, Janet Ann 253
Holmes, Willard R. 21
Holmgren, Mike 378
Home Front series 197
Home teaching 245
     Companionship, longest-paired 246
     Families visited, most in shortest time 245
     Route, longest 247
     Service as, longest 247
     Visited 100 percent, by a companionship 246
     Visited 100 percent, by a High Priests' Group 246
     Visited 100 percent, by a ward 246
     Visited 100 percent, by an individual 245

Homefront series 116
Homeowners, highest percentage in U.S. 290
Hoope, Edward W. 296
Horne, Grant 177
Horne, Natalie 58
Horseshoe Toss 419
House, oldest in Utah 288
Household, largest 50
Households, fewest unmarried 50
Households, most 50
Hovenden, Amy 320
Howells, William 276
Huber, Clayton S. 328-329
Hughes, Howard 31, 358
Hughes, Stephanie 40
Hughes, Vilda Mauss 52
Hulme, Phil 34
Human, 5-billionth 57
Hunsaker, Lynn 123
Hunsaker, T. Earl 252
Hunt, Becky 388
Hunter, Howard W. 213, 268
Huntsman, Jon 304
Hurdles (track event) 366
Hurst, Bruce 390
Hurtado, Wilfredo Rojas 277
Husbands, best 62
Hutchins, Colleen Kay 120

I

Ice Cream, consumption 39
Ice, most cracked 402
Indian Placement Program, first person 67
Indian tribe, Catawba 68
Indian, highest political office 65
Instruments, most played 23
Interior, Secretary of 133
Inventions 307
    Brake system, anti-lock 316
    Dialysis Breakthrough 310
    Diamonds, first man-made 309
    Diapers, first disposable 314
    Explosives, slurry 312
    Games, first computer 314
    Guitar, first electric 311
    Guns, world's best 312
    Hearing Aid 309
    Invention, Dog Gone Garbage Bags 317
    Invention, licking bubbles 317
    Invention, most expensive 317
    Mannequins 316
    Monitor, first SIDS 316
    Music, stereo 309
    Odometer 315
    Skinfolds measurement 316
    Software, WordPerfect 317
    Steel, chromium and stainless 315
    TD Nickel 316
    Television 307
    Toys, Wheelo 315
    Traffic Light, first 307
    Treadmill, cardiac-testing 314
    Woodworking, first T-square for 316
Iorg, Dane 390
Iorg, Garth 390
IQ, highest 60
Iron Curtain 175
Irrigation 351
Irvine, Jerry 413
Ivins, Anthony W. 275

J

Jack, Tarra and Tomara 54
Jackson, Elizabeth 370
Jackson, Jesse 160
Jacob, LaDawn Anderson 120
Jacobs, Clarence 319
Jacobs, Elmer 319
Jail, shortest sentence 327
Japan, expensive real estate 290
Jarvik, Robert K. 338
Jarvis, Howard 139
Jarvis, Olive 256
Javelin Throw 375
Jenkins, Ab 373, 420
Jenkins, Randy 36
Jennings, Ken 110
Jensen, "Dinosaur" Jim 349
Jensen, Gary 24
Jensen, Kimberly Ann 123
Jensen, Larry 251
JETS, singing group 56, 175
JETTS17, singing group 56
Jewkes, Delos 104
Jockey, horse 418
Johnson, Jennifer 389
Johnson, Maureen 55
Johnson, Mike 376
Johnson, Shannon 55
Johnson, Tina 123
Johnson, V.O. "Johnny" 73
Johnson, Vernon S. 23
Joke, most widely circulated 97
Jonathan, Don Leo 401
Jones, Bill 96
Jones, Daniel W. 275

Jones, Raymond F. 145
Jones, Richard 198, 203, 422
Jones, Stanley 13
Jones, Wiley C. 275
Jorgensen, Gaylon 371
Jorgensen, John Henry 21
Josephson, Marba C. 59
Joslin, Dea Ann 396
Joyner, Wally 390
Judicial 327
Juliana, Queen 161
Jump Rope 413

K

Kan, Yue-Sai 17
Karate 403
Katseanes, Kristopher G. 388
Keith, Donnie and Darren 54
Kekanakailokookoaihana, Solomon 34
Keller, Margaret McPherson 241
Kelsch, Jodie K. 49
Kelsch, Kim 55
Kelsch, Renee 49
Kemp, Gary F. 35
Kennedy, David 132-133
Kennedy, Pres. John F. 155
Kennedy, Senator Ted 153
Keola, Debbie 16
Kerper, Martin 278
Kha, Le Van 258
Khrushchev, Nikata 156
Kick Line 12
Kidney machine, artificial 310
Killebrew, Harmon 389, 391
Kimball, Heber C. 248, 276
Kimball, Spencer W. 83, 215
King, Ann 123
King, Lindsay Brooke 123
King, Coretta Scott 159
Kirkham, Don 301
Kitashima, Mervlyn 120
Kitchens, Todd 280
Kite, Greg 386
Kite, highest 19
Kluit, Gerritt and Corri 231
Knight, Amanda Inez 270
Knight, Gladys 171
Knight, Ray 390
Knockwood, Freeman 66
Knot Tying, fastest 31
Knotts, Hilda 256
Koford, Jim 116
Kohler, Bertha 238

Kolob Arch 345
Komatsu, Adney Y. 62
Konyushenko, Oleg 401
Kosoff, Melanie 415
Krahenbuhl, Tanner 422
KSL 20, 182
Kuka, Jared 126
Kunalan, Canagasabai 364, 366
Kunz, Dr. Phillip, and Jay 19
Kuoha, Sam Alama 402
Kuresa, Iofipo R. 136

L

Labor, Department of 134
Lady of the Year 119
Lambert, James Cannon 284
Lamoreaux, Lenora Huntsman 54
Lanesen, Sheri 370
Laneson, Craig 370
Languages, most 76
Languages, most known 21
Lansing, Joi 107
Lap Sit 12
Largo, Mrs. Charlie 66
Larsen, Clint 372
Larson, Derilyn 271
Larson, Glen 106
Larson, Kyle 271
Las Vegas 344
Lavulite 345
Law School Graduate, first Indian, BYU 67
Law Student, first BYU Black 63
Law, Vance 390
Law, Vernon and Vance, father-son all-stars 391
LDS.org 267
Leaders, political 130
Leavitt, Michael 130
LeBaron, Homer M. 302
Lee, Benjamin 297
Lee, George P. 66, 68
Lee, Gregory L. and Susan 76
Lee, Rex 273, 327
Leishman, Ron 189
Leman, Homer 365
Lemmon, Capt. Robert H. 36
Lemperle, John 316
Lettermen (singing group) 174
Levi, Ezra 129
Library, Family History 263
Lincoln, Abraham 152
Lind, Don 147, 200
Lind, Don, sacrament in space 257
Lindlof, Johan M. and Alma 251

Lindner, Cheryl 241
Lindsay, Julee 406
Load, largest - modern 16
Load, largest - pioneer 13
Loayza, Norman 343
Long Jump, running 373
Long Jump, standing 373
Lookingland, Michael 107
Lopez, Danny 394
Lott, Tiffany 366, 376
Loudest Mormons 59
Lowe, George H., III 412
Lucia, Connie Della 124
Ludwig, Mark 286
Luge, winter Olympics event 409
Lund, Andrea 125
Lund, Lori 412
Lundmark, Kenneth 372
Lungren, Benjamin 337
Lungs, best in the world 57
Lynch, Liz 368
Lyon, Joseph 340

M

Maass, Josephine 35
Machir, Ryan 181
Magleby, McRay 187
Mahoney, Jenny 241
Mahoney, Krista 400
Malin, Staci 396
Maloy, Thelma 238
Man, oldest 46
Man, shortest 48
Man, tallest 48
Mann, Ralph 366
Mannova, Michaela 370
Mansilla, Enrique 277
Manuia, Jayson 407
Marathon 372
Marathon, Boston, wheelchair division 377
Marathon, Days of '47 371
Mariteragi, Garff and Ura Tehoiri 53
Marksman 35
Marquardt, George W. 79
Marriages, LDS have better 50
Marriott Jr, J. Willard 326
Marriott, J. Willard 265, 303
Marsh, Henry 369
Marsh, LuJean Taggart 184
Martin, Tony 109
Martinez, Maria 249
Martins, Helvica 63
Martins, Marcus H. 63

Martyr, first 219
Matis, Nadine Thomas 120
Matusow, Harvey Job 315
Mauss, Vinal Grant 52
Mayer, Mike and Joe 108
Mayor, Nauvoo 139
McAfee, James 326
McBride, Tanya 61
McCabe, Rose 121
McCreary, Craig E. 328
McCune, Matthew 275
McDaniel, James William 90
McDonald, Lyle M. 318
McGee, Amy Kathryn 419
McHenry, Eric Scott 57
McKay, David O. 164, 213-214, 323, 345
McKenna, Wendy 120
McKenna, Wendy Goodrich 119
McKim, Vance 87
McKinley, Brent 144
McKinnon, Tanya 124
McOmber, Douglas 132
McQuade, Kristin 373
Medical 338
    Cancer, skin and lip 341
    Heart transplant, first among family 339
    Heart valve, longest running artificial 339
    Heart, first artificial 338
    Kidney transplants, "firsts and onlys" 339
    Nuclear bomb testing, cancer among LDS 340
    Penicillin 340
    Word of Wisdom 340
Medical Practice 342
    Burn Victim, most persistent 343
    Injections 343
    March of Dimes 343
    Student, youngest medical 343
    Surgery, pre-natal 342
    Twins, head-conjoined 342
Meeks, Melynie and Tom 52
Meeting places, north and south 232
    Alaska's North Slope 232
    Chile, Puntas Arenas Branch 233
    Inuvik Branch 232
    Kotzebue, Alaska 232
    McMurdo Station, Antarctica, 233
    North Pole Ward 232
    Thule Air Base 232
    Trondheim, Norway 233
Meik, James P. 275
Melrose, Beverly 41
Memmot, Bob and Connie 57
Memory, superlative 58
Menlove, Amy 375
Mercer, Lavinia Webber 253
Merrill, Kieth 115

Merrill, Susan 124
Mertes, Lori 373
Mexico, Tecalco Stake 221
MIA, longest serving leader 237
Mibey, Kip 57
Mickelson, Ken 337
Microfilming 262
Mile, fastest run 367
Miles, driven accident free 20
Miles, Vera 85
Military 68
Military March, longest 77
Military, first married couple enlistees 76
Military, Highest Ranking 69
Milk Drinkers 40
Milkshake, largest 39
Mill, first flour 94
Millennial Star 261
Miller, Dean L. 208
Miller, Johnny 407
Miller, Judie Boyd 39
Miller, Larry H. 16
Millet, Lillian 263
Millington, Quinn 415
Millman, Neil 24
Mills, Byron G. 85
Miss All-American Cheerleader 124
Miss America 120
Miss American Honey Queen 125
Miss Black U.S.A. Scholarship Pageant 123
Miss Cambodia 122
Miss Cheerleader U.S.A. 124
Miss Chinatown U.S.A. 122
Miss Dance/Drill International 124
Miss Gorgeous Eyes 123
Miss Indian America 121
Miss Indian World 121
Miss La Petite 123
Miss National Contact Lens 125
Miss Navajo 121
Miss New Zealand 121
Miss Pioneer (Days of '47 Queen) 122
Miss Rodeo America 124
Miss Rodeo Queen 124
Miss Teen USA 122
Miss U.S. Latina 122
Miss U.S.A. 121
Miss Universe 118
Miss Universe, Non-American 119
Mission President, first black 64
Mission, first among blacks 64
Missionaries, first black 63
Missionaries, first from Western Africa 64
Missionaries, first to 274
   Argentina 276
   Brazil 276

Fiji 275
France 276
Great Britain 276
India 275
Mexico 275
Newfoundland 274
Pacific 275
Poland 274
Missionaries, unusual companionships 280
Missionary Tools 278
   Boat 279
   Flags 279
   Hamster 278
   Helicopter 278
   Mules and Horses 278
   Phantom Jet 279
   Ship 280
   Taxi Cab 278
   Yacht 279
Missionary Work 270
   Bike-Riding Mission President 273
   Calls in foreign tongue 271
   Discourse, first 270
   Elder, first use of 270
   Foreign, first 271
   Frugal 273
   Full-Time missions, most 271
   Handcart 271
   Hearing-impaired 273
   Heart recipient 272
   Iron Curtain 274
   Lightning 272
   Mission, most international 272
   Missionaries, most brother-sister sets - ward 272
   Missionaries, most in one family 271
   Missionary Couple, youngest 272
   Missionary, first 270
   Missionary, first Sister 270
   Most Missionaries, same time/place/family 272
   Percentage, highest - ward 272
   Reagan, Ronald 274
   Supreme Court Case 273
   Temple Riders 274
Missionary, first from 275
   Bolivia 277
   Japan 277
   Peru 277
   Philippines 277
   South Africa 277
   Sri Lanka 277
   Swaziland 277
   Tonga 275
   Uruguay 276
Missionary, first South African 63
Mitchell, Hal 384
Miyashiro, Ron 223

Moikeha family 271
Molen, Gerald R. 100
Moles, Dorothy Elaine 67
Money, most for a toy design 21
Montesquieu Prize 302
Montgomery, Rollan, Leland, Anthon, Faunt 222
Montierth, Amy 123
Moon, Judy 39
Moon, Mormons who put men on the 328
　Engineer 328
　Flight Surgeon 330
　Food 329
　Slurped in Space 328
　Tooling 329
Moore, Terry 31, 107, 359
Moorman, Esther 141
Moral, Mario Robles del 82
Mormann, Jackson F. 141
Mormon Battalion 77
Mormon Cricket 95
Mormon Island 344
Mormon Meteor 420
Mormon Trail, deaths 94
Mormon, Book of (see Book of Mormon) 142
Mormon, Book of, longest movie quote 103
Mormons and Cancer 341
Morris, George Q 216
Morris, Jack 390-391
Morrison, Cherrie 55
Motocross 422
Mount Everest 411
Mount Joseph Smith, a.k.a. Mt. Palomar 344
Movie Stars 99
Movie, first feature length 100
Movies, And Should We Die 112
Movies, It's A Wonderful Life 102
Movies, Nielsen Ratings 109
Movies, The Ten Commandments 104
Mower, riding - longest ride 34
Moyes, Jerry 307
Mr. America 125
Mr. Clean 126
Mr. Natural America 125
Mr. Olympia 125
Mr. U.S.A. National "Natural" Body Builder 126
Mr. Universe 125
Mrs. America 119
Mrs. International U.S.A. 119
Mrs. National U.S.A 119
Mrs. U.S.A. 119
Ms. United Nations 124
Mt. Palomar, a.k.a. Mt. Joseph Smith 344
Murakami, Toshio 277
Murphy, Dale 390-391
Murray, James 265
Murray, LaRue Cottle 321

Music 169
　Album, first Gold 170
　Album, first Platinum 169
　Brass Ensemble 175
　Guitar in Carnegie 178
　Musical Group, first 170
　Orchestra, first 171
　Organist, national league baseball 176
　Pianist, youngest 178
　Polkas 178
　Singing soloist, profesional football 176
　Single, fastest-selling 175
　Ward Choir, oldest 177

N

Naegle, John C. 272
Nakhirunkanok, Porntip 119
Name, longest last 34
Names, LDS 140
NASA 330
Nash, Mark 400
Nauvoo Temple, burned 286
NBA 387
Nebaur, Alexander 341
Nebeker, Vern L. 221
Needlework, most 41
Neeleman, David 306
Neely, Lillian Lyedella Stanley 67
Neely, Shirley Ann 67
Neilsen, Norman L. 126
Nelson, Craig 406
Nelson, Lee 37
Nemelka, Dick 387
Newell, Gregory J. 132
Newspaper, first English 167
NFL Head Coach 378
Niagara Falls, only man to stop the 336
Nibley, Hugh 59
Nicholas, Michael 269
Nielson, Albert 339
Nielson, Effie 416
Nielson, Larry 411
Nielson, Mabel Field 47
NIT basket ball tournament 388
Nuclear attack relocation plan 79
Nugent, Victor 254
Nyborg, Keith Foote 134

O

Olivera, Jose 253
Olsen, Merlin 108, 384

Olympic athletes and medal winners 362
Olympic Winter Games (2002) 17, 116, 364
Opera, youngest singer 176
Orellrana, Ricardo Garcia 253
Organist, most enduring 177
Organist, youngest 177
Orr, Kevin and Damon 54
Orton, George 411
Orullian, LaRae 88
Orullian, Venus Aposhian 47
Osako, Kei 84
Osborn, Kristyn, Kelsi, and Kassidy 169
Osborne, Mark 403
Oscar 115
Osipo Somaray family 271
Osmond family, Hollywood Star 106
Osmond family, music careers 172
Osmond family, television movie 109
Osmond, Marie 112
Ottesen, Ronald G. 28
Outland Trophy 384
Oyler, David C. 414, 424
Oyler, Michael 424

P

Pack, Keena 299
Packard, A. Lisle 28
Packard, Ron 132
Packer, Newell and Eleanor Foxall 237
Padilla, Doug 367-368, 370-371
Page Jr., A. Curtis 274
Page, Kim and Kent 49
Pageant, Hill Cumorah 128
Pageants 118
Pageants, least expensive gown 125
Painter, fantasy 187
Painting, deepest traveled 186
Painting, heaviest 187
Pakistan, Islamabad Branch, Asia Area 84
Parachute Jumper, oldest female 28
Parade, largest 13
Parcell, Jan Gladene 124
Parker, Ed 158, 243, 403
Parker, Linda 261
Parks, Bert 127
Partridge, Edward 222
Partridge, Ernest 319
Party, oldest birthday 29
Pasquali, Paul 178
Passmor, Jared 373
Patriarch 257
Patterson, Myra Tolman 263
Paulson, John M. and Elsie 56

Pearce, Brad 407
Pearl of Great Price, papyri 332
Pedraja, Carlos 277
Pee Wee Miss of America 123
Pimentel, Roger 423
Pen and Pencil 11
Periodicals 162
    Children's Friend 162
    Improvement Era 163
    Relief Society Bulletin 162
Peron, Juan D. 161
Perpetual Emigration Fund 28
Perry, Anne 143
Perry, L. Tom 59, 270
Persistent, most 228
Peru, Cuzco 46
Peters, Mary 41
Peterson, Catherine Cryer 120
Peterson, Chesley 74
Peterson, Ester Eggertsen 134
Peterson, Joshua J. 85
Peterson, Lezla 366
Peterson, Peter and Celestia Terry 46
Peterson, Ronald M. 302
Peterson, Vilah 39
Phelps, Cynthia 175
Phillips, Earlet 124
Phillips, John 25
Photography 183
Pi, algorithm to calculate 300
Pickles (comic strip) 189
Pie, largest 38
Pierce, Walter Hugh 139
Pilcher, Annie Starling 35
Pillsbury Bake-off 39
Pilot, fast female 31
Pilot, hang glider 25
Pilot, oldest commercial 28
Pilots, Top Gun 76
Pincock, Norman W. 330
Pinegar, Maureen 39
Pioneers 88
Pioneers, first company in Salt Lake 88
Pioneers, first half-acre plowed 89
Pioneers, last handcart company 91
Pioneers, longest sea voyage 89
Pious XII, Pope 154
Poet Laureate 144
Pole Sit, longest 33
Pole Vault 374
polio immunizations 343
Polk, Randy 345
Pollei, Steven K. 84
Polo, Dumisane 394
Polynesian Center 129
Poole, Harold 73

Pope, Paula Meyers 363-364
Porter, David 408
Porter, Lezlie Noel 119
Porter, Roger 136
Post Office, Axtell, Utah 293
Postage Stamps 165
   Artist, U.S. stamp 166
   Cancellation 166
   Dempsey, Jack 165
   Farnsworth, Philo T. 165
   Olympics 166
   Seagull Monument 165
   Sesquicentennial 166
   Symbols of the Early Pioneers 166
   Tabernacle Choir 165
Postal Service 133
Poster, most widely known 187
Poulsen, Michael and Shauna 55
Praita 279
Pratt, Addison 275
Pratt, Helaman 275
Pratt, Orson 218, 271, 315, 336
Pratt, Ray L. 276
Presley, Elvis 158, 243
Prettiest Schoolgirl 125
Price, Vincent 104
Priest, Baker 133
Priesthood, aerial meeting 238
Priesthood, extended to blacks 64
Priesthood, first to receive Aaronic 237
Priesthood, most generations ordained 240
Primary, first 91
Primary, longest in 239
Prince, W. Wayne 82
Prison Warden 139
Prisoners, most LDS 97
Pro Wrestler 401
Projectors, largest users of 16
Publishing 143
   Columnists 164
   Hymn Book, earliest 164
   Longest published publication 163
   Printing Press, largest 163
   Printing Press, oldest 163
   Scripture, newest 163
Pugh, Troy Jens 86
Pukui, Mary Kawena 302
Pulitzer, first 143
Puppies, nation's "first" 42
Purnell, Kenneth 31
Putts, Roland 178
Pyrah, Jason 367, 369

Q

Quadruplets 52
Quanda, James 327
Quarterback, NFL 380
Quechua 286
Queen's Guards 76
Quilt, most traveled 41
Quinton, Wayne E. 310, 314
Quintuplets 51

R

Radio 195
   Broadcasting station, first 195
   Network, world's largest radio 196
   Radio Spot, most famous 195
   Talk show host, largest audience 196
Radio Broadcast 230
Radio broadcast, first long-distance stereo 335
Radio broadcast, first satellite 335
Radio, first broadcast 334
Railroad, first transcontinental 93
Rambova, Natacha 105
Rampas, Encarnacion Banares 46, 250
Ramsey, Lewis A. 187
Ramsey, Ralph 193
Rannells, Shirley 397
Rat Fink 186
Reader, fastest 61
Reader, most prolific 59
Readers, largest audience of 15
Reagan, Ronald 153, 385
Real Estate 138, 291
   Church building, most expensive 291
   Most Expensive Temple 291
   Outbidding Billionaires 292
   Parcel, largest 291
   Parcel, most expensive 291
Records, how to submit 5, 7
Redmond, Lee 60
Reeder, Cindy 368
Reese, Fred 81
Reid, Rose Marie 127
Reid, Tori 386
Republican Party, national chairman 137
Restaurants, largest chain 15
Revolt, taxpayer 139
Rey, Alvino 311
Reynolds, Alice Louise 320
Rhodes, Heidi 404
Rial, Francisco Guillermo 276

Rich, Richard 114
Richards, Alma W. 362, 372, 375
Richards, Franklin D. 216
Richards, Kathleen 297
Richards, Kristin 394
Richards, Mrs. Reed H. 119
Richards, Richard 137
Ricks College (now BYU-Idaho) 321
Ricks, Eldon 73
Riding-Mower, longest ride 34
Rifle 312
Roberts, E. L. 412
Roberts, Eugene L. 321
Roberts, Fred 386
Robertson, William Cass 250
Robinson, David A. 247
Robinson, Lance 417
Robinson, Rosetta B. 319
Rocks and the Earth 345
    Adam-ondi-Ahman 347
    Arch, largest 345
    Cave, historic LDS 346
    Cave, most secret ... until now 346
    Gem 345
    Hole, most significant 345
    Stone, most significant 345
Rockwell, Orrin Porter 327
Rodeo Clown 419
Roderick, Lee 302
Rogers, Aurelia Spencer 91
Rogers, Russell L. 199
Rohatinsky, Joshua 370
Romney, George W. 303
Rooney, Terry 136
Roping, calf 417
Roroni, Leilani Marsh 425
Ros, Oun 122
Rose, Lori 263
Ross, Kathy 176
Ross, Milton H. 58
Roth, Ed "Big Daddy" 186
Routson, Samuel Aaron 317
Rowing 422
Rowland, Grace 237
Rozier, Dick 372
Ruesch, Chad 272
Rules 6
Run, 1,000/1,500/3,000-Meter 368
Run, 1,600-Meter Relay 367
Run, 5,000/10,000-meter 371
Run, 800-Meter/800-yard 366
Run, one mile 367
Run, two mile 368
Ryan, Colleen 244
Ryan, Jeffrey 84

S

S.S. Flying Cloud 280
Sacrament 257
    Airborne Cup Delivery 258
    bread delivery, most consistent 258
    Group, largest served to 257
    Space, first served in 257
    Vietnam 258
Sadler, Arthur 81
Sahim, Duad 275
Saitoh, Yuki 173
Sakamaki, LeGrand 415
Salisbury, Sean 381
Salote, Queen 162
Salt Lake Temple, attacked 286
Salvioli, Rafael 246
Samoa, national legislative assembly 136
Sampson-Davis, Benjamin Crosby 64
San Bernardino, California 344
Sanborn, Mabel Y. 219
Sanders, Col. Harland 14
Sanderson, Cael 364, 401
Sandwich, longest 37
Santucho, Nicholas 46
Sasaki, Arnold 60, 320
Saunders, Alma Olly 396
Schettler, Cornelius Daniel 178
Schiffman, Derek 86
Schindler, Emil A. J. 276
Schlappi, Michael 377
Schultz, Karen 124
Schuster family 256
Schweitzer, Dr. Albert 160
Science Fiction 144
Scott, Doris 129
Scott, Larry 125
Scott, Richard G. 216
Scott, Russell C. 406
Scout, first 81
Scout, oldest 81
Scouting 81
Scouting Award, highest, Spain 82
Scouting, Cub Scout World Athletic Champs 86
Scouting, Disney's "Follow Me, Boys" 85
Scouting, first troop 82
Scouting, Fuji Scout Award 84
Scouting, Girl Scouts 87
Scouting, Girl Scouts President 88
Scouting, highest camp 86
Scouting, highest Cub Scout leader 86
Scouting, highest medal 82
Scouting, largest encampment 86

Scouting, Most Eagle Scouts 84
Scouting, most merit badges 85
Scouting, most Wolf electives 87
Scouting, Rover Badge 84
Scouting, youngest Eagle scout 86
Scouting, youngest to earn all merit badges 85
Scouts, Explorer President 84
Scouts, first Indian to earn Eagle 68
Scouts, Japan Jamboree 83
Scouts, national director 83
Scowcroft, Brent 130-131, 136
Sculpture Art 190
    Angel Moroni 194
    Eagle Gate 193
    Fraughton, Ed 192
    Mormon Battalion figure 192
    Mount Rushmore 191
    Presidential Medallion 191
    Statue, Brigham Young 193
    Sunstones 190
    Wood 193
Seamstress, most prolific 41
Searfoss, Richard A. 200
Seargeant, Tracy 298
Searle, Jennifer and Scott 52
Sears, Jane 363
Sease, Chester 83
Secretary of State, Assistant 132
Selkirk, Minnie 28
Sell, Bertha 276
Seminary 242
    Elvis Presley 243
    England, first graduate 245
    First 242
    First Seminary Teacher and Class 243
    International 242
    Korea 245
    Mortuary 243
    Prison 244
    Reunions 244
Seminary, most twins 53
Senator, first 131
Senator, first woman 132
Service-Minded, most 97
Sessions, Thomas 351
Settlements 292
Severson, Christopher 87
Sewing, largest project 41
sexes, male-female ratio 61
Shaang, Francis Cheung King 251
Shamy, Aaron 412
Shaw, Wayne T. 49
SheDaisy 169
Sheets, Elijah 224
Sheffield, Charlotte 121
Shields, Budd 397

Shingleton, Wendy 410
Ships, S.S. Brigham Young 70
Ships, S.S. Joseph Smith 71
Ships, USS Utah 71
Shock, electrical 37
Shorthand, fastest 30
Shot Put 375
Shotguns 313
Shrubs, oldest 326
Shumway, Janae and Bruce 54
Sieger, Ralph 176
Silvester, Jay 374
Simons, Claude 248
Simper, Jonathan 339
Singer, major-league soloist 25
Singing, longest continuous 141
Sirikit, Queen 157
Size, greatest difference in couple 49
Skateboarding 411
Skiing, blind skier 410
Skiing, longest forward somersault 408
Skiing, water 410
Skinner, Gloria 33
Skousen, Ben 293
Skousen, Brent W. 311
Skousen, David C. 331
Skousen, Eric N. 344
Skousen, Jewel A. 311
Skousen, Joe 293
Skousen, Kathleen 311
Skousen, Kathy Bradshaw 97
Skousen, Patricia 97
Skousen, Paul B. 5, 353, 424
Skousen, Rita 345
Skousen, W. Cleon 143, 165, 320, 327
Skylab 334
Sleeping Bag 18
Smith, Aaron 296
Smith, Craig 280
Smith, Eldred G. 228
Smith, George Albert 214
Smith, Jesse N. 221
Smith, Jessie Evans 171
Smith, Joseph 237, 268, 326
Smith, Joseph, only photograph? 184
Smith, Merrett 183
Smith, Milan D. 221
Smith, Paul 245
Smith, Samuel F. 221
Smith, Samuel H. 270
Smokey the Bear 137
Smoot, Reed 103, 131
Sneed, Woodrow Blaine 67
Snelgrove, Laird 318
Snider, Ernest L. 246
Snoopy 181

Snow, Stephen J. 75
Social Security Number 36
Solicitor General, U.S. 327
Sophia, Queen 160
Sorenson, James 306
Souter, Steve 31
South Africa, town council 136
Souza, Maria Margarida de 251
Space shuttle 27
Spaulding, Teresa 48
Speed Records, automobile 420
Spellers, One Ward 300
Spelling Bee, National 299
Spencer, Amy 342
Spjute, Rex 25
Sports 361
  Automotive/Motorcycles 420
  Baseball/Softball 389
  Basketball 386
  Bowling 420
  Boxing 392
  Chess 423
  Cycling 405
  Dog Sled Race 410
  Field Events 374
  Football 378
  Golf 406
  Gymnastics 400
  High Jump/Long Jump 372
  Hiking 412
  Jump Rope 413
  Martial Arts 402
  Mountain Climbing 411
  Olympics 362
  One Mile Run 367
  Paralympics 376
  Rodeo/Equestrian/Jockey 417
  Rowing 422
  Rugby 386
  School Spirit 398
  Skating 411
  Skiing 408
  Skiing, water 410
  Softball, Little League 391
  Surfing 398
  Swimming/Diving 395
  Tennis 407
  Track 364
  Volleyball 394
  Weightlifting/Strength 413
  Wheaties Box Heroes 364
  Wrestling 401
  YO-YO 423
Sputnik, first LDS to hear 331
Stained Glass 195
Stake, first among blacks 64

Stanliff, Mrs. Luett J. 254
Stapley, Effie 241
Stapp, Curtis C. 21
State, most livable 61
State, youngest population 50
Steele family 130
Steeplechase 370
Stewart, Harold and Vera 271
Stewart, Howard 334
Stewart, James Z. 275
Stewart, Jimmy 103
Stimpson, Joseph H. 74
Stoddard, Henry H. 221
Stone, Mike 33
Stoneman, Heather 423
Stoof, Reinhold 276
Stradling, Gary 301
Strasers, Robert 73
Stratford Sr., Eldredge Wayne 340
Strongest, men 413
Strongest, women 415
Structure, Utah's first 287
Studer, Wally 420
Study Group, longest continuously-meeting 239
Stum, Robert W. 101
Submarine, Salt Lake City 72
Subscriptions, most 24
Summers, Nathan 296
Sunday School 354
Sunday School, first 90
Sunday School, longest serving teacher 240
Sunflower, tallest 326
Sunstone 357
Super Bowl 362
Superintendent, youngest 239
Superman 188
Supersaurus 349
Sutter's Mill 352
Swain, Mark 107
Swann, Alexandra 296
Swanson, Connie Jean 139
Sweat, Steve 85
Swenson, Paul and David 26
Swimsuit competition 126
Swimsuits, most beautiful 127
Swimsuits, ugliest 127
Swing, largest wooden 293

T

Tabernacle Choir 178, 335
  "Mormon" Voice 180
  Audience, largest live 180
  Audience, largest televised 178

Broadcast, longest 181
Conductor, dog 181
Conductor, oldest 179
Conductor, youngest 181
Gold albums 178
Grammy 178
Member, oldest 180
Organ Players 179
Organ, Tabernacle 182
Soviet Visitors 183
Tribute to a Conductor 179
Tabernacle, first 288
Tabernacle, Salt Lake 288
Dome 288
First Structural Change 290
Organ 289
Tahquette, Nellie Lucille Burgess 67
Taim, Olev 136
Talker, loudest 59
Talker, quickest 59
Talksdorf, Charles Lon 58
Tamani, Saimoni 365
Tanner, Kristen 122
Tanner, Mary Richards 237
Tanner, Nathan Eldon 134, 350
Tanner, Robert 33
Tarasov, Afanasy Ivanovich 154
Tate, Sheri 119
Taylor, Ray N. 279
Taylor, Samuel W. 102
Teacher, longest-serving Gospel Doctrine 240
Teacher, oldest 238
Teeter-Totter, longest nonstop ride 33
Telegraph, first 92
Telephone number, the best in D.C. 359
Telescope, earliest LDS 336
Telescope, location of world's largest 344
Television, "Peanuts" 115
Television, aerobics 111
Television, Disney Sunday Movie 113
Television, documentary 112
Television, game show 110
Television, game-show announcer 110
Television, game-show host 110
Television, Homefront series 108
Television, I Love Lucy Show 108
Television, largest contract 111
Television, longest-running commercial 110
Television, morning show host 111
Television, soap character 110
Television, stupid human tricks 112
Television, The Last Leaf 109
Television, The Survivor 112
Television, world's first 307
Temple, Nauvoo 247, 286
Temple, Nuku'alofa Tonga 249

Temples 281
All Continents 283
Ancient Language 286
Asia 283
Attack 286
Busiest 281
Dedicated by One Man 284
Destroyed by fire, Samoa 287
Farthest North 283
First (and only?) Baby Born in a Temple 285
First in Europe 283
First Wed in Los Angeles Temple 285
First Wed in Swiss Temple 285
First Wed In the Salt Lake Temple 284
Iron Curtain 282
Largest 281
Longest Wait 282
Most Dedicated in Shortest Time 282
Most Viewed 281
One Administration 283
Site Rejections 283
Youngest in a ground-breaking 286
Tenney, Allyson 119
Tennis 407
Thaler, David 301
Thanksgiving, first 95
Thatcher, James W. 176
Thatcher, Prime Minister Margaret 157
Thinkers 298
Agriculture 302
Best Spellers 298
Chemistry 300
Hawaiian Language 302
Mathematics 300
National Geographic Bee 298
Nintendo Player 299
Physics 301
Political Thinking 302
Software 301
Soil 301
Weeds 301
Thomas, Dian, do it yourselfer 140
Thomas, Elaine 122
Thompson, B.J. 137
Thompson, Elbert O. 341
Thompson, Janie 174
Thompson, John 386
Tilleman, Karl 388
Timbimboo, Moroni 66
Time Capsule 354
Timpanogos Mountain 412
Toilet Flush 15
Tolstoy, Leo 158
Toone, Jared 86
Torgan, Moroni Bing 135
Torp, Velma Mauss 52

Torvosaurus tanneri (a dinosaur) 350
Tourists, most to a Temple 22
Tower, tallest 20
Towhid-Ul-Alam 254
Town Criers 138
Toy, the "Wheelo" 315
Train Ride, boring 214
Trash, from the White House 353
Treasurer, United States 133
Trees 322
   "Mormon" Desert Tree 324
   Cabin, oldest log 324
   David O. McKay Oak 323
   Lone Cedar Tree. 322
   Oldest 323
   Russian Olive, largest 324
   Trees planted, most 324
   Violin Trees 324
Triathlon 375
Triple Jump 373
Triplets, first in Tahiti 53
Triplets, longest surviving 52
Tripp, Ryan 34
Trottier, Douglas, Darrell, Liena, Lisa 256
Trueba, Andres Martinex 161
Tucker, Jana 375
Tulips 326
Tumbling 400
Turkey Cook 40
Turnbull, Mary 256
Tuttle, Theodore 25
Twain, Mark 155
Twins 53
Twins, most born in shortest time 54
Twins, most in family 53
Twins, most in Stake Presidency 53
Twins, most in ward 54
Twins, oldest 47
Twins, oldest male-female 47
Tyler, Lorraine 260
Typing, fastest 30
Typing, longest continuous 33

U

U.S. Post Office 263
Udall, Stewart 133
Udy, Marvin J. 315
Ugliest Man contest 126
Underwood, Louis W. 237
Unicycle, longest ride 34
University of Utah 295
University, largest private in U.S. 317
Utah, census figures 45
Utah State Prison 244

V

Valentine, Rose Ellen 341
Valentino, Rudolph 105
Van Atta, Dale 164
Vatale, Dennis 342
vaults 264
Vehikite, Kenneth Lucas 414
Velluto, Sal 190
Vickers, Betty 417
Victoria, Queen 153
Video games, world's first 314
Vidmar, Peter 363, 400
Vienna Boys Choir 176
Villamor, Vincent 185
Villesenor, Atanasia 250
Violist 175
Visiting Teaching, largest route 241
Visiting Teaching, longest 100 percent, ward 241
Visiting Teaching, longest 100% individual 241
Visitors, most to Temple Square 23
Visitors, museum 24

W

Waddell, Mary McAllister 284
Wagstaff, Darol 408
Waldholtz, Enid Greene 134
Walk, 50-kilometer 376
Walk, fastest across U.S. 376
Walk, longest 35
Walker, Paul 101
Walker, Robert 107
Walker, Sid L. 38
Walker, Steven 373
Wall, largest Mormon 354
Wallace, RaNelle 343
Wallace, Todd 299
Wallentine, Van Ness, Max, Robert, C. Booth 224
Walter & Hayes Band 175
Walters, Jacob 86
Walton, Dean 33
Wang, Shu-Hwa 373
Ward, international 229
Ward, most divided 226
Ward, most mobile 226
Ward, smallest 225
Wardle, Lucy 397
Wards, oldest 226
Waring, Fred 179
Water Skiing, barefoot 410
Water Speed Records 410
Watson, Delores "Lorie" 422

Watson, Margo 119
Watt, Andrew K. 316
Watt, George Darling 252
Weichers, Gregory 86
Weirich, Matthew 37
Weiss, Penelope 39
Welch, Chad, Richard, Matthew, Jason, Justin 256
Welch, Jolene and Jeff 52
Welfare 259
    Animals 260
    Apricots project, largest 262
    Canning, largest 259
    Cleanup, largest 260
    Food Budget, lowest 260
    Grape project, largest 262
    Olympic Winter Games 260
    Orchard project, largest 260
    Penguins 261
    Ronald Reagan 259
    Service project, largest 259
    Valuable Find at DI 261
Welfare, Dutch help Germans 261
Wells, Gary 76
Wells, Rulon S. 276
Wells, Sharlene (married: Hawkes) 26, 140
West, Mrs. Marion W. 177
Weston, Ryan 400
Westover, Madeline 40
What E'er Thou Art, Act Well Thy Part 346
Wheaties 364
Wheelchair basketball champion 377
Wheelchair, athletes 377
Wheelchair, marathon 378
Wheelie, longest 33
Whitaker, Johnny 107
White, Danny 380
White, Maurice 275
White, Robert Ensign 296
Whitehead, Leroy 53
Whitesides, Leanne 371
Whitmore, Kay R. 302
Whitney, Trish 297
Wigglesworth, Ted 256
Wiglesworth, Kelly 112
Wildcat, Bobette Kay 121
Wiley, Paris 316
Wilkey, Merle 223
Wilkins, Reg 184
Wilkinson, Ernest L. 320
Willes, Mark H. 303
Willes, William 275
Williams, James M. 298
Williams, K.C. 22
Willison, Brenda 138
Wilson, David 86
Wimbledon 407

Winder, Barbara 241
Winder, Carol 39
Windmill, home sweet home 231
Windsor, Marie 107
Winn, Marion and Erma 46
Wire, Lester Farnsworth 307
Wolfe, Deborah 119
Wolfgramm, Maikeli and Vake 56
Wolverton, Dave 144
Woman, oldest 46
Woman, tallest 48
Women, first to vote 134
Women's organization, largest 240
Woodbury, Robert P. 247
Woods, T. George 82
Wooley, Fannie 270
Woolf, George 418
Word, the only "Mormon" 166
Work Ethic 136
Worker, oldest 29
World record, first in sports 364
World War II 185
World's Majorette Queen 124
Wray, Fay 107
Wrestler, Arm/Wrist 402
Wright, Amos L. 336
Wright, Ester 125
Wright, Susan Elizabeth 120
WWI 69
WWII 69

X

Y

Yates, Thomas J. 243
Yates, William Butler 402
Yen, Hosteen Ele 66
Yerman, Jack 367
Yorgason, Brent and Blaine 113
York, Sgt. Alvin C. 159
Yoshino, Yotaro 277
Yost, Paul A. 69
Young Women 242
    First Telecast 242
    Head Prefect 242
    Largest Female-Teens' Organization 242
Young Women, oldest president 238
Young Women, sacrament served to 257
Young, Brigham 140, 213, 248, 280
Young, Bryon D. 376
Young, John Willard 216

Young, Lorna 125
Young, Margaret 122
Young, Steve 364, 380
Young, Wayne 400
Youngberg, Rachel 176
Yo-Yo 423
Yugoslavia, ambassador 135

Zandamela, Paulo Cipriano 277
ZoBell, Norma Bernice 237

Index by Ward, Stake, Branch or Mission

A

Alabama, Hoover Ward 396

Alaska, Soldotna Ward 11

Argentina, Ramos Majia 2nd Ward, Buenos Aires West Stake 134

Arizona, 9th Ward, Phoenix North Stake 246

Arizona, Apache Junction 6th Ward, Apache Junction Stake 176

Arizona, Buckeye 2nd Ward, Buckeye Stake 373

Arizona, Citrus Heights Ward, Mesa Red Mountain Stake 125

Arizona, Duncan Stake 407

Arizona, Glendale Sixth Ward, Glendale North Stake 36

Arizona, Mesa 1st Ward, Mesa North Stake 339

Arizona, Mesa 27th Ward 278

Arizona, Mesa 38th Ward 120

Arizona, Mesa 43rd Ward, Mesa Central Stake 241

Arizona, Mesa 45th Ward, Mesa South Stake 388

Arizona, Mesa 47th Ward, Mesa Central Stake 316

Arizona, Mesa 4th Ward, Maricopa 240

Arizona, Mesa 53rd Ward 246

Arizona, Phoenix 21st Ward, West Maricopa Stake 110

Arizona, Phoenix 2nd Ward 389

Arizona, Phoenix 36th Ward, Glendale Stake 365

Arizona, Springerville Ward 231

Arizona, St. David Ward 87

Arizona, Sunrise Ward, Tucson Stake 378

Arizona, Tempe 1st Ward, Tempe 81

Arizona, Tempe 8th Ward 377

Arizona, Thatcher 1st Ward, Thatcher Stak 54

Arizona, University 2nd Ward, Tempe Stake 33

Arkansas, Little Rock 2nd Ward 207

Australia (Western), Albany Branch, Manjimup 225

Australia West Gippsland Branch, Moe, Victoria 225

Australia, Elizabeth Ward, Modbury Stake 241

Australia, Hedland Branch 244

Australia, Kangaroo Island Branch, Marion Stake 258

Australia, Port Headland Branch, Perth Mission 247

Australia, Port Hedland Branch, Port Hedland 225

Australia, Ryde Ward, Sydney, Greenwich Stake 33

Australia, Wels Branch 35

B

Brazil, Areoporto Branch, Sao Paulo West Stake 297

Brazil, Fortaleza Stake 135

Brazil, Rio de Janeiro Andarai Stake 424

Brazil, San Paulo 424

BYU 49th Ward, Provo, Utah 120

BYU 4th Ward 20

BYU 7th Stake 39

C

California, Alpine Ward, El Cajon Stake 402

California, Apple Valley 4th Ward, Victorville Stake 419

California, Banning Ward, Palm Springs Stake 419

California, Brentwood Ward, Stockton Stake 262

California, Chatsworth 2nd Ward 373

California, Chico Stake 35

California, Chula Vista II Ward, San Diego South Stake 120

California, Claremont 2nd Ward, La Verne Stake 302

California, Coronado Branch, San Diego Stake 36

California, Danville 1st Ward 305

California, El Cajon 7th Spanish Ward 178

California, El Centro Ward, California North Stake 122

California, Fairfield Stake 52

California, Fresno 8th Ward 372

California, Fresno 9th Ward, Fresno Stake 123

California, Glendale Stake 119

California, Glendora 4th Ward 373

California, Grass Valley 2nd Ward, Auburn Stake 123

California, Harbor Ward, Torrance Stake 107

California, Huntington Park West Stake 221

California, Irvine 2nd Ward, Santa Ana Stake 122, 133

California, La Canada 1st Ward, La Crescenta Stake 201

California, Lake Prot Ward, Ukiah Stake 400

California, Laurelglen Ward, Bakersfield Stake 413, 416

California, Long Beach 5th Ward 392

California, Long Beach Stake 248

California, Loomis 1st Ward 300

California, Los Altos 3rd Ward 397

California, Mission Hills Ward, Granada Hills Stake 241

California, Niguel 1st Ward, Laguna Niguel Stake 119
California, Orinda Ward, Oakland Stake 87
California, Oroville 1st Ward, Chico Stake 329
California, Pacific Beach Ward, San Diego Stake 397
California, Rafael Stake 396
California, Redding 12th Ward, Redding Stake 33
California, San Bernardino 2nd Ward, San
    Bernardino Stake 82
California, San Bruno Ward, San Mateo Stake 207
California, San Diego 5th, 10th, and 12th Wards 243
California, San Diego 8th Ward, San Diego Stake 414
California, San Jose 13th Ward 13
California, San Jose 24th Ward 176
California, San Jose 9th Ward, Saratoga Stake 190
California, San Luis Obispo 2nd Ward 398
California, Santa Ana Stake 297
California, Santa Barbara Stake 53
California, Santa Clarita Stake 116
California, Santa Cruz Ward, Saratoga Stake 366
California, Santa Fe Springs Ward, Cerritos Stake 411
California, Saratoga 1st Ward, Saratoga Stake 301
California, Southwest Branch, Downey Stake 65
California, Studio City 2nd Ward, North
    Hollywood Stake 115
California, Tustin 3rd Ward, Orange Stake 422
California, Victoria Ward, Riverside Stake 296
California, Westwood 2nd Ward, Los Angeles
    Stake 183
California, Yucaipa 2nd Ward, San Bernardino
    East Stake 123
California, Yucaipa 3rd Ward, San Bernardino
    East Stake 419
Canada, Bergland Branch, Ontario 224
Canada, Calgary 3rd Ward, Alberta 31
Canada, Fort St. John Branch, Calgary Mission 225
Canada, Horsefly, British Colombia 227
Canada, Prince George Branch, Canada
    Vancouver Mission 402
Canada, Raymond 1st Ward, Magrath, Alberta,
    Stake 419
Canada, Raymond Wards 237
Canada, Richmond Hill Ward, Brampton,
    Ontario, Stake 396
Canada, Stirling 1st Ward, Raymond, Alberta,
    Stake 236
Canada, Sydney Branch, Nova Scotia 239
Canada, Victoria, British Columbia Stake 174
Colorado Springs, Colorado, North Stake 373
Colorado, Castle Rock Ward 410
Colorado, Englewood Ward, Denver Stake 406
Colorado, Lakewood Stake 88
Colorado, Littleton 6th Ward, Columbine Stake 54
Colorado, Monument Ward, Springs North Stake 27
Colorado, Southglenn 1st Ward, Littleton Stake 366

D

Dakota, Fargo Stake 221

E

East Germany, Freiburg Stake 221
England, Bradford 2nd Ward, Huddersfield Stake 136
England, Brighton Ward 256
England, Hyde Park Ward, London Hyde Park
    Stake 404
England, Leicester 2nd Ward 245
England, Member of Parliament 136
England, Newcastle-Upon-Tyne Ward 28
England, Peterborough 2nd Ward, Northampton 138

F

Florida, Boynton Beach Ward, Pompano Beach
    Stake 296
Florida, Ft. Myers 2nd Ward, Ft. Myers Stake 129
Florida, Jacksonville Beach Ward, Jacksonville
    East Stake 39
Florida, Oak Grove Branch 227

G

Greece, Athens Branch 226

H

Hawaii Kai 2nd Ward, Honolulu Stake 404
Hawaii, Ainaola Ward 407
Hawaii, BYU-Hawaii 2nd Ward, BYU-Hawaii
    1st Stake 84
Hawaii, Kea'au Ward, Hilo Stake 405
Hawaii, Kilauea 2nd Ward, Hilo Stake, 415
Hawaii, Wailuku Branch 34
Hong Kong mission 272

I

Iceland, Reykjavik Branch 24
Idaho Falls 4th Ward 23
Idaho Falls, Idaho, 25th Ward 85
Idaho, Boise 12th Ward 418

Idaho, Chubbuck 4th Ward 400
Idaho, College 18th Ward, Rexburg College 3rd
    Stake 368
Idaho, Downey Ward, Portneuf Stake 256
Idaho, Grangeville Ward, Lewiston Stake 375
Idaho, Groveland 2nd Ward, Blackfoot South
    Stake 299
Idaho, Iona 1st Ward 85
Idaho, Melba Ward, Nampa, Idaho, South Stake 30
Idaho, Meridian 6th Ward 402
Idaho, Pocatello 32nd Ward 237
Idaho, Pocatello 4th Ward, Pocatello East Stake 236
Idaho, Ricks College 20th Ward, Ricks College
    2nd Stake 375
Idaho, Rigby 2nd Ward 240
Idaho, St. Anthony Ward, St. Anthony Stake 123
Idaho, Thomas 2nd Ward, Blackfoot West Stake 389
Idaho, Washakle Ward, Malad Stake 66
Illinois, Arlington Heights 1st Ward,
    Schaumburg Stake 414
Illinois, Freeport Ward, Rockford Stake 86
Illinois, Normal 1st Ward, Peoria Stake 423
Illinois, Shaumburg Stake 424
Indiana, Elwood Branch, Indianapolis North Stake 414
Indiana, Evansville 2nd Ward, Evansville Stake 21
Indiana, Muncie 1st Ward, Indianapolis North
    Stake 296
Iowa, Ames 2nd Ward 301
Iowa, Des Moines Ward 224

J

K

Kansas, Topeka 3rd Ward, Topeka Stake 402
Kentucky, Hopkinsville 1st Ward, Hopkinsville
    Stake 402

L

M

Maryland, Cantonsville Ward 132
Maryland, Potomac North Ward 302
Michigan, East Lansing University Ward,
    Lansing Stake 301
Michigan, Lansing Ward, Lansing Stake 316
Michigan, Royal Oaks Ward, Detroit Stake 124

Minnesota, Crystal 1st Ward, Minneapolis Stake 86
Minnesota, St. Paul 2nd Ward 301
Missouri, Commerce Branch, Joplin Stake 417
Missouri, Pittsburgh Ward, Joplin Stake 41
Montana, Columbia Falls Ward, Kalispell Stake 404
Montana, Corvallis Ward, Missoula Stake 374
Montana, Kalispell 1st Ward 35, 122

N

Nebraska, Omaha 1st Ward, Winter Quarters Stake 410
Netherlands, Hague Stake 221
Netherlands, Heerlen Servicemen Branch 242
Netherlands, Heerlen Servicemen Ward, Utrecht
    Stake 298
Nevada, 31st Ward, Las Vegas Stake 123
Nevada, Alma 9th Ward, Mesa Stake 25
Nevada, Elk Ridge 2nd Ward 417
Nevada, Las Vegas 1st Ward 327
Nevada, Las Vegas 23rd Ward 124
Nevada, Las Vegas 31st Ward, Las Vegas Stake 410
Nevada, Las Vegas 37th Ward, East Stake 404
Nevada, Las Vegas 42nd Ward, Paradise Stake 272
Nevada, Las Vegas 72nd Ward, Green Valley Stake 403
Nevada, Legacy Ward, Las Vegas Green Valley
    Stake 422
Nevada, Mountain Shadows Ward, North Las
    Vegas Stake 122
Nevada, Pahrump Ward 256
Nevada, Sparks 2nd Ward, Sparks Stake 189
Nevada, Sparks West Ward 376
New Mexico, Southwest Indian Mission 66
New Mexico, White Rock Ward, Santa Fe Stake 301
New York, Albany Ward, Albany Stake 403
New York, Manhattan Ward 35
New York, Plainview 2nd Ward, Long Island Stake 278
New York, Rochester Palmyra Stake 302
New York, Scarsdale Ward, 188
New Zealand, Auckland Harbour Stake 265
New Zealand, Invercargill 1st Branch 425
New Zealand, Temple View 1st Ward, Temple
    View Stake 387
New Zealand, Temple View Ward, Hamilton Stake 53
Nigeria, Aba Stake 64
North Carolina, Dunn Branch, Raleigh Stake 61
North Carolina, Greensboro Stake 302

O

O'Dell, Wayne 126
Oaks, Dallin H. 218
Oaks, Mrs. Merrill C. 120
Oaks, Robert C. 69

Obinna, Anthony 65
Observatory, first 290
Ohio, Dayton East Stake 269
Ohio, Medina Ward 41
Ohio, Medina Ward, Akron Stake 141
Ohio, Reynoldsburg Ward 25
Oklahoma, Choctaw Ward City South Stake 419
Oregon, Canby 2nd Ward City Stake 373
Oregon, Dayton Second Branch, McMinnville Stake 396
Oregon, McKay Creek Ward, Hillsboro Stake 52
Oregon, Vale 1st Ward, Nyssa Stake 222

P

Pennsylvania, Altoona Branch, Pennsylvania Mission 229
Pennsylvania, Audubon 2nd Ward, Philadelphia Stake 141
Pennsylvania, East Erie Branch 177
Peru, Miraflores Ward, Lima Stake 343

Q

R

Rhode Island, Westminster 1st Ward 124

S

Singapore, Singapore Branch, Southeast Asia Mission 364
Slovenia, Ljubljana Branch 406
South Africa, Mdantsane Branch Cape Town Mission 394
South Carolina, Charleston 2nd Ward, Charleston Stake 124
Sweden, Norrokoping Branch of the Swedish Mission 239
Switzerland, Geneva Ward 229
Switzerland, Petit Saconnex Ward 229

T

Tahiti, Mahu Branch 227
Tahiti, Papeete First Branch, French Polynesian Mission 53
Taiwan, Pei Tou Branch 224
Tennessee, Brainerd Ward, Chattanooga Stake 126
Texas, Alamogordo Ward, El Paso Stake 297
Texas, Alvin Ward, Houston East Stake, 329
Texas, Bay City Ward, Bay City Stake 397
Texas, Broadway 1st Ward, Houston East Stake 176
Texas, Bryan 1st Ward, College Station Stake 124
Texas, Colleyville Ward, Hurst Stake 122
Texas, Coppell Ward, Lewisville Stake 296
Texas, Dallas 4th Ward, Richardson Stake 301
Texas, Dallas 4th Ward, Richardson Stake. 125
Texas, Fort Worth 5th Ward, Fort Worth Stake 419
Texas, Friendswood 2nd Ward, Friendswood Stake 201
Texas, Lewisville 1st Ward, Lewisville Stake 297
Texas, Midland Ward, Texas, West Stake 31
Texas, Plum Creek Ward, Austin Oak Hills Stake 51

U

Utah, 10th Ward, Sandy Hillcrest Stake, 406
Utah, 17th Ward, Salt Lake Stake 41, 248
Utah, 22nd Ward, Salt Lake Stake 85
Utah, 35th Ward, Pioneer Stake 238
Utah, 8th Ward 224
Utah, Bear Lake Ward, Garden City 226
Utah, Beaver 6th Ward, Beaver, Utah, Stake 34
Utah, Blanding 1st Ward 54
Utah, Blanding 3rd Ward 54
Utah, Blanding Indian Branch 54
Utah, Bluffdale 2nd Ward, Bluffdale, Utah, Stake 32
Utah, Bluffdale Ward, West Jordan Stake 177
Utah, Bountiful 46th Ward, Bountiful Mueller Park Stake 58
Utah, Bountiful 56th Ward, Mueller Park Stake 131
Utah, Bountiful Height Stake 54th Ward 125
Utah, Brigham City 7th Ward 76
Utah, Butler 20th Ward, Salt Lake City Butler West Stake 52
Utah, Butler 5th Ward, Butler Stake 224
Utah, BYU 147th Ward, BYU 11th Stake 413
Utah, Canyon View, Orem 1st Ward 417
Utah, Castle Dale 3rd Ward, Castle Dale 317
Utah, Cedar City West Stake 261
Utah, Cottonwood 14th Ward, Salt Lake Big Cottonwood Stake 375
Utah, East Mill Creek 14th Ward 119
Utah, East Mill Creek 3rd Ward, East Mill Creek Stake 54
Utah, Eastridge 4th Ward, Draper Eastridge Stake 376
Utah, Edgemont 17th Ward, Provo 321
Utah, Fairmont Ward, Granite Stake 177
Utah, Farmington 19th Ward, Farmington South Stake 119
Utah, Farmington 3rd Ward, Farmington Stake 417

Utah, Forest Dale Ward, Granite Stake 58
Utah, Fountain Green Ward 177
Utah, Fruit Heights 1st Ward 119
Utah, Garden Park, Salt Lake City, 1st Ward 378
Utah, Garland 1st Ward 41
Utah, Granite 4th Ward 208
Utah, Gunlock Ward, St. George Stake 246
Utah, Harper Ward, North Box Elder Stake 246
Utah, Heatheridge 5th Ward, Orem Heatheridge
    Stake 394
Utah, Heber 3rd Ward, Heber City East Stake 124
Utah, Heber City 5th Ward 85
Utah, Highland Ward, Ogden East Stake 123
Utah, Holladay 24th Ward, Holladay North Stake 412
Utah, Homestead Ward, Murray South Stake 299
Utah, Hunter 6th Ward 85
Utah, Hyrum 3rd Ward, Hyrum North Stake 86
Utah, Hyrum 5th Ward 256
Utah, Jordan River 5th Ward, Jordan River Stake 408
Utah, Jordan River 5th Ward, South Jordan
    River Ridge Stake 191
Utah, Juab Stake Seminary, Nephi 53
Utah, Kanesville 3rd Ward, Hooper Stake 226
Utah, Lakeridge 4th Ward, Orem Lakeridge Stake 374
Utah, Layton 10th Ward, 406
Utah, Leeds Ward, St. George Pine View Stake 376
Utah, Leeds Ward, St. George Pine View Stake, 366
Utah, Lorin Farr 4th Ward, Ogden Lorin Farr
    Stake 372
Utah, Lynn Ward, Raft River Stake 225
Utah, Magna 10th Ward 371
Utah, Magna Stake 263
Utah, Manila 4th Ward, Pleasant Grove Manila
    Stake 373
Utah, Manti 3rd Ward, Manti Stake 84
Utah, Mantua Ward 224
Utah, Mill Road Ward, Heber City East Stake 401
Utah, Monument Park 4th Ward, Salt Lake
    Foothill Stake 237
Utah, Monument Park Stake 338
Utah, Morgan Stake 236
Utah, Murray 1st Ward 79
Utah, Oakridge 1st Ward, Farmington Oakridge
    Stake 86
Utah, Ogden 41st Ward, Ogden East Stake 124
Utah, Ogden 55th Ward 85
Utah, Orem 27th Ward 342
Utah, Orem 63rd Ward 187
Utah, Orem 6th Ward, North Orem Stake 224
Utah, Orem 89th Ward 422
Utah, Park Avenue Ward 38
Utah, Parley's 1st Ward, Parley's Stake 42, 143, 179
Utah, Parley's Stake 265
Utah, Pine Valley Ward 230
Utah, Pleasant Green 3rd Ward, Oquirrh Stake 224
Utah, Price 4th Ward, Carbon Stake 240

Utah, Princeton Ward, Park Stake 239
Utah, River Ridge 3rd Ward 97, 293
Utah, Rosecrest Ward, Salt Lake Canyon Rim
    Stake 406
Utah, Salem 2nd Ward 224
Utah, Salt Lake City Poplar Grove Ward 246
Utah, Salt Lake Holladay Stake 119
Utah, Salt Lake Millcreek 2nd Ward 122
Utah, Salt Lake Mount Olympus 3rd Ward 122
Utah, San Juan Stake 54
Utah, Sandy 37th Ward, Sandy, Utah, East Stake 30
Utah, Sandy Crescent Sixth Ward 52
Utah, Sandy First Ward 53
Utah, South Jordan 49
Utah, South Jordan 18th Ward, South Jordan,
    Utah Stake 403
Utah, Spanish Fork 13th Ward, Spanish Fork Stake 224
Utah, Spanish Fork 3rd Ward, Palmyra Stake 123
Utah, Springville 4th Ward 237
Utah, St. George 16th Ward 417
Utah, St. George 6th Ward, St. George East Stake 248
Utah, St. George 7th Ward, St. George East Stake 249
Utah, St. George Green Valley Stake 122
Utah, Sunset 6th Ward, Provo West Stake 187
Utah, Taylor 3rd Ward, Taylor Stake 263
Utah, Timpview 6th Ward, Orem Timpview Stake 370
Utah, Tridell Ward, Ashley Stake 272
Utah, Uintah 5th Ward, Ogden Weber Stake 272
Utah, Union 5th Ward, Sandy Willow Creek Stake 86
Utah, Val Verda 3rd Ward in Bountiful 177
Utah, Waterloo Ward, Granite Stake 82
Utah, West Weber Ward, Ogden Weber North
    Stake 124
Utah, Wilford 2nd Ward, Salt Lake City 416
Utah, Willard Ward, Willard Stake 177
Utah, Willow Canyon 3rd Ward, Sandy East Stake 124
Utah, Willow Creek 5th Ward, Sandy 423
Utah, Winder 20th Ward, Salt Lake County 119
Utah, Winder 7th Ward, Winder Stake 60
Utah, Winder 9th Ward, Winder Stake 43
Utah, Winder Ward, Winder Stake 256
Utah, Yale 2nd Ward, Bonneville Stake 374

V

Vermont, Ascutney Ward 315
Virginia, Alexandria Ward 137
Virginia, Arlington Ward 303
Virginia, Fair Oaks Ward, Fairfax Stake 353
Virginia, Falls Church Ward, Potomac Stake 123
Virginia, Herndon Ward, Oakton Stake 317
Virginia, Salem Ward, Roanoke Stake, 414
Virginia, Springfield Ward, Annandale 75

W

Washington, Basin City Ward, Pasco Stake 123
Washington, Bothell Stake 416
Washington, D.C., Georgetown Ward 34
Washington, D.C., Potomac South Ward 302
Washington, Eatonville Ward, East Stake 21
Washington, Federal Way 1st Ward, Federal
          Way, Washington, Stake 338
Washington, Ferndale 2nd Ward, Bellingham Stake 86
Washington, Longview 1st Ward, Longview Stake 365
Washington, Moses Lake 4th Ward, Grand
          Coulee Stake 53
Washington, Olympia 4th Ward 411
Washington, Salmon Creek Ward, Vancouver
          West Stake 298
Washington, Seattle 1st Ward, Seattle Stake 310
Washington, South Hill 3rd Ward, Puyallup
          South Stake 86
Washington, Wall Walla 3rd Ward 120
Wyoming, Afton 3rd Ward 87
Wyoming, Basin Ward, Worland Stake 397
Wyoming, Big Horn Stake 255
Wyoming, Casper 4th Ward, Casper Stake 373
Wyoming, Randolph 2nd Ward, Kemmerer Stake 124

X, Y, Z